RUSSIA

BUSINESS AND INVESTMENT OPPORTUNITIES YEARBOOK

VOLUME 1

PRACTICAL INFORMATION, OPPORTUNITIES, CONTACTS

International Business Publications, USA
Washington DC, USA - Moscow

RUSSIA

BUSINESS AND INVESTMENT OPPORTUNITIES YEARBOOK

VOLUME 1 PRACTICAL INFORMATION, OPPORTUNITIES, CONTACTS

UPDATED ANNUALLY

Cover Design: International Business Publications, USA

We express our sincere aappreciation to all government agencies and international organizations which provided information and other materials for this guide

2014 Edition Updated Reprint International Business Publications, USA
ISBN 1-57751-949-3

This guide provides basic information for starting or/and conducting business in the country. The extraordinary volume of materials covering the topic, prevents us from placing all these materials in this guide. For more detailed information on issues related to any specific investment and business activity in the country, please contact Global Investment Center, USA
Please acquire the list of our business intelligence and marketing reports and other business publications. We constantly update and expand our business intelligence and marketing materials. Please contact the center for the updated list of reports on over 200 countries.

in the USA: **Global Investment Center, USA.**
P.O.Box 15343, Washington, DC 20003
Phone: (202) 546-2103, Fax: (202) 546-3275, E-mail: rusric@erols.com
For additional analytical, marketing and other information please contact Global Investment Center, USA

Printed in the USA

RUSSIA
BUSINESS AND INVESTMENT OPPORTUNITIES YEARBOOK
VOLUME 1
PRACTICAL INFORMATION, OPPORTUNITIES, CONTACTS

TABLE OF CONTENTS

STRATEGIC AND DEVELOPMENT PROFILES

IMPORTANT FACTS

Capital (and largest city)	Moscow 55°45′N 37°37′E55.75°N 37.617°E
Official language(s)	Russian official throughout the country; 27 others co-official in various regions
Ethnic groups (2010)	81% Russians 3.7% Tatars 1.4% Ukrainians 1.1% Bashkirs 1% Chuvashes 11.8% others and unspecified
Demonym	Russian
Government	Federal semi-presidential constitutional republic
- President	Vladimir Putin
- Prime Minister	Dmitry Medvedev
Legislature	Federal Assembly
- Upper house	Federation Council
- Lower house	State Duma
Formation	
- Rurik Dynasty	862
- Kievan Rus'	882
- Vladimir-Suzdal Rus'	1169
- Grand Duchy of Moscow	1283
- Tsardom of Russia	16 January 1547
- Russian Empire	22 October 1721
- Russian Soviet Federative Socialist Republic	7 November 1917
- Union of Soviet Socialist Republics	10 December 1922
- Russian Federation	25 December 1991
Area	
- Total	17,075,400 km^2 (1st) 6,592,800 sq mi
- Water (%)	13 (including swamps)
Population	
- 2012 estimate	143,100,000 (9th)
- Density	8.3/km^2 (217th) 21.5/sq mi
GDP (PPP)	2011 estimate
- Total	$2.383 trillion
- Per capita	$16,736
GDP (nominal)	2011 estimate
- Total	$1.850 trillion
- Per capita	$12,993
Gini (2008)	42.3 (83rd)
HDI	0.755 (high) (66th)
Currency	Ruble (RUB)
Time zone	(UTC+3 to +12 (exc. +5))
Date formats	dd.mm.yyyy
Drives on the	right

ISO 3166 code	RU
Internet TLD	.ru, .su, .рф
Calling code	+7

Russia also officially known as the **Russian Federation** (Russian: is a country in northern Eurasia. It is a federal semi-presidential republic, comprising 83 federal subjects.

From northwest to southeast, Russia shares borders with Norway, Finland, Estonia, Latvia, Lithuania and Poland (both via Kaliningrad Oblast), Belarus, Ukraine, Georgia, Azerbaijan, Kazakhstan, China, Mongolia, and North Korea. It also has maritime borders with Japan by the Sea of Okhotsk, and the US state of Alaska by the Bering Strait. At 17,075,400 square kilometres (6,592,800 sq mi), Russia is the largest country in the world, covering more than one eighth of the Earth's inhabited land area. Russia is also the ninth most populous nation with 143 million people as of 2012.

Extending across the whole of northern Asia and most of eastern Europe, Russia spans nine time zones and incorporates a wide range of environments and landforms. Russia has the world's largest reserves of mineral and energy resources and is the largest producer of oil and natural gas globally. Russia has the world's largest forest reserves and its lakes contain approximately one-quarter of the world's fresh water.

The nation's history began with that of the East Slavs, who emerged as a recognizable group in Europe between the 3rd and 8th centuries AD. Founded and ruled by a Varangian warrior elite and their descendants, the medieval state of Rus arose in the 9th century. In 988 it adopted Orthodox Christianity from the Byzantine Empire, beginning the synthesis of Byzantine and Slavic cultures that defined Russian culture for the next millennium. Rus' ultimately disintegrated into a number of smaller states; most of the Rus' lands were overrun by the Mongol invasion and became tributaries of the nomadic Golden Horde.

The Grand Duchy of Moscow gradually reunified the surrounding Russian principalities, achieved independence from the Golden Horde, and came to dominate the cultural and political legacy of Kievan Rus'.

By the 18th century, the nation had greatly expanded through conquest, annexation, and exploration to become the Russian Empire, which was the third largest empire in history, stretching from Poland in Europe to Alaska in North America.

Following the Russian Revolution, Russia became the largest and leading constituent of the Soviet Union, the world's first constitutionally socialist state and a recognized superpower, which played a decisive role in the Allied victory in World War II. The Soviet era saw some of the most significant technological achievements of the 20th century, including the world's first human spaceflight. The Russian Federation was founded following the dissolution of the Soviet Union in 1991, but is recognized as the continuing legal personality of the Soviet state.

The Russian economy is the world's ninth largest by nominal GDP and sixth largest by purchasing power parity, with the 3rd largest nominal military budget. Russia is one of the world's fastest growing major economies. It is one of the five recognized nuclear weapons states and possesses the largest stockpile of weapons of mass destruction.

Russia is a great power and a permanent member of the United Nations Security Council, a member of the G8, G20, the Council of Europe, the Asia-Pacific Economic Cooperation, the Shanghai Cooperation Organisation, the Eurasian Economic Community, the Organisation for Security and Cooperation in Europe (OSCE), the World Trade Organisation (WTO), and is the leading member of the Commonwealth of Independent States.

Background:	Founded in the 12th century, the Principality of Muscovy, was able to emerge from over 200 years of Mongol domination (13th-15th centuries) and to gradually conquer and absorb surrounding principalities. In the early 17th century, a new Romanov Dynasty continued this policy of expansion across Siberia to the Pacific. Under PETER I (ruled 1682-1725), hegemony was extended to the Baltic Sea and the country was renamed

	the Russian Empire. During the 19th century, more territorial acquisitions were made in Europe and Asia. Repeated devastating defeats of the Russian army in World War I led to widespread rioting in the major cities of the Russian Empire and to the overthrow in 1917 of the imperial household. The Communists under Vladimir LENIN seized power soon after and formed the USSR. The brutal rule of Josef STALIN (1928-53) strengthened Russian dominance of the Soviet Union at a cost of tens of millions of lives. The Soviet economy and society stagnated in the following decades until General Secretary Mikhail GORBACHEV (1985-91) introduced glasnost (openness) and perestroika (restructuring) in an attempt to modernize Communism, but his initiatives inadvertently released forces that by December 1991 splintered the USSR into 15 independent republics. Since then, Russia has struggled in its efforts to build a democratic political system and market economy to replace the strict social, political, and economic controls of the Communist period. While some progress has been made on the economic front, recent years have seen a recentralization of power under Vladimir PUTIN and an erosion in nascent democratic institutions. A determined guerrilla conflict still plagues Russia in Chechnya.

GEOGRAPHY

Location:	Northern Asia (that part west of the Urals is included with Europe), bordering the Arctic Ocean, between Europe and the North Pacific Ocean
Geographic coordinates:	60 00 N, 100 00 E
Map references:	Asia
Area:	total: 17,075,200 sq km land: 16,995,800 sq km water: 79,400 sq km
Area - comparative:	approximately 1.8 times the size of the US
Land boundaries:	total: 20,017 km border countries: Azerbaijan 284 km, Belarus 959 km, China (southeast) 3,605 km, China (south) 40 km, Estonia 294 km, Finland 1,340 km, Georgia 723 km, Kazakhstan 6,846 km, North Korea 19 km, Latvia 217 km, Lithuania (Kaliningrad Oblast) 227 km, Mongolia 3,485 km, Norway 196 km, Poland (Kaliningrad Oblast) 206 km, Ukraine 1,576 km
Coastline:	37,653 km
Maritime claims:	territorial sea: 12 nm exclusive economic zone: 200 nm continental shelf: 200-m depth or to the depth of exploitation

Climate:	ranges from steppes in the south through humid continental in much of European Russia; subarctic in Siberia to tundra climate in the polar north; winters vary from cool along Black Sea coast to frigid in Siberia; summers vary from warm in the steppes to cool along Arctic coast
Terrain:	broad plain with low hills west of Urals; vast coniferous forest and tundra in Siberia; uplands and mountains along southern border regions

Elevation extremes:	lowest point: Caspian Sea -28 m highest point: Gora El'brus 5,633 m
Natural resources:	wide natural resource base including major deposits of oil, natural gas, coal, and many strategic minerals, timber note: formidable obstacles of climate, terrain, and distance hinder exploitation of natural resources
Land use:	arable land: 7.33% permanent crops: 0.11% other: 92.56%

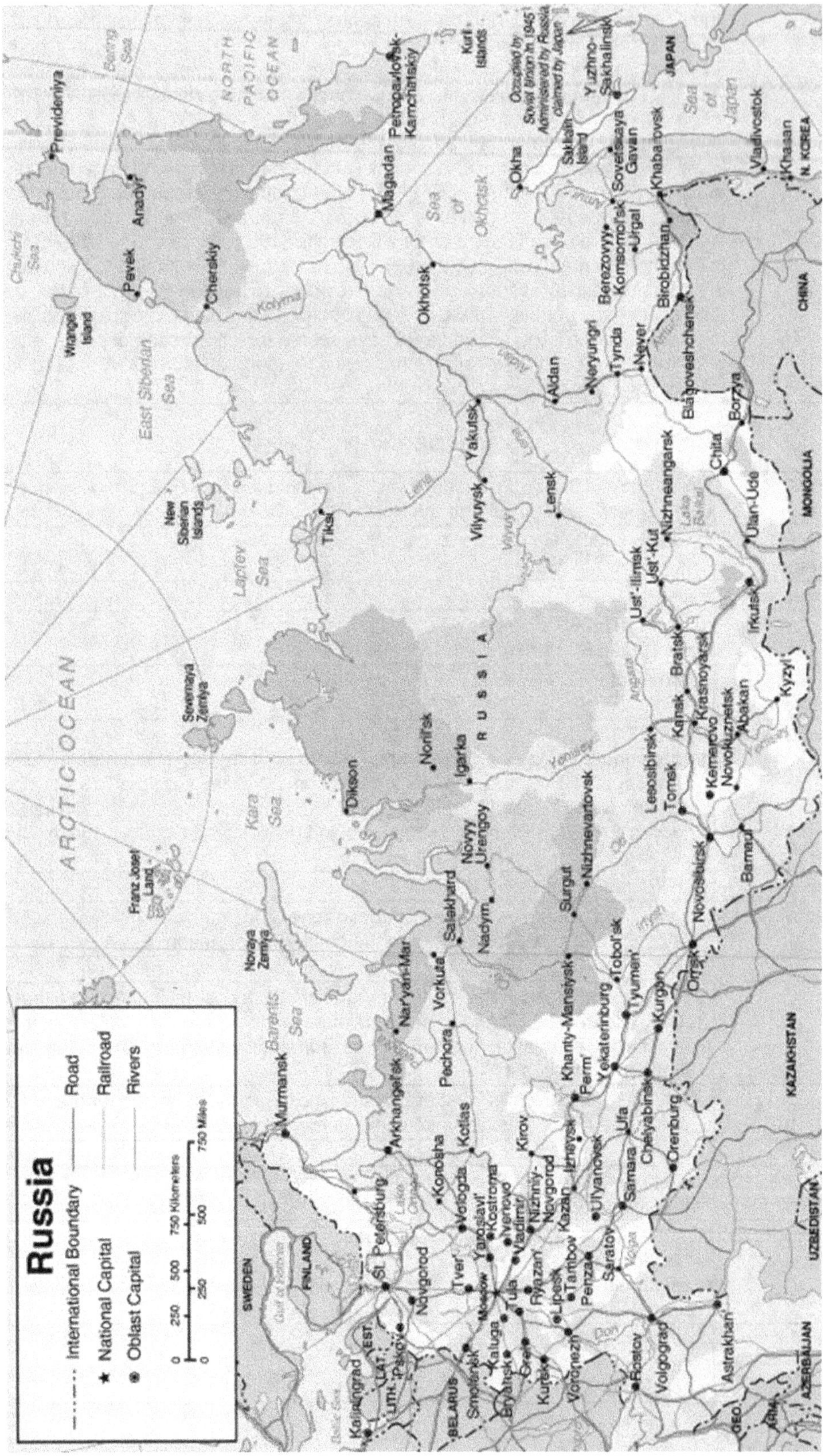
Russia
International Boundary
National Capital
Oblast Capital
Road
Railroad
Rivers
0 250 500 750 Kilometers
0 250 750 Miles

Irrigated land:	46,630 sq km
Natural hazards:	permafrost over much of Siberia is a major impediment to development; volcanic activity in the Kuril Islands; volcanoes and earthquakes on the Kamchatka Peninsula; spring floods and summer/autumn forest fires throughout Siberia and parts of European Russia

Environment - current issues:	air pollution from heavy industry, emissions of coal-fired electric plants, and transportation in major cities; industrial, municipal, and agricultural pollution of inland waterways and seacoasts; deforestation; soil erosion; soil contamination from improper application of agricultural chemicals; scattered areas of sometimes intense radioactive contamination; groundwater contamination from toxic waste; urban solid waste management; abandoned stocks of obsolete pesticides
Environment - international agreements:	party to: Air Pollution, Air Pollution-Nitrogen Oxides, Air Pollution-Sulfur 85, Antarctic-Environmental Protocol, Antarctic-Marine Living Resources, Antarctic Seals, Antarctic Treaty, Biodiversity, Climate Change, Endangered Species, Environmental Modification, Hazardous Wastes, Law of the Sea, Marine Dumping, Ozone Layer Protection, Ship Pollution, Tropical Timber 83, Wetlands, Whaling signed, but not ratified: Air Pollution-Sulfur 94, Climate Change-Kyoto Protocol
Geography - note:	largest country in the world in terms of area but unfavorably located in relation to major sea lanes of the world; despite its size, much of the country lacks proper soils and climates (either too cold or too dry) for agriculture; Mount El'brus is Europe's tallest peak

PEOPLE

Population:	143,782,338
Age structure:	0-14 years: 15% (male 11,064,109; female 10,518,595) 15-64 years: 71.3% (male 49,534,076; female 52,958,107) 65 years and over: 13.7% (male 6,177,580; female 13,529,871)
Median age:	total: 37.9 years male: 34.7 years female: 40.7 years
Population growth rate:	-0.45%
Birth rate:	9.63 births/1,000 population
Death rate:	15.17 deaths/1,000 population
Net migration rate:	1.02 migrant(s)/1,000 population
Sex ratio:	at birth: 1.06 male(s)/female under 15 years: 1.05 male(s)/female 15-64 years: 0.94 male(s)/female 65 years and over: 0.46 male(s)/female total population: 0.87 male(s)/female
Infant mortality rate:	total: 16.96 deaths/1,000 live births male: 19.58 deaths/1,000 live births female: 14.18 deaths/1,000 live births
Life expectancy at birth:	total population: 66.39 years male: 59.91 years female: 73.27 years
Total fertility rate:	1.26 children born/woman
HIV/AIDS - adult prevalence rate:	0.9%
HIV/AIDS - people living with HIV/AIDS:	700,000
HIV/AIDS - deaths:	9,000

Nationality:	noun: Russian(s) adjective: Russian
Ethnic groups:	Russian 81.5%, Tatar 3.8%, Ukrainian 3%, Chuvash 1.2%, Bashkir 0.9%, Belarusian 0.8%, Moldavian 0.7%, other 8.1% (1989)
Religions:	Russian Orthodox, Muslim, other
Languages:	Russian, other
Literacy:	definition: age 15 and over can read and write total population: 99.6% male: 99.7% female: 99.5%

GOVERNMENT

Country name:	conventional long form: Russian Federation conventional short form: Russia local long form: Rossiyskaya Federatsiya local short form: Rossiya former: Russian Empire, Russian Soviet Federative Socialist Republic
Government type:	federation
Capital:	Moscow
Administrative divisions:	49 oblasts (oblastey, singular - oblast), 21 republics (respublik, singular - respublika), 10 autonomous okrugs (avtonomnykh okrugov, singular - avtonomnyy okrug), 6 krays (krayev, singular - kray), 2 federal cities (singular - gorod), and 1 autonomous oblast (avtonomnaya oblast') : oblasts: Amur (Blagoveshchensk), Arkhangel'sk, Astrakhan', Belgorod, Bryansk, Chelyabinsk, Chita, Irkutsk, Ivanovo, Kaliningrad, Kaluga, Kamchatka (Petropavlovsk-Kamchatskiy), Kemerovo, Kirov, Kostroma, Kurgan, Kursk, Leningrad, Lipetsk, Magadan, Moscow, Murmansk, Nizhniy Novgorod, Novgorod, Novosibirsk, Omsk, Orenburg, Orel, Penza, Perm', Pskov, Rostov, Ryazan', Sakhalin (Yuzhno-Sakhalinsk), Samara, Saratov, Smolensk, Sverdlovsk (Yekaterinburg), Tambov, Tomsk, Tula, Tver', Tyumen', Ul'yanovsk, Vladimir, Volgograd, Vologda, Voronezh, Yaroslavl' : republics: Adygeya (Maykop), Altay (Gorno-Altaysk), Bashkortostan (Ufa), Buryatiya (Ulan-Ude), Chechnya (Groznyy), Chuvashiya (Cheboksary), Dagestan (Makhachkala), Ingushetiya (Magas), Kabardino-Balkariya (Nal'chik), Kalmykiya (Elista), Karachayevo-Cherkesiya (Cherkessk), Kareliya (Petrozavodsk), Khakasiya (Abakan), Komi (Syktyvkar), Mariy-El (Yoshkar-Ola), Mordoviya (Saransk), Sakha [Yakutiya] (Yakutsk), North Ossetia (Vladikavkaz), Tatarstan (Kazan'), Tyva (Kyzyl), Udmurtiya (Izhevsk) : autonomous okrugs: Aga Buryat (Aginskoye), Chukotka (Anadyr'), Evenk (Tura), Khanty-Mansi, Komi-Permyak (Kudymkar), Koryak (Palana), Nenets (Nar'yan-Mar), Taymyr [Dolgano-Nenets] (Dudinka), Ust'-Orda Buryat (Ust'-Ordynskiy), Yamalo-Nenets (Salekhard) : krays: Altay (Barnaul), Khabarovsk, Krasnodar, Krasnoyarsk, Primorskiy (Vladivostok), Stavropol' : federal cities: Moscow (Moskva), St. Petersburg (Sankt-Peterburg) : autonomous oblast: Yevrey [Jewish] (Birobidzhan) note: administrative divisions have the same names as their administrative centers (exceptions have the administrative center name following in parentheses)
Independence:	24 August 1991 (from Soviet Union)
National holiday:	Russia Day, 12 June (1990)
Constitution:	adopted 12 December 1993
Legal system:	based on civil law system; judicial review of legislative acts
Suffrage:	18 years of age; universal
Executive branch:	chief of state: President Vladimir Vladimirovich PUTIN (since 7 May 2012)

	head of government: Dmitriy Anatolyevich MEDVEDEV (since 8 May 2012); First Deputy Premier Igor Ivanovich SHUVALOV (since 12 May 2008); Deputy Premiers Arkadiy Vladimirovich DVORKOVICH (since 21 May 2012), Olga Yuryevna GOLODETS (since 21 May 2012), Aleksandr Gennadiyevich KHLOPONIN (since 19 January 2010), Dmitriy Nikolayevich KOZAK (since 14 October 2008), Dmitriy Olegovich ROGOZIN (since 23 December 2011), Vladislav Yuryevich SURKOV (since 27 December 2011) cabinet: the "Government" is composed of the premier, his deputies, and ministers; all are appointed by the president, and the premier is also confirmed by the Duma note:there is also a Presidential Administration (PA) that provides staff and policy support to the president, drafts presidential decrees, and coordinates policy among government agencies; a Security Council also reports directly to the president elections: president elected by popular vote for a six-year term (eligible for a second term); election last held 4 March 2012 (next to be held in March 2018); note - the term length was extended from four to six years in late 2008 and went into effect after the 2012 election; there is no vice president; if the president dies in office, cannot exercise his powers because of ill health, is impeached, or resigns, the premier serves as acting president until a new presidential election is held, which must be within three months; premier appointed by the president with the approval of the Duma election results: Vladimir PUTIN elected president; percent of vote - Vladimir PUTIN 63.6%, Gennadiy ZYUGANOV 17.2%, Mikhail PROKHOROV 8%, Vladimir ZHIRINOVSKIY 6.2%, Sergey MIRONOV 3.9%, other 1.1%; Dmitriy MEDVEDEV approved by Duma 299 to 144
Legislative branch:	bicameral Federal Assembly or Federalnoye Sobraniye consists of an upper house, the Federation Council or Sovet Federatsii (166 seats; members appointed by the top executive and legislative officials in each of the 83 federal administrative units - oblasts, krays, republics, autonomous okrugs and oblasts, and the federal cities of Moscow and Saint Petersburg; members to serve four-year terms) and a lower house, the State Duma or Gosudarstvennaya Duma (450 seats; as of 2007, all members elected by proportional representation from party lists winning at least 7% of the vote; members elected by popular vote to serve four-year terms) elections: State Duma - last held on 4 December 2011 (next to be held in December 2015) election results: State Duma - United Russia 49.6%, CPRF 19.2%, Just Russia 13.2%, LDPR 11.7%, other 6.3%; total seats by party - United Russia 238, CPRF 92, Just Russia 64, LDPR 56
Judicial branch:	Constitutional Court; Supreme Court; Superior Court of Arbitration; judges for all courts are appointed for life by the Federation Council on the recommendation of the president
Political parties and leaders:	Communist Party of the Russian Federation or CPRF [Gennadiy Andreyevich ZYUGANOV]; Liberal Democratic Party of Russia or LDPR [Vladimir Volfovich ZHIRINOVSKIY]; Motherland Bloc (Rodina) [Dmitriy ROGOZIN]; People's Party [Gennadiy RAYKOV]; Union of Rightist Forces or SPS [Anatoliy Borisovich CHUBAYS, Yegor Timurovich GAYDAR, Irina Mutsuovna KHAKAMADA, Boris Yefimovich NEMTSOV]; United Russia [Boris Vyacheslavovich GRYZLOV]; Yabloko Party [Grigoriy Alekseyevich YAVLINSKIY]
Political pressure groups and leaders:	NA
International organization participation:	APEC, ARF, ASEAN (dialogue partner), BIS, BSEC, CBSS, CE, CERN (observer), CIS, EAPC, EBRD, G- 8, IAEA, IBRD, ICAO, ICC, ICCt (signatory), ICFTU, ICRM, IDA, IFC, IFRCS, IHO, ILO, IMF, IMO, Interpol, IOC, IOM (observer), ISO, ITU, LAIA (observer), MIGA, MINURSO, MONUC, NAM (guest), NSG, OAS (observer), ONUB, OPCW, OSCE, Paris Club, PCA, PFP, SCO, UN, UN Security Council, UNAMSIL,

	UNCTAD, UNHCR, UNIDO, UNITAR, UNMEE, UNMIK, UNMIL, UNMISET, UNMOVIC, UNOCI, UNOMIG, UNTSO, UPU, WCO, WFTU, WHO, WIPO, WMO, WToO, WTrO (observer), ZC
Diplomatic representation in the US:	chief of mission: Ambassador Yuriy Viktorovich USHAKOV chancery: 2650 Wisconsin Avenue NW, Washington, DC 20047 telephone: (202) 298-5700, 5701, 5704, 5708 FAX: (202) 298-5735 consulate(s) general: New York, San Francisco, and Seattle
Diplomatic representation from the US:	chief of mission: Ambassador Alexander VERSHBOW embassy: Bolshoy Devyatinskiy Pereulok No. 8, 121099 Moscow mailing address: PSC-77, APO AE 09721 telephone: (095) 728-5000 FAX: (095) 728-5090 consulate(s) general: Saint Petersburg, Vladivostok, Yekaterinburg
Flag description:	three equal horizontal bands of white (top), blue, and red

ECONOMY

Russia has undergone significant changes since the collapse of the Soviet Union, moving from a globally-isolated, centrally-planned economy towards a more market-based and globally-integrated economy, but stalling as a partially reformed, statist economy with a high concentration of wealth in officials' hands. Economic reforms in the 1990s privatized most industry, with notable exceptions in the energy and defense-related sectors. The protection of property rights is still weak and the private sector remains subject to heavy state interference. Russia is one of the world's leading producers of oil and natural gas and is also a top exporter of metals such as steel and primary aluminum.

Russia's manufacturing sector is generally uncompetitive on world markets and is geared toward domestic consumption. Russia's reliance on commodity exports makes it vulnerable to boom and bust cycles that follow the volatile swings in global prices. The economy, which had averaged 7% growth during 1998-2008 as oil prices rose rapidly, was one of the hardest hit by the 2008-09 global economic crisis as oil prices plummeted and the foreign credits that Russian banks and firms relied on dried up.

Slowly declining oil prices over the past few years and difficulty attracting foreign direct investment have contributed to a noticeable slowdown in GDP growth rates. In late 2013, the Russian Economic Development Ministry reduced its growth forecast through 2030 to an average of only 2.5% per year, down from its previous forecast of 4.0 to 4.2%. In 2014, following Russia's military intervention in Ukraine, prospects for economic growth declined further, with expections that GDP growth could drop as low as zero.

GDP (purchasing power parity):

$2.553 trillion (2013 est.)
country comparison to the world: 7
$2.52 trillion (2012 est.)
$2.437 trillion (2011 est.)
note:data are in 2013 US dollars

GDP (official exchange rate):

$2.113 trillion (2013 est.)

GDP - real growth rate:

1.3% (2013 est.)
country comparison to the world: 165
3.4% (2012 est.)
4.3% (2011 est.)

GDP - per capita (PPP):
$18,100 (2013 est.)
country comparison to the world: 77
$17,800 (2012 est.)
$17,100 (2011 est.)
note:data are in 2013 US dollars

Gross national saving:
28.3% of GDP (2013 est.)
country comparison to the world: 33
29.5% of GDP (2012 est.)
30.6% of GDP (2011 est.)

GDP - composition, by end use:
household consumption: 51.3%
government consumption: 18.8%
investment in fixed capital: 22%
investment in inventories: 1.4%
exports of goods and services: 29.6%
imports of goods and services: -23%
(2013 est.)

GDP - composition, by sector of origin:
agriculture: 4.2%
industry: 37.5%
services: 58.3% (2013 est.)

Agriculture - products:
grain, sugar beets, sunflower seeds, vegetables, fruits; beef, milk

Industries:
complete range of mining and extractive industries producing coal, oil, gas, chemicals, and metals; all forms of machine building from rolling mills to high-performance aircraft and space vehicles; defense industries (including radar, missile production, advanced electronic components), shipbuilding; road and rail transportation equipment; communications equipment; agricultural machinery, tractors, and construction equipment; electric power generating and transmitting equipment; medical and scientific instruments; consumer durables, textiles, foodstuffs, handicrafts

Industrial production growth rate:
0.1% (2013 est.)
country comparison to the world: 165

Labor force:
75.29 million (2013 est.)
country comparison to the world: 8

Labor force - by occupation:
agriculture: 9.7%
industry: 27.8%
services: 62.5% (2012)

Unemployment rate:
5.8% (2013 est.)
country comparison to the world: 55

5.5% (2012 est.)

Population below poverty line:
11% (2013 est.)

Household income or consumption by percentage share:
lowest 10%: 5.7%
highest 10%: 42.4% (2011 est.)

Distribution of family income - Gini index:
42 (2012)
country comparison to the world: 50
41.7 (2011)

Budget:
revenues: $439 billion
expenditures: $450.3 billion (2013 est.)

Taxes and other revenues:
20.7% of GDP (2013 est.)
country comparison to the world: 157

Budget surplus (+) or deficit (-):
-0.5% of GDP (2013 est.)
country comparison to the world: 57

Public debt:
7.9% of GDP (2013 est.)
country comparison to the world: 151
8% of GDP (2012 est.)
note:data cover general government debt, and includes debt instruments issued (or owned) by government entities other than the treasury; the data include treasury debt held by foreign entities; the data include debt issued by subnational entities, as well as intra-governmental debt; intra-governmental debt consists of treasury borrowings from surpluses in the social funds, such as for retirement, medical care, and unemployment, debt instruments for the social funds are not sold at public auctions

Fiscal year:
calendar year

Inflation rate (consumer prices):
6.8% (2013 est.)
country comparison to the world: 184
5.1% (2012 est.)

Central bank discount rate:
8.25% (31 December 2012 est.)
country comparison to the world: 33
8% (31 December 2011)
note:this is the so-called refinancing rate, but in Russia banks do not get refinancing at this rate; this is a reference rate used primarily for fiscal purposes

Commercial bank prime lending rate:
9.3% (31 December 2013 est.)

country comparison to the world: 95
9.1% (31 December 2012 est.)

Stock of narrow money:
$452.8 billion (31 December 2012 est.)
country comparison to the world: 13
$399.3 billion (31 December 2011 est.)

Stock of broad money:
$1.061 trillion (31 December 2012 est.)
country comparison to the world: 18
$893.1 billion (31 December 2011 est.)

Stock of domestic credit:
$947 billion (31 December 2013 est.)
country comparison to the world: 17
$922.6 billion (31 December 2012 est.)

Market value of publicly traded shares:
$874.7 billion (31 December 2012 est.)
country comparison to the world: 16
$796.4 billion (31 December 2011)
$1.005 trillion (31 December 2010 est.)

Current account balance:
$74.8 billion (2012 est.)
country comparison to the world: 4
$71.43 billion (2012 est.)

Exports:
$515 billion (2013 est.)
country comparison to the world: 10
$528 billion (2012 est.)

Exports - commodities:
petroleum and petroleum products, natural gas, metals, wood and wood products, chemicals, and a wide variety of civilian and military manufactures

Exports - partners:
Netherlands 14.6%, China 6.8%, Germany 6.8%, Italy 6.2%, Turkey 5.2%, Ukraine 5.2%, Belarus 4.7% (2012 est.)

Imports:
$341 billion (2013 est.)
country comparison to the world: 17
$335.7 billion (2012 est.)

Imports - commodities:
machinery, vehicles, pharmaceutical products, plastic, semi-finished metal products, meat, fruits and nuts, optical and medical instruments, iron, steel

Imports - partners:
China 16.6%, Germany 12.2%, Ukraine 5.7%, Japan 5%, United States 4.9%, France 4.4%, Italy

4.3% (2012 est.)

Reserves of foreign exchange and gold:
$515.6 billion (01 December 2013 est.)
country comparison to the world: 6
$537.6 billion (31 December 2012 est.)

Debt - external:
$714.2 billion (30 September 2013 est.)
country comparison to the world: 22
$636.4 billion (31 December 2012 est.)

Stock of direct foreign investment - at home:
$552.8 billion (31 December 2013 est.)
country comparison to the world: 16
$497.8 billion (31 December 2012 est.)

Stock of direct foreign investment - abroad:
$439.2 billion (31 December 2013 est.)
country comparison to the world: 17
$387.2 billion (31 December 2012 est.)

Exchange rates:
Russian rubles (RUB) per US dollar -
31.82 (2013 est.)
30.84 (2012 est.)
30.368 (2010 est.)
31.74 (2009)
24.853 (2008)

ENERGY

Electricity - production:
1.057 trillion kWh (2013 est.)
country comparison to the world: 4

Electricity - consumption:
1.038 trillion kWh (2012 est.)
country comparison to the world: 4

Electricity - exports:
19.14 billion kWh (2012 est.)
country comparison to the world: 11

Electricity - imports:
2.661 billion kWh (2012 est.)
country comparison to the world: 50

Electricity - installed generating capacity:
223.1 million kW (2012 est.)
country comparison to the world: 5

Electricity - from fossil fuels:

67.7% of total installed capacity (2012 est.)
country comparison to the world: 112

Electricity - from nuclear fuels:
17.8% of total installed capacity (2012 est.)
country comparison to the world: 12

Electricity - from hydroelectric plants:
15.1% of total installed capacity (2012 est.)
country comparison to the world: 100

Electricity - from other renewable sources:
0% of total installed capacity (2012 est.)
country comparison to the world: 117

Crude oil - production:
10.44 million bbl/day (2013 est.)
country comparison to the world: 3

Crude oil - exports:
4.72 million bbl/day (2013 est.)
country comparison to the world: 2

Crude oil - imports:
16,380 bbl/day (2012 est.)
country comparison to the world: 69

Crude oil - proved reserves:
80 billion bbl (1 January 2013 est.)
country comparison to the world: 8

Refined petroleum products - production:
4.812 million bbl/day (2010 est.)
country comparison to the world: 4

Refined petroleum products - consumption:
3.196 million bbl/day (2012 est.)
country comparison to the world: 6

Refined petroleum products - exports:
2.92 million bbl/day (2012 est.)
country comparison to the world: 1

Refined petroleum products - imports:
24,300 bbl/day (2013 est.)
country comparison to the world: 97

Natural gas - production:
669.7 billion cu m (2013 est.)
country comparison to the world: 2

Natural gas - consumption:
457.2 billion cu m (2013 est.)
country comparison to the world: 2

Natural gas - exports:
196 billion cu m (2013 est.)
country comparison to the world: 1

Natural gas - imports:
32.5 billion cu m (2012 est.)
country comparison to the world: 17

Natural gas - proved reserves:
47.8 trillion cu m (1 January 2013 est.)
country comparison to the world: 1

Carbon dioxide emissions from consumption of energy:
1.788 billion Mt (2011 est.)

COMMUNICATIONS

Telephones - main lines in use:
42.9 million (2012)
country comparison to the world: 6

Telephones - mobile cellular:
261.9 million (2012)
country comparison to the world: 5

Telephone system:
general assessment: the telephone system is experiencing significant changes; there are more than 1,000 companies licensed to offer communication services; access to digital lines has improved, particularly in urban centers; Internet and e-mail services are improving; Russia has made progress toward building the telecommunications infrastructure necessary for a market economy; the estimated number of mobile subscribers jumped from fewer than 1 million in 1998 to more than 235 million in 2011; fixed line service has improved but a large demand remains
domestic: cross-country digital trunk lines run from Saint Petersburg to Khabarovsk, and from Moscow to Novorossiysk; the telephone systems in 60 regional capitals have modern digital infrastructures; cellular services, both analog and digital, are available in many areas; in rural areas, the telephone services are still outdated, inadequate, and low density
international: country code - 7; Russia is connected internationally by undersea fiber optic cables; satellite earth stations provide access to Intelsat, Intersputnik, Eutelsat, Inmarsat, and Orbita systems (2011)

Broadcast media:
6 national TV stations with the federal government owning 1 and holding a controlling interest in a second; state-owned Gazprom maintains a controlling interest in a third national channel; government-affiliated Bank Rossiya owns controlling interest in a fourth and fifth, while the sixth national channel is owned by the Moscow city administration; roughly 3,300 national, regional, and local TV stations with over two-thirds completely or partially controlled by the federal or local governments; satellite TV services are available; 2 state-run national radio networks with a third majority-owned by Gazprom; roughly 2,400 public and commercial radio stations (2007)

Internet country code:

.ru; note - Russia also has responsibility for a legacy domain ".su" that was allocated to the Soviet Union and is being phased out

Internet hosts:
14.865 million (2012)
country comparison to the world: 10

Internet users:
40.853 million (2009)
country comparison to the world: 10

TRANSPORTATION

Airports:
1,218 (2013)
country comparison to the world: 5

Airports - with paved runways:
total: 594
over 3,047 m: 54
2,438 to 3,047 m: 197
1,524 to 2,437 m: 123
914 to 1,523 m: 95
under 914 m: 125 (2013)

Airports - with unpaved runways:
total: 624
over 3,047 m: 4
2,438 to 3,047 m: 13
1,524 to 2,437 m: 69
914 to 1,523 m: 81
under 914 m:
457 (2013)

Heliports:
49 (2013)

Pipelines:
condensate 122 km; gas 163,872 km; liquid petroleum gas 1,378 km; oil 80,820 km; oil/gas/water 40 km; refined products 13,658 km; water 23 km (2013)

Railways:
total: 87,157 km
country comparison to the world: 2
broad gauge: 86,200 km 1.520-m gauge (40,300 km electrified)
narrow gauge: 957 km 1.067-m gauge (on Sakhalin Island)
note:an additional 30,000 km of non-common carrier lines serve industries (2006)

Roadways:
total: 1,283,387 km
country comparison to the world: 5
paved: 927,721 km (includes 39,143 km of expressways)
unpaved: 355,666 km (2012)

Waterways:
102,000 km (including 48,000 km with guaranteed depth; the 72,000 km system in European Russia links Baltic Sea, White Sea, Caspian Sea, Sea of Azov, and Black Sea) (2009)
country comparison to the world: 2

Merchant marine:
total: 1,143
country comparison to the world: 11
by type: bulk carrier 20, cargo 642, carrier 3, chemical tanker 57, combination ore/oil 42, container 13, passenger 15, passenger/cargo 7, petroleum tanker 244, refrigerated cargo 84, roll on/roll off 13, specialized tanker 3
foreign-owned: 155 (Belgium 4, Cyprus 13, Estonia 1, Ireland 1, Italy 14, Latvia 2, Netherlands 2, Romania 1, South Korea 1, Switzerland 3, Turkey 101, Ukraine 12)
registered in other countries: 439 (Antigua and Barbuda 3, Belgium 1, Belize 30, Bulgaria 2, Cambodia 50, Comoros 12, Cook Islands 1, Cyprus 46, Dominica 3, Georgia 6, Hong Kong 1, Kiribati 1, Liberia 109, Malaysia 2, Malta 45, Marshall Islands 5, Moldova 5, Mongolia 2, Panama 49, Romania 1, Saint Kitts and Nevis 13, Saint Vincent and the Grenadines 11, Sierra Leone 7, Singapore 2, Spain 6, Vanuatu 7, unknown 19) (2010)

Ports and terminals:
major seaport(s): Kaliningrad, Nakhodka, Novorossiysk, Primorsk, Vostochnyy
river port(s): Saint Petersburg (Neva River)
oil terminal(s): Kavkaz oil terminal
container port(s) (TEUs): Saint Petersburg (2,365,174)

MILITARY

Military branches:
Ground Troops (Sukhoputnyye Voyskia, SV), Navy (Voyenno-Morskoy Flot, VMF), Air Forces (Voyenno-Vozdushniye Sily, VVS); Airborne Troops (Vozdushno-Desantnyye Voyska, VDV), Missile Troops of Strategic Purpose (Raketnyye Voyska Strategicheskogo Naznacheniya, RVSN) referred to commonly as Strategic Rocket Forces, and Aerospace Defense Troops (Voyska Vozdushno-Kosmicheskoy Oborony or Voyska VKO) are independent "combat arms," not subordinate to any of the three branches; Russian Ground Troops include the following combat arms: motorized-rifle troops, tank troops, missile and artillery troops, air defense of the Ground Troops (2014)

Military service age and obligation:
18-27 years of age for compulsory or voluntary military service; males are registered for the draft at 17 years of age; service obligation is 1 year (conscripts can only be sent to combat zones after 6 months of training); reserve obligation for non-officers to age 50; enrollment in military schools from the age of 16, cadets classified as members of the armed forces
note: the chief of the General Staff Mobilization Directorate announced in May 2013 that for health reasons, only 65% of draftees called up during the spring 2013 draft campaign were fit for military service, and over 12% of these were sent for an additional medical examination (by way of comparison, 69.9% in 2012 and 57.7% in 2011 were deemed fit for military service); approximately 50% of draft-age Russian males receive some type of legal deferment each draft cycle (2014)

Manpower available for military service:
males age 16-49: 34,765,736
females age 16-49: 35,410,779 (2013 est.)

Manpower fit for military service:
males age 16-49: 22,597,728
females age 16-49: 23,017,006 (2013 est.)

Manpower reaching militarily significant age annually:

male:
female:

Military expenditures:
4.47% of GDP (2012)

country comparison to the world: 8
4.13% of GDP (2011)
4.47% of GDP (2010)

TRANSNATIONAL ISSUES

Russia remains concerned about the smuggling of poppy derivatives from Afghanistan through Central Asian countries; China and Russia have demarcated the once disputed islands at the Amur and Ussuri confluence and in the Argun River in accordance with the 2004 Agreement, ending their centuries-long border disputes; the sovereignty dispute over the islands of Etorofu, Kunashiri, Shikotan, and the Habomai group, known in Japan as the "Northern Territories" and in Russia as the "Southern Kurils," occupied by the Soviet Union in 1945, now administered by Russia, and claimed by Japan, remains the primary sticking point to signing a peace treaty formally ending World War II hostilities; Russia's military support and subsequent recognition of Abkhazia and South Ossetia independence in 2008 continue to sour relations with Georgia; Azerbaijan, Kazakhstan, and Russia ratified Caspian seabed delimitation treaties based on equidistance, while Iran continues to insist on a one-fifth slice of the sea; Norway and Russia signed a comprehensive maritime boundary agreement in 2010; various groups in Finland advocate restoration of Karelia (Kareliya) and other areas ceded to the Soviet Union following World War II but the Finnish Government asserts no territorial demands; Russia and Estonia signed a technical border agreement in May 2005, but Russia recalled its signature in June 2005 after the Estonian parliament added to its domestic ratification act a historical preamble referencing the Soviet occupation and Estonia's pre-war borders under the 1920 Treaty of Tartu; Russia contends that the preamble allows Estonia to make territorial claims on Russia in the future, while Estonian officials deny that the preamble has any legal impact on the treaty text; Russia demands better treatment of the Russian-speaking population in Estonia and Latvia; Lithuania and Russia committed to demarcating their boundary in 2006 in accordance with the land and maritime treaty ratified by Russia in May 2003 and by Lithuania in 1999; Lithuania operates a simplified transit regime for Russian nationals traveling from the Kaliningrad coastal exclave into Russia, while still conforming, as an EU member state with an EU external border, where strict Schengen border rules apply; preparations for the demarcation delimitation of land boundary with Ukraine have commenced; the dispute over the boundary between Russia and Ukraine through the Kerch Strait and Sea of Azov is suspended due to the occupation of Crimea by Russia; Kazakhstan and Russia boundary delimitation was ratified on November 2005 and field demarcation should commence in 2007; Russian Duma has not yet ratified 1990 Bering Sea Maritime Boundary Agreement with the US; Denmark (Greenland) and Norway have made submissions to the Commission on the Limits of the Continental shelf (CLCS) and Russia is collecting additional data to augment its 2001 CLCS submission

Refugees and internally displaced persons:
IDPs: at least 34,900 (armed conflict, human rights violations, generalized violence in North Caucasus, particularly Chechnya and North Ossetia) (2013)
stateless persons: 178,000 (2012); note - Russia's stateless population consists of Roma, Meskhetian Turks, and ex-Soviet citizens from the former republics; between 2003 and 2010 more than 600,000 stateless people were naturalized; most Meskhetian Turks, followers of Islam with origins in Georgia, fled or were evacuated from Uzbekistan after a 1989 pogrom and have lived in Russia for more than the required five-year residency period; they continue to be denied registration for citizenship and basic rights by local Krasnodar Krai authorities on the grounds that they are temporary illegal migrants

Trafficking in persons:
current situation:
tier rating:

Illicit drugs:

limited cultivation of illicit cannabis and opium poppy and producer of methamphetamine, mostly for domestic consumption; government has active illicit crop eradication program; used as transshipment point for Asian opiates, cannabis, and Latin American cocaine bound for growing domestic markets, to a lesser extent Western and Central Europe, and occasionally to the US; major source of heroin precursor chemicals; corruption and organized crime are key concerns; major consumer of opiates

IMPORTANT INFORMATION FOR UNDERSTANDING RUSSIA

PROFILE

Geography
Area: 17 million sq. km. (6.5 million sq. mi.); about 1.8 times the size of the United States.
Cities: *Capital*--Moscow (pop. 10.4 million). *Other cities*--St. Petersburg (4.6 million), Novosibirsk (1.4 million), Nizhniy Novgorod (1.3 million).
Terrain: Broad plain with low hills west of Urals; vast coniferous forest and tundra in Siberia; uplands and mountains (Caucasus range) along southern borders.
Climate: Northern continental.

People
Nationality: *Noun and adjective*--Russian(s).
Population (August 2011): 142.9 million.
Annual population growth rate (2011 est.): -0.07%.
Ethnic groups (2002 census): Russian 79.8%, Tatar 3.8%, Ukrainian 2%, Bashkir 1.2%, Chuvash 1.1%, other 12.1%.
Religion: Russian Orthodox, Islam, Judaism, Roman Catholicism, Protestant, Buddhist, other.
Language: Russian (official); more than 140 other languages and dialects.
Education (total pop.): *Literacy*--99.4%.
Health: *Life expectancy* (2011 est.)--63.03 years men, 74.87 years women.
Work force (75.49 million, 2010 est.): *Services*--58.1%, *industry*--31.9%, *agriculture*--10%.

Government
Type: Federation.
Independence: August 24, 1991.
Constitution: December 12, 1993.
Branches: *Executive*--president, prime minister (chairman of the government). *Legislative*--Federal Assembly (Federation Council, State Duma). *Judicial*--Constitutional Court, Supreme Court, Supreme Court of Arbitration, Office of Procurator General.
Political parties: There are seven registered political parties in Russia: United Russia, the Communist Party (KPRF), the Liberal Democratic Party (LDPR), Just Russia, Yabloko, Patriots of Russia, and Right Cause. Yabloko, Patriots of Russia, and Right Cause did not win enough votes in the December 2011 election to be represented in the Duma. The next Duma election will be held in December 2016.
Subdivisions: 83 federal subjects (members of the Federation), including 21 republics, 9 krays, 46 oblasts, 2 federal cities, 1 autonomous oblast, and 4 autonomous okrugs.
Suffrage: Universal at 18 years.

Economy
GDP (2010): $1.477 trillion.
Growth rate (2011): 4%.
Natural resources: Petroleum, natural gas, timber, furs, precious and nonferrous metals.
Agriculture: *Products*--Grain, sugar beets, sunflower seeds, meat, dairy products.
Industry: *Types*--Complete range of manufactures: automobiles, trucks, trains, agricultural equipment, advanced aircraft, aerospace, machine and equipment products; mining and extractive industry; medical and scientific instruments; construction equipment.
Trade (2010): *Exports*--$376.7 billion: petroleum and petroleum products, natural gas, woods and wood

products, metals, chemicals. *Major markets*--EU, CIS, China, Japan. *Imports*--$191.8 billion: machinery and equipment, chemicals, consumer goods, medicines, meat, sugar, semi-finished metal products. *Major partners*--EU, CIS, Japan, China, U.S. *U.S. exports*--$6.0 billion. *Principal U.S. exports to Russia* (2010)--oil/gas equipment, meat, motor vehicles and parts, aircraft, electrical machinery, automatic data processing machines and parts, medical equipment, plastics, cosmetics, and chemicals. *U.S. imports*--$25.7 billion. *Principal U.S. imports from Russia* (2010)--oil, chemicals (including fertilizer), radioactive materials, iron/steel, precious stones, nickel, aluminum, fish and crustaceans, alcoholic beverages, and base metals.

PEOPLE

Russia's 142.9 million citizens descend from more than 100 ethnic groups. Russian is the official language of Russia and is one of the six official languages of the United Nations. Russian is also the language of such giants of world literature as Pushkin, Tolstoy, Dostoevsky, Chekhov, Pasternak, and Solzhenitsyn.

Russia's educational system has produced nearly 100% literacy. About 8.1 million students attended Russia's 1,108 institutions of higher education in 2008, but continued reform is critical to producing students with skills to adapt to a market economy. Because great emphasis is placed on science and technology in education, Russian mathematical, scientific, and space and aviation research is still generally of a high order. The number of doctors in relation to the population is high by American standards, although medical care in Russia, even in major cities, is generally far below Western standards. The unraveling of the Soviet state in its last decades and the physical and psychological traumas of transition during the 1990s resulted in a steady decline in the health of the Russian people. Currently Russia faces a demographic crisis as births lag far behind deaths. While its population is aging, the high number of deaths of working-age males due to cardiovascular disease is a major cause of Russia's demographic woes. A rapid increase in HIV/AIDS infections and tuberculosis, added to rising deaths from cancer, compounds the problem. In 2011, life expectancy at birth was estimated at 63.03 years for men and 74.87 years for women. The large annual excess of deaths over births, if unabated, could cut Russia's population by 30% over the next 50 years, though inward migration could change this picture. At the end of 2010, there were 60 million Internet users in Russia, with the number growing by 15% a year. Industry watchers forecast that Russia will be Europe's largest Internet market within the next 2 years.

The Russian labor force, amounting to nearly 76 million workers in 2010, is undergoing tremendous changes. Although well educated and skilled, it is largely mismatched to the rapidly changing needs of the Russian economy. Official unemployment dropped to its lowest rate of 5.4% in May 2008, and labor shortages appeared in some high-skilled job markets. The economic crisis that began in late 2008, however, quickly reversed this trend and the ranks of unemployed swelled to an International Labor Organization (ILO)-estimated 8.2% in 2009; 1.8 million Russians lost their jobs in the first quarter of 2009 alone. By the end of 2010, the Russian economy showed signs of recovery, with the unemployment rate falling to 7.4% by the end of the second quarter, according to the Russian Government statistics agency, Rosstat. Following the 1991 collapse of the Soviet Union and the economic dislocation it engendered, the standard of living fell dramatically. Real disposable incomes then doubled between 1999 and 2009, and experts estimate that the middle class constitutes approximately one-fourth of the population. The economic crisis, however, interrupted this trend, as real disposable incomes grew by only 1.9% in 2009 and wages fell by 2.8% during the same period. The stock of wage arrears, which peaked during the crisis at almost 9 billion rubles, had fallen by almost half by February 2010. Government anti-crisis measures to bolster wages, pensions, and other benefits helped reduce the poverty rate in 2009 to an estimated 14%, bringing the number of people living below the subsistence minimum (equivalent to about $169 per month) to below 20 million. The official poverty rate was estimated as 13.1% by the World Bank at the end of 2010. According to Russian statistics, the poverty level increased to 14.9% of the population in the first half of 2011 because of an increase in the official poverty threshold and because average real income fell slightly in 2011.

Moscow is Russia's capital and largest city. Moscow is also increasingly important as an economic and business center; it has become Russia's principal magnet for foreign investment and business presence. Its cultural tradition is rich, and there are many museums devoted to art, literature, music, dance, history, and science, as well as hundreds of churches and dozens of notable cathedrals.

The second-largest city in Russia is St. Petersburg, which was established by Peter the Great in 1703 to be the capital of the Russian Empire as part of his Western-looking reforms. The city was called Petrograd during World War I and Leningrad after 1924. In 1991, as the result of a city referendum, it was renamed St. Petersburg. Under the tsars, the city was Russia's cultural, intellectual, commercial, financial, and industrial center. After Lenin moved the capital back to Moscow in 1918, the city's political significance declined, but it remained a cultural, scientific, and military-industrial center. The Hermitage, formerly the Winter Palace of the tsars, is one of the world's great fine arts museums.

Russia has an area of about 17 million square kilometers (6.5 million sq. mi.); in geographic terms, this makes Russia the largest country in the world by more than 2.5 million square miles. But with a population density of about 22 persons per square mile (9 per sq. km.), it is sparsely populated, and most of its residents live in urban areas.

HISTORY

Although human experience on the territory of present-day Russia dates back to Paleolithic times, the first lineal predecessor of the modern Russian state was founded in 862. The political entity known as Kievan Rus was established in Kiev in 962 and lasted until the 12th century. In the 10th century, Christianity became the state religion under Vladimir, who adopted Greek Orthodox rites. Consequently, Byzantine culture predominated, as is evident in much of Russia's architectural, musical, and artistic heritage. Over the next centuries, various invaders assaulted the Kievan state and, finally, Mongols under Batu Khan destroyed the main population centers except for Novgorod and Pskov in the 13th century and prevailed over the region until 1480. Some historians believe that the Mongol period had a lasting impact on Russian political culture.

In the post-Mongol period, Muscovy gradually became the dominant principality and was able, through diplomacy and conquest, to establish suzerainty over European Russia. Ivan III (1462-1505) referred to his empire as "the Third Rome" and considered it heir to the Byzantine tradition. Ivan IV (the Terrible) (1530-1584) was the first Russian ruler to call himself tsar, a word derived from the Old Russian term for Caesar. He pushed Russia eastward with his conquests but his later reign was marked by the cruelty that earned him his familiar epithet. He was succeeded by Boris Godunov, whose reign commenced the so-called Time of Troubles. Relative stability was achieved when Mikhail Romanov established the dynasty that bore his name in 1613.

During the reign of Peter the Great (1689-1725), modernization and European influences spread in Russia. Peter created Western-style military forces, subordinated the Russian Orthodox Church hierarchy to the tsar, reformed the entire governmental structure, and established the beginnings of a Western-style education system. He moved the capital westward from Moscow to St. Petersburg, his newly-established city on the Baltic. His introduction of European customs generated nationalistic resentments in society and spawned the philosophical rivalry between "Westernizers" and "Slavophiles" that remains a key dynamic of current Russian social and political thought.

Catherine the Great continued Peter's expansionist policies and established Russia as a European power. During her reign (1762-96), power was centralized in the monarchy, and administrative reforms concentrated great wealth and privilege in the hands of the Russian nobility. Catherine was also known as an enthusiastic patron of art, literature and education and for her correspondence with Voltaire and other Enlightenment figures. Catherine segregated the large Jewish population Russia inherited during the partitions of Poland (1772-95) into an area known as "The Pale of Settlement," where great numbers of Jews were concentrated and later subject to vicious attacks known as pogroms.

Alexander I (1801-1825) began his reign as a reformer, but after defeating Napoleon's 1812 attempt to conquer Russia, he became much more conservative and rolled back many of his early reforms. During this era, Russia gained control of Georgia and much of the Caucasus. Throughout the 19th century, the Russian Government sought to suppress repeated attempts at reform and attempts at liberation by various national movements, particularly under the reign of Nicholas I (1825-1855). Its economy failed to compete with those of Western countries. Russian cities were growing without an industrial base to generate employment, although emancipation of the serfs in 1861 foreshadowed urbanization and rapid industrialization late in the century. At the same time, Russia expanded into the rest of the Caucasus, Central Asia and across Siberia. The port of Vladivostok was opened on the Pacific coast in 1860. The Trans-Siberian Railroad opened vast frontiers to development late in the century. In the 19th century, Russian culture flourished as Russian artists made significant contributions to world literature, visual arts, dance, and music. The names of Dostoyevsky, Tolstoy, Gogol, Repin, and Tchaikovsky became known to the world.

Alexander II (1855-1881), a relatively liberal tsar, emancipated the serfs, reformed the judiciary, and established elected local councils (zemstvos). His 1881 assassination, however, prompted the reactionary rule of Alexander III (1881-1894). At the turn of the century, imperial decline became evident. Russia was defeated in the unpopular Russo-Japanese war in 1905. The Russian Revolution of 1905 forced Tsar Nicholas II (1894-1917) to grant a constitution and introduce limited democratic reforms. The government suppressed opposition and abetted anti-Semitic pogroms. Attempts at economic change, such as land reform, were incomplete.

1917 Revolution and the U.S.S.R.
The ruinous effects of World War I, combined with internal pressures, sparked the March 1917 uprising that led Tsar Nicholas II to abdicate the throne. A provisional government came to power, headed by Aleksandr Kerenskiy. On November 7, 1917, the Bolshevik Party, led by Vladimir Lenin, seized control and established the Russian Soviet Federated Socialist Republic. Civil war broke out in 1918 between Lenin's "Red" army and various "White" forces and lasted until 1920, when, despite foreign interventions and a war with Poland, the Bolsheviks triumphed. After the Red army conquered Ukraine, Belarus, Azerbaijan, Georgia, and Armenia, a new nation, the Union of Soviet Socialist Republics (U.S.S.R.), was formed in 1922.

First among its political figures was Lenin, leader of the Bolshevik Party and head of the first Soviet Government, who died in 1924. In the late 1920s, General Secretary of the Communist Party of the Soviet Union (CPSU) Josef Stalin emerged as the dominant figure in the aftermath of intra-party rivalries; he maintained complete control over Soviet domestic and international policy until his death in 1953. In the 1930s, Stalin oversaw the forced collectivization of tens of millions of its citizens in state agricultural and industrial enterprises. Millions died in the process from state-created famines. Millions more were executed or died in the vast penal and labor system known as the Gulag. Initially allied to Nazi Germany, which resulted in significant territorial additions on its western border, the U.S.S.R. was attacked by the Axis on June 22, 1941. More than twenty million Soviet citizens died during World War II in the successful effort to defeat the Axis, in addition to over two million Soviet Jews who perished in the Holocaust. After the war, the U.S.S.R. became one of the Permanent Members of the UN Security Council. In 1949, the U.S.S.R. developed its own nuclear arsenal.

Stalin's successor, Nikita Khrushchev, served as Communist Party leader until he was ousted in 1964, and presided over an era of cautious liberalization known as the Thaw. Aleksey Kosygin became Chairman of the Council of Ministers, and Leonid Brezhnev was made First Secretary of the CPSU Central Committee in 1964. In 1971, Brezhnev rose to become "first among equals" in a collective leadership. During this period, the Soviet economy entered a period of stagnation from which it never recovered. Brezhnev died in 1982 and was succeeded by Yuriy Andropov (1982-84) and Konstantin Chernenko (1984-85). In 1985, Mikhail Gorbachev became the next (and last) General Secretary of the CPSU. Gorbachev introduced policies of *perestroika* (restructuring) and *glasnost* (openness). But his efforts to reform the creaky Communist system from within failed. The people of the Soviet Union were not content with half-freedoms granted by Moscow; they demanded more and the system collapsed. Boris Yeltsin was elected the first president of the Russian Federation in 1991. Russia, Ukraine, and Belarus formed the Commonwealth of Independent States in December 1991. Gorbachev resigned as Soviet President on December 25, 1991.

The Russian Federation
After the December 1991 dissolution of the Soviet Union, the Russian Federation became its successor state, inheriting its permanent seat on the UN Security Council, most of its military assets, as well as the bulk of its foreign assets and debt. By the fall of 1993, politics in Russia reached a stalemate between President Yeltsin and the parliament elected in the waning days of the Soviet Union. The parliament had succeeded in blocking, overturning, or ignoring the President's initiatives on drafting a new constitution, conducting new elections, and making further progress on democratic and economic reforms.

In a dramatic speech in September 1993, President Yeltsin dissolved the Russian parliament in contravention of the existing constitution, and called for new national elections and a new constitution. In response, the parliament sought to depose Yeltsin and instigate an armed insurrection. Yeltsin ordered the army to respond with force to capture the parliament building and crush the insurrection. In December 1993, voters elected a new parliament and approved a new constitution that had been drafted by the Yeltsin government. Yeltsin remained the dominant political figure, although a broad array of parties, including ultra-nationalists, liberals, agrarians, and communists, had substantial representation in the parliament and competed actively in elections at all levels of government.

In late 1994, the Russian security forces launched a brutal operation in the Republic of Chechnya against rebels who were intent on separation from Russia. The protracted conflict, which received close scrutiny in the Russian media, raised serious human rights and humanitarian concerns abroad as well as within Russia, with violations committed on both sides of the fighting. After numerous unsuccessful attempts to institute a cease-fire, in August 1996 the Russian and Chechen authorities negotiated a settlement that resulted in a complete withdrawal of Russian troops and the holding of elections in January 1997. A peace treaty was concluded in May 1997. Following a number of terrorist incidents blamed on Chechen separatists, the Russian Government launched a new military campaign into Chechnya in 1999. By spring 2000, federal forces claimed control over Chechen territory, but fighting continued as rebel fighters regularly ambushed Russian forces in the region. Throughout 2002 and 2003, the ability of Chechen separatists to battle the Russian forces waned but they claimed responsibility for numerous terrorist acts. In 2005 and 2006, key separatist leaders were killed by Russian forces. Large-scale violence was quelled after Ramzan Kadyrov was confirmed as Chechen President in 2007, though many human rights groups accused him of committing serious human rights violations. In April 2009, the Russian Government announced the end of counterterrorism operations in Chechnya; however, the specter of potential conflict in the North Caucasus was raised again by the March 2010 bombing of the Moscow Metro, the January 2011 explosion in Moscow's Domodedovo airport, and the continuing violence in the republic of Dagestan.

On December 31, 1999 Boris Yeltsin resigned, and Vladimir Putin was named Acting President. In March 2000, he won election in his own right as Russia's second president with 53% of the vote. Putin moved quickly to reassert Moscow's control over the regions, whose governors had confidently ignored edicts from Boris Yeltsin. He ended direct elections for regional leaders and sent his own "plenipotentiary representatives" (commonly called 'polpred' in Russian) to ensure that Moscow's policies were followed in recalcitrant regions and republics. He won enactment of liberal economic reforms that rescued a faltering economy and stopped a spiral of hyperinflation. Putin achieved wide popularity by stabilizing the government, especially in marked contrast to what many Russians saw as the chaos of the latter Yeltsin years. The economy grew both because of rising oil prices and, in part, because Putin was able to achieve reforms in banking, labor, and private property. During this time, Russia also moved closer to the U.S., especially after the terrorist attacks of September 11, 2001. In 2002, the NATO-Russia Council was established, giving Russia a voice in NATO discussions.

U.S.-Russian relations cooled over the ensuing years given concerns over domestic developments in Russia, including political freedoms and human rights, as well as over foreign policy differences. Dmitriy Medvedev was elected President in March 2008 and inaugurated in May. Relations during the first few months of his presidency were affected by the August 2008 Russia-Georgia war and subsequent decision by Russia to recognize the territories of South Ossetia and Abkhazia. As a result, U.S.-Russian contact decreased significantly and the NATO-Russia Council was suspended temporarily.

With the change of U.S. administration in January 2009, U.S.-Russian relations have markedly improved as both sides sought to change the tone of the relationship and to cooperate in areas of mutual interest. At a July 2009 summit in Moscow, Presidents Barack Obama and Medvedev created the U.S.-Russia Bilateral Presidential Commission to pursue joint projects and improve cooperation between the two countries. Recent years have also seen increased cooperation with U.S. and NATO, leading to a new strategic concept proposed at the November 2010 Lisbon Summit that strives to develop a "true strategic partnership between NATO and Russia." In February 2011, the New START Treaty, which significantly reduced each country's deployable nuclear weapons, came into effect. The new 123 Agreement between the U.S. and Russia establishes a legal framework for advancing joint work on peaceful uses of nuclear energy. The U.S., NATO, and Russia have also worked closely together to bring stability to Afghanistan. To address Iran's failure to abide by its international commitments regarding its nuclear program, the U.S. and Russia coordinated multilateral approaches to demonstrate to Iran the consequences of its intransigence.

GOVERNMENT AND POLITICAL CONDITIONS

In the political system established by the 1993 constitution, the president wields considerable executive power. There is no vice president, and the legislative branch is far weaker than the executive. The bicameral legislature consists of the lower house (State Duma) and the upper house (the Federation Council). The president nominates the highest state officials, including the prime minister, who must be approved by the Duma. The president can pass decrees without consent from the Duma. He also is head of the armed forces and of the Security Council.

Elections to the Duma, the 450-seat lower house of parliament, were held most recently on December 4, 2011, and presidential elections on March 4, 2012. The pro-government party, United Russia, polled 49 percent of the Duma vote, which translated to 53 percent of seats under Russia's proportional representation system. This was a much weaker result than in 2007, when the party won more than two thirds of seats, enabling it to change the Constitution at will. The three minority parties elected to the Duma in 2007- the Communists, Just Russia and the Liberal Democratic Party – all increased their representation in the 2011 election. Three other parties – Yabloko, Right Cause, and Patriots of Russia – contested the elections but did not meet the 7 percent threshold for representation.

The Party of People's Freedom, a liberal opposition party, had its party registration invalidated and could not participate in the elections. In contrast to 2007, the Organization for Security and Cooperation in Europe's (OSCE) Office of Democratic Institutions and Human Rights (ODIHR) sent a mission to observe the Duma elections. The ODIHR mission's post-election statement identified discrepancies in voting, counting, and tabulation procedures, and noted that the elections took place in an atmosphere which seriously limited political competition. Frequent abuses of administrative resources and media coverage strongly in favor of United Russia combined to hinder political pluralism. The next Duma election must occur before December 2016, as a December 2008 law extended the mandate of the Duma, beginning with the 2011 elections, to five years from four.

On September 24, 2011 Prime Minister Vladimir Putin announced his intention to seek a new term as Russia's president. Putin was elected to a third term – he served the constitutional maximum two consecutive terms from 2000-2008 – as Russia's president on March 4, 2012. He officially garnered 63.4 percent of the vote against four rivals, including leaders of the minority parties in the Duma and a self-nominated candidate, Mikhail Prokhorov. The OSCE/ODIHR observed the election and noted similar shortcomings to those noted in the Duma elections, including the lack of genuine competition and biased media coverage affecting the fairness of the election. The December 2008 law that extended the Duma's mandate also lengthened the term of Russia's president, beginning with the 2012 election, to six years, so the next presidential election is scheduled for 2018.

Russia is a federation, but the precise distribution of powers between the central government and the regional and local authorities is still evolving. The Russian Federation consists of 83 administrative units, including two federal cities, Moscow and St. Petersburg. The constitution explicitly defines the federal government's exclusive powers, but it also describes most key regional issues as the joint responsibility of the federal government and the regional administrative units. In 2000, President Putin grouped the regions into seven federal districts, with presidential appointees established in Moscow and six provincial capitals. In March 2004, the constitution was amended to permit the merger of some regional administrative units. A law enacted in December 2004 eliminated the direct election of the country's regional leaders. Governors are now nominated by the president and subject to confirmation by regional legislatures.

Judicial System

The Russian judicial system consists of the Constitutional Court, courts of general jurisdiction, military courts, and arbitrage courts (which hear commercial disputes). The Constitutional Court of the Russian Federation is a court of limited subject matter jurisdiction. The 1993 constitution empowers the Constitutional Court to arbitrate disputes between the executive and legislative branches and between Moscow and the regional and local governments. The court also is authorized to rule on violations of constitutional rights, to examine appeals from various bodies, and to participate in impeachment proceedings against the president. The July 1994 Law on the Constitutional Court prohibits the court from examining cases on its own initiative and limits the scope of issues the court can hear. The system of general jurisdiction courts includes the Supreme Court of the Russian Federation, regional level courts, district level courts and justices of the peace.

The Duma passed a Criminal Procedure Code and other judicial reforms during its 2001 session. These reforms help make the Russian judicial system more compatible with its Western counterparts. The reforms reintroduced jury trials in certain criminal cases and created a more adversarial system of criminal trials that protect the rights of defendants more adequately. Another significant advance in the Code is the transfer, from the Procuracy to the courts, of authority to issue search and arrest warrants. There are concerns, however, that prosecutors have selectively targeted individuals for political reasons, as in the prosecution of Yukos Oil CEO Mikhail Khodorkovskiy.

In spite of some efforts to increase judicial independence (for example, through a considerable salary increase for judges several years ago), many judges still see their role not as impartial and independent arbiters, but as government officials protecting state interests. See below for more information on the commercial court/business law.

Human Rights

Russia's human rights record remains uneven and poor in some areas. Despite significant improvements in conditions following the end of the Soviet Union, problem areas remain. In particular, the Russian Government's policy in the North Caucasus has been a cause for international concern. Although the government has recognized the legitimacy of international human rights standards, the institutionalization of procedures to safeguard these rights has lagged. There are, however, some indications that the law is becoming an increasingly important tool for those seeking to protect human rights.

The judiciary is not independent, is often subject to manipulation by political authorities, and is plagued by large case backlogs and trial delays. Lengthy pretrial detention remains a serious problem. Russia has one of the highest prison population rates in the world, at 613 per 100,000. There are credible reports of beating and torture of inmates and detainees by law enforcement and correctional officials, and brutality perpetrated by the prisoners themselves, some of whom are informally granted authority to enforce order within the prisons. Prison conditions fall well below international standards and extreme overcrowding is common. In 2001, President Putin ordered a moratorium on the death penalty. There are reports that the Russian Government might still be violating promises it made upon entering the European Council, especially in terms of prison control and conditions. A 2008 law established an independent association of prison monitors, which began work in 2009. The association has had mixed results in its work, with some prison officials cooperating, and others obstructing its work. Highly publicized cases, such as the November 2009 death of lawyer Sergey Magnitsky, who died in pre-trial detention due to lack of access to medical care, have increased pressure on the authorities to ensure effective prison monitoring.

In the North Caucasus, there have been credible allegations of violations of international human rights and humanitarian law committed by both government and non-government forces. Despite an official end to the counterterrorism campaign in Chechnya in April 2009, there was an upsurge in violence in the North Caucasus starting in 2009 and continuing to the present, especially in the republic of Dagestan. Russian authorities have introduced some improvements, such as requiring the presence of civilian investigators during all large-scale military operations and targeted search and seizure operations. Human rights groups and non-governmental organization (NGO) leaders in the region claim that most abuses remain uninvestigated and unpunished and have spread more broadly in the North Caucasus. Chechen leader Ramzan Kadyrov, in power since 2007, was unanimously approved by the Chechen parliament for a new 5-year term beginning in April 2011. Kadyrov has reportedly begun imposing strict Islamic rules on women in the Russian republic, including mandatory headscarves and other restrictive dress code and workplace policies. In 2010, there were paintball attacks in the Chechen capital of Grozny on women who did not have their heads covered, but were otherwise modestly dressed.

The Russian constitution provides for freedom of religion, the equality of all religions before the law, and the separation of church and state. More than 70% of Russians identify themselves as Russian Orthodox. While Muslims, Jews, and other religious minorities continue to encounter prejudice and societal discrimination, they have not been inhibited by the government in the free practice of their religion. High-ranking federal officials have condemned anti-Semitic hate crimes, but law enforcement bodies have not always effectively prosecuted those responsible. The Federal Registration Service and some local officials continue to prevent some religious minority groups from registering locally or from acquiring property. Jehovah's Witnesses, readers of Said Nursi, and Scientologists have all reported problems with registration and harassment. All have also had religious literature declared extremist by regional courts.

The constitution provides for freedom of speech and of the press; however, in practice government pressure on the media persists, resulting in numerous infringements of these rights. The government uses direct ownership or ownership by large private companies with links to the government to control or influence the major media outlets, especially television, through direct control and through self-censorship by editors and journalists. This results in restricted access to information about issues deemed sensitive, including coverage of opposition political parties and movements. Unsolved murders of journalists, including the murder of respected investigative reporter Anna Politkovskaya in October 2006, have caused significant international concern and increased the reluctance of journalists to cover controversial subjects. In another unsolved case, environmentalist journalist Mikhail Beketov was beaten nearly to death in November 2008 after he published articles attacking local authorities' development plans for the Khimki forest. The November 2010 beating of Kommersant reporter Oleg Kashin led President Medvedev to pledge to capture those who committed the crime and prompted over 200 journalists to sign a petition to the President asking for protection.

The 2006 law on NGOs created a burdensome registration process for all NGOs, with stricter requirements for foreign-funded NGOs and more relaxed requirements for religious organizations. Authorities also have used a separate law against extremism as a pretext for closing opposition NGOs and media entities, doing so for the first time in January 2007. In 2010, the State Duma passed a law easing registration requirements for NGOs, but critics alleged that this law was largely symbolic, as it did nothing to reinstate the tax-exempt status of foreign grants.

The constitution guarantees citizens the right to choose their place of residence and to travel abroad. Some big-city governments, however, have restricted this right through residential registration rules that closely resemble Soviet-era restrictions. These restrictions, though, are widely circumvented, as evidenced by the large number of undocumented foreign workers in these cities. The freedom to travel abroad and emigrate is respected although restrictions may apply to those who have had access to state secrets, or who have court orders against them for default on debts. Since 1994, the U.S. President has found Russia to be in full compliance with the provisions of the Jackson-Vanik Amendment.

Principal Government Officials

Pres., **Vladimir Vladimirovich PUTIN**
Premier, **Dmitriy Anatolyevich MEDVEDEV**
First Dep. Premier, **Igor Ivanovich SHUVALOV**
Dep. Premier, **Arkadiy Vladimirovich DVORKOVICH**
Dep. Premier, **Olga Yuryevna GOLODETS**
Dep. Premier, **Aleksandr Gennadiyevich KHLOPONIN**
Dep. Premier, **Dmitriy Nikolayevich KOZAK**
Dep. Premier, **Dmitriy Olegovich ROGOZIN**
Dep. Premier, **Vladislav Yuryevich SURKOV**
Min. of Agriculture, **Nikolay Vasilyevich FEDOROV**
Min. of Civil Defense, Emergencies, & Natural Disasters, **Vladimir Andreyevich PUCHKOV**
Min. of Communications & Mass Media, **Nikolay Anatolyevich NIKIFOROV**
Min. of Culture, **Vladimir Rostislavovich MEDINSKIY**
Min. of Defense, **Anatoliy Eduardovich SERDYUKOV**
Min. of Economic Development, **Andrey Removich BELOUSOV**
Min. of Education & Science, **Dmitriy Viktorovich LIVANOV**
Min. of Energy, **Aleksandr Valentinovich NOVAK**
Min. of Far East Development, **Viktor Ivanovich ISHAYEV**
Min. of Finance, **Anton Germanovich SILUANOV**
Min. of Foreign Affairs, **Sergey Viktorovich LAVROV**
Min. of Health, **Veronika Igoryevna SKVORTSOVA**
Min. of Industry & Trade, **Denis Valentinovich MANTUROV**
Min. of Internal Affairs, **Vladimir Aleksandrovich KOLOKOLTSEV**
Min. of Justice, **Aleksandr Vladimirovich KONOVALOV**
Min. of Labor & Social Protection, **Maksim Anatolyevich TOPILIN**
Min. of Natural Resources & Ecology, **Sergey Yefimovich DONSKOY**
Min. of Regional Development, **Oleg Markovich GOVORUN**

Min. of Sport, **Vitaliy Leontyevich MUTKO**
Min. of Transportation, **Maksim Yuryevich SOKOLOV**
Min. for Liaison With Open Govt., **Mikhail Anatolyevich ABYZOV**
Dir., Foreign Intelligence Service (SVR) (Acting), **Mikhail Yefimovich FRADKOV**
Dir., Federal Security Service (FSB) (Acting), **Aleksandr Vasilyevich BORTNIKOV**
Head, Govt. Apparatus, **Vladislav Yuryevich SURKOV**
Sec., Security Council, **Nikolay Platonovich PATRUSHEV**
Procurator Gen., **Yuriy Yakovlevich CHAYKA**
Chmn., Central Bank of Russia, **Sergey Mikhaylovich IGNATYEV**
Ambassador to the US, **Sergey Ivanovich KISLYAK**
Permanent Representative to the UN, New York, **Vitaliy Ivanovich CHURKIN**

The Russian Federation maintains an **embassy** at 2650 Wisconsin Ave., NW, Washington, DC 20007 (tel. 202-298-5700) and a consular section at 2641 Tunlaw Road, Washington, DC (tel. 202-939-8907/8913/8918). Russian consulates also are located in Houston, New York, San Francisco, and Seattle.

ECONOMY

Rank	8th (nominal) / 6th (PPP) (2013)
Currency	Russian ruble (RUB)
Fiscal year	calendar year
Trade organizations	WTO, CIS, APEC, EURASEC, G-20 and others
	Statistics
GDP	$2.118 trillion (nominal) $3.461 trillion (PPP) (WB)
GDP growth	0.7%
GDP per capita	$14,818 (2013) (nominal) $23,589 (2012-2014) (PPP) (WB)
GDP by sector	agriculture: 4.4% industry: 37.6% services: 58%
Inflation (CPI)	7.8%
Population below poverty line	11.2%
Labour force	75.5 million
Labour force by occupation	Agriculture: 4.4%, Industry: 37.6%, Services: 58%
Unemployment	4.9%
Average gross salary	32,715 rubles
Main industries	
Ease-of-doing-business rank	92nd
	External
Exports	$542.5 billion
Export goods	petroleum and petroleum products, natural gas, metals, wood and wood products, chemicals, and a wide variety of civilian and military manufactures
Main export partners	Netherlands 14.6% People's Republic of China 6.8% Germany 6.8% Italy 6.2% Turkey 5.2% Ukraine 5.2% Belarus 4.7%
Imports	$358.1 billion
Import goods	consumer goods, machinery, vehicles, pharmaceutical products, plastic, semi-finished metal products, meat, fruits and nuts, optical and medical instruments, iron, steel
Main import partners	People's Republic of China 16.6% Germany 12.2% Ukraine 5.7% Japan 5% United States 4.9%

	France 4.4%
	Italy 4.3%
FDI stock	$552.8 billion
Current account	$34.1 billion
Gross external debt	$720.9 billion
	Public finances
Public debt	7.9% of GDP
Revenues	$469 billion
Expenses	$414 billion
Credit rating	Standard & Poor's: BBB (Domestic) BBB- (Foreign) BBB- (T&C Assessment) Outlook: Negative Moody's: Baa1 Outlook: Negative Fitch: BBB Outlook: Negative
Foreign reserves	$467.2 billion

Economy of Russia is a mixed economy with state ownership in strategic areas of the economy. Market reforms of the 1990s privatized much of Russian industry and agriculture, with notable exceptions in the energy and defense-related sectors.

Russia is unusual among the major economies in the way it relies on energy revenues to drive growth. The country has an abundance of natural resources, including oil, natural gas and precious metals, which make up a major share of Russia's exports. As of 2012 oil and gas sector accounted for 16% of the GDP, 52% of federal budget revenues and over 70% of total exports

Russia has a large and sophisticated arms industry, capable of designing and manufacturing high-tech military equipment, including a fifth-generation fighter jet. The value of Russian arms exports totalled $15.7 billion in 2013—second only to the US. Top military exports from Russia include combat aircraft, air defence systems, ships, submarines.

Russian economy is the sixth largest in the world by PPP. Between 2000 and 2012, Russia's energy exports fuelled a rapid growth in living standards, with real disposable income rising by 160%.

In dollar-denominated terms this amounted to more than sevenfold increase in disposable incomes since 2000. However, these gains have been distributed unevenly as 110 wealthiest individuals were found to own 35% of all financial assets held by Russian households. Since 2008 Moscow has been repeatedly named the "billionaire capital of the world" by Forbes.

According to the IMF, the Russian economy was already in recession from early 2014 mainly as a result of the 2014 Crimean crisis and the subsequent capital flight. But this turned out to be false and the IMF revised it's rhetoric to *close to being in recession* and a forecast of 0.2% growth in 2014 and 1.0% through 2015

The Russian economy underwent tremendous stress in the 1990s as it moved from a centrally planned economy to a free market system. Difficulties in implementing fiscal reforms aimed at raising government revenues and a dependence on short-term borrowing to finance budget deficits led to a serious financial crisis in 1998. Lower prices for Russia's major export earners (oil and minerals) and a loss of investor confidence due to the Asian financial crisis exacerbated financial problems. The result was a rapid and steep decline (60%) in the value of the ruble, flight of foreign investment, delayed payments on sovereign and private debts, a breakdown of commercial transactions through the banking system, and the threat of runaway inflation.

The Russian economy bounced back quickly from the 1998 crisis and enjoyed over 9 years of sustained growth averaging about 7% due to a devalued ruble, implementation of key economic reforms (tax, banking, labor and land codes), tight fiscal policy, and favorable commodities prices. Household consumption and fixed capital investments both grew by about 10% per year during this period and replaced net exports as the main drivers of demand. Inflation and exchange rates stabilized due to a prudent fiscal policy (Russia ran a budget surplus from 2001-2008). Foreign exchange reserves grew to almost $600 billion by mid-2008, the third-largest in the world, of which more than $200 billion were classified as stabilization funds designed to shelter the budget from commodity price shocks. The balance of payments experienced twin surpluses until mid-2008 in the current and capital accounts, which accounted for the phenomenal growth of reserves. As of July 1, 2006, the ruble became convertible for both current and capital transactions. Russia repaid its entire Soviet-era Paris Club debt of $22 billion in late 2006, but by October 2008 foreign external debt totaled $540 billion, of which $500 billion was owed by banks and corporations, including state-owned enterprises.

The global economic crisis hit Russia hard, starting with heavy capital flight in September 2008, which caused a crisis in its stock market. Several high-profile business disputes earlier in 2008, such as TNK-BP and Mechel, as well as the Georgian war helped drive capital out of Russia. By mid-September, Russia's stock market had collapsed, as businesses sold shares to raise collateral for margin calls required by international lending institutions. As the global financial crisis gathered steam in the fall of 2008, the accompanying steep fall in global demand, commodity prices, and tightening of credit served to almost bring Russia's economic growth to a halt in the fourth quarter of 2008, to 1.1% down from 9.5% during the same period in 2007. The Central Bank of Russia responded by pumping liquidity into Russian banks, which helped avert a banking crisis. At the same time, the government attempted a managed devaluation, which successfully avoided a run on the ruble and bank deposits but at the cost of a steep decline in foreign exchange reserves to $387 billion by mid-February 2009. This in turn prompted the S&P and Fitch rating agencies to downgrade Russia's sovereign debt to the lowest investment grade. By 2010, however, the Russian economy had begun a modest recovery, bolstered by government anti-crisis policies, the global rebound, and a rise in oil prices. Russia's leaders put renewed emphasis on promoting innovation as key to economic modernization as well as on the need to diversify the economy away from oil and gas.

Government Spending/Taxation

The Russian federal budget ran growing surpluses from 2001-2007, as the government taxed and saved much of the rapidly increasing oil revenues. The government overhauled its tax system for both corporations and individuals in 2000-2001, introducing a 13% flat tax for individuals and a unified tax for corporations, which improved overall collection. Responding to demands from the oil sector, the government reduced the tax burden on oil production and exports, but only marginally. Tax enforcement of disputes continues to be uneven and unpredictable. In 2007 the federal budget surplus was 5.5% of GDP, and in 2008 the government ended the year with a surplus of 4.1% of GDP. Although the government revised its budget projections during 2009 to reflect lower oil prices and the effects of the economic crisis, it ended the year with a budget deficit amounting to 7.9% of GDP, which it financed from the Reserve Fund, one of the government's two stabilization funds. The government's anti-crisis package in 2008 and 2009 amounted to about 6.7% of GDP, according to World Bank estimates. The package provided support to the financial sector and enterprises--through liquidity injections to banks and tax cuts/fiscal support to enterprises--as well as modest support for households and small and medium enterprises (SMEs) and increased unemployment benefits. By the end of 2010, due to improving economic conditions, Russia had lowered its budget deficit to 3.9% of GDP. Due to relatively high oil prices through the first half of the year, many officials believed there would not be a budget deficit for 2011.

Population

Russia's population was 142.9 million as of August 2011. Life expectancy remains low compared to developed countries, averaging 63.03 years for men and 74.87 years for women in 2011. The UN predicts that Russia may lose one-third of its population by 2050. Cardiovascular diseases, cancer, traffic accidents, and violence continue to be major causes of death among working age men. Many premature deaths are attributed to excessive alcohol consumption and smoking. A truly healthy Russia will require serious improvements in the health sector and some major changes in current cultural norms. To combat the looming demographic crisis, in October 2007 then-President Putin approved the concept of demographic policy for the years 2008-2025. The program aims to increase life expectancy, reduce mortality, increase the birth rate, improve the population's health, and develop a sound migration policy. The government instituted the National Priority Health Project and "mother's capital" in order to slow the population decline. These programs had short-term success; Russia's natural population decline, the absolute difference between births and deaths, diminished from more than 800,000 in 2005 to roughly 200.000 in 2010, as the birthrate grew from 10.2 to 12.5 per 1,000 in the same period. In April 2008, the government signed the World Health Organization's Framework Convention on Tobacco Control, then approved a tobacco control policy in September 2010 designed to reduce extremely high smoking rates. Results of the 2010 Global Adult Tobacco Survey showed tobacco is the third-leading cause of premature death in Russia, amounting to 17% of all deaths. Nearly 40% of Russia's adult population, or nearly 44 million people, are smokers, more than any other country surveyed on a per capita basis.

HIV/AIDS

Rhere were 592,110 HIV cases officially registered in Russia, though some experts believe the actual number may be over 1 million HIV cases. Statistics show 58,663 new HIV cases documented in Russia in 2010, which is not a significant change from 58,448 new cases recorded in 2009. However, the prevalence of HIV cases was 369 per 100,000 people in 2010, higher than the 2009 indicator of 323 per 100,000. The chief form of transmission continues to be intravenous drug use, which accounted for over 59.2% of new HIV cases in 2010, slightly down from 61.3% in 2009, suggesting an increase in transmission from at-risk groups into the general population via sexual contact. More than 40% of new HIV cases are identified in females, and transmission through heterosexual sex has grown rapidly.

The Government of Russia implements HIV treatment and prevention programs through its National Priority Health Project and Federal Targeted Program. The government currently spends over $250 million per year on HIV/AIDS treatment programs and allocated over $42 million for the period of 2007-2010 to support HIV/AIDS vaccine research. Approximately 74,000 patients are receiving antiretroviral therapy, and the government projects that number will exceed 100,000 patients by 2012. Russia's government-procured antiretroviral therapy (ART) supplies have been affected by a series of shortages and inconsistent delivery to ART recipients.

Commercial Law

Russia has a body of conflicting, overlapping and rapidly changing laws, decrees and regulations, which has resulted in an ad hoc and unpredictable approach to doing business. In this environment, negotiations and contracts from commercial transactions are complex and protracted. Uneven implementation of laws creates further complications. Regional and local courts are often subject to political pressure, and corruption is widespread.

Natural Resources

The mineral-rich Ural Mountains and the vast oil, gas, coal, and timber reserves of Siberia and the Russian Far East make Russia rich in natural resources. However, most resources are located in remote and climatically unfavorable areas that are difficult to develop and far from Russian ports. Nevertheless, Russia is a leading producer and exporter of minerals, gold, and all major fuels. Natural resources, especially energy, dominate Russian exports. Over two-thirds of Russian exports to the United States are fuels, mineral oil, or metals.

Industry

Russia is one of the most industrialized of the former Soviet republics. However, years of very low investment have left much of Russian industry antiquated and highly inefficient. Besides its resource-based industries, it has developed large manufacturing capacities, notably in metals, food products, and transport equipment. Russia is now the world's third-largest exporter of steel and primary aluminum. Russia inherited most of the defense industrial base of the Soviet Union, so armaments remain an important export category for Russia. Efforts have been made with varying success over the past few years to convert defense industries to civilian use, and the Russian Government is engaged in an ongoing process to privatize many of the state-owned enterprises.

Agriculture

Although Russia has 9% of the world's arable land and abundant fresh water, the relative lack of investment and modernization has made agriculture one of Russia's lagging economic sectors. But significant change has occurred in recent years. Grain production for export is concentrated in the south of European Russia, with additional grain for domestic consumption grown throughout the rest of non-Arctic Russia west of the

Urals as well as western Siberia. Over the past 5 years Russia has improved its competitive position and is now the world's third-largest exporter of wheat. Livestock production was in decline from 1990 to 2006, when new government support policies were instituted to stimulate domestic meat production. Since the start of the National Priority Program in 2006 the Russian Government has invested to increase poultry, pork, beef, and milk production in Russia, primarily through subsidized loans (worth approximately $3 billion from 2006-2010) to large private enterprises. In January 2010, President Medvedev signed the Food Security Doctrine, which sets targets for domestic production of meat, dairy, oilseeds, grain, fruit, and vegetables and provides a justification for sustained government subsidies to agriculture. One of the main continuing constraints to both agricultural investment and productivity, however, is the absence of clearly defined agricultural property rights and the lack of private land ownership. Agriculture priorities continued to be subsidizing livestock and poultry production.

Investment/Banking

Foreign direct investment (FDI) in 2009 fell to less than $40 billion after reaching an all-time high of $75 billion in 2008. Much of the FDI in recent years was Russian capital "returning home," from havens like Cyprus and Gibraltar, and these flows reversed during the economic downturn. Moreover, although the annual flow of FDI into Russia was in line with those of China, India, and Brazil, Russia's per capita cumulative FDI lagged far behind such countries as Hungary, Poland, and the Czech Republic. In 2010, net FDI inflow rose to $43 billion, still well below the levels seen in 2008. In the first quarter of 2011, it amounted to $12.8 billion, the CBR reported.

Although still small by international standards, the Russian banking sector before the crisis was growing fast and becoming a larger source of investment funds. To meet a growing demand for loans, which they were unable to cover with domestic deposits, Russian banks borrowed heavily abroad in 2007-2008, accounting for 57% of the private-sector capital inflows in 2007. Ruble lending has increased since the October 1998 financial crisis, and in 2007 loans were 66% of total bank assets, with consumer loans posting the fastest growth at 57% that same year. In 2004, Russia enacted a deposit insurance law to protect deposits up to 100,000 rubles (about $3,700) per depositor. Amendments to the law in the fall of 2008 increased the Deposit Insurance Agency's 100%-coverage for deposits up to 700,000 rubles. The vast majority of Russians keep their money in the banking sector. The combination of liberalized capital controls and ruble appreciation against the dollar in 2005-2008 persuaded many Russians to keep their money in ruble- or other currency-denominated bank deposits. In 2010 private deposits grew by 31.2% and corporate deposits and accounts by 16.4%. In 2011 private deposit growth slowed down such that over the first 8 months of the year, private deposits went up 9.2% (versus 16.5% in the first 8 months of 2010) while corporate deposits and accounts were up by 9.1% (versus 5.0%).

Even with the banking sector's recent growth, financial intermediation in the overall economy remains underdeveloped. Contradictory regulations across the banking and securities markets have hindered efforts to transfer resources from capital-rich sectors, such as energy, to capital-poor sectors, such as agriculture and manufacturing. The sector is dominated by large state banks, and concentrated geographically in Moscow and the Moscow region. Thus financial service providers face little competition for resources and charge relatively high interest rates for favored, large corporate borrowers.

This state of affairs makes it difficult for entrepreneurs to raise capital, and banks generally perceive small and medium commercial lending as risky. Most of the country's financial institutions are inexperienced with assessing credit risk, though the situation is improving. The low level of trust, both between the general public and banks as well as among banks, makes the system highly susceptible to crises. After an uncertain year in 2009, by spring 2010 Russian officials announced an end to anti-crisis bank support, and a World Bank report said that "a systemic banking crisis had been averted, the liquidity crunch eased and depositor confidence reestablished." The report cautioned, however, that systemic weaknesses exposed during the crisis--especially excessive dependence on foreign borrowing and non-performing loans--still needed to be addressed.

Trade

After hitting lows in 2009, trade between the U.S. and Russia grew to $31.7 billion in 2010, an increase of 35% from 2009. U.S. imports from Russia grew 41% year over year to $25.7 billion while exports to Russia increased just 13% to $6.0 billion. The rapid increase in U.S. imports from Russia from 2009 to 2010 can be attributed to the low base year and nascent economic recovery in the United States, but also to the rising price of oil and other commodities. Oil and oil products represent over two-thirds of the value of all U.S.

imports from Russia. Russia is currently the 37th-largest export market for U.S. goods. Russian exports to the U.S. were fuel oil, inorganic chemicals, aluminum, and precious stones. U.S. exports to Russia were machinery, vehicles, meat (mostly poultry), aircraft, electrical equipment, and high-tech products.

Russia's overall trade surplus in 2009 was $112 billion--compared with $180 billion in 2008 and $129 billion in 2007. In 2010 the trade surplus increased to $152 billion and continued to grow in 2011 to reach $118 billion by July 2011 (versus $96.4 billion at the same time in 2010), although import growth was beginning to outpace export growth. World prices continue to have a major effect on export performance, since commodities--particularly oil, natural gas, metals, and timber--comprise nearly 90% of Russian exports. Russian GDP growth and the surplus/deficit in the Russian Federation state budget are closely linked to world oil prices.

Russia is in the process of negotiating terms of accession to the World Trade Organization (WTO). The U.S. and Russia concluded a bilateral WTO accession agreement in late 2006, and negotiations continue on meeting WTO requirements for accession. Both Prime Minister Vladimir Putin and the General Director of the WTO, Pascal Lamy, stated in early 2011 that they felt Russia would join within the year.

According to the 2010 U.S. Trade Representative's National Trade Estimate, Russia continues to maintain a number of barriers with respect to imports, including tariffs and tariff-rate quotas; discriminatory and prohibitive charges and fees; and discriminatory licensing, registration, and certification regimes. Discussions continue within the context of Russia's WTO accession to eliminate these measures or modify them to be consistent with internationally accepted trade policy practices. Non-tariff barriers are frequently used to restrict foreign access to the market and are also a significant topic in Russia's WTO negotiations. In addition, Russia's lax enforcement of intellectual property rights had led to large losses for U.S. audiovisual and other companies and is an ongoing irritant in U.S.-Russia trade relations. Russia continues to work to bring its technical regulations, including those related to product and food safety, into conformity with international standards.

DEFENSE

The **Armed Forces of the Russian Federation** (Russian: Вооружённые Си́лы Росси́йской Федера́ции, tr. *Vooruzhonnije Síly Rossíyskoj Federátsii*) are the military services of Russia, established after the dissolution of the Soviet Union. On 7 May 1992, Boris Yeltsin signed a presidential decree establishing the Russian Ministry of Defence and placing all Soviet Armed Forces troops on the territory of the RSFSR under Russian control. The commander-in-chief of the armed forces is the president of Russia. Although the Russian armed forces were formed in 1992, the Russian military dates its roots back to the times of the Kievan Rus'.

The number of troops is specified by decree of the President of Russia. On 1 January 2008, a number of 2,019,629 units, including military of 1,134,800 units, was set. In 2010 the International Institute for Strategic Studies (IISS) estimated that the Russian Armed Forces numbered about 1,040,000 active troops and in the region of 2,035,000 reserves (largely ex-conscripts). As opposed to personnel specified by decree, actual personnel in the forces and paid was reported by the Audit Chamber of Russia as 766,000 in October 2013. As of December 2013, the armed forces are at 82 percent of the required manpower.

According to SIPRI, Russia spent nearly $72 billion on arms in 2011. Russia is planning further increases in its military spending, with draft budgets showing a 53% rise in real terms up to 2014. However, SIPRI adds that many analysts are doubtful whether the industry will be able to deliver on such ambitious plans after decades of stagnation following the collapse of the Soviet Union

The Russian Government has stated its desire to build a professional army, but implementation has been progressing slowly. Russia's efforts to transform its Soviet-legacy military into a smaller, lighter, and more mobile force continue to be hampered by an ossified military leadership, discipline problems and human rights violations, corruption, limited funding, and demographics. The August 2008 conflict with Georgia highlighted the need for Russia to modernize its armed forces, which currently number 850,000, according to General Staff leadership.

In October 2008, Defense Minister Serdyukov announced the start of the "New Look" reorganization of the

Russian military, which included a significant cut to the officer corps (more than 60%), a joint operations command structure, and a reduction of support and operational units, while calling for a new non-commissioned officer (NCO) corps, improvements in social issues within the military (namely pay and housing), and advanced training and education. Concurrently, the Kremlin called for a vast modernization and rearmament program under the State Armament Plan, with Putin promising 20.7 trillion rubles ($670 billion) through 2020, which would triple current defense spending. Russia's ability to fund such a program, particularly if in competition with other national priorities, is highly questionable.

In an effort to make military service more attractive, the tour of duty for conscripts was reduced to 1 year (from 18 months) beginning in 2008, and the military is offering increased pay and benefits to raise the number of professional servicemen, while slashing the size of the officer corps. Current plans envision a transition to a mixed force, in which professional soldiers will make up approximately 70%, including in select units, and conscripts will make up 30% of the force. There is also an effort to develop an NCO corps, but the military faces difficulties recruiting NCOs and has done little to develop the mechanisms and capability to sustain such a force. Military spending continues to grow (the government announced in February 2011 that it would spend more than $650 billion upgrading hardware), but deep structural problems remain.

Russian military salaries are low, although the government has promised to increase them, in some cases by as much as three times, starting January 1, 2012. Theoretically, the army provides all necessities, but housing and food shortages continue to plague the armed forces. Problems with both discipline and brutal hazing are common as well. Such conditions continue to encourage draft evasion and efforts to delay military service. Moreover, military officials complain that new recruit cohorts are plagued by increasing incidences of poor education, communicable diseases, and criminality. HIV infection rates in the Russian army are estimated to be between two and five times higher than in the general population, and tuberculosis is a persistent problem.

FOREIGN RELATIONS

In the years after the dissolution of the Soviet Union, Russia took important steps to become a full partner in the world's principal political groupings. On December 27, 1991, Russia assumed the permanent UN Security Council seat formerly held by the Soviet Union. Russia also is a member of the Organization for Security and Cooperation in Europe (OSCE) and the Euro-Atlantic Partnership Council (EAPC). Russia and the European Union (EU) signed a Partnership and Cooperation Agreement in 1994. Russia also joined the North Atlantic Treaty Organization (NATO) Partnership for Peace initiative in 1994. The NATO-Russia Founding Act established the Permanent Joint Council (PJC) in 1997, with the NATO-Russia Council superseding the PJC in 2002. Russia, despite misgivings, did not actively oppose enlargement of NATO by members of the former Warsaw Pact and the Baltic states, which had been forcibly integrated into the Soviet Union. However, Russia has stressed its strong opposition to the membership aspirations of Ukraine and Georgia.

Over the past several years Russia has increased its international profile, played an increasing role in regional issues, and been more assertive in dealing with its neighbors. In recent years, Russia has not shied from using its significant oil and gas exports as sources of political influence. The August 2008 conflict between Russia and Georgia marked a new low point in relations between the two countries, with Russia unilaterally recognizing the Georgian breakaway regions of Abkhazia and South Ossetia as independent countries. Russia continues to support separatist regimes in Georgia and Moldova.

U.S.-RUSSIA RELATIONS

By the end of 2008 and in the wake of the Russia-Georgia war, U.S.-Russia relations were at a low and characterized by mutual frustration and an adversarial drift. The change in the U.S. administration in January 2009 provided a diplomatic opportunity for both sides to change the tone of the relationship and cooperate in areas of mutual interest. Presidents Barack Obama and Dmitriy Medvedev first met in April 2009 on the margins of a multilateral summit to address the global financial crisis, where they resolved to negotiate the New START Treaty. In July of that year, the two leaders met for a bilateral summit where they reached additional agreements on nuclear security, cooperation on Afghanistan, military-to-military cooperation, a joint commission on POW/MIAs, and the formation of the Bilateral Presidential Commission. The New

START Treaty entered into force in February 2011. Subject to final approval by the Russian Government, bilateral agreements have also been concluded on cooperation in intercountry adoptions between the U.S. and Russia as well as liberalization in laws and practices governing entry visas.

The Bilateral Presidential Commission, which Presidents Obama and Medvedev established in July 2009, is dedicated to improving coordination between the two countries, identifying areas of cooperation, and pursuing joint projects and actions that strengthen strategic stability, international security, economic well-being, and the development of ties between the Russian and American people. It is intended to serve as a regular and structured mechanism to advance the highest-priority bilateral objectives through 20 working groups and numerous sub-working groups chaired by senior government officials from a variety of agencies and ministries. Working groups have been formed on the following topics: agriculture; arms control and international security; business development and economic relations; civil society; counterterrorism; counternarcotics; defense relations; education, culture, sports, and mass media; emergency situations; energy; environment; health; innovation; intelligence; military cooperation; nuclear energy and nuclear security; policy steering; science and technology; space cooperation; and rule of law. More information can be found at **http://www.state.gov/p/eur/ci/rs/usrussiabilat/index.htm**.

The United States and Russia share interests in all of these areas but, as the world's leading nuclear powers, the countries share a particular interest and responsibility in the areas of nuclear energy, security, and nonproliferation. The U.S. and Russia work closely on initiatives to address the threat of nuclear terrorism and keep terrorists from acquiring nuclear materials. Both Russia and the U.S. continue to try to bring Iran's nuclear programs into compliance with International Atomic Energy Agency (IAEA) rules and United Nations Security Council Resolutions 1737, 1747, 1803, and 1929. On North Korea, Russia is a participant in the Six-Party Talks aimed at the verifiable denuclearization of the Korean Peninsula.

Despite this cooperation, there remain areas in which the U.S. and Russia disagree, including Moscow's recognition of the independence of South Ossetia and Abkhazia. The recently improved relations with Russia provide an improved atmosphere to address this disagreement and others.

U.S. Assistance to Russia
For more detailed information on U.S. Government assistance to Russia, please see the **annual reports** to Congress on U.S. Government Assistance to and Cooperative Activities with Eurasia, which are available in the Bureau of European and Eurasian Affairs section on the State Department's website. A fact sheet on U.S. assistance to Russia can be found at **http://www.state.gov/p/eur/rls/fs/167370.htm**.

Principal U.S. Embassy Officials
Ambassador--Michael McFaul
Deputy Chief of Mission--Sheila Gwaltney
Counselor for Political Affairs--Michael Klecheski
Counselor for Economic Affairs--Stuart Dwyer
Counselor for Commercial Affairs--John McCaslin
Counselor for Consular Affairs--Doron D. Bard
Counselor for Management Affairs--Michael Hoza
Counselor for Public Affairs--Michael J. Hurley
Counselor for Environment, Science, Technology, and Health--Lynette Poulton
Director, U.S. Agency for International Development--Charles North
Legal Attache--David Rubincan
Law Enforcement Section--Tom Firestone and Luke Dembosky
DHS/Citizenship and Immigration Services (CIS)--Susan Aikman
Department of Energy--Christine Buzzard
National Aeronautics and Space Administration (NASA)--Patrick Buzzard
Senior Defense Official and Defense Attache--Rear Admiral Douglas Venlet

TRAVEL

Travel Alerts, Travel Warnings, Trip Registration
The U.S. Department of State's Consular Information Program advises Americans traveling and residing abroad through Country Specific Information, Travel Alerts, and Travel Warnings. **Country Specific**

Information exists for all countries and includes information on entry and exit requirements, currency regulations, health conditions, safety and security, crime, political disturbances, and the addresses of the U.S. embassies and consulates abroad. **Travel Alerts** are issued to disseminate information quickly about terrorist threats and other relatively short-term conditions overseas that pose significant risks to the security of American travelers. **Travel Warnings** are issued when the State Department recommends that Americans avoid travel to a certain country because the situation is dangerous or unstable.

For the latest security information, Americans living and traveling abroad should regularly monitor the Department's Bureau of Consular Affairs Internet web site at http://travel.state.gov, where current Worldwide Caution, Travel Alerts, and Travel Warnings can be found. The travel.state.gov website also includes information about passports, tips for planning a safe trip abroad and more. More travel-related information also is available at http://www.usa.gov/Citizen/Topics/Travel/International.shtml.

The Department's Smart Traveler app for U.S. travelers going abroad provides easy access to the frequently updated official country information, travel alerts, travel warnings, maps, U.S. embassy locations, and more that appear on the travel.state.gov site. Travelers can also set up e-tineraries to keep track of arrival and departure dates and make notes about upcoming trips. The app is compatible with iPhone, iPod touch, and iPad (requires iOS 4.0 or later).

The Department of State encourages all U.S. citizens traveling or residing abroad to enroll in the State Department's Smart Traveler Enrollment Program (STEP). A link to the registration page is also available through the Department's Smart Traveler app. U.S. citizens without internet access can enroll directly at the nearest U.S. embassy or consulate. By enrolling, you make your presence and whereabouts known in case it is necessary to contact you in an emergency and so you can receive up-to-date information on security conditions.

Emergency information concerning Americans traveling abroad may be obtained by calling 1-888-407-4747 toll free in the U.S. and Canada or the regular toll line 1-202-501-4444 for callers outside the U.S. and Canada.

Passports
The National Passport Information Center (NPIC) is the U.S. Department of State's single, centralized public contact center for U.S. passport information. Telephone: 1-877-4-USA-PPT (1-877-487-2778); TDD/TTY: 1-888-874-7793. Passport information is available 24 hours, 7 days a week. You may speak with a representative Monday-Friday, 8 a.m. to 10 p.m., Eastern Time, excluding federal holidays.

INVESTMENT AND BUSINESS CLIMATE

Russia's annexation of Crimea in March 2014 is not recognized by the U.S. government and led to the placement of USG sanctions on various Russian government officials and a limited number of entities, as well as the imposition of stricter licensing controls on certain products exported to Russia. Policy discussions with the Russian government regarding measures to increase bilateral trade and investment ties and in multilateral forum such as the G8 were also halted in the aftermath of Russia's illegal actions in Ukraine.

The government of Russia continues to express interest in attracting higher levels of domestic and foreign investment. Looking to domestic investment, the Russian Government has established a number of regulations which penalize Russian individuals and firms for investing abroad, in part possibly to offset lower levels of foreign direct investment in Russia during 2014. As detailed below, the Russian Government has worked actively on the technical level to improve the business and investment climate. Despite numerous new programs and initiatives, progress has been uneven and the government has yet to take action to make much needed overall structural reforms. Russian government officials have publicly and privately expressed their desire for foreign investment and technology transfer. At the same time, the government continues to limit foreign investment in "strategic" sectors and by maintaining control over half of Russia's GDP through state-owned enterprises.

American firms seeking to invest in the Russian Federation should be aware that the Russian investment climate continues to be marked by high levels of corruption and political risk, making thorough due diligence and good legal counsel essential for any potential investment. A variety of regulations also require Russian government approval for foreign firms to invest in "strategic sectors" and, in some cases, ban majority foreign ownership. The Russian legal system and jurisprudence is improving but recent changes in the structure of the Russian high court have cast doubts on its ultimate autonomy. Given Russia's continued actions in Ukraine, additional sanctions from the international community cannot be ruled out, which could have effects on potential investments. Additionally, senior Russian government officials have threatened that they could retaliate against sanctions, although they have not specified in what manner.

1. OPENNESS TO, AND RESTRICTIONS UPON, FOREIGN INVESTMENT

Russia's annexation of Crimea in March 2014 is not recognized by the U.S. government and led to the placement of USG sanctions on various Russian government officials and a limited number of entities, and the postponement of key bilateral and multilateral engagement on economic reforms. The United States announced the first round of sanctions against influential Russian government officials and entities in early March and has added additional names to the sanctions list on subsequent occasions. Policy discussions with the Russian government regarding measures to increase bilateral trade and investment ties were also halted in the aftermath of Russia's illegal actions in Ukraine.

In late March, Senator Andrei Klishas of the Federation Council, the upper chamber of Russia's national legislature, said the Council plans to draft legislation which would allow the confiscation of property, assets, and accounts of American and EU companies, including private companies, as a retaliatory measure on possible sanctions from the U.S. and EU. While no specific legislation has been proposed or passed, such an announcement clearly adds an additional element of uncertainty to any investment prospect in Russia because it would signal the willingness of the Russian government to violate national and international norms when it finds it to be politically expedient.

However, the government of Russia continues to express interest in attracting higher levels of domestic and foreign investment by private companies. Looking to domestic investment, the Russian Government has established a number of regulations which penalize Russian individuals and firms for investing abroad, possibly to offset lower foreign direct investment in Russia during 2014. It is unclear what success this policy initiative, called "de-offshorization" by President Putin, has had to date. In the first quarter of 2014, capital outflow from Russia reached approximately $63.7 billion, the highest quarterly outflow since the last quarter of 2008 during the height of the global financial crisis.

As detailed below, the Russian Government has also worked actively on the technical level to improve the business and investment climate. Despite numerous new programs and initiatives, progress has been uneven and the government has yet to take action to make much needed structural reforms.

Russia's illegal annexation of Crimea has dampened growth prospects for the Russian economy. The International Monetary Fund predicts the Russian economy will grow by a sluggish 0.2 percent in 2014. Given the uncertainty surrounding Russia's actions in Ukraine, the World Bank provided two estimates for GDP in 2014. The low risk scenario anticipates 1.1 percent GDP growth and the high risk scenario anticipates a contraction of 1.8 percent for 2014. Russia finished 2013 with 1.3 percent growth, the lowest rate since the 2009 financial crisis and well under half of the 3.6 percent the Russian government forecasted at the beginning of the year. Russia's economy continues to be particularly vulnerable to fluctuations in global energy prices and continued weakness in the European economy, as the EU represents more than 50 percent of Russia's total trade volume. According to the United Nations Conference on Trade and Development (UNCTAD) Global Investment Trends Monitor from January 2014, FDI inflow into Russia jumped 83 percent to $94 billion in 2013 from $51 billion in 2012.

Russian government officials have repeatedly stressed that foreign investment and technology transfer are critical to Russia's economic modernization. At the same time, the government continues to limit foreign investment in sectors deemed to have strategic significance for national defense and state security via the Strategic Sectors Law of 2008. The law originally specified 42 activities and has since been amended on five separate occasions. As of April 2014, 45 activities require government approval for foreign investment. Foreign investors wishing to increase or gain ownership above certain thresholds need to seek prior approval from a government commission headed by Russia's Prime Minister. While the Commission has approved 129 of 137 applications for foreign investment since 2008, the number of transactions approved with conditions has been increasing significantly.

Russia continues to promote the use of high-tech parks, special economic zones and industrial clusters which offer additional tax and infrastructure incentives to attract investment. One of President Putin's stated goals, to move Russia from 120th (in 2010) to 20th on the World Bank's Doing Business Index by 2020, saw progress with Russia climbing to 92nd in the 2014 publication. It will likely climb in the ranks again due largely to improvements in obtaining a connection to electricity for new businesses and in the ease of registering a business.

Russia's policy to foster innovation continues but the enthusiasm and funding for this policy appears to be waning. The flagship project, the Skolkovo Innovation Center, was designed to be the Russian equivalent of Silicon Valley and has been assured funding through 2015 with future funding uncertain. Roughly a dozen American firms have made sizable commitments to investment in the tech park portion of the project and the Massachusetts Institute of Technology continues to run a multi-million dollar program with Skolkovo Institute of Science and Technology (SkolTech) to design educational curricula and research programs, innovation activities, administrative policies and structures, recruiting processes, and campus operations and infrastructure. So far, tangible results from the project have been modest. On top of this, in 2013, the Skolkovo Foundation, which runs the endowment portion of the project, faced accusations of corruption though no case was ever brought to court. In early 2014 the Russian government announced a new initiative to create an innovation center on Russky Island in Vladivostok. It remains to be seen if this latest project will yield results.

While a legal structure exists to support foreign investors, the laws are not always enforced in practice. The 1991 Investment Code and 1999 Law on Foreign Investment guarantee that foreign investors enjoy rights equal to those of Russian investors, although some industries have limits on foreign ownership (see Establishment section). Russia has sought to enhance consultation mechanisms with international businesses (for example through the Foreign Investment Advisory Council whose members are CEOs of large companies) regarding the impact of the country's legislation and regulations on the business and investment climate. In June 2012, President Putin created the position of Ombudsman for Entrepreneur's Rights, which was designed to be an additional measure of protection and advocacy for entrepreneurs, and the relevant implementation legislation was signed into law by President Putin on May 7, 2013. Still, the country's investment dispute resolution mechanisms remain a work in progress, and at present can seem non-transparent and unpredictable (see Dispute Settlement section).

The government continues to hold significant blocks of shares in many privatized enterprises with state-owned enterprises (SOEs) accounting for approximately 50 percent of Russia's GDP in 2013. In June 2013, the Russian government unveiled its 2014-2016 Privatization Plan, the most recent update of Russia's original privatization plan that was drafted in 2010 and amended in 2012. However, the government has taken little action to implement additional privatizations, arguing current valuations for SOEs are too low to justify proceeding with a privatization. The new plan significantly rolled back the scope of privatizations and involves, to a large extent, the Russian government maintaining "golden shares" in some of the most prestigious SOEs. To date, treatment of foreign investment in new privatizations has been inconsistent: foreign participation has often been confined to limited positions in the companies. Subsequently, many have faced problems with inadequate protection for minority shareholders and corporate governance. Potential foreign investors are advised to work directly and closely with appropriate local, regional, and federal agencies that exercise ownership or authority over companies whose shares they may want to acquire. (See State-Owned Enterprises)

In September 2012, the United States and Russia signed a new bilateral visa agreement which extended the validity of a tourist visa to 36 months for both American and Russian travelers. This agreement also reduced the documentary requirements for Americans applying for a visa and eliminated the need for an invitation letter in some cases. The process for the approval and renewal of visas and residence permits for foreign businessmen and investors remains cumbersome with numerous documentary requirements. Additionally, there are regulations in specific industries that require a certain percentage of staff be Russian citizens, which may have a negative impact on foreign investors. The situation is improving, however. As part of Russia's efforts to encourage investment in innovative sectors, the GOR has eased the regulations on visas and residence permits for "highly-skilled" workers, and eliminated yearly quotas for foreign workers who fall into this category (defined by salary, position and education level). Potential investors are advised to consult the State Department's Country-Specific Information on travel to Russia, which includes the latest information on Russian visas.

Corruption remains a major challenge for Russia. Targeted efforts in 2012 to root out corruption by public officials and within business transactions led to widely-reported investigations in the Ministry of Defense and the Ministry of Agriculture. Russia's ranking improved six spots to 127th in Transparency International's 2013

Corruption Perceptions Index (CPI). The National Anti-Corruption Plan for 2012–2013 contains guidance and recommendations for the government on counteracting corruption, including the establishment of a legal framework for lobbying and increasing the transparency of state officials' personal finances and acceptance of gifts. Specifically, the bill requires all civil servants to declare large expenditures or face termination. These officials must also present information on the expenditures of their spouses and children if the expenditures involve acquisitions of land, vehicles or securities. Expenditures that do not match the declared income will be investigated by law enforcement agencies. If an individual fails to prove that the property in question was acquired legally, the property will be confiscated and turned over to the state. Bribing a public official has been illegal in Russia since May 2011 (see Corruption section).

Global Benchmarks

The following table includes the most recent data from indices measuring the investment and business climate in Russia:

Measure	Year	Index/Ranking
Transparency International Corruption Index	2013	127 of 175 countries
Heritage Economic Freedom	2013	140 of 184 countries, "Mostly Unfree"
World Bank Doing Business	2014	92 of 185 economies
Trade Policy (Heritage Economic Freedom)	2013	74.6 out of highest score of 100
Starting a Business (World Bank Doing Business)	2014	88 of 189 economies
Land Rights Access (World Bank Doing Business)	2014 2014	Construction Permits: 178 of 189 economies Registering Property: 17 of 189 economies
Freedom Rating (Freedom House)		5.5 out of 7 (scale of 1-7, 1 being the best) Status: Not Free Political Rights: 6 Civil Liberties: 5

2. CONVERSION AND TRANSFER POLICIES

While the ruble is the only legal tender in Russia, companies and individuals generally face no significant difficulty in obtaining foreign exchange. Only authorized banks may carry out foreign currency transactions but finding a licensed bank is not difficult. According to currency control laws, the Central Bank retains the right to impose restrictions on the purchase of foreign currency, including the requirement that the transaction be completed through a special account. The Central Bank does not require security deposits on foreign exchange purchases. Russia has no capital controls and there are no barriers to remitting investment returns abroad, including dividends, interest, and returns of capital. Nonetheless, investors should seek expert advice at the time of an investment.

Currency controls exist on all transactions that require customs clearance, which in Russia applies to both import and export transactions and certain loans. A business must open a "deal passport" with the authorized Russian bank through which it will receive and service the transaction or loan. A "deal passport" is a set of documents that importers and exporters provide to authorized banks which enable the bank to monitor payments with respect to the transaction or loan and to report the corporation's compliance with currency control regulations to the Central Bank. Russia's regulations regarding deal passports are prescribed under Instructions of the Central Bank of Russia number 117-I of June 15, 2004. In early 2011, the Central Bank of Russia expanded the list of grounds under which a deal passport does not have to be submitted. On June 4, 2012, the Central Bank issued Instruction number 138-I, which introduced some changes to the regulation. In particular, an authorized bank is no longer required to submit additional documentation if the authorized bank is debiting money for a currency operation from an existing bank account of a resident or non-resident. In case of multilateral agreements with multiple parties and participation of non-residents, only one resident deal participant is obligated to execute a deal passport for this agreement rather than all resident parties being required to submit documentation. The Central Bank further amended the regulation by issuing Directive number 3016-U of June 14, 2013, which came into effect in the fall of 2013. A deal passport is now needed only if the value of the underlying contract is equal to or exceeds the equivalent of $50,000.

3. EXPROPRIATION AND COMPENSATION

The 1991 Investment Code prohibits the nationalization of foreign investments, except following legislative action and where deemed to be in the national interest. Such nationalizations may be appealed to Russian courts, and the investor must be adequately and promptly compensated. At the sub-federal level, expropriation has occasionally been a problem, as has local government interference and a lack of enforcement of court rulings protecting investors. Some Russian parliamentary deputies suggested in March 2014 that Russia might expropriate Western firms in reaction to U.S. and EU sanctions but there has been no government action to that end.

4. DISPUTE SETTLEMENT

Russia has a body of conflicting, overlapping, and frequently changing laws, decrees and regulations, which complicates the environment for dispute resolution. Independent dispute resolution in Russia can be difficult to obtain since the judicial system is still developing. Courts are sometimes subject to political pressure. According to numerous reports, corruption in the judicial system is widespread and takes many forms, ranging from bribes of judges and prosecutors to fabrication of evidence. However, corruption likely does not play a role in the vast majority of cases, most of which involve relatively low stakes.

Until mid- 2014, Russia will continue to have two parallel court structures: one, which is specialized in commercial cases and known as the Arbitrage Courts, answers to the Higher Arbitrage Court and a second criminal and civil court system that answers to the Russian Supreme Court. At the end of June 2014, the Higher Arbitrage Court will be eliminated and the lower arbitrage courts will thereafter answer to the Russian Supreme Court. Many in the business community have expressed concern about this change, as the Arbitrage Courts have been known for their professionalism and reputation for judicial independence (although they were not completely free from corruption). The process of appointment to the Higher Arbitrage Court – done via regional structures and not federal structures – also was more independent from the centralization of power in the Russian government. When this change is implemented, the legal chain for the lower arbitration courts will run through to the Supreme Court, which consists of federally-appointed judges who are widely believed to pay particularly keen attention to the wishes of the Kremlin. It is too early to tell if these changes will make it more difficult for foreign investors to receive independent dispute resolution under this new system. It is also unclear how the elimination of the Higher Arbitrage Court will affect the existence of the lower arbitrage courts. No indication was given if these specialized courts will also eventually be eliminated at the lower levels. However, it is clear that the level of judicial independence of the courts will have been reduced.

In an attempt to address some of these challenges facing the business community, the GOR created the Office of the Ombudsman for Entrepreneur Rights in 2012 which is headed by Boris Titov, a businessman and former Chairman of the business group Delovaya Rossiya. Titov's remit includes advocating for foreign and domestic business rights in court and requesting suspension of official actions if a business feels its rights were violated. Each Russian Federal District also has an Investment Ombudsman who reports to the national Ombudsman and oversees efforts to improve the business climate, including the protection of foreign and domestic investors. The government has also encouraged international business leaders, as part of their work in the Foreign Investment Advisory Council, to participate in the discussion of dispute resolution mechanisms and individual commercial disputes. While these steps offer some promise, overall, the country's investment dispute mechanisms remain underdeveloped and largely non-transparent.

In 2008, then-President Medvedev carried out a series of legal reforms that aimed to reduce corruption in the courts. These measures included a law that requires judges to disclose their income and real estate assets, including those owned by their spouses and minor children. Another component of included a series of amendments to the Code of Criminal Procedure – in 2008, 2009, and 2010 – to limit pre-trial detention of individuals accused of economic crimes. Implementation of these reforms has yielded mixed results. Prosecutors have sometimes avoided them by charging defendants under articles technically not covered by the amendments and judges have sometimes refused to apply them. Nevertheless, available statistics reveal a substantial decrease in the number of pre-trial detentions in cases involving economic crimes since the legislation was passed. In June 2013, President Putin announced plans for a widespread amnesty for those convicted of economic crimes. However, by years' end, only a relatively small number of persons had been released under this program.

Commercial arbitration courts are required by law to decide business disputes relatively quickly, and many cases are decided on the basis of written evidence and little or no live testimony of witnesses. The arbitration court workload is dominated by relatively simple non-contentious cases involving the collection of debts between firms and disputes with the taxation and customs authorities, pension fund, and other state organs. Tax-paying firms often prevail in their disputes with the government in court. The number of routine cases limits the time available to decide more complex cases. The court system has special procedures for the seizure of property before trial, such that it cannot be disposed of before the court has heard the claim, as well as for the enforcement of financial awards through the banks. Many observers believe that over the twenty year period that the arbitration court system has existed, its judges have grown more competent and better at writing decisions. Many lawyers nonetheless report that due to insufficient training, especially in complex business disputes, many judges often make poorly reasoned or simply incorrect decisions. As with international arbitral procedures, the weakness in the Russian arbitration system lies in the enforcement of decisions. Few firms pay judgments against them voluntarily and rumors of corruption concerning bailiffs, who are charged with enforcing decisions, are frequent, although hard evidence is scarce.

Federal Law 262, in effect since 2010, requires courts to publish their decisions online and otherwise make information about their activities publicly available. All Russian courts now have websites, which generally include a schedule of cases to be heard, the name of the judge, the location of the court, form documents that can be used by prospective litigants, and copies of decisions. Personal information is expunged before case decisions are posted online. The better of these court websites allow citizens to calculate filing fees and search for analogous decisions. The arbitrage courts have played a leadership role in providing information online and using information technology. Electronic filing allows citizens to sign up to receive e-mail notifications of developments in cases of interest to them. NGOs have rated the compliance of courts with their obligations under the law and found that the information provided varies greatly in quality from one region to another, but have noted a willingness by some courts to respond to queries and criticisms by improving their sites. Although there are gaps and failures to provide information, overall judicial transparency has increased since the law took effect in 2010.

Many attorneys refer Western clients who have investment or trade disputes in Russia to international arbitration in Stockholm or to courts abroad. A 1997 Russian law allows foreign arbitration awards to be enforced in Russia, even if there is no reciprocal treaty between Russia and the country where the order was issued. Russia is a member of the International Center for the Settlement of Investment Disputes (ICSID) and accepts binding international arbitration. Russia is also a signatory to the 1958 New York Convention on the Recognition and Enforcement of Foreign Arbitral Awards (UNCITRAL). However, international arbitral awards still require Russian courts to enforce awards and bailiffs to attach assets; these courts have yet to become consistently effective enforcers of court judgments, whether domestic or international.

In January 2011, a new law took effect that authorizes the use of mediation in various kinds of disputes, including commercial ones, and provides for the confidentiality of mediation proceedings and for their enforceability in court. Although there are still issues concerning implementation, this represents an important step towards further development of alternative dispute resolution in Russia.

According to a Federal Law of December 2011, a specialized court for intellectual property (IP) disputes began to function in 2013. This court, embedded in the system of arbitration (commercial) courts, will hear cases on intellectual property rights (IPR), including those challenging statutory instruments on IP, in the first instance and cassation. In September 2012 the Higher Qualification Board of Judges (a body within the Russian judicial corps responsible for nominating judges to be further appointed by the President) nominated 20 judges to form the new IPR Court, and the Chief Judge of the IPR Court was appointed by the President in December 2012. The elimination of the Higher Arbitrage Court has now raised doubts about how the decisions of the IP Court will be reviewed.

The IP Court has reportedly adjudicated around 360 cases as a trial court, and over 200 cases as the court of the 3rd instance (second level of appeal) out of over 900 suits admitted to the court since it started operation in July 2013. Several legal experts and litigation practitioners have cited the good quality of its dispute resolution, the high qualification of its judges and the good attention to detail in the court.

5. PERFORMANCE REQUIREMENTS AND INCENTIVES

Performance requirements are not generally imposed by Russian law and are not widely included as part of private contracts in Russia. However, they have appeared in the agreements of large multinational companies investing in natural resources and in production-sharing legislation. There are no formal requirements for offsets in foreign investments. Since approval for investments in Russia frequently depends on relationships with government officials and on a firm's demonstration of its commitment to the Russian market, this may result in offsets in practice.

The Central Bank of Russia has imposed caps on foreign employees in foreign banks. The ratio of Russian employees in a subsidiary of a foreign bank is set at no less than 75 percent; if the executive of the subsidiary is a non-resident, at least 50 percent of the bank's managing body should be Russian citizens.

In early 2014, the Russian government drafted a directive requiring all state-controlled assets including SOEsto come up with a series of key performance indicators (KPIs) to guide their development strategy going forward. In rolling out the initiative, the government made it clear that if KPIs were not met, personnel changes would be made. This measure is meant to push state corporations toward a more efficient operating strategy. The Russian government also declined to increase the size of the government budgetary subsidies to each state corporation, with a view to forcing these companies to run more efficiently.

6. RIGHT TO PRIVATE OWNERSHIP AND ESTABLISHMENT

Both foreign and domestic legal entities may establish, purchase, and dispose of businesses in Russia, except in certain sectors that are regarded as affecting national security. There is a blanket ban on purchases of property in border areas for national security reasons. Some Russian Duma deputies called for a ban on foreigners purchasing land without the permission of the Federal Management Service, but no legislative action has been taken in this regard yet.

The Russian government limits foreign investment in sectors deemed to have strategic significance for national defense and state security via the Strategic Sectors Law of 2008 (Law No. 57-FZ). The law has been amended on four occasions, most recently in February 2014. The law currently specifies 45 strategic activities that require government approval for foreign investment. Foreign investors wishing to increase or gain ownership above certain thresholds in any of the sectors listed need to seek prior approval from a government commission headed by Russia's Prime Minister. In 2012 (most recent information published), the Russian government considered 44 petitions from foreign investors of which 22 were pre-approved, 18 were returned to the petitioner for additional information, and four were withdrawn. The government denied in April 2013 a petition from the U.S. company Abbott Laboratories to purchase Russia's Petrovax in a deal that was strongly supported by Petrovax. Russia also established via Executive Order No. 1009 of August 4, 2004 a separate list of strategic companies which includes the largest and most profitable Russian companies. Companies identified on this list have some level of government ownership; the Executive Order sets forth the requirements to privatize these firms. The 2012 addition of Russian privately-held internet company Yandex to the strategic companies list highlights the broad interpretation of what is required to protect state security and national defense.

Real Estate

The Constitution and a 1993 presidential decree give Russian citizens rights to own, inherit, lease, mortgage, and sell real property. Foreigners enjoy similar rights with certain restrictions, notably with respect to the ownership of farmland and areas located near federal borders. Mortgage legislation enacted in 2004 facilitates the process for lenders to evict homeowners who do not stay current in their mortgage payments. Thus far, this law has been successfully implemented and is generally effective. Mortgage lending is in its initial stages, and after a sharp contraction in 2008-09, the total value of mortgages in Russia is around three percent of GDP. In 2013, mortgage lending grew by 31 percent compared to 2012, with new issuances amounting to $42.5 billion in 2013.

7. PROTECTION OF PROPERTY RIGHTS

In Russia, the protection of intellectual property rights (IPR) is enforced on the basis of civil, administrative, criminal or customs legislation. The Civil Code sets up the statutory damages for IPR infringement and/or incurred damages for copyright, trademarks and geographical indications. The Code of Administrative Offenses concerns IPR infractions that violate public or private interest or rights, but do not meet the criteria of the Criminal Code. An administrative investigation may be initiated at the request of an IPR owner or by law enforcement authorities (police or customs) suspecting possible IPR infringement. Administrative cases are dealt with by general jurisdiction courts or state arbitration (commercial) courts that have jurisdiction over economic disputes. The IPR provisions of the Criminal Code apply to large-scale infringements of copyright, patent and trademark rights that cause gross damages, as defined by the Criminal Code.

Enforcement

The United States Government has expressed concerns that IPR enforcement continued to decrease overall in 2013, following a dramatic decline in 2012, and remained plagued by a lack of transparency and effectiveness. Stakeholders express concern about the manufacture, transshipment, and retail availability of counterfeit goods, including counterfeits of agricultural chemicals, electronics, information technology, auto parts, consumer goods, machinery and other products. Enforcement actions combatting end user piracy have sharply declined, including a decrease in raids, initiations of criminal cases and issuances of court verdicts.

Copyright violations (audiovisual and sound recordings, computer software) remain a serious problem, particularly in the online environment. Although dwarfed in volume by pirated products online, legitimate DVD sales are on the rise, thanks in part to cheaper legitimate products, a growing consumer preference for high quality goods, and law enforcement action against physical piracy. Russian police on occasion carry out end-user raids against businesses using pirated products, namely software. However, at times, police have used IPR enforcement as a tactic to elicit bribes or harass NGOs.

For additional information about treaty obligations and points of contact at local IP offices, please see WIPO's country profiles at http://www.wipo.int/directory/en/.

Embassy point of contact: William Muntean moscow.office.box@mail.doc.gov

Local lawyers list: http://moscow.usembassy.gov/root/pdfs/list---attorneys.pdf

Bankruptcy

Russia has had a law providing for bankruptcy of enterprises since the early 1990s. Law enforcement officials, however, tend to view bankruptcy with suspicion and reported 500 cases of financial crimes involving bankruptcy in 2011. In November 2012, the State Duma passed in its first reading (three readings are required for passage) a personal bankruptcy bill, but the bill has not been adopted. The bill states that a citizen who finds himself in financial difficulty can submit a bankruptcy statement to the court. The court may then grant the individual the right to pay the debt in installments for a term of up to five years. An individual with debts exceeding 50,000 rubles ($1,389) and whose arrears amount to three months can be declared bankrupt. In this case, the individual cannot apply for a bank loan without citing his bankruptcy for the five years after his bankruptcy status was declared. The individual is then given six months to come up with a debt restructuring plan subject to the approval of both the creditors and the court. Once the plan is approved, all late payment fees and penalties will be waived and assets unfrozen. Only in the case of a person who has no assets and no income may the debt be completely written off. The bill also stipulates a ban on declaring oneself bankrupt more than once in five years. The Duma is expected to consider the bill in the first half of 2014.

8. TRANSPARENCY OF THE REGULATORY SYSTEM

Russia's legal system remains in a state of flux, with various parts of the government continuing to implement new regulations and decrees on a broad array of topics, including the tax code and requirements related to regulatory and inspection bodies. Negotiations and contracts for commercial transactions, as well as due diligence processes, are complex and protracted. Investors must do careful research to ensure that each contract fully conforms to Russian law. In some cases, Russian law has contradictory provisions. Contracts must likewise seek to protect the foreign partner against contingencies that often arise. Keeping up with legislative changes, presidential decrees, and government resolutions is a challenging task. Uneven implementation of laws creates further complications; various officials, branches of government, and jurisdictions interpret and apply regulations inconsistently and the decisions of one may be overruled or contested by another. As a result, reaching final agreement with local political and economic authorities can be a long and burdensome process. Companies should be prepared to allocate sufficient funds to engage local legal counsel to set up their commercial operations in Russia.

Taxes

Russia's tax system has recently undergone major changes. The Russian government has brought its tax legislation into line with OECD requirements, which has simplified the system and prevents double taxation on transfer prices. However, businesses continue to raise concerns regarding audits. Multiple audits, repeated requests for documentation, and technical weaknesses of some claims have been identified as serious impediments to the conduct of business. Russia's Law on Transfer Pricing entered into force on January 1, 2012, and fully phased in all provisions by the start of 2014. Some experts caution the new provisions could result in additional disputes with the tax authorities.

Public Comment

All draft laws that go through the Russian Duma are published on the Duma's website. Sometimes, but not consistently, ministries and other Russian government bodies also publish proposed legislation (including draft laws, government decrees and regulations) on their websites. The scope of Russia's Open Government initiative was severely reduced after the Russian government announced in May 2013 that it would no longer be a part of the international Open Government Partnership due to unspecified differences regarding the terms of the partnership. In a statement announcing the decision, Kremlin spokesperson Dmitry Peskov said that Russia remained committed to providing more transparency in government and might reconsider joining the partnership at a later date. Russian Ministries have become more active in seeking input from industry experts and business groups, including the Foreign Investment Advisory Council, when developing business-related laws and regulations.

Strategic Sectors

Statements made by key Russian officials in November 2012 suggest the government will take additional action to roll back administrative barriers to foreign investment in Russian strategic companies. The Federal Antimonopoly Service (FAS) has prepared various amendments, still awaiting approval by the State Duma, intended to simplify the procedures for state supervision of foreign investment in Russian strategic companies and to eliminate ambiguities in the interpretation and application of existing legislative provisions. The proposed amendments include the following: (1) removal of food and beverage production from the list of strategic activities involving the use of infectious agents (e.g., cultured bacteria in yogurt production). FAS is considering similar revisions to exempt certain entities involving selected activities (e.g., foreign banks vis-a-vis distribution and servicing of encryption devices required for their operations); (2) eliminating the need for prior approval by the Government Commission for certain share increases or transactions in cases where the foreign investors hold 75 percent or more of a Russian strategic company's shares; (3) eliminating the need for prior approval for intra-group transactions by foreign investors controlled by the same entity; (4) allowance of automatic permit extensions for foreign investors already holding a permit (typically with a 2-year term) to invest in a strategic enterprise; (5) elimination of the need for government approval for acquisitions by Russian-controlled purchasers from foreign-controlled sellers (currently, only Russian-to-Russian transactions are exempt, but not acquisitions by Russian-controlled purchasers from foreign-controlled sellers); (6) clearer rules on state supervision and approval of transactions involving the placement of securities of Russian strategic companies (including depositary receipts) on stock exchanges, including foreign stock exchanges. However, it is unclear if and when such proposals would be advanced in the current economic and political climate.

9. EFFICIENT CAPITAL MARKETS AND PORTFOLIO INVESTMENT

Banks continue to make up a disproportionate share of Russia's financial system. Although Russia has roughly 900 banks, the sector is dominated by state-owned banks, particularly Sberbank and VTB. The six largest banks (in terms of assets) in Russia are state-controlled, and the top five held 53.7 percent of all bank assets in Russia as of March 1, 2014. The growing role of the state in the banking sector continues to distort the competitive environment, impeding Russia's financial sector development. The successful implementation of the Deposit Insurance System in 2004 has proved a critical psychological boon to the banking sector, reflected in the overall growth of deposits. This has significantly enhanced the stability of the banking sector's deposit base. At the beginning of 2014, aggregate assets of the banking sector amounted to 86.0 percent of GDP and aggregate capital was 10.6 percent of GDP. Russia's banking sector has recovered from the global economic crisis, with corporate loan growth reaching 17.0 percent and retail loan growth 27.4 percent in the 12 months running up to March 1, 2014. The share within Russia's banking sector of non-performing and troubled loans (categories III-V), which during the 2008-2009 financial crisis increased substantially, stabilized in 2010 at around 20% and began to slowly decline in the second half of 2011, so that as of March 1, 2014, it was equal to 14.0 percent. These positive trends notwithstanding, Russian banks reportedly still operate on short time horizons, limiting capital available for long-term investments.

On September 1, 2013, the Central Bank of Russia became the consolidated financial markets regulator (replacing the Federal Financial Markets Service) for Russia's capital markets and financial institutions. Whereas the Central Bank previously had primary responsibility for banks, the new Financial Markets Service of the Bank of Russia, the so-called mega-regulator, has responsibility for other non-bank financial institutions including pension funds, insurance companies, and asset management companies, as well as the securities markets. Consolidated supervision is expected to improve overall regulation and oversight of the capital markets.

Along these lines, the Central Bank has closed down a growing number of banks in recent months as part of a crackdown on the banking sector, as the Central Bank attempts to tighten oversight of banks and rein in shadow banking activity. The Central Bank revoked licenses for 54 banks from June 2013 through March 2014, with many banks cited for violating anti-money laundering or countering the financing of terrorism (AML/CFT) laws. This effort is succeeding in not only much needed banking sector consolidation, but also in weeding out bad banks that have been complicit in money laundering and facilitating the so-called "grey transactions" that have been part of capital outflows from Russia.

To fill the gap in capital available for long-term investments, authorities have also sought to improve the regulatory environment for non-bank institutional investors. This has had some success, though non-bank financials remain small relative to the size of the financial sector. Pension funds are viewed as the most promising source of long-term capital. Pension funds have had strong inflows, in recent years, though they have shown little risk appetite, primarily investing in sovereign debt, corporate debt, and bank deposits, thus limiting their utility as a source of long-term capital. A recent decision by the government to freeze inflows to funded pensions has increased uncertainty, undermining confidence in the industry. The government plans to allow inflows to resume to private pension funds once they have been audited and restructured. This could bolster confidence in the industry over the long term.

Russia's two main stock exchanges – the Russian Trading System (RTS) and the Moscow Interbank Currency Exchange (MICEX) – merged in December 2011. The MICEX-RTS bourse conducted an initial public offering on February 15, 2013, auctioning an 11.82% share. Russian authorities and shareholders of MICEX and RTS believe the merged entity, now branded the Moscow Exchange, has the potential to become a global player. While most large Russian companies currently choose to list their stocks in London and elsewhere abroad, the Russian government has begun a campaign to encourage state-owned companies to use the Moscow Exchange as a vehicle for privatization.

The Law on the Securities Market includes definitions of corporate bonds, mutual funds, options, futures, and forwards. Companies offering public shares are required to disclose specific information during the placement process, as well as on a quarterly basis. In addition, the law defines the responsibilities of financial consultants who assist companies with stock offerings and holds them liable for the accuracy of the data presented to shareholders.

Russian financial authorities are attempting to deepen the ruble-denominated domestic debt market to make it more attractive to foreign investors. In December 2011, the Central Bank issued a resolution allowing, effective January 1, 2012, government bonds (OFZ) to be traded outside Russian exchanges (over the counter). In February 2013, Euroclear and Clearstream, two international securities depositories, began settling transactions of OFZ bonds, Russia's primary sovereign debt security. Euroclear and Clearstream have since also begun settling transactions of Russian corporate and municipal debt, and may soon be able to settle equity transactions as well, possibly by early 2015. This has increased access to Russian securities markets for foreign investors by negating the need to have onshore brokerage and custody accounts.

10. COMPETITION FROM STATE-OWNED ENTERPRISES

State-owned enterprises (SOEs) accounted for roughly half of Russia's GDP in 2013 and the Russian government's policy is for the most part focused on maintaining the status quo, rather than supporting competition. In June 2013, the Russian government unveiled their 2014-2016 Privatization Plan, the most recent update of Russia's original privatization plan that was published in 2010 and amended in 2012. The new plan rolled back previous commitments to fully privatize oil giant Rosneft, VTB bank, energy company Zarubezhneft and hydroelectric company Rushydro. Instead of selling all stakes in those companies by 2016 the Russian government will continue to own a 50.1 percent of each company, a "golden share." Plans for Russian Railways, the Russian Agricultural Bank and Rosagroleasing were also scaled back. However, a decision was made to fully privatize Rostelecom and a total of 431 enterprises were added to the block for privatization by 2016. Most of the sales involve selling off minority share positions, privatization through dilution of shares rather than divestment and retaining golden shares to maintain government veto power. To date, treatment of foreign investment in new privatizations has been inconsistent; at times, foreign participation has often been confined to limited positions. Subsequently, many have faced problems with inadequate protection for minority shareholders and corporate governance. Potential foreign investors are advised to work directly and closely with appropriate local, regional, and federal agencies that exercise ownership or authority over SOEs whose shares they may want to acquire.

Corporate Governance

Due to the significance of SOEs within Russia's economy, corporate governance within those companies is a significant factor in Russia's economic growth. A specific variant of SOE, state corporations, are 100% owned by the Russian government and operate under special legislation. The Russian economy also features thousands of other companies owned in part or whole by the Russian government that operate under different legal arrangements, such as unitary enterprises and joint stock companies. In early 2014, the Russian government drafted a directive requiring all state corporations to come up with a series of key performance indicators (KPIs) to guide their development strategy going forward. In rolling out the initiative, the government made it clear that if KPIs were not met personnel changes would be made. This measure is aimed at pushing state corporations toward more efficient operating strategies. The Russian government also declined to increase the size of the government subsidy supporting each state corporation, also with the aim of forcing these companies to run more efficiently. Private enterprises are theoretically allowed to compete with SOEs on the same terms and conditions, and in some sectors, including where state ownership is minimal, competition is robust. But in other areas the playing field can be tilted. Issues that hamper efficient operations and fair competition with SOEs include a lack of transparency, lack of independence and unclear responsibilities of boards of directors, misalignment of managers' incentives and company performance, inadequate control mechanisms on managers' total remuneration or their use of assets transferred by the government to the SOE, and minimal disclosure requirements.

SWFs

There are two sovereign wealth funds in Russia: the Reserve Fund ($87.46 billion, or 4.3% of GDP as of April 1, 2014, up from 3.9% of GDP as of April 1, 2013) and the National Wealth Fund ($87.5 billion, or 4.3% of GDP as of April 1, 2014, up from 4.1% of GDP as of April 1, 2013). The Ministry of Finance manages both funds' assets in accordance with established procedures; the Central Bank of Russia acts as operational manager. Both funds are audited by Russia's Chamber of Accounts and the results are reported to the

Federal Assembly. The Reserve Fund, at 4.3% of GDP, remains below the target of 7% of GDP and is, under currently loosening fiscal policy policies, expected to fall. In February 2014, the Finance Ministry announced plans to spend RUB 212.2 billion on FX purchases for the Reserve Fund. Since the beginning of the year, 38 billion rubles ($1.1 billion) have been spent on currency purchases. The Ministry said that currency purchases for the country's Reserve Fund were tied to the position of the ruble within the currency's euro-dollar trading corridor. Due to the high volatility of the markets, triggered by the tensions around the situation in Ukraine and Crimea, the Ministry suspended such purchases March 4.

11. CORPORATE SOCIAL RESPONSIBILITY

While not standard practice, Russian companies are beginning to show an increased level of interest in their reputation as good corporate citizens. When seeking to acquire companies in Western countries or raise capital on international financial markets, Russian companies face international competition and scrutiny, including on corporate social responsibility (CSR) standards. Consequently, most large Russian companies currently have a CSR policy in place, or are developing one, despite the lack of pressure from Russian consumers and shareholders. CSR policies of Russian firms are usually published on corporate websites and detailed in annual reports. However, these CSR policies and strategies --are still in an early stage relative to those of Western counterparts. Most companies choose to create their own NGO or advocacy group rather than contribute to an already existing organization. The Russian government is a powerful stakeholder in the development of certain companies' CSR agendas, predictably, some companies choose to support local health, educational and social welfare organizations favored by the government.

The Federal Service for Financial Markets established a corporate governance code in 2002 and has endorsed an OECD White Paper on ways to improve practices in Russia. International business associations such as the American Chamber of Commerce in Russia, the U.S.-Russia Business Council, the Association of European Businesses in Russia, the International Business Leaders Forum, and Russian business associations, all stress corporate governance as an important priority for their members and for Russian businesses overall. One association, the Russian Union of Industrialists and Entrepreneurs, developed a Social Charter of Russian Business in 2004 in which over 200 Russian companies and organizations have since joined.

12. POLITICAL VIOLENCE

Political freedom has been significantly curtailed during the past year, including rising hostility toward almost all opposition media outlets and increasing harassment of non-governmental organizations. In the aftermath of Ukraine's EuroMaidan protest which led to the ouster of Kremlin-friendly Ukrainian President Viktor Yanukovich, the Russian government and Russian society as a whole has been gripped by nationalist rhetoric. Soviet-era phrases such as "national traitors" and the "fifth column," which for the Government refers to persons and groups within Russia which they regard as fomenting revolution on behalf of outside forces but in reality may include those opposed to government policy, have reappeared. It remains difficult to predict the next actions of the Russian government, ruled with increasing authoritarianism by President Putin. Political risk is arguably the biggest drag on the Russian economy through the end of 2014.

On the media front, in December 2013, RIA Novosti, the only remaining semi-independent Russian wire service, was abruptly dissolved and reorganized into a new organization to be called "Rossiya Segodnya." The new organization will take marching orders directly from the Kremlin and is charged with producing a specifically Russian view on world events. In early 2014, popular opposition-minded cable channel Dozhd was cut from every major cable and satellite network due to an internet poll that was deemed to be "unpatriotic." The channel continues to produce online content but retains only 20 percent of its original audience, and little advertising revenue without access to cable networks. In a call-in show in April, President Putin indicated a reprieve for the embattled channel but it is still unclear how much longer Dozhd will be able to continue to operate in its limited state.

Public protests continue to occur sporadically in Moscow though they are often disrupted by spur of the moment construction work at the protest site and heavy police presence. The most recent large-scale protest was in February 2014 when 30,000 persons took to the street to protest the illegal Russian annexation of Crimea. There have been smaller protests regarding media freedom and eCommerce issues in 2014 that drew a few thousand participants as well as protests in support of opposition politician Alexey Navalny, who has faced a variety of legal charges due to his activism. The Russian government has also been more inclined to use government-sponsored counter-protests to gain support for their actions. Counter protests in support of Russia's illegal annexation of Crimea drew less than 5,000, although the Russian media erroneously reported the participation figure as much higher.

Some individuals who took part in Moscow's Bolotnaya Ploshchad protest in May 2012 are currently serving jail sentences of up to 4 years for offensives including violence against police officers and participating in an unsanctioned rally. Opposition leaders insist that the individuals were arrested at random and their prosecution was meant to intimidate Russians and prevent future protest actions. Aleksey Navalny, anticorruption whistleblower and member of the opposition Coordination Council, was convicted in October 2013 of stealing $500,000 worth of state-owned timber in a trial that was maligned by opposition leaders and international organizations as little more than a show trial. However, he was released and his five-year sentence was suspended so he could run in the Moscow mayoral elections. His conviction and release resulted in large rallies in Moscow. He has since spent ten days in jail for participation in an unsanctioned rally and is currently under house arrest on a new set of trumped up fraud charges. Although the use of strong-arm tactics is not unknown in Russian commercial disputes, the U.S. Embassy is not aware of cases where foreign investments have been attacked or damaged for purely political reasons. Russia continues to struggle with an ongoing insurgency in Chechnya, Ingushetiya and Dagestan. These republics and neighboring regions in the northern Caucasus have a high risk of violence and kidnapping.

In yet another sign of the worsening civil rights situation in Russia, prominent economist and Rector of the New Economic School Sergei Guriev fled Russia in April 2013. He currently lives in exile in Paris. He has written extensively in the Western press regarding his decision, which was motivated primarily by increasing harassment by the Russian government for support of opposition politicians. He is only one of many examples of high-profile people who have fled Russia because they fear repercussions for holding opinions different from the government's.

The remaining two imprisoned members of the Russian punk rock group "Pussy Riot" were released on December 12, 2013 as a part of a Presidential amnesty to celebrate the 20th anniversary of the Russian constitution. Since their release they have been arrested and subsequently released for their participation in additional protest actions in Moscow and in Sochi, on the margins of the 2014 Winter Olympic Games. They have also been physically abused in public multiple times, with authorities refusing to press charges against their assailants despite video evidence of the crimes. Also released as a part of the amnesty was Russian oligarch Mikhail Khordorkovsky, who was convicted in 2005 of fraud in the controversial Yukos case and sentenced to nine years in prison. He was convicted on secondary charges in 2010 which extended his term to 2014 and a third case was in the process of being brought before the courts. Upon release, Khordorkovsky departed Russia for Germany and currently resides in Switzerland.

13. CORRUPTION

The Russian government stepped up its campaign against corruption in 2012. In March 2012, then-Russian President Medvedev adopted the National Anti-Corruption Plan for 2012–2013. The plan contained guidance and recommendations for the government, federal executive bodies and other government agencies on counteracting corruption, including the establishment of a legal framework for lobbying and increasing the transparency of state officials' personal finances and acceptance of gifts. Additionally, in 2012, Russia adopted a law requiring individuals holding public office, state officials, municipal officials and employees of state organizations to submit information on the funds spent by them and members of their families (spouses and underage children) to acquire certain types of property, including real estate, securities, stock and vehicles. The law also required public servants to disclose the source of the funds for these purchases and to confirm the legality of the acquisitions. In addition, the State Duma adopted a law in 2013 that required state officials, deputies, senators and governors to disclose information on their foreign property holdings and to close foreign bank accounts.

Speaking at the Russian General Prosecutor's Office on the occasion of the 291st anniversary of its establishment, Sergei Ivanov, Chief of the Presidential Administration, mentioned that in 2012, over 7,000 persons charged with corruption had received prison sentences and a greater number of corruption cases were initiated. One high level case led to the firing of Defense Minister Anatoly Serdyukov, who was reportedly at the center of multiple corrupt schemes on a very large scale. However, after a year of investigation, no charges have been filed. Various reports in the media speculated that Serdyukov had been given amnesty, or alternatively, that the investigation had been limited to suspicious of negligence rather than more serious crimes. Failure to hold high government officials accountable for corruption sends a strong signal throughout the system that certain persons are untouchable and protected by the highest authorities. This phenomenon undermines the rule of law in Russia.

Indeed, a long-running dispute between the Russian Prosecutor General, Yuri Chaika, and the Chairman of the Investigative Committee, Alexander Bastrykin, flared up in the Spring 2014. Chaika publicly accused the Investigative Committee of being unwilling to handle serious corruption matters. However, even the General Procuracy has experienced public embarrassment on this issue, when Hewlett Packard Russia pleaded guilty in the United States in April 2014 to bribing Russian prosecutors ten years earlier in exchange for a computer systems procurement contract. Media reports suggested that Russia has not been very helpful in investigating cases under the U.S. Foreign Corrupt Practices Act (FCPA).

Russia is a signatory to the UN Convention against Corruption, the Council of Europe's Criminal Law Convention on Corruption, and, as of 2012, the OECD Anti-Bribery Convention. The OECD Convention calls for the implementation of national legislation to criminalize commercial bribery and to prohibit both offering bribes to foreign government officials and accepting such bribes. It provides no exceptions for "grease payments," and includes foreign entities doing business in Russia, meaning these entities could be subject to liability under their own country's law, as well as Russia's. The convention also calls for increasing the penalties that may be imposed upon an individual or entity found in violation. Fines and terms of incarceration contemplated by the Convention vary, depending upon the type of bribe and the official involved. During 2011-2012, Russia passed national legislation to bring itself into better compliance with its commitments under the OECD Convention and UNCAC. For instance, Article 13.1 of the Federal Law on Corruption allows removal of government officials for failure to take measures to combat corruption. Article 13.3, very broadly requires all legal entities in the Russian Federation implement an ethics and compliance program to combat corruption and conflict of interest. This law also applies to Russian government budgetary entities like schools.

Some analysts have expressed concern that lack of depth in the compliance culture in Russia will render the law a formality that does not function in reality. The implementation and enforcement of the many measures required by these conventions have not yet been fully tested. In recent years, there appears to be a greater number of prosecutions and convictions of mid-level bureaucrats for corruption, but real numbers were difficult to obtain and high-ranking officials were rarely prosecuted. After the close of the 2014 Winter Olympic Games in Sochi, anti-corruption blogger and opposition political candidate Alexey Navalny released a detailed report alleging wide-spread corruption and graft from those government and private individuals involved in construction of the Olympic venues. According to reports, the Prosecutor General's Office opened over 50 criminal cases related to the Olympic Games and has imposed administrative penalties on over 100 persons and companies. It is likely that many of these cases touch only lower level bureaucrats and not high-ranking government officials or prominent businessmen close to the Kremlin who won the lucrative construction contracts for the Olympics.

It is important for U.S. companies, irrespective of size, to assess the business climate in the relevant market in which they will be operating or investing, and to have an effective compliance programs or measures to prevent and detect corruption, including foreign bribery. U.S. individuals and firms operating or investing in Russia should take the time to become familiar with the relevant anticorruption laws of both Russia and the United States in order to properly comply with them, and where appropriate, they should seek the advice of legal counsel.

Additional country information related to corruption can be found in the U.S. State Department's annual Human Rights Report available at http://www.state.gov/g/drl/rls/hrrpt/.

Assistance for U.S. Businesses

The U.S. Department of Commerce offers several services to aid U.S. businesses seeking to address business-related corruption issues. For example, the U.S. Commercial Service can provide services that may assist U.S. companies in conducting their due diligence as part of a company's overarching compliance program when choosing business partners or agents overseas. The U.S. Commercial Service can be reached directly through its offices in major U.S. and foreign cities, or through its Website at: www.trade.gov/cs.

The Departments of Commerce and State provide worldwide support for qualified U.S. companies bidding on foreign government contracts through the Commerce Department's Advocacy Center and State's Office of Commercial and Business Affairs. Problems, including alleged corruption by foreign governments or competitors, encountered by U.S. companies in seeking such foreign business opportunities can be brought to the attention of appropriate U.S. government officials, including local embassy personnel and through the Department of Commerce Trade Compliance Center "Report A Trade Barrier" Website at: tcc.export.gov/Report_a_Barrier/index.asp.

The U.S. Government seeks to level the global playing field for U.S. businesses by encouraging other countries to take steps to criminalize their own companies' acts of corruption, including bribery of foreign public officials, by requiring them to uphold their obligations under relevant international conventions. A U.S. firm that believes a competitor is seeking to use bribery of a foreign public official to secure a contract should bring this to the attention of appropriate U.S. agencies, as noted below.

U.S. Foreign Corrupt Practices Act (FCPA)

In 1977, the United States enacted the FCPA, which makes it unlawful for a U.S. person, and certain foreign issuers of securities, to make a corrupt payment to foreign public officials for the purpose of obtaining or retaining business for or with, or directing business to, any person. The FCPA also applies to foreign firms and persons who take any act in furtherance of such a corrupt payment while in the United States. For more detailed information on the FCPA, see the FCPA Lay-Person's Guide at: www.justice.gov/criminal/fraud/fcpa/docs/lay-persons-guide.pdf.

The Department of Justice (DOJ) FCPA Opinion Procedure enables U.S. firms and individuals to request a statement of DOJ's present enforcement intentions under the anti-bribery provisions of the FCPA regarding any proposed business conduct. The details of the opinion procedure are available on DOJ's Fraud Section Website at: www.justice.gov/criminal/fraud/fcpa.

Although the Department of Commerce has no enforcement role with respect to the FCPA, it supplies general guidance to U.S. exporters who have questions about the FCPA and about international developments concerning the FCPA. For further information, see the Office of the Chief Counsel for International Counsel's website, at: http://www.ogc.doc.gov/trans_anti_bribery.html.

Other Instruments

It is U.S. Government policy to promote good governance, including host country implementation and enforcement of anti-corruption laws and policies pursuant to their obligations under international agreements. Since enactment of the FCPA, the United States has been instrumental to the expansion of the international framework to fight corruption. Several significant components of this framework are the OECD Convention on Combating Bribery of Foreign Public Officials in International Business Transactions (OECD Anti-Bribery Convention), the United Nations Convention against Corruption (UN Convention), the Inter-American Convention against Corruption (OAS Convention), the Council of Europe Criminal and Civil Law Conventions, and a growing list of U.S. free trade agreements.

OECD Anti-Bribery Convention

The OECD Anti-Bribery Convention entered into force in February 1999. There are 38 parties to the Convention including the United States (see http://www.oecd.org/dataoecd/59/13/40272933.pdf). The Convention obligates the Parties to criminalize bribery of foreign public officials in the conduct of international business. The United States meets its international obligations under the OECD Anti-Bribery Convention through the FCPA. In 2011, Russia passed anti-corruption legislation that clearly criminalized foreign bribery and acceded to the Anti-Bribery Convention in 2012.

Local Laws

U.S. firms should familiarize themselves with local anticorruption laws, and, where appropriate, seek legal counsel. While the U.S. Department of Commerce cannot provide legal advice on local laws, the Department's U.S. Commercial Service can provide assistance with navigating the host country's legal system and obtaining a list of local legal counsel.

Transparency International (TI) publishes an annual Corruption Perceptions Index (CPI). The CPI measures the perceived level of public-sector corruption in 183 countries and territories around the world. The CPI is available at: http://cpi.transparency.org/cpi2011/. TI also publishes an annual Global Corruption Report which provides a systematic evaluation of the state of corruption around the world. It includes an in-depth analysis of a focal theme, a series of country reports that document major corruption related events and developments from all continents and an overview of the latest research findings on anti-corruption diagnostics and tools. Seehttp://www.transparency.org/publications/gcr. Transparency International-Russia also posts corruption-related research materials and findings on the following sites, all specific to Russia: www.transparency.org.ru/INTER/index.asp and www.askjournal.ru.

The World Bank Institute publishes Worldwide Governance Indicators (WGI). These indicators assess six dimensions of governance in 213 economies, including Voice and Accountability, Political Stability and Absence of Violence, Government Effectiveness, Regulatory Quality, Rule of Law and Control of Corruption. See http://info.worldbank.org/governance/wgi/sc_country.asp. World Bank Business Environment and Enterprise Performance Surveys may also be of interest.

The World Economic Forum publishes the Global Enabling Trade Report, which presents the rankings of the Enabling Trade Index, and includes an assessment of the transparency of border administration (focused on bribe payments and corruption) and a separate segment on corruption and the regulatory environment. See http://www.weforum.org/reports/global-enabling-trade-report-2012.

Global Integrity, a nonprofit organization, publishes its annual Global Integrity Report, which provides indicators with respect to governance and anti-corruption. The report highlights the strengths and weaknesses of national level anti-corruption systems. The report is available at: http://www.globalintegrity.org/report.

14. BILATERAL INVESTMENT AGREEMENTS

While the United States and Russia signed a bilateral investment treaty (BIT) in 1992, it is not in force due to lack of ratification by the Russian Duma. In January 2014, Russia and the United States began talks on ways to improve the bilateral investment relationship. Those talks were suspended after Russia's illegal invasion of Crimea in February 2014. Russia has BITs with 75 countries, 54 of which are currently in force.

The United States and Russia have shared an income tax treaty since 1992, which is designed to address the issue of double taxation and fiscal evasion with respect to taxes on income and capital. Full text of the treaty: http://www.irs.gov/pub/irs-trty/russia.pdf. There is some concern that taxation requirements have sometimes been used in Russia as a way to "raid" or illegally take possession of foreign companies, particularly small and medium enterprises.

15. OPIC AND OTHER INVESTMENT INSURANCE PROGRAMS

Since 1992, the U.S. Overseas Private Investment Corporation (OPIC) has been authorized to provide loans, loan guarantees (financing), and investment insurance against political risks to U.S. companies investing in Russia. OPIC's political risk insurance and financing help U.S. companies of all sizes invest in Russia. OPIC insures against three political risks: expropriation; political violence; and currency inconvertibility. OPIC recently announced that political risk insurance now covers private equity fund investments. To meet the demands of larger projects in Russia and worldwide, OPIC can insure up to $250 million per project and up to $300 million for projects in the oil and gas sector with offshore, hard currency revenues. Projects in the oil and gas sector with offshore, hard currency revenues may be approved for an exposure limit up to $400 million if the project receives a credit evaluation (shadow rating) of investment grade or higher. The individual per project exposure limit for financing is $250 million. The maximum combined (insurance and financing) exposure limit to OPIC on a single project is $400 million. OPIC has no minimum investment size requirements. OPIC also makes equity capital available for investments in Russia by guaranteeing long-term loans to private equity investment funds. Detailed information about OPIC's programs can be accessed at www.opic.gov. Russia is also a member of the World Bank's Multilateral Investment Guarantee Agency.

16. LABOR

The Russian labor market remains fragmented, characterized by limited labor mobility across regions and consequent wage and employment differentials. Earnings inequalities are substantial, enforcement of labor standards is relatively weak, and collective bargaining is underdeveloped. Employers regularly complain about shortages of qualified skilled labor. This is due in part to weak linkages between the education system and the labor market. In addition, the economy suffers from a general shortage of highly skilled labor. Businesses face increasing labor costs as competition over a limited pool of workers intensifies. On the other hand, private business must compete with SOEs, where Russians have indicated in recent surveys they would prefer to work due to salaries and benefits. The public sector, which maintains inefficient and unproductive positions, accounts for about 25 percent the workforce. The 2002 Labor Code governs labor standards in Russia. The enforcement of worker safety rules continues to be a major issue, as enterprises are often unable or unwilling to invest in safer equipment or to enforce safety standards.

The rate of actual unemployment (calculated according to ILO methodology) in 2013 was low at 5.5 percent. Average unemployment in urban districts (4.7 percent as of December) was much lower than in rural districts (8.3 percent). In 2013, two regions in the North Caucasus had the highest unemployment rates in the country: Ingushetia (43.7 percent) and Chechnya (26.9 percent). In stark contrast, the unemployment rate was 1.5 percent in St. Petersburg and 1.7 percent in Moscow.

17. FOREIGN TRADE ZONES/FREE PORTS

Russia has 26 Special Economic Zones (SEZs), which fall in one of four categories: industrial and production zones; technology and innovation zones; tourist and recreation zones; and port zones. Enterprises operating within SEZs enjoy a range of benefits that the Ministry of Economic Development (MED) – which manages the SEZ program – estimates can save investors up to 30% of the cost of doing business. Specifically, investors enjoy streamlined administrative requirements and procedures, a more favorable customs regime (including the waiver of import duties and refunds of the value-added-tax), and reduced tax rates on income, property, land, and transport. SEZ investors also receive discounts on infrastructure expenses, including facilities and utilities costs. Such benefits are extended for an agreed introductory period, often lasting five years.

Progress in attracting foreign investors to SEZs is uneven. The majority of SEZ investments are still listed as "planned," meaning investors are still able to back out of commitments. The lack of interest from foreign investors in addition to environmental concerns led to the closure of the proposed Kaliningrad tourist and recreational zone SEZ in late 2012. The Russian government has been hesitant to go forward with major SEZ infrastructure projects. Detailed information about the benefits and results of Russia's SEZs can be found at the MED's SEZ website: http://www.economy.gov.ru/minec/activity/sections/sez/main/.

Independent of the SEZs, in 2010 then-President Medvedev launched an initiative to establish the Skolkovo Innovation Center in the Moscow suburbs to promote investment in high-technology startup businesses, research, and commercialization of technological innovation. Inspired by the model of Silicon Valley, Skolkovo "resident companies" can receive a broad range of benefits, including exemption from profit tax, value-added tax, property taxes, and import duties, and partial exemption from social fund payments. Applicants for residency are evaluated and selected by an international admission board; company performance is monitored to ensure continued qualification for benefits. According to the Skolkovo Foundation, over 1,000 startups have been selected as residents thus far, although very few are physical present at Skolkovo now. The infrastructure for Skolkovo is still being built.

18. FOREIGN DIRECT INVESTMENT AND FOREIGN PORTFOLIO INVESTMENT STATISTICS

Table 1 shows flows of foreign investment into Russia by country for the first nine months of 2013, compared to the same period in 2012. Total foreign investment increased by 15 % year-on-year. According to Russian statistical practice, total foreign investment numbers include direct investment (FDI), portfolio investment, and other investment (largely trade credits). FDI flows into Russia also increased in 2013, rising by 52%; the largest share came from Cyprus according to available data. FDI from the Netherlands and Cyprus is consistently high, reflecting the fact that most FDI coming from these countries is likely either returning or reinvested Russian capital through subsidiaries or off-shore "shell" vehicles. The data in the table below is from the Central Bank of Russia. While official statistics for 2014 are not yet available, anecdotal evidence suggests that uncertainty spawned by the crisis in Ukraine as well as market fluctuations in Russia will drive FDI numbers down for this year.

Table 1: Top Investors - By Year (in $ million)

Country	Jan-Sep 2013		Jan-Sep 2012		Jan-Sep 2011	
	Total	FDI	Total	FDI	Total	FDI
Switzerland		754	43,252	88	69,115	70.1
Netherlands	12,812	2,655	15,676	909	13,218	3,023
Cyprus	17,612	7,772	11,788	3,842	12,972	2,758
Germany	6,338	2,411	3,799	1,119	8,169	1,480
UK	12,158		10,618	500	6,336	176
All Others			29,330	5,819	23,976	4,228
Total	132,385	18,610	114,463	12,277	133,784	11,736

The numbers in Table 2 represent the accumulated stock of total foreign investment in Russia by originating country, including FDI, portfolio, and "other" investment as of September 30, 2013, compared to the amount accumulated a year prior. Source: Central Bank of Russia.

Table 2: Top Investors - Accumulated Basis (in $ million)

Country	As of Sep 30, 2013		As of Sep 30, 2012		As of Sep 30, 2011	
	Total	FDI	Total	FDI	Total	FDI
Cyprus	67,635	44,160	78,566	53,357	69,057	47,290
Netherlands	67,113	23,385	59,223	21,723	46,295	23,328
Luxembourg	47,197	1,319	39,808	1,191	35,051	643
Germany	21,969	12,119	24,757	11,393	29,779	11,386
China	32,383	1,492	27,792	1,346	27,356	1,238
All Others			123,198	46,298	115,650	42,529
Total	379254	122500	353,344	135,308	323,178	126,415

Table 3 shows total foreign investment by region over the first nine months of 2013, compared to the same period in 2012. Moscow continues to attract the lion's share of investments, mainly due to the concentration of companies' headquarters and consumers with high purchasing power. Source: Central Bank of Russia, including direct, portfolio and "other" investments.

Table 3 – Foreign Investment – Top Regions (in $ million)

	Jan-Sep 2013			Jan-Sep 2012			Jan-Sep 2011		
	Amount	%	Rank	Amount	%	Rank	Amount	%	Rank
Moscow (city)	78,383	59.20%		63,211	55.20%		84,878	63.40%	1

Tyumen Region	4,669	3.50%		6,975	6.10%		9,821	7.30%	2
Sakhalin Region	1,008	1.50%		8,541	7.50%		6,570	4.90%	3
St. Petersburg	8,974	6.80%		6,580	5.70%		3,972	3.00%	4
Belgorod Region	1,433	1.10%		465	0.10%		3,171	2.40%	5
Others							25,371	19.00%	
Total	132,385	100%		114,463	100%		133,784	100%	

Table 4 shows investment by sector over the first nine months of 2013, compared to the same period in 2012. Total investment increased in six of the ten top sectors. Data for investment into the financial sector was not available. Source: Central Bank of Russia

Table 4: Foreign Investment: Top Sectors (in $ million)

Industry/Sector	Jan-Sep 2013		Jan-Sep 2012		Jan-Sep 2011	
	%	Amount	%	Amount	%	Amount
Finance	11.77%	15,579	33.46%	38,300	49.10%	65,711
Extraction of Fuel	5.06%	6,702	10.60%	12,136	9.60%	12,850
Wholesale and Retail Trade	16.97%	22,463	15.79%	18,074	9.20%	12,363
Production of coke and oil products	34.42%	45,563	10.78%	12,338	7.50%	9,997
Metallurgy	7.50%	9,932	6.05%	6,927	4.40%	5,902
Transport and Communications	2.41%	3,190	2.95%	3,377	4.10%	5,494
Real Estate and Related Services	4.79%	6,337	6.25%	7,150	3.60%	4,782
Chemical Industry	3.67%	4,858	2.09%	2,387	2.70%	3,636
Food Industry	2.08%	2,755	1.38%	1,583	1.50%	1,964
Production of vehicles	3.90%	5,164	2.45%	2,802	1.40%	1,845
All Others	7.43%	9,842	9.20%	9,389	6.90%	9,240
Total	100.00%	132,385	100.00%	114,463	100.00%	133,784

Table 5 shows stocks of Russian FDI abroad as of September 30, 2013 and September 30, 2012, as well as flows of Russian FDI abroad for the first nine months of 2013, compared to the same period in 2012. Russian FDI stocks decreased in the Netherlands and the United States but increased in Cyprus, the United Kingdom and Luxembourg (data from 2011 was unavailable for Luxembourg and the United Kingdom). Source: Central Bank of Russia

Table 5: Top Destinations of Russian FDI - By Year (in $ million)

Country	as of Sep 30, 2013		as of Sep 30, 2012		as of Sep 30, 2011	
	Stock	Flow	Stock	Flow	Stock	Flow
Netherlands	22,284	6,388	31,049	6,848	25,067	8,427
Cyprus	33,595	14,974	25,686	10,834	14,280	842
Switzerland	8,190	36,446	8,115	38,641	2,814	328
United States	4,004	545	7,880	642	6,663	439
United Kingdom	9,157	3,550	6,270	7,528	N/A	N/A
Luxembourg	6,846	7,873	6,206	213	N/A	N/A
Belarus	5,501	2,831	5,820	5,877	2,685	629

SELECTED U.S. AND RUSSIAN CONTACTS

Contact Point at the US Trade Center
William Muntean
Senior Trade Officer
Bolshoy Deviatinsky Pereulok No. 8,
Moscow 121099, Russian Federation
+7 (495) 728-5000
moscow.office.box@mail.doc.gov

RUSSIAN GOVERNMENT AGENCIES:

*Ministry of Trade and Industry:
Yuri Dmitrievich Maslyukov, Minister-Designate
18/1, Ovchinnikovskaya Nab., Moscow
Tel: (095) 220-1064; Fax: (095) 220-1684, 231-9220
*Note: The Russian Government announced that in August 1998, the Ministry for Foreign Economic Relations and Trade would be abolished, and that some of its functions would be assumed by a new Ministry of Trade and Industry. Mr. Maslyukov was appointed by President Yeltsin in July 1998.

Ministry of Finance:
Mikhail Mikhailovich Zadornov, Minister of Finance
Ulitsa Ilyinka 9, Entrance 1, Moscow
Tel: (095) 298-9130; Fax: (095) 925-0889

Ministry of Fuel and Energy:
Sergei Vladimirovich Generalov, Minister of Fuels and Energy
7, Kitaigorodskiy Proyezd, Moscow 103074
Tel: (095) 220-4659; Fax: (095) 975-2045 (International Dept.)

Ministry of Agriculture and Food:
Viktor A. Semyonov, Minister of Agriculture and Food
Orlikov Pereulok, 1/11, Moscow

Tel: (095) 207-4243; Fax: (095) 207-8362

State Customs Committee:
Vitaly G. Draganov, Chairman, State Customs Committee
1a, Komsomolskaya Ploshchad, Moscow 107842
Phone: (095) 975-1918; Fax: (095) 975-4823

State Committee for Standardization, Metrology and Certification (GOSSTANDART
Gennady Petrovich Voronin, Chairman
9, Leninskiy Prospekt, Moscow 117049
Phone: (095) 236-6208, -4044; Fax: (095) 236-6231, 237-6032

Russian Copyright Agency:
Georgiy Artashessovich Ter-Gazariyants, Chairman of the Board;
Vadim Serafimovich Dunin, Head of Foreign Relations Department
6a, Bolshaya Bronnaya Ul., Moscow 103670
Phone: (095) 203-2996, -4599; Fax: (095) 200-1263

Committee for Patents and Trademarks (Rospatent
Alexander Dmitrievich Korchagin, General Director
2/6 Cherkasskiy Pereulok, Moscow
Tel: (095) 206-6203; Fax: (095) 923-4093

State Investment Corporation:
Yuriy Vladimirovich Petrov, Chairman
35, Myasnitskaya Ul., Moscow 103685
Phone: (095) 925-6796; Fax: (095) 207-6936
Regional Governments:

Moscow City Administration:
Iosif N. Ordzhonikidze,
Deputy Mayor and Minister for External Relations
13 Tverskaya Ulitsa, 103032, Moscow
Tel: 095-229-6360; Fax: (095) 883-6208

Moscow Registration Chamber:
Vladimir Ivanovich Sobolyev, Chairman
Mokhovaya Ul., 11, Bld. 8-E, Moscow 103009
Tel/Fax: (095) 202-2787;

Roald Nestorovich Lebedinskiy,
Dir., Registration/Accreditation (information in English)
Tel: (095) 132-0500

Tatyana Kuzminichna Nikonorkina, Expert for Registration of Companies with Foreign Capital
(information in Russian)
Tel: (095) 202-4042

St. Petersburg City Administration:
Gennady I. Tkachev, Chairman, External Relations Committee
1, Smolniy, St. Petersburg 193060
Phone: (812) 276-1204; Fax: (812) 276-1633

Ilya I. Klebanov, First Vice Governor
Chairman, Cmte. on Economy and Industrial Policy
16 Voznesensky Prospect, St. Petersburg, Russia 190000
Phone: (812) 315-5152; Fax: (812) 319-9292.

Igor Yu. Artemiev, First Vice Governor
Chairman, Committee on Finance
16 Voznesensky Prospect, St. Petersburg, Russia 190000
Phone: (812) 319-9308; Fax: (812) 319-9967.

Leninrad Oblast Administration:
Inna L. Bigotskaya, Chief of Protocol Department
External Relations Committee,
67, Suvorovskiy Prospekt, St. Petersburg 193311
Phone: (812) 274-4859; Fax: (812) 274-2463.

Mark A. Vybornov, Chairman,
Committee on Foreign Economic Relations and Investments
67, Suvorovskiy Prospekt, St. Petersburg 193311
Phone: (812) 278-5587 or 274-4742; Fax: (812) 274-5986.

Yekaterinburg Oblast Administration:

Igor Ivanovich Arzyakov, Dir., Foreign Relations Department
1, Oktyabrskaya Ploshchad, Yekaterinburg 620031
Phone: (3432) 51-54-97, 58-96-56; Fax: (3432) 51-98-70

Yekaterinburg City Administration:
Vladimir I. Lomovtzev, Dir., Foreign Relations Department
1, Oktyabrskaya Ploshchad, Yekaterinburg 620031
Phone: (3432) 51-13-07, 51-43-83; Fax: (3432) 51-90-05

Primorskiy Territorial Administration:
Andrey Gennadyevich Zagumyonnov, Chairman
Committee for Foreign Economic Relations and Regional Trade
of the Dept. for Foreign Economic Relations and Tourism
22 Svetlanskaya ulitsa, 690110, Vladivostok
Phone: (4232) 22-08-52
Fax: (4232) 22-10-19

Khabarovsk Territorial Administration:
Sergey I. Lopatin, Chief, Foreign Economic Relations Dept.
56 ul.K.Marksa, Khabarovsk
Phone/fax: (4212) 32-41-21

Sakhalin Regional Administration:
Vitaly Nikolaevich Elizariev, Director
Department of Foreign Economic Relations
32 Kommunisticheskiy prospect, "Sakhincenter", office 236
693000 Yuzhno-Sakhalinsk 693000
Phone: (4242) 72-74-94
Fax: (4242) 72-74-93; International fax: 7 509-95-1236

State Duma (Lower chamber of Parliament

--Cmte. on Budget, Taxes, Banking and Finance:
Alexander Zhukov, Chairman
2, Georgiyevskiy Pereulok, Moscow
Tel: (095) 292-3618; Fax: (095) 292-5601

--Cmte. on Property, Privatization and Economic Activity:
Pavel Grigoryevich Bunich, Chairman
2, Georgiyevskiy Pereulok, Moscow
Tel: (095) 229-9559; Fax: (095) 229-6996

--Cmte. on Industry, Construction, Transport and Energy:
Vladimir Kuzmich Gusev, Chairman
2, Georgiyevskiy Pereulok, Moscow
Tel: (095) 292-0365; Fax: (095) 292-3763

TRADE ASSOCIATIONS/CHAMBERS OF COMMERCE IN RUSSIA:

American Chamber of Commerce in Russia (Amcham)
Scott M. Blacklin, President
Kosmodamianskaya Nab. 52, Building 1, 8th floor, Moscow
Phone: (095) 961-2141; Fax: (095) 961-2142

American Chmbr. of Commerce in Russia, St. Petersburg Chapter:
Slava Bytchkov, Executive Director
25, Nevsky pr., St. Petersburg, 191186
Tel: (812) 326-2590; Fax: (812) 326-2591

St. Petersburg International Business Association (SPIBA)
Anna Kessner, Executive Administrator
27, Naberezhnaya Moiki, 5th Floor, St. Petersburg, 191186
Tel: (812) 325-9091; Fax: (812) 325-9933

Vladivostok International Business Association (VIBA)
Andrew Wilson, President
c/o U.S. and Foreign Commercial Service, Vladivostok
32 Pushkin Street, Vladivostok, Russia 690000
Phone: (4232) 300-093; Fax: (4232) 300-092
e-mail: csvlad@online.ru

Council for Trade and Economic Cooperation (CIS-USA)
Boris Petrovich Alekseyev, President
3, Naberezhnaya Shevchenko, Moscow 121248
Phone: (095) 243-5514, -5470; Fax: (095) 230-2467

Russian Chamber of Commerce and Industry
Stanislav Alekseyevich Smirnov, President;
Yuriy Nikolayevich Denissenkov, Head,
Sergey B. Kulyba, Expert on Accreditation,
Protocol Department
6, Ilyinka Ul., Moscow 103684
Phone: (095) 929-02-86,-60,-61,-62,-63;
Fax: (095) 929-0356

Primorskiy Territory Chamber of Commerce
Vladimir Borisovich Brezhnev, Chairman
13a Okeanskiy prospekt, Vladivostok
Phone: (4232) 26-96-30
Fax: (4232) 22-72-26

Khabarovsk Territory Chamber of Commerce and Industry
Mikhail Kruglikov, President
113, Shevronova Ulitsa, Khabarovsk 680000
Phone: (4212) 33-03-11, 33-11-30; Fax: (4212) 33-03-12

U.S. GOVERNMENT PERSONNEL HANDLING BUSINESS ISSUES IN RUSSIA:

U.S. EMBASSY IN MOSCOW:

--John Peters, Minister Counselor for Commercial Affairs
U.S. and Foreign Commercial Service
Bolshaya Molchanovka 23/28, Moscow 121019
Phone: (095) 967-3414; Fax: (095) 967-3416
Satellite phone: 7 (502) 224-1105;
Satellite fax: 7 (502) 224-1106

--Michael Matera, Minister Counselor for Economic Affairs
21, Novinskiy Bulvar, Moscow 121099
Phone: (095) 956-4220; Fax: (095) 956-4146

--Asif Chaudry, Minister Counselor for Agricultural Affairs
21, Novinskiy Bulvar, Moscow 121099
Phone: (095) 956 4103; (502) 221 1245
Fax: (095) 975 2339; (502) 224 1356

--James Waller, Treasury Attache
21, Novinskiy Bulvar, Moscow 121099
Phone: (095) 956-4258; Fax: (095) 956-4146

--U.S. Agency for International Development
Office of Privatization and Economic Restructuring
U.S. Embassy, Moscow
21 Novinskiy Bulvar., Moscow 121099
Phone: (095) 956-4281

U.S. and Foreign Commercial Service, St. Petersburg
James McCarthy, Principal Commercial Officer
25, Nevsky prospekt., St. Petersburg, Russia 191186
Tel: (812) 326-2560; Fax: (812) 326-2561/62

American Business Center, St. Petersburg
Zhanna Agasieva, Assistant Manager
25, Nevsky prospekt, St. Petersburg, Russia 191186
Tel: (812) 326-2570; Fax: (812) 326-2571

U.S. and Foreign Commercial Service, Vladivostok
Richard Steffens, Principal Commercial Officer
32 Pushkin Street, Vladivostok, Russia 690000
Satellite phone/fax: (509) 851-1211
Phone: (4232) 300-093; Fax: (4232) 300-092
e-mail: csvlad@online.ru

American Business Center, Vladivostok
Inna Nazarova, Assistant Manager
2, Batareynaya Ul., Vladivostok
Satellite phone/fax: (509) 851-1212
Phone: (4232) 25-46-25; Fax: (4232) 25-46-61

U.S. Consulate-General in Yekaterinburg
Alexander Deyanov, Commercial Assistant
15A Gogol Street, Third Floor
Yekaterinburg, Russia
Phone: (3432) 564-619; Fax: (3432) 564-515

Phone: (3432) 564-736 (Foreign Commercial Service)

Federal Aviation Administration (FAA)
Dennis B. Cooper, Senior Representative
American Embassy, Brussels
27 Boulevard du Regent, B-1000 Brussels, Belgium
Phone: 322 508-2700; Fax: 322 230-06428
Phone: (095) 956-4036; Fax: (095) 956-4293

WASHINGTON-BASED U.S. GOVERNMENT CONTACTS FOR RUSSIA:

Business Information Service for the Newly Independent States (BISNIS)
Anne Grey, Director
U.S. Department of Commerce, Rm.7413,
Washington, D.C. 20230
Phone: (202) 482-4655; Fax: (202) 482-2293

U.S. Export-Import Bank
David Fiore, Loan Officer
811 Vermont Avenue, N.W., Washington, D.C. 20571-0999
Phone: (202) 565-3815; Fax: (202) 565-3816

Overseas Private Investment Corporation
Peter Ballinger, Manager, NIS Investment Development
1100 New York Avenue, N.W., Washington, D.C. 20527
Phone: (202) 336-8618; Fax: (202) 408-5145

U.S. Trade and Development Agency
Daniel Stein, Regional Director
U.S. Department of State, SA-16, Rm.301
Washington, D.C. 20523-1602
Phone: (703) 875-4357; Fax: (703) 875-4009

U.S. Department of State, Office of Russian Affairs
Thomas K. Huffaker, Chief Economist
2201 C Street, N.W., Washington, D.C. 20520
Phone: (202) 647-6747; Fax: (202) 736-4710

U.S. Department of Commerce -- Market Access and Compliance
Russia and Independent States Division
Jack Brougher, Director,
U.S. Department of Commerce, Rm.3318,
Washington, D.C. 20230
Phone: (202) 482-3952; Fax: (202) 482-3042

U.S. Agency for International Development
Office of Privatization and Economic Restructuring
Washington, D.C. 20523
Phone: (202) 736-4410

U.S. Department of Agriculture
Russian Area Officer
14th St. and Independence Avenue S.W.,
Washington, D.C. 20250
Phone: (202) 720-3080

U.S. Bureau of Export Administration
Export Counselling Division
U.S. Department of Commerce, Rm.3898,
Washington, D.C. 20230
Phone: (202) 482-4811; Fax: (202) 482-3911

Special American Business Internship Training Program (SABIT)
Liesel Duhon, Director
U.S. Department of Commerce, Rm.3006,
Washington, D.C. 20230
Phone: (202) 482-0073; Fax: (202) 482-4098

U.S.-Based Multipliers and International Organizations
with Interests in Russia:

U.S.-Russia Business Council
Eugene K. Lawson, President
1701 Pennsylvania Ave., N.W. Suite 650,
Washington, D.C. 20046
Phone: (202) 956-7670; Fax: (202) 956-7674

Russian-American Chamber of Commerce
Deborah Palmieri, President
6200 South Quebec St., Suite 210,
Englewood, Colorado 80111

Phone: (303) 689-8642; Fax: (303) 689-8762

Foundation for Russian-American Economic Cooperation
Carol Vipperman, President
1932 First Avenue, Suite 803
Seattle, WA 98101
Tel: (206) 443-1935; Fax (206) 443-0954

National Association of State Departments of Agriculture
Richard Kirchhoff, Executive Vice President
1156 15th Street, N.W. Suite 1020,
Washington, D.C. 20045
Tel: (202) 296-9680; Fax: (202) 296-9686

The World Bank
Thomas Kelsey, U.S. Department of Commerce liaison
1818 H Street, NW, Washington, DC, 20433
Phone: (202) 458-0118; Fax: (202) 458-0118

International Finance Corporation (IFC)
Mark Constantine
1850 Eye Street, NW, Washington, DC 20433
Phone: (202) 473-9331; Fax: (202) 676-1513
Moscow Office: Roger Gale
6, Neglinnaya St., Moscow
Tel: 7-095-928-5328; Fax: 7-095-927-6832

International Bank for Reconstruction and Development
U.S. Department of Commerce Liaison
to the U.S. Executive Director's Office
1818 H Street, N.W., Room D-13004
Washington, D.C. 20433
Phone: (202) 458-0118; Fax: (202) 477-2967

Office of Multilateral Development Banks,
U.S.& Foreign Commercial Service
U.S. Department of Commerce, Room H-1107
Washington, D.C. 20230
Phone: (202) 482-3399; Fax: (202) 273-0927

European Bank for Reconstruction and Development (EBRD)
One Exchange Square, London EC2A 2EH, United Kingdom
Dean Peterson, U.S. Department of Commerce Liaison
Tel: 011-44-171-338-6569; Fax: 011-44-171-338-6487

MARKET RESEARCH

A comprehensive and up-to-date listing of market research reports prepared by the U.S. & Foreign Commercial Service in Russia is available on the NTDB (National Trade Data Bank). The following listing is of key publications from 1998, and publications under consideration for 1999:

SECTOR ANALYSES (ISAS

Advertising
Agricultural Machinery and Tractors
Automotive Aftermarket
Aviation Industry
Computer and Office Equipment
Construction Equipment in Northwest Russia
Construction Materials and Services on Sakhalin Island
Construction Materials in the Urals Region
Consumer Goods (General)
Consumer Appliances
Cosmetics
Electronic Components
Financial Services and Insurance
Food Processing and Packaging Equipment
Food Processing Equipment in the Urals Region
Furniture Manufacturing in the Urals Region
Hotel and Restaurant Equipment
Internet Services
Laboratory Diagnostic Equipment
Metallurgy in the Urals Region
Meters and Controls for Heating and Ventilation
Mining Equipment Interior Building Products
Packaging Equipment
Petroleum Markets (Retail)
Pharmaceuticals
Satellite Equipment and Services
Transportation Services

Travel and Tourism Services (Russian Far East)

COMMODITY REPORTS AND MARKET BRIEFS:

Annual Marketing Plan Information Report (annual)
Livestock (annual and semi-annual)
Poultry (annual)
Fresh Deciduous Fruit (annual)
Agricultural Situation Report (annual)
Seafood (annual)
Sugar (annual and semi-annual)
Foreign Buyer List Annual Report
Dairy (annual)
Planting Seeds (annual)
Forest Products (annual)
Grain & Feed (annual)
Oilseeds and Products (annual)
Cotton (annual)

SELECTED INVESTMENT AND BUSINESS OPPORTUNITIES

MARKET FOR HOTEL AND RESTAURANT EQUIPMENT

The hotel and restaurant equipment market in Russia is booming! Contributing to this boom is the hospitality industry, one of the fastest growing segments in the Russian economy, fueled by a growing economy and increased consumer spending. The food service industry alone is expected to continue growing at the average annual rate of between 30-40 percent for the next few years. With the average monthly per capita spending on 'eating out' increasing by more than 25 percent in 2009, industry experts estimate that the total turnover for the Moscow restaurant market will hit $3 billion in 2010 (it ranged between $2-2.5 billion in 2009). And to top it all off, more than 390 new hotels are to be built in Russia's largest cities by 2010, 240 in Moscow alone. Market conditions are favorable for U.S. companies to take advantage of the opportunities in this dynamic industry.

MARKET DEMAND

Russia's market for hotel and restaurant equipment has been growing rapidly over the last several years and is expected to continue. With over 390 new hotels to be built by 2010 in Moscow and St. Petersburg alone, there are significant opportunities for U.S. companies in this market.

In the food service sector, the fast food and quick & casual restaurants segments are showing the greatest growth rate. In Moscow, consumer spending on 'eating out' increased by 25 percent in 2009 (the last year figures are available for).

Similarly, the restaurant sector has also been expanding rapidly. Along with this continued growth in demand, there is a new recognition of the advantages technologically advanced equipment that is designed to improve efficiency and reduce expenses, contributing to improving a restaurant's competitive edge. Even though the market is very price sensitive, experts indicate growth in the demand for quality equipment of the leading manufacturers. Industry insiders are of the opinion that the high-and low-end equipment segments of the market are almost saturated, and that there are better opportunities in the mid-price range.

Market Data

The Russian economy has expanded steadily over the last several years (averaging 6 to 7 percent growth per annum). Sharp increases in consumer disposable income and expanding tourism have lead to boom in Russia's hotel and restaurant industries.

SUB-SECTOR PROFILES

The Restaurant Market

Though the Russian hotel and restaurant market has shown significant growth over the past few years, it is still modest in size and has significant potential for further growth and development. The current market size of Russian restaurant sector is estimated to be $5 billion annually. The food service sector has been rapidly developing since the early 1990's not only in the larger cities such as Moscow, St. Petersburg also in the small ional cities as well.

Russia is a large country undergoing dynamic development, which varies greatly from region to region, depending on each region's economic situation. Fast food selections are becoming more varied, with many traditional Russian, as well as international eateries appearing. Catering and food delivery services are also expanding rapidly. The demand for efficient equipment, specific to food delivery, which allows companies to minimize expenses and remain competitive, is strong. The food services sector has become an attractive investment area as well, with growth expected to continue for another 5 to 7 years.

According to the Moscow City government, there are about 10,000 restaurants in Moscow. Industry experts estimate that the total turnover of the Moscow restaurant market ranged between $2-2.5 billion in 2009, and is expected to hit $3 billion in 2010. The average monthly per capita spending on 'eating out' increased in 2009 by more than 25 % to $23.60 over 2008.

Regardless of a wide variety of offerings, new restaurants are opening. The most dynamic segment is the branded medium priced and quick & casual restaurants. Growing at a notably slower place are the expensive and elite restaurants.

Food service equipment is in constant demand. Presently, a wide selection of imported and domestic food service equipment is being offered on the Russian market. Food service equipment is divided into three major categories: premium/high priced equipment, medium, and low priced equipment.

According to market research conducted by Step-By-Step, 62 percent of the market share is low-priced equipment represented by domestic producers, 35 percent is mid-price range equipment, which is usually imported, and premium/high-priced equipment segment holds only 3 percent of the market share.

The food service industry is expected to continue to expand at the average annual rate of between 30 40 percent for the next few years, offering good opportunities for U.S. exporters of food service equipment.

The Hotel Market

With its large population, huge industrial and abundant natural resources, Russia is potentially one of the biggest markets in the world. The country has attracted and will continue to attract increasing numbers of business travelers and tourists.

Although Russia's hotel industry has grown significantly and achieved spectacular results within the last decade, it is still modest in size compared to that of Western countries, and is still not yet able to accommodate the growing number of guests. Starting in the mid 90's, almost all well-known international hotel operators, such as Kempinski Hotel & Resorts, Marriott International, Rezidor SAS Hospitality Intercontinental, Hayatt International, and Starwood Hotels & Resorts started operations in the major Russian cities, targeting the needs of upscale foreign business travelers and tourists. To date, the number of mid-tier and budget hotels has still not satisfied the demand of both Russian and foreign middle-class business travelers, nor the increasing number of tourists. Demand for quality three star and economy hotels, is the highest and most urgent.

According to official statistics, the Moscow hotel market is comprised of approximately 183 hotels that can accommodate 66,800 guests. According to the city's plan for hotel development 240 more hotels (of differing categories) will be built in Moscow by 2010, increasing the total number of rooms to 200,000.

In terms of regional development, the hotel boom is spreading to St. Petersburg, and other major Russian cities. According to Biznes (Moscow business newspaper), St. Petersburg plans to build 150 new hotels by 2010, and 10 new hotels will be open in Yekaterinburg by the end of 2010.

In Moscow, annual revenues of the hospitality industry are estimated at nearly $5 billion. The Moscow City government is keen on developing the industry further. The increasing volume of tourists (both business and leisure), the growing number of hotels and restaurants, as well as the increasing tendency of Russians to dine out is expected to stimulate the continued growth of the hospitality sector in Russia.

Competitive Factors

There are no companies, domestic or foreign, in a position to monopolize the Russian market for hotel and restaurant equipment.

According to experts in the industry, the Russian market for hotel and restaurant equipment is growing steadily. While several years ago foreign suppliers had one or two authorized distributors, today, the trend is toward increasing the number of authorized distributors, which creates competition not only among suppliers, but also among distributors. Another trend of note is that in order to maintain market positions and to stay competitive, distributors are now including in their offers – technical training, equipment adjustments, and maintenance services.

New players to the market will have to make a significant effort to enter the market. Partnerships with solid, well-known Moscow equipment trading companies is one way for U.S. companies to penetrate the market. There are a number of highly professional firms dealing with food-service equipment that offer a wide range of equipment, including turnkey restaurant projects. Companies such as Russian Project, Stars of Catering, Delovaya Rus', Soyuzagrocomplekt, Praktika, New Line, and Perfic are all capable of handling complicated certification issues (if they arise), advise on promotional strategies, and minimize the expenses related to importing equipment into Russia. In general U.S. hotel/restaurant equipment is well received, enjoying a good reputation for high quality and reliability, comfort, labor saving features, and high productivity.

Best Prospects

Below is a list of some of the equipment utilized in the hospitality industry which is expected to be in demand due to the continued growth in the hospitality equipment market:

HS 8516 60	electric commercial/industrial		stoves, ovens and ranges electric
	commercial/industrial	stoves,	ovens and ranges
HS 851400	convection ovens		

HS 841800 freezers, refrigerating machinery, refrigerating and freezing showcases

HS 841981 hot beverage service machines, including commercial coffee makers

HS 850900 vacuum cleaners, floor polishers, kitchen waste disposals, food mixers, juice extractors, shakers, slicers, blenders, grinders HS 8450 00 laundry-type washing machines

Russian company reps are very familiar with European suppliers of hotel/restaurant products and equipment and the latest technological breakthroughs in the industry. Russians companies attend industry trade shows, where are 90 percent of the foreign exhibitors are European. Historically there has not been much interest in American suppliers, however that has changed. Russian trading companies are now interested in widening their pool of suppliers, to include American and other Western suppliers. With the anticipated significant growth in the building of hotels in Russia, there is a corresponding need for quality, long-lasting equipment ranging from security systems to kitchenware.

In addition to the growth spurt in the hotel industry, the market for household appliances and kitchen equipment is also increasing. The market for best prospects will be developing relatively quickly. The consistent continued growth of the Russian economy and the increase of personal earnings are fuelling the growth of the hospitality sector and according to industry observers it is expected to continue until 2010.

The following major European companies are represented in the Russian market:
German companies Rational, Kuppersbusch, Miele, MBM, and Palux; from Finland, Hackman Metos; Croacian company, Koncar; from Spain, Fagor; Swedish company Electolux and Soget, Gico, Berto's, Lainox, UNOX, Modular, Cimbali, Zanussi companies from Italy. The highest demand is for Italian equipment, which fits ideally the parameters of good quality and reasonable price.

US equipment present in the Russian market through distribution agreements includes Alto-Shaam, Hatco, HennyPenny, Broaster Foods, Kitchenaid, Frymaster, Ballantyne and Bar-Line.

Key Suppliers

Based on trade statistics and interviews with local importers of equipment for the hospitality industry, the market of imported equipment is primarily captured by European suppliers. U.S. imports for 2009 totaled a mere 0.35 %.

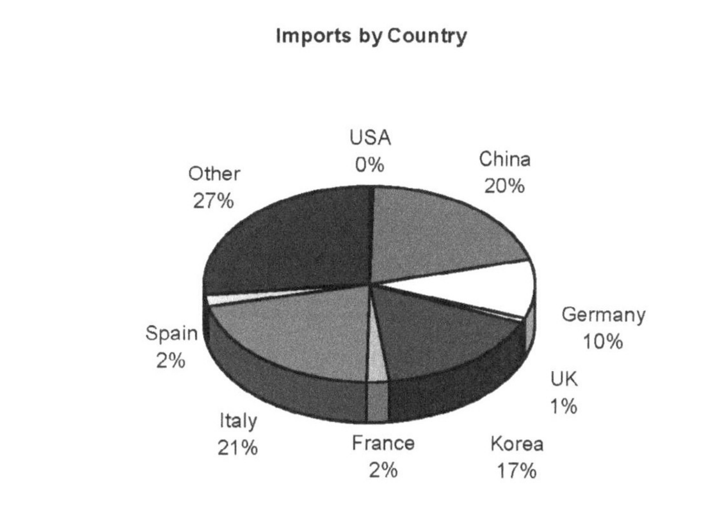

Note: These statistics refer only to the HS codes identified in the Best Prospects section and include all subgroups, i.e., hotel, restaurant and household equipment and appliances. Available statistics do not make a distinction between the subgroups, only HS codes.

To request statistics on other HS codes see Key Contacts at the end of this report.

Prospective Buyers

-Hotels (estimated -12,000)
-Restaurants (estimated -100,000)
-Industrial kitchens (institutional food caterers – number unknown)

Market Entry

The most important factors that must be taken into consideration by U.S. companies seeking to penetrate the Russian market are price and after sales service. Price is always important, and currently the strong Ruble and Euro make U.S. products more competitive.

The following are recommended marketing techniques that have proven very effective for U.S. companies entering the Russian market:

* Direct contact with Russian trading firms specializing in hotel/restaurant equipment; Face to face meetings are very important. Conduct business negotiations in Russian. (CS Russia strongly recommends the services of an interpreter and can make arrangements upon request.)

* Exhibiting at industry trade shows. (When exhibiting it is important to have Russian language promotional materials, and Russian speaking assistants to facilitate working with contacts at exhibitions.) The following trade shows are popular with Russians in the industry:

o **PIR held in Moscow, Russia**

o **HOST held in Milan, Italy**

o **Hostelco held in Barcelona, Spain**

* Advertise through industry / specialized journals. The following magazines provide important industry specific articles, new trends and developments, etc.

o **Restorannyi Bisnes**
o **Restorannye Vedomosti**
o **Gosteprimstvo**
o **Restorator**
o **Otel**
o **Gostinichnoye Delo.**
* **Participate in, or host a seminar.**

DISTRIBUTION PRACTICES

Organized distribution channels are well developed in the major population centers, such as Moscow and St. Petersburg. The most effective channel for entry into the Russian hospitality equipment market is through a Russian agent or distributor, who has previous experience in the hospitality equipment field and the Russian market. These companies are familiar with the local market conditions and the financial abilities of prospective customers. Many of these firms also have sales or show rooms and provide pre-sales adjustments and after-sales service of the equipment.

MARKET ISSUES & OBSTACLES

The import barriers for food service equipment are significant. Food service equipment is subject to import duties, which varies from 15 percent to 20 percent. Value added tax (VAT) of 18 percent is added to the contract value after the import duty is paid.

RUSSIAN FAR EAST TRADE EVENTS 2008

This report provides current information on several key Russian Far East (RFE) trade events with a particular focus on the Primorskiy Krai. The Krai administration is playing a lead role in integrating the broader RFE region into the Asia-Pacific business community. The Krai will receive significant federal funds over the next several years to develop infrastructure for the Asia Pacific Economic Conference (APEC) Summit planned for Vladivostok in 2012. These investments are largely directed towards municipal infrastructure modernization including bridges, road construction, and the modernization of the Vladivostok airport. Regional administrators have also secured several special territorial inducements from the Federal government to attract private investment including a legal gambling zone and a special port zone. The many related infrastructure investment projects will be the key focus of the Pacific Economic Congress (URL: http://www.pacific-congress.ru/) to be held in Vladivostok on July 26 -27, 2008.

The Khabarovsk International Economic Forum (URL: http://www.dvforum.ru/) will be held on September 31-October 1st. Khabarovsk is the second largest City in the region and is a key finanacial and political center for the region's booming timber, mining, and fishing industries. Located less than 30 kilometers from the border with China, Khabarovsk has benefited from the cross-border trade and is rapidly emerging as an industrial and educational center in the region. The city will celebrate its 150th anniversary this year andseveral major infrastructure investments will be discussed at the Froum including development of the Vanino sea-port, construction of several highways, reconstruction of regional airports, construction of several high-capacity wood processing complexes, erection of a bridge over the Amur river near Khabarovsk, and development of the Tungusskiy potable water deposit to supply Khabarovsk city with water.

Another international event worth note is the Fifth Special Conference and Exhibition on Fisheries Development (URL: http://www.fish-forum.ru/) that will occur in Vladivostok, September 3 - 5, 2008. Fishing currently accounts for almost four-fifths of Vladivostok's commercial production. The Regional Government recently instituted a major initiative to help develop the sector and to spur the development of fish-processing in the region. Fish-processing enterprises can receive eight-year investment credits for the purchase of technological equipment and the modernization of fish-processing production. Companies can also receive compensation to offset some interest costs from the regional budget.

The Commercial Service staff based in Vladivostok will update this report regularly to allow US firms to benefit from the large numbers such events draw from across the widely dispersed RFE population. Though these cities are over 10 hours by plane from Moscow, they are quick flights from the commercial centers in Korea, Japan, and China. Companies with activities in these countries are strongly encouraged to avail themselves of the many opportunities that will be presented during these conferences. Participation in such events can provide an excellent platform to tap into this remote but high potential regional market. The US Commercial Office in Vladivostok is always ready to coordinate and facilitate the participation of US exporters in these worthwhile events.

RESOURCES & CONTACTS WEB LINKS ON RUSSIAN EXHIBITIONS:

- http://www.english.expomenu.ru/
- http://www.english.visitexpo.ru/
- http://www.exponet.ru/exhibitions/countries/rus/topics/index.en.html
- http://www.businesscom.ru
- http://www.sibexpo.ru

For More Information on the trade opportunities in the region, please contact Mark O'Grady,

U.S. Commercial Service, Moscow at 7-495-737-5030 or via e-mail at mark.ogrady@mail.doc.gov or the U.S. Commercial Office in Vladivostok, Russia via e-mail at: tatyana.soboleva@mail.doc.gov; Phone: 7-4232-499-381; Fax: 7-4232- 300-092; or visit our website: http://www.buyusa.gov/russia/en

RUSSIAN PHARMACEUTIOCAL MARKET

The report briefly overviews major developments in the Russian pharmaceutical market, analyses the market size and major growth factors. It also analyzes major effects of the government-funded Additional Drug Supply (DLO) Program on the market structure and segmentation. The report outlines the best strategies for U.S. pharmaceutical companies under significantly increased influence of political decisions on the market potential and structure. End summary.

MARKET SIZE AND POTENTIAL

The Russian pharmaceutical market has demonstrated steady and uninterrupted growth in 2010 and 2012. According to the estimates by TSMI Pharmexpert, a leading pharmaceutical business analytics and market research company, in 2010 the total volume of the market grew by 27.4 percent and reached $10.7 billion. Most experts are confident that in 2012 the pharmaceutical industry will continue its steady and fast growth. Currently, Russia has one of the fastest growing pharmaceutical markets in the world. However per capita consumption of drugs is still low by Western standards. Annual per capita consumption of drugs is estimated at 2,100 rubles (about USD 82), or 2 percent of the average income. In comparison, in Europe this figure is 7 percent while in the United States – 9 percent.

MAJOR GROWTH FACTORS

The Russian pharmaceutical market is divided between key pharmaceutical producers. According to the July 23, 2012 edition of Profil magazine, a leading business weekly publication in Russia, the top ten major producers control about 30 percent of the commercial sales of pharmaceuticals. The top fifty producers control over 70 percent of the sales. Despite growing rates of commercial pharmaceutical sales and expanding presence of major pharmaceutical manufacturers in the Russian market, the state has continued to play a commanding role in the market over the last several years, especially since the launch of the Additional Drug Supply (DLO) Program that began in January 2009. To implement the DLO Program, the government put together a list of 500 international non-patented drugs to be provided to the Program participants free of charge. These drugs are able to treat several hundred different diseases, including those whose treatment is considered expensive. Currently the state has become the key growth factor of the market. In 2010 the government through funding hospital drug purchases, various reimbursement programs and DLO accounted for 47 percent of the total market having purchased pharmaceuticals out of federal budget funds at $5 billion. The rest of the market is covered by commercial sales.

The DLO segment was estimated at $2.7 billion, or 25 percent of the total market. The government spending for drugs for invalids and pensioners rose by 95 percent in 2010 as a direct result of implementation of DLO program. The average price of one pack of drugs prescribed under DLO increased more than two times and reached about 320 rubles. In 2010, a Russian citizen's average yearly spending for drugs was 1,150 rubles ($45) while at the same time the state spent on every participant in the DLO program an average of 8000 rubles ($314). The DLO program not only stimulated fast growth of the market, it has also changed mentality of its main players. Political decisions on spending for healthcare have become more important market development factors than economic growth, improved well-being of population, increased investment and consolidation of companies.

Government drug reimbursement programs have radically changed the position of many foreign drug manufacturers. For example, thanks to participation in DLO program F. Hoffman-la-Roche and Teva Pharmaceutical managed to increase their share in the market two-fold, Janssen Pharmaceutical – more than three times.

MARKET STRUCTURE AND SEGMENTS

The previous year has been marked by a heavy participation of a number of foreign manufacturers in the DLO program. However heavy dependence on the DLO market segment had negative effects for some of the players because of shortfalls in DLO funding. The 2010 budget allocated for DLO was exhausted within the first six months of the program and has led to significant arrears in payments. A large number of outstanding debts to pharmaceutical companies remain unpaid. In mid 2012, the government has only repaid a small portion of its DLO debts to the pharmaceutical manufacturers. This situation with unpaid drug supplies is predicted to repeat itself in 2012. The total volume of outstanding drugs supplies, which got stuck in the commodity turnover chain, amounted to $4 billion. It is difficult to predict how these outstanding debts will affect the market in the future. Federal representatives have indicated that the debts will be covered from the regional budgets, but it is not clear where the money will come from in the many regions dependent on federal subsidies in the first place.

Recently the government made a decision to actually eliminate the DLO Program on the federal level. It is decided that from January 1, 2008, procurement of free drugs to invalids and pensioners will be funded from regional budget funds. The federal government will be only responsible for supply of drugs to smaller categories of sick such as patients with hemophilia, oncological hematology, transplanted organs, etc. The projected 2008-2010 federal budget makes provision for such healthcare expenditures growth, which will only compensate inflation. This means that there will be practically no growth unless regional budgets expand their healthcare spending significantly.

Another important move is the recent discussion about creation of a state distribution corporation, Pharmaceutical Logistical Complex (FLK), which will be responsible for purchasing pharmaceuticals under DLO Program. The idea of the Pharmaceutical Logistical Complex is to improve the quality of drug purchases, cope with deficiencies of some drugs and save budget funds, which under the old system will go to national distributors. In the new system distributors switch from being the key national players in the DLO Program to particles in the logistical chain to deliver pharmaceuticals from their regional warehouses to pharmacies. FLK will become the key element of this system signing contracts with pharmaceutical manufacturers to supply their products to regions in cooperation with regional partners – distributors, which won regional tenders for participation in the DLO. Experts believe that the new structure will hardly solve the outstanding DLO debt problem and bring more order and transparency into the Program.

The highest portion of the market is occupied by commercial sales (53 percent). However the growth rates of the commercial sector have been much lower than those of the DLO sector (20 versus 95 percent in 2010). The commercial sector totally relies on the growing incomes of the population and not government programs. As a result, competition in the commercial segment is growing and major drug suppliers have been investing increased funds into advertising.

Hospital purchases of drugs, which are part of the government purchases, have been stagnant in the last years and now account for only 15 percent of the total market. On the other hand, the pharmacy segment of the market is developing rapidly, faster than pharmaceutical manufacturing or wholesale trade. The top ten pharmacy networks control, according to different estimates, from 20 to 40 percent of total retail sales. According to July 23, 2012 edition of Profil, it is estimated that pharmacy networks will control 60 percent of the total market by 2010.

The share of expensive innovative drugs used to treat severe illnesses in the total volume of DLO program is high and reaches 40 percent while the share of innovative drugs in the total market is 17 percent. Such drugs are primarily used to treat three broad groups of diseases: 1) central nervous system, 2) cancer/tumor and immune system, and 3) blood diseases. In order to control and manage expenses for innovative drugs the government plans to withdraw a significant volume of innovative drugs from the DLO and move them to special newly established subprograms under the National Priority Health Project. Each such subprogram will be dedicated to a specific serious illness. At the same time the government started to revise DLO lists to replace high-end expensive drugs with generic analogs. Most analysts believe that innovative and therefore most expensive drug segment will not increase significantly in the next several years.

RECOMMENDATIONS

In 2009-2011 the payment for drug purchases have been made through Federal and Regional Mandatory Medical Insurance Funds based on the lists of supplied drugs provided by distributors. The DLO Program functions as follows: 1) distributors purchase medicines based on credit terms from manufacturers and supply them to regional pharmacies; 2) regional pharmacies provide the distributors with prescriptions for the medicines they receive from patients, 3) distributors submit the filled prescriptions to established Insurance Funds which pay for the drugs supplied by distributors, 4) the distributors then make their payments to the suppliers.

Thus, distributors play a key role in the DLO program. They have become the key financial intermediaries in the market and are able to influence major suppliers of drugs and their access to DLO. Heavy dependence on the DLO Program has led to problems for a significant number of foreign suppliers due to imbalances in implementation and financing of DLO in 2010-2012. In many regions, contracts to deliver drugs under DLO were purportedly awarded without tenders, or with only appearance of ones, to companies close to high-level officials in the Ministry of Health. The drugs and equipment in question were often supplied at inflated prices with accusations that profits flowed back to government officials.

Despite the DLO outstanding debts, very few manufacturers involved in DLO supplies have decided to leave that market since it continues to present a guaranteed state channel of distribution. U.S. companies are recommended to take into account a wide combination of market growth and structural factors. Specifically, they should not underestimate the significant role of DLO in the short and mid-term perspectives as well stabilization of the growth of the innovative drug segment. In this regard, U.S. companies are recommended to develop a strategy, which balances pros and cons of the different market segments and does not overlook the importance of political decisions. U.S. companies are also recommended to take into account the fact that starting from January 1, 2008, DLO will be transferred to the regional level. Therefore regions should play a growing role in the U.S. companies overall Russia's strategy.

According to the author's estimate, political factors and government reimbursement programs will continue to play a significant role. However in the long run, the importance of DLO will be diminishing, and the commercial and innovative segments will be increasing. Industry experts believe that, in the future, pharmacies will play an increasingly active and influential role in implementation of government programs. The role of distributors, who currently are the key players of the market, will continue to diminish. Wholesalers will continue for some time to be important market players, especially in the regions. The role of the regional insurance funds is expected to increase in the long-term perspective.

RUSSIA: CONSUMER GOODS MARKET IN UPPER VOLGA NIZHNY NOVGOROD REGION[1]

The objective of this report is to provide U.S. companies with an overview of the consumer goods industry in Russia, Upper Volga region, current major projects and potential market opportunities. The information provided will be useful not only to U.S. exporters of physical goods who include domestic distribution in their business model, but also to exporters and investors who are assessing the market potential. This report also provides information about certification, registration and customs procedures, if applicable, and provides with the appropriate process description, government entities and documentation necessary to export consumer goods in Russia, Upper Volga Region.

1. GENERAL MARKET OVERVIEW

1.1 U.S. – Nizhny Novgorod region trade: trends & opportunities

According to the official statistics, the trade turnover between the United States and Russia amounted to US$ 10.9 billion in 2009, and totaled almost US$ 13 billion in 2010. The share of the U.S. exports constituted approximately 40% of the total trade turnover between the two countries.

There is no official statistics on the U.S. – Nizhny Novgorod trade turnover, as the United States is not on the list of major exporters or importers to the region. However, one may estimate the annual trade turnover at US$ 170 – 200 million.

---

[1] Author: Roman Vvedensky, BISNIS representative in Nizhny Novgorod, Russia

ITand engineering products represent the main sales items from the region to the U.S., and the list of U.S. exports includes, but is not limited to, production machinery (both, new and refurbished), industrial goods, used cars and trucks, engineering products, spare parts and supplies. A good lot of U.S. industrial products are exported to the region via Moscow and StPetersburg; the share of direct U.S. exports to the region is smaller.

A Chrysler plant was the recent largest U.S. sales deal in the region. The plant will be launched in Nizhny Novgorod in early 2008, next to the old site of the Ford plant, sold to Russia in 1930s. Used cars and trucks are some of the main items of durable consumer goods, sold to Nizhny Novgorod region from the U.S.A. Local experts estimate the annual trade in used cars, shipped from the U.S.A., in US$ 57 million, and the volume is growing. Another major product category of U.S. consumer goods exports is food products (mainly, frozen chicken and meat products), but they are shipped to the region, primarily, from Moscow and StPetersburg, as this business is controlled by a group of Moscow based companies. Products for the automotive aftermarket, home tools & appliances are the third group of U.S. consumer goods, shipped to the region in a reasonable amount.

Prospects for U.S. exports growth to the region are high, primarily in industrial sectors, where new opportunities get open in traditional industries (mainly, in aerospace and automotive), new industries (i.e. hi tech and logistics), as well as in local infrastructure (road maintenance & construction, water supply & treatment, waste processing), and social infrastructure (health care & education).

Penetration of related U.S. goods to the local market will contribute to better awareness of local consumers about good features of U.S. products, which in turn influence local consumer preferences. Better presence of any U.S. quality product in the local market increases consumer confidence in U.S. goods, and influences a consumer's shopping choice. A shortlist of mostly recognized U.S. brands in Russia of 1970s included Montana jeans, CocaCola and Marlboro cigarettes. The shortlist of mostly known U.S. brands in Russia currently has been modified to Microsoft software, a Boeing jet, and a Hummer vehicle. What will be the next basket of most popular U.S. products (Hollywood movies are not subject of this report) It will be logical to assume that certain hi tech products, home appliances, and luxury items, manufactured by a U.S. company or under a U.S. license, will retain some place in a local consumer basket.

According to the current statistics the share of foreign food products and consumer goods is 19 percent of all imports to the region. The ratio of food products to consumer goods is close to 5050. The actual share of foreign consumer goods sold in the local market is higher and it is approximately 60 percent of the new consumer goods products. The share of the food products is 30 percent.

The breakdown by consumer goods product categories is as follows:

90% in licensed computer software

80% in footwear,
70% in apparel, sports and recreation goods,
60% in electronics, pharmaceutical & cosmetics goods, live flowers, and DIY

products,
50% in new cars and goods for children,
40% in furniture, home appliances, and office supplies,
30% in food products,
10% in jewelry and decoration items.

With an exception of food products the highly priced goods are of foreign origin. Domestic and foreign products are both presented in a middlepriced segment of consumer goods. The low priced segment is composed of domestic goods and foreign goods from China and Turkey, sold at open markets. Secondhand apparel and footwear comprise the lowest segment of the consumer goods market. Imported used cars can be found both, in high and middle priced segments (depending on a brand, type, and technical condition of a vehicle), while used boats (mainly, yachts) are proposed in the highend of the market. Foreign footwear and leather items are, mainly, imported to Nizhny Novgorod region from Italy; Apparel – also from Italy, and from other European companies (assembled at their Chinese factories). Sports goods – from international companies i.e. Nike, Puma, Adidas, Reebok, and some others (assembled at their factories in China & SouthEast Asia). Electronics – from international companies (assembled at their factories in Europe, China & SouthEast Asia). Cosmetics and pharmaceutica l are imported mostly from Europe and partly from Asia (i.e. India). Currently, U.S. manufacturers have a visible representation in the sector of electrical tools and instruments in the DIY segment of the market. Foreign food is supplied to Nizhny Novgorod mostly from Eastern and Northern Europe, except frozen chicken and meat, which is shipped from the U.S.A. and South America.

According to the official statistics, the trade turnover in consumer goods exceeded US$ 4.6 billion in Nizhny Novgorod last year, and this year it may further grow to US$ 5.5 billion. It should be mentioned that the statistics refers to turnover of consumer goods in the wholesale and retail sectors of the local market and it may have no data on retail trade turnover at small outlets and openair markets, i.e. bazaars, grocery stores and fleemarkets. Independent experts estimate the turnover of the Nizhny Novgorod market in consumer goods at US$ 6.25 billion in 2010, and they forecasted an increase to US$7.45 billion in 2012. Recent price growth on a range of food products (milk & diary products, oil, fruits) may level up this assessment. According to the local experts, the retail trade turnover of food products equals approximately US$ 1.7 1.8 billion in the region.

1.2 Distribution Networks, Retail and Wholesale

This section of the report includes brief information on major trading chains and malls, located at the crossroads of trade flows in Nizhny Novgorod.

A U.S. company, interested to enter the retail market of Nizhny Novgorod, should clearly understand that the geographical distance is a principal challenge for doing business in the region. Products with a short shelf life may not be the best choice for shipment to Nizhny Novgorod. The city is at 3040 days distance from the U.S. eastern coast, 2224 days for sea transportation, 510 days for customs clearance, 15 days for delivery to Nizhny Novgorod from Moscow or StPetersburg. This time frame also includes storage, processing and transportation time. The time of delivery to the stores may be shortened to 57 days in case of transportation by air, and with customs clearance at one of the dozen terminals in Nizhny Novgorod. Currently the local supermarket chains have alternative sources of local suppliers of food, cosmetics, and related products. Large western supermarkets, such as *Metro Cash & Carry*, *Real*, *Auchan*, *Olsen*, *Eurospar*, *X5 Retail,* which have recently entered the Nizhny Novgorod market, signed contracts with national and foreign distributors of food, beverages and some other consumer goods from abroad. An U.S. company may find good opportunities with these trading chains in case it has an efficient distribution network in European Russia, or if it runs a warehouse facility somewhere in Central Russia or close to the Volga valley.

It is worth mentioning that Nizhny Novgorod has been rapidly growing its logistics infrastructure. This year, the Nizhny Novgorod region has been ranked 13th among all other Russian regions by the volume of retail trade, and #6 by the volume of wholesale trade.

The region has a convenient location at the crossroads of the NorthSouth and the WestEast transportation channels of European Russia. The volume of cargo, shipped through the region by rail, highways, waterways, and by air has been constantly growing.

The head offices of national leaders in rail and waterways cargo transportation, *Gorky Railroads* and *Volga*

Shipping Company are located in Nizhny Novgorod. The *Volga Shipping Company* has a fleet of eleven container ships, each carrying 5060 40ft containers, to deliver cargo directly to the port of Nizhny Novgorod by seaand waterways. The railroad company also actively participates in delivery of foreign cargo, unloaded in the port of StPetersburg, and shipped inward Russia.

Nizhny Novgorod has one more infrastructure advantage, crucial for trade and distribution of consumer goods in European Russia. The city is situated in the center of a 310mile range area, which inhabits 43 million of people (almost 30 percent of the total Russian population), 24 million of which live in urban locations. In 2010 the average level of consumer spending per capita in this area totaled US$ 2,200 per year. The area is also characterized by a developed transportation and distribution systems. The maximum distribution range of Nizhny Novgorodbased companies is currently limited to 350370 miles, which is a distance covered by a cargo vehicle within a daytime. The cargo flow along two major highways of the region M5 (MoscowChelyabinsk), and M7 (MoscowUfa) – is accessed by 6,0008,000 tractor trailers per day.

A quick growth of the trade sector and a shortage of logistics space encouraged foreign and national investment in logistic projects in the Nizhny Novgorod region. Lower construction and operation costs, compared to Moscow, which is located only 260 miles to the west of Nizhny Novgorod, also contribute to the development of the logistic network in the area. This information may be of value to those U.S. companies, that are considering entry to the market of Central Russia and the Volga valley with their consumer goods. The list of major logistic projects in the region includes, but it is not limited to;

• *HermitageCenter logistics terminal*

The Moscowbased company *Hermitage Construction & Management* plans to build a Class A logistics terminal with a total area of 40,000 square meters. Total investment in the project is estimated at US$ 42 million. The logistic terminal will include premises for different categories of goods with a focus on food products and white electronics. The mall will be erected at Tchaadaeva street, which is close to the exit to Moskovskoye (Moscow) highway, which connects Nizhny Novgorod and the Russian capital.

• *DomCenter*

Nizhny Novgorod based company *Dom Center* announced a US$ 240 million project of a logistics center. It will be located between two settlements (*Severny and Lesnaya Polyana*) on Moskovskoye (Moscow) highway, next to Nizhny Novgorod. The center will cover over 1,000,000 square meter land parcel, residing 24 warehouses, office buildings, a hotel, and parking sites. The total area of facilities is 300,000 – 350,000 square meters. The logistic center will focus on storage and processing of construction and DIY goods, white electronics, IT products, and furniture.

• *Garbo World Cargo Center* (GWCC)

The German company signed an agreement with the region's government to build a Class A terminal next to the Nizhny Novgorod airport Strigino. Total investment is estimated at Euro 3540 million. A 21acre land parcel is allocated for the project, which provides for construction of 45,000 – 50,000 square meters of modern logistic facilities.

Currently, the total area of warehouses and logistics terminals totals 360,000 square meters in the Nizhny Novgorod region, where 70 percent of facilities are concentrated in the city of Nizhny Novgorod. The list of major operating customs and logistic centers includes Terminal (which is part of Logoprom holding company), ROSTEKNizhny Novgorod, Nizhny Novgorod International Airport terminal, and Privolzhskoye Agentstvo Tamozhennogo Oformlenya (Volga Agency for Customs Clearance). Local experts forecast that demand for Class A logistics centers will exceed their supply in the local market within the next five years due to a rapid growth of retail trade and train chains in the area. They estimate the existing unsatisfied demand in Class A terminals at 50% from the current supply.

Logistics business is a good potential opportunity for U.S. companies in the Nizhny Novgorod region, because the local sector is developing, and it experiences a good demand in international expertise, qualified skills in development and managements of logistic centers, and investment support for projects' implementation. A U.S. company, interested to propose its services/products in the logistics market, may approach local operators and developers of existing and new projects in Nizhny Novgorod, to start business negotiations. A U.S. company may also cooperate with the local government, which considers development of logistic and transport infrastructure as one of major priorities of its economic policy.

A U.S. expertise is also a demanded commodity by a trade sector of the local economy. As stated by the rep of Nizhny Novgorod Store Association, the U.S.A. is a cradle of modern technologies in goods distribution and trade. Actively launched in Russia less than a dozen years ago, they completely modified the local trade sector, and led to success those companies, which pioneered in their introduction and development in the Nizhny Novgorod market. For example, almost half of trade outlets and boutiques in the city operate under franchise or subfranchise agreements with international companies or their masterfranchisees in Moscow. The names of major malls, shopping centers, their anchor tenants, and distribution chains are provided in further chapters of the report. A U.S. company may study the list of presented brands at major shopping centers, and negotiate with the local companies, which trade in these brands in the region.

It is not a rare case, when an owner/owners of a successful trade business, may set up a new company to trade in related goods, promoted by other national/international brands in the local market. Nizhny Novgorod Store Association, which works closely with the Russian Franchise Association (http://www.rarf.ru/eng/) may also render a consulting support on the local retail trade market. When studying websites of local trade firms, a U.S. company may come across with a technical inconvenience – most of the provided information is done in the Russian language, because it is aimed at local customers or focused on the domestic market. Assistance from an EnglishRussian translator may be required to receive recent news and info updates on local development and management companies as well as wholesale and retail traders.

The major distribution chains of the region may be grouped under the following categories:

• White electronics & home appliances

National: *M.Video, DOMO, El Dorado*

Local: *Expert, Electronica*

• Hypermarket & Supermarket chains International: *Metro Cash & Carry, Real, Auchan, Olsen, Ramstore, EuroSpar, X5 Retail, Perekryostok, Pyaterochka, Lenta* National: *Kopeyka, Magnit, Mosmart, Carusel* Local: *Andreevsky, XXI Vek, Narodny, Medved, , Raitsentr, Saus, Sladkaya Zhizn, VKT, Frukty & Produkty, Steakmart, Myasnov, Otdokhni*

Drugs and Pharmaceuticals
National: *Rigla, Pharmacy 36.6*
Local: NAS /Nizhny Novgorod Drugstore Association/, *Avicenna*

Furniture and DIY products International: *IKEA, OBI, Olsen* National: *Starik Khottabych, Calypso, Mebel Plus* Local: Order, Vintik & Shpuntik (Screw & Rabbet), Karina, Mebelny Centre 2000

Electronics, Cellular phones, digital devices, and accessories

DIXIS, Euroset, Svyaznoy, Tsyfrograd

• Cosmetics Ile de Beaute, L'Etoile, Yves Rocher

- *Apparel, footwear, accessories, fashion goods*

The list of the latter is pretty vast, and the references may be found on the web sites of major malls of Nizhny Novgorod, provided at the end of the report. A U.S. company, interested in the list of brands, presented in the local market, should primarily check it with the following sites:

MEGA (150 stores and boutiques, including *IKEA, OBI, Auchan, M.Video, Detsky Mir /Kids' World/*, and many others) http://megamall.ru/mega5/ *ETAZHI* (fashion plaza, and boutiques trading in apparel, footwear, accessories)

http://www.etagi.ru *RESPUBLICA* (over 50 brand stores) – http://www.respublikann.ru - *FANTASTIKA* (under construction – over 50 brand stores) www.stnn.ru/about/project - *SHOKOLAD* (over 30 brand stores) http://www.ramstore.ru/eng/store/regions/n

novgorod.html

The malls also host electronics stores, sports goods stores, home appliances, supermarkets, recreation centers, and food courts.

Sportmaster (http://www.sportmaster.ru) is the major national chain store, which trades in sports goods, outfit, sports apparel & footwear, leisure products, presented in the region. Positioned as a seller of middlepriced goods of recognized sports brands, the company launched a new trade project under the name of SportLandia to sell lower priced sports goods, unfamiliar to local consumers: Nordway, Dinamix, Timeout, Tundra, Joss, as well as some familiar brands.

1.3 Market peculiarities

Consumer preferences in Nizhny Novgorod, the city with 1.34 million population, does not differ much from consumer preferences in other large provincial cities of the Volga valley and the Urals (e.g. Kazan, Samara, Perm, Yekaterinburg, Chelyabinsk), which have approximately the same climate and similar parameters of income per capita/household. Yekaterinburg may reveal certain deviations in consumers' choice due to higher local income rates, compared to the other cities. The previous chapter provides with the names of major retail traders, which are anchor tenants of local malls across the area. International and national companies are now presented in all large cities; the names of local supermarket chains may differ between regions.

A similar structure of trade business and almost the same list of key players rule the game in major urban centers. Sales seasons start twice a year: in JanuaryFebruary, and in late JulyAugust. The winter sales season is usually more productive for stores and outlets as there are two other popular national holidays after the New Year. Although they are named differently in Russia, they are close in content to Father's Day (celebrated in late February), and to Mother's Day (celebrated in early March). Valentine's Day in mid-February is growing popular in this country, and it also contributes to growing sales in live flowers, fragrances, cosmetics, confectionary, and goods with a romantic fleur. Summer sales season is usually less active because of a vacation period, and a lack of national holidays, which incur buying gifts. Stores and boutiques carry out regular incentive programs between two major sales seasons: discount cards, special proposals/rates/discounts for a customer's birthday, buytwogetthethirdfree, etc. Electronics and home appliances stores also run promotion and sales events, when goods of a certain brand are sold at discounted prices within a certain month. Some stores (mainly for, computers & electronics) offer season discounts to high school and university students.

Young people are an active group of customers, but their consumer activity is naturally limited by a low income. They are more sensitive to new or the latest fashion products, which includes apparel, footwear, cellular phones, CDs, and DVDs. The second group of demanded products for young people includes PCs, laptops, PDAs (personal digital advisors), cameras, fashion jewelry and decorations. The third group of consumer sensitive goods is vehicles, where a car is on the top of the list, and a scooter is at its affordable bottom. Vehicles may be both used and new, depending on a household paying capacity, and the amount of pocket money. Buying a car for a young person is not very common in the local market although the amount of 'fresh' drivers is growing. At present, there are over half a million of cars, registered in the Nizhny Novgorod region. The share of young drivers is still beyond 10% of the total amount.

Goods for children are a fastgrowing segment in local trade. The amount of stores and their network has been actively developed in Nizhny Novgorod since 20032008, following an increase in birth rates, and an improved income capacity of local customers. All major brands of children stores are presented at Nizhny Novgorod malls, and they include a number of chain stores, which are international (e.g. Mothercare http://www.mothercare.ru), national

(e.g. Kenguru http://www.keng.ru , BananaMama http://www.bananamama.ru/ , Detsky Mir http://www.detmir.ru , HobbyCenter http://www.hobbycenter.ru/index.php?name=english), and local (e.g. Mama + Ya, and some others). Their major clients are people in the middleage consumer segment with higher purchasing power and most representation. They consume all types of durable and nondurable consumer products, presented in the market, depending on their paying capacity and consumer preferences. Giving way to young people in sensitivity to new proposals of the trade market, middleage consumers overweigh them in spending capacity. Middleage people constitute approximately 45% of the region's population, which makes 1.5 million of active consumers. Over a million of them live in Nizhny Novgorod and other cities of the region.

People of elder age usually have a low income in the Nizhny Novgorod region, and their consumption basket is primarily open for two categories of goods: food products, and pharmaceuticals.

Consumer goods sector of Nizhny Novgorod region have some particular features, which can make it a potential market for certain U.S. products. Nizhny Novgorod is located at the confluence of Volga and Oka rivers, which provides natural opportunities for yachting and boating during the months of May through October. At present, there are 56 local stores, trading in new foreign and Russian boats. The same stores also sell boat accessories, including gasoline and electric motors, and spare parts. Business proposals on used motorboats and other hydrovessels may raise a certain interest, as the niche of foreign used vessels is almost vacant. Used snowmobiles are another perspective niche. They may be sold thru the network of local boat stores, which trades in new snow vehicles. Bombardier and Yamaha are the most popular brands of snowcycles in the local market.

Similarly to other large cities in Russia, Nizhny Novgorod experiences a growing demand in consumer products, necessary for country cottage construction and finishing. Traditionally, country cottage houses are made from timber and, sometimes, from sandlime brick. This rapidly growing niche may consume products in various price categories: from high to low. The products should be aimed to finish a cottage house from inside and from outside, and they should cover the issues of insulation, roofing, heating, water supply & sewage, safety, and lightening. The intellectual house appliances report a growing demand in the local market.

1.4 Major Developments in the industry

Development of logistic infrastructure and construction of new malls are major events for the local trade market. The logistic topic was referred to at chapter 1.1 of the current report. It may be supplemented with the list of international and national courier, shipping, and forwarding companies, which contribute to the trade sector development of the Nizhny Novgorod region.

Courier services:

DHL (www.dhl.ru)
Federal Express (www.fedex.com)
EMS Garant Post (www.garantpost.ru)

Pony Express (www.ponyexpress.ru)
TNT (www.tnt.ru)
UPS (www.ups.com)

Forwarding & shipping companies:

Bizpak (www.bizpack.ru)
Free Lines Company (www.freelines.ru)
AvtotransCargo Nizhny Novgorod (www.atcargo.ru)
Avtooboz (www.avtooboz.ru)
Golion MT (www.golion.ru)
Dalk (www.dalknn.ru) Lunny Svet (www.vozimvse.ru)
MeridianTransAvto (www.meridian52.ru)
Perevozka SPb (www.perevozkaspb.ru)

The list of new construction in Nizhny Novgorod in 20082010 includes Mosmart supermarket (with the total area of 30,000 square meters), two supermarkets Okey (10,000 square meters each), Lobachevsky Plaza mall & office center (16,000 square meters), third part of Fantastika mall (over 70,000 square meters), HolidayCenter mall & leisure center (140,000 square meters), OZ mall & leisure center (156,000 square meters), and a number of other malls and recreation facilities in the city.

The monthly lease rates at malls, located in the downtown area of Nizhny Novgorod, vary from US$ 50 to US$ 100 per square meter at the moment. Malls, located in the suburbian area, come up with lower rates. Opening of new malls, shopping and leasure centers may slow down a lease rate growth, and, moreover, it may lead to a little decrease at some trade sites. Major supermarkets in Nizhny Novgorod, with few exceptions, owns their buildings. Most of outlets, boutiques, and supermarkets, opened at malls and shopping centers, lease their premises.

A growing range of proposals in highly priced segments of consumer goods is a recent tendency of the local market. The mall ETAZHI hosted the first fashion plaza in the city, which sells apparel, footwear, accessories, and jewelry of leading luxury brands from Europe. Lobachevsky Plaza, a new mall, constructed next to the local Kremlin, is likely to become another location, selling luxury items in Nizhny Novgorod. Medical (therapeutic) cosmetics are another growing niche of expensive products. They are supplied mostly by recognized brands from France & Israel, and sold at local outlets in the malls, beauty saloons, or at some drugstores.

Car showrooms, trading in expensive models (Porsche, Jaguar) were opened the city last year. The local BMW showroom has been reporting growing sales for the last five years. Trade in middlepriced new cars is also booming in Nizhny Novgorod, like in other large cities, and currently, local consumers are to stay on a waiting list for 37 months to buy a desired model.

Consumer boom in durable goods was ignited by a launch of accessible consumer loan programs by local and national banks in Nizhny Novgorod four years ago. Now, every large and middle store or outlet has a desk or several desks of credit consultants, which facilitate provision of consumer loans to the customers.

2. PRIMARY DISTRIBUTION CHANNELS

According to the local experts assessment, over 7580% of retail trade in consumer goods and food products is carried out thru malls, detached stores, supermarkets, and outlets in the Nizhny Novgorod region. The remaining share comes up with openair markets, which are focused primarily on food products, inexpensive apparel and footwear, and home appliances. Major malls and shopping centers concentrate half of retail trade in the region, and their share will be growing as they are more convenient for shopping, and they offer a diversified package of sales services to attract clients thru the whole year. Soon after opening of a new mall, it is surrounded by trading outlets, drugstores and service centers, which benefit from a growing flow of customers in the area. A U.S. company interested to enter the Nizhny Novgorod consumer goods market should analyze location of its sales points, for it has a higher chance for success, when the latter are located at malls or major shopping centers, or close to them.

There is also a shopping street – Bolshaya Pokrovskaya – in the city, which resides outlets of major multinational and national brands, trading in apparel, footwear, cosmetics & fragrances, accessories (e.g. watches), jewelry, mobile phones, and some other consumer goods. The lease rate is high in the area, as well as the sales turnover. Currently, there are two more pedestrian quarters in the city, developed as shopping centers: one close the Volga embankment, and another in the center of Sormovo county of Nizhny Novgorod.

The list and the contact info on major malls and shopping centers of Nizhny Novgorod are provided at the end of the report. The websites also contain information on the anchor tenants. As mentioned above, most of local outlets and boutiques are run under franchising or subfranchising agreements, while larger stores are usually set as branches of national and international companies (the latter are usually registered as Russian subsidiaries). Data on local companies, trading in a lowpriced segment of the market, is less transparent, and a U.S. company should plan a field visit to Nizhny Novgorod to meet with potential distributors in this sector. Probability of setting a meeting with small and middlesized local companies is high, as they experience a growing competition, and they are looking for new available options/proposals to increase their competitive edge in the market.

There is one more helpful distribution channel for expensive and middlepriced consumer goods in Nizhny Novgorod and nationwide. It is advertising of the goods, promoted by a

U.S. company to the market, thru a regional edition of the national consumer magazine *Ya Pokupayu*. The magazine is published and distributed in major malls and shopping centers of 19 cities of Russia. The English info on the magazine is available at http://en.apress.ru and http://en.apress.ru/yapok.

Other forms of distribution include catalogue trade and Internettrade. Till recently, Internettrade has been focused on such commodities & services as books, DVDs, CDs, delivery of food from some local supermarkets and restaurants, and money transfers. Still, this form of trade may be further developed, and a U.S. company may find opportunities both for distribution of products thru the net, and for selling its services and consultancy to local and national operators to develop the electronic trade system.

Catalogue trade has existed in the local market since mid1990s. Now, it is actively migrating to an Internet-trade format. The form of trade is popular with its longterm customers, and with active Internet surfers, interested in fashionable but affordably priced apparel & footwear. The list of most popular national catalogues includes, but is not limited to *Otto* and *Quelle*. More information on the catalogues is available at their websites:

Otto: http://www.ottobest.ru; -
Quelle:http://www.quelle.ru/ru/extern/index.html?EMBPERL_UID=:41635014d8aac
57696f1d76d48b33b64&fsreloaded=1&

The importance of Internet as a trade vehicle is growing in the region. Now, the amount of Internet users is estimated at approximately 250,000 people in Nizhny Novgorod.

There are some other formats of trade and distribution, which have a minimum representation in Nizhny Novgorod i.e. liquidation factories/stores, which trades in new commodities, offered with large discounts. This distribution model is demanded in Nizhny Novgorod, which resides 120,000 university and college students, studying during the day. Alongside with other lowincome groups of people (which totals over 250,000 people in Nizhny Novgorod), they are regular customers of secondhand store chains in Nizhny Novgorod and other cities of the region. Local secondhand shops trade mainly in apparel, and they offer no other commodities like electronics, furniture, and home appliances. This commodity niche also represents good opportunities for a U.S. company in the region.

List of helpful contacts:

Nizhny Novgorod Store Association (Soyuz Magazinov Nizhnegorodskoy Oblasty)

2, Ivana Romanova street, Nizhny Novgorod, 603002, Russia Tel.: +7 (831) 228 06 80, Fax: +7 (831) 246 55 63, 246 79 20 Email: info@snm.nnov.ru http://www.snm.nnov.ru/

Director Oxana V. Dektyaryova
Chairman – Vadim G. Nosov (Nosov@r52.ru)

MEGA Mall (anchor tenants IKEA, Auchan, OBI, M.Video)

Settlement Fedyakovo, Kstovo district, Nizhny Novgorod region, Russia

http://www.megamall.ru/
http://megamall.ru/mega5/ Nizhny Novgorod webpage
http://megamall.ru/mega5/guide/route/
http://megamall.ru/mega5/en/ English version

IKEA Nizhny Novgorod (Shopping centre MEGA) /furniture/

Settlement Fedyakovo, Kstovo district, Nizhny Novgorod region, 607687, Russia Tel.: +7 (831) 57 77 71 Fax: +7 (831) 96 01 68

http://www.ikea.com
http://www.ikea.com/webapp/wcs/stores/servlet/IkeaNearYouView?storeId=23&langId=-31&StoreNumber=437 Nizhny Novgorod weblink

Director of IKEA Nizhny Novgorod Inge Juliusson

AUCHAN Nizhny Novgorod (Shopping centre MEGA) /supermarket/

Settlement Fedyakovo, Kstovo district, Nizhny Novgorod region, 607687, Russia Tel.: +7 (831) 4162411 Fax: + (831) 4162413 Email: reception_nn@auchan.ru http://www.auchan.ru/ru/vacancies/regions/nn/ - Nizhny Novgorod weblink **OBI** – Fedyakovo Nizhny Novgorod (Shopping centre MEGA) /DIY supermarket/

Settlement Fedyakovo, Kstovo district, Nizhny Novgorod region, 607650, Russia Tel.: +7 (831) 220 13 00 Fax: +7 (831) 220 13 08 Email: marktru011@obi.ru http://www.obi.ru/ru/markets/maerkte/011/index.html Nizhny Novgorod webpage

M.VIDEO

Stores:
26, Vedenyapina street, 603000, Nizhny Novgorod, Russia (shopping centre Park Avenue)
9, Revolyutsiy square, 603000, Nizhny Novgorod, Russia (shopping centre Respublika)
Settlement Fedyakovo (Shopping centre MEGA)

Tel.: 88002012775 (tollfree)

http://nnovgorod.mvideo.ru/contacts/
http://nnovgorod.mvideo.ru/shops/
http://english.mvideo.ru/ English version

Group of companies ELECTRONICA (development; trade in electronics & household appliances) http://www.e.nn.ru/shops/shops/ list of all shops with contacts http://www.e.nn.ru/ official site of company

Shopping centre ZOLOTAYA MILYA (Golden Mile) – EUROSPAR market, ELECTRONICA stores, GOLD`S FITNESS sportclub, Sormovsky leisure center 105, Kominterna street, Nizhny Novgorod, 603003, Russia Tel/fax: +7 (831) 296 00 16 email: info@goldmile.nnov.ru http://www.goldmile.nnov.ru/ http://www.goldmile.nnov.ru/?id=90 all contacts of shopping centre

SLADKAYA ZHIZN /SPAR Middle Volga/ (wholesale and retail trade) 4, Komsomolskoye chausse, Nizhny Novgorod, 603950, Russia Tel.: +7 (831) 257 80 80 email: Gusev@swlife.nnov.ru http://www.swlife.nnov.ru/ http://www.swlife.nnov.ru/eng English version General director – Albert G. Gusev mob.ph.: 8 951 901 13 74

MAGNIT (food supermarket chain) 15/2, Solnechnaya street, Krasnodar, 350072, Russia Tel.: +7 (861) 210 98 10 Email: info@gw.tander.ru http://www.magnitinfo.ru/ http://www.magnitinfo.ru/customers/branches/ list of all branches in the RF

ETAGI Mall

63, Belinskogo street, Nizhny Novgorod, 603024, Russia

Management company TRUSTARENDA

63, Belinskogo street, Nizhny Novgorod, 603024, Russia General director of TrustArenda company – Elena V. Nagornaya

Direction of Shopping centre ETAGI Tel.: +7 (831) 416 7757, 416 77 67 Email: project@etagi.ru, www@etagi.ru http://www.etagi.ru/

Group of companies STOLITSANIZHNY

General director – Victoria V. Moskvichova
Tel.: 2785717 (18)
Email: vicmos@stnn.ru

Lease department of STOLITSANIZHNY

Tel.: +7 (831) 296 09 99 Email: snnr@mtsnn.ru

Management company BIZNESDOM

Tel.: + (831) 2785717, 2785718 (20),
Mob.ph.: +79519132753
Email: korotkova.yv@stnn.ru , vicmos@stnn.ru

Shopping centre FANTASTIKA (Real, METRO Group)

187, Rodionova street, Nizhny Novgorod, 603000, Russia

www.stnn.ru/about/project

METRO CASH & CARRY Nizhny Novgorod

http://www.metrocc.ru/

http://www.metrocc.ru/servlet/PB/menu/1064015_l7/index.html Nizhny Novgorod web page

Shopping centre METRO – Nizhny Novgorod 3A, Meschersky boulevard, Nizhny Novgorod, 603070, Russia Tel.: +7 (831) 278 00 00 Fax: +7 (831) 2757964 Email: acquisition.store21@metro.com.ru

Shopping centre METRO – Nizhny Novgorod 4A, Nartova street, Nizhny Novgorod, 603057, Russia Tel.: +7 (831) 220 19 00 Fax: +7 (831) 220 19 64 Email: acquisition.store50@metro.com.ru

RESPUBLIKA Mall

9, Revolyutsiy square, 603000, Nizhny Novgorod, Russia

Direction of SC RESPUBLIKA
Tel.: +7 (831) 277 92 92, 277 92 50

Management company TORGOVAYA PLOSCHAD (SALES AREA)
61, Belinskogo street, Nizhny Novgorod, 603000, Russia
Email: mail@respublikann.ru
http://www.respublikann.ru/
http://www.respublikann.ru/?id=286 list of all contacts of SC RESPUBLIKA
General director of management company TORGOVAYA PLOSCHAD – Alexander V. Kokovich

RAMSTORE Nizhny Novgorod Mall 124, Belinskogo street, Nizhny Novgorod, 603000, Russia Tel.: +7 (831) 278 70 30 Fax: +7(831) 278 71 30 Email: ramenka@ramenka.ru http://www.ramstore.ru/store/regions/nnovgorod.html http://www.ramstore.ru/eng/store/regions/n-novgorod.html English version

Ramenka Investment department

Building 9, 16, Leningradskoye chausse, Moscow Tel.: +7 (495) 937 04 47 Fax: +7 (495) 937 87 81 For other partnership questions: Tel.: +7 (495) 937 04 40 Email: ramenka@ramenka.ru

Management company TORGOVY KVARTAL (TRADE QUARTER), Moscow Tel.: +7 (495) 265 74 62 Fax: +7 (495) 263 05 83 Email: office@tk.ru http://www.tk.ru/

Shopping centre SHOKOLAD

124, Belinskogo street, Nizhny Novgorod, 603000, Russia

Shopping centre GAGARINO (Nizhny Novgorod)

http://www.tk.ru/regions/nizhnii_novgorod_gagarino/

X5 Retail Group (management company of allRussian retailers: PEREKRYOSTOK, PYATEROCHKA, LENTA)
Headoffice of X5 Retail Group:
Prins Bernhardplein 200
1097 JB Amsterdam
The Netherlands

Corporate centre of X5 Retail Group in Moscow:
Building 4, 28, Srednaya Kalitnikovskaya street, Moscow, 109029, Russia
Tel.: +7 (495) 662 88 88, 789 95 95
Fax: +7 (495) 662 88 88, additional: 41265

Email: info@x5.ru http://www.perekrestok.ru/shops/nnovgorod/ (all shops in Nizhny Novgorod and region)

Shopping centre PEREKRYOSTOK

3A, Plotnikova street, Nizhny Novgorod, 603000, Russia Tel.: +7 (831) 277 85 42 Fax: +7 (831) 277 85 28

Shopping centre PEREKRYOSTOK

122, Moscovskoye chausse, Nizhny Novgorod, 603000, Russia Tel.: +7 (831) 220 13 21 Fax: +7 (831) 220 13 22

Shopping centre MURAVEY (anchor tenants MAGNIT, EL DORADO, ECOLAS)

33. Prospekt Lenina street, Nizhny Novgorod, 603000, Russia Lease department Tel.: +7 (831) 275 93 23

EL DORADO (electronics & home appliances) 3, Polkovaya street, Moscow, 127018, Russia Russian information service unit Tel.: 88005551111 (tollfree) PRdepartment (Moscow) Tel.: +7 (495) 787 78 00 E-mail: press@eldorado.ru http://www.eldorado.ru/ http://www.eldorado.ru/help/eldorado/contacts.php list of all contacts http://www.eldorado.ru/info/shops/index.php?city=11289 – Nizhny Novgorod weblink

ECOLAS (footwear) Head office (RostovnaDonu) General director – Sergey V. Kirpichnikov Tel.: +7 (863) 2955858 Email: secretar@ecolas.ru http://www.ecolas.ru/

Director of Nizhny Novgorod branch office – Sergey V. Zhuliev Tel.: +7 (831) 244 01 25 Email: dir@nn.ecolas.ru http://www.ecolas.ru/?page=RuNN&Sid=SID– Nizhny Novgorod weblink

RAITSENTR (food supermarket chain) Head office (Nizhny Novgorod) 10/1, Germana Lopatina street, Nizhny Novgorod, 603163, Russia Tel.: +7 (831) 460 99 05, 460 99 06 Email: office@rcenter.nnov.ru http://raycenter.ru/

VKT (wholesale and retail trader; logistics center)
Head office (Nizhny Novgorod)
2B, Geologov street, Nizhny Novgorod, 603141, Russia

Tel.: +7 (831) 463 96 39, 463 96 66,
Fax: +7 (831) 463 96 85

Email: vkt@vkt.nnov.ru
http://www.639639.ru/
http://www.639639.ru/site.aspx?IID=349380&SECTIONID=349340 – English version

SAUS (food supermarket chain) General director – Alexander A. Bochkarev Deputy general director – Natalya V. Kalinina 7, Naberezhnaya Fedorovskogo (Fedorovskogo embankment), Nizhny Novogorod, 603109, Russia Tel.: + 7 (831) 278 01 75, 278 01 79, 278 01 90 Mob. ph.: + 7 (904) 789 92 20 Fax: + 7 (831) 278 01 85 Email: kadrsaus@mail.ru (staff office) http://saus.rusmarket.ru/

USG Resources

Roman Vvedensky BISNIS Representative Nizhny Novgorod Teatralnaya square 5/6 Office 22 Nizhny Novgorod 603005, 20230NULL Russia

Phone: 78314192726 FAX: 78312192726 Email: volgabisnis@sinn.ru

REGIONAL IT MARKET

This report analyzes the recent market trends of the Russian regional IT market. Regional consumption of IT services and solutions has moved ahead of Moscow, most likely due to the fact that most Moscowbased companies have already achieved their key automation goals and are now investing in their regional production and distribution facilities. In 2009, the size of IT market was estimated at $1112 billion, a 25.4% increase over 2008. IT sales are growing steadily in the regions, increasing 5% in 2009. The most promising regions for IT are the Urals, the Republic of Tatarstan, Northwest Russia, and the special economic zones. U.S. IT companies are currently present in all the regions of the Russian Federation, selling directly or through distributors. The overall growth of the economy and the continued development of a competitive marketplace provide U.S. exporters good opportunities for IT sales.

Market Demand

Market Overview: According to industry sources, 2009 was another successful year for the Russian IT sector. By yearend 2010, the IT market is projected to reach $13.5$14 billion. Industry analysts predict 19% annual growth, doubling by 2009. IT hardware purchases increased by 30% in 2009, and now comprise 70% of Russian IT market spending. Disk data storage systems remain the fastest growing sector; desktops are the driving force in the market due to increased sales to home and government consumers. The volume of desktop computers will continue to dominate the market, but as desktop prices decline, laptop computer revenues may take the lead. IT services accounted for one fifth of all IT expenditures in Russia in 2009, migrating from a focus on system deployment to management and security. Sales of offtheshelf software grew by 19.6% in 2009, the smallest share of the Russian IT market. However small this niche is, it is expected to continue growing by 1920% annually for the next several years.

Regional Markets: Regional consumption of IT services and solutions has moved ahead of Moscow, most likely due to the fact that most companies based in Moscow have already achieved their key automation goals and are now investing more in their regional production and distribution facilities. Typically, large regional contracts are signed with Moscowbased companies and then are partially subcontracted to companies in the regions. To protect their interests and to address their mutual concerns, industry associations have been established in several regions of Russia. The regional markets develop differently than they have in Moscow and St. Petersburg. Historically, Moscow and St. Petersburg served as a gateway for international business. After the collapse of the Soviet Union and the rush to develop a market economy, companies located in the regions had the freedom to engage in international business directly. There have been obstacles though – a lack of infrastructure, and the access to international carriers and major international transport hubs. Then there is the proximity to government offices, ministries, certification bodies and customs headquarters, which only Moscow is privy too.

Large foreign companies, like HP and IBM have developed a network of regional offices in other cities in Russia. Some companies have at least one office in each of the seven federal districts of Russia. Other companies prefer to act through their local businesspartners. Microsoft, for example has built a presence in 20 Russian cities, employing 80 people. CNews, the leading Russian hitech website and magazine estimated that in 2009, 71% of large IT companies in Russia were based in Moscow, and 29% in the regions. Regional market share increased 5%, compared to 2008.

Industry specialists have identified several independent regional IT markets, where more business decision are made locally, thereby allowing some independence to react to local market conditions. Among these regions are St. Petersburg and the region, Tatarstan, Bashkortostan, the Urals, and Volga region.
Regional ICT market Page 2 of 10

2009 IT Sales in the Regions

City	$ Sales (thousands)	% Of market share
St. Petersburg	425,717	44.8 %
Novosibirsk	187,236	19.7 %
Yekaterinburg	71,874	7.6 %
Perm	47,448	5 %
Nizhniy Novgorod	42,044	4.4 %
Tomsk	62,778	6.6 %
Voronezh	42,418	4.5 %
Kazan	29,571	3.1 %
Naberezhnyie Chelny	22,572	2.4 %
Vladivostok	8,609	0.9 %

Source: CNews Analytics, 2010

Regional Trends:

The IT regional market was affected by the following trends:

Russian government initiatives to develop Special Economic Zones

Continued industrial growth spurred increased IT spending by regional governments and large industrial enterprises.
Distributors are strengthening their positions in the regions
Multinationals are expanding their presence in the regions

Special Economic Zones (SEZ):

The Russian Government instituted initiatives to create special economic zones to stimulate economic growth, encourage foreign investment by applying simplified legal procedures for foreign investors, and granting tax breaks. SEZ investors are also entitled to privileges on real estate and other property in order to buy land and to obtain speedy approval for construction. Six zones are scheduled for completion by the end of 2012. According to FC News Information Agency, the Zelenograd SEZ expects to register 3 to 4 companies by the fall of 2010. Cisco, a leading supplier of networking equipment and network management applications for the Internet, intends to invest $500 million in the zone within the next two years. SEZ's in Tatarstan, St Petersburg, Dubna, Lipetsk and Tomsk each expect to register companies for their respective zones. Russian companies are expected to account for about 70% of the residents in the SEZs with foreign companies making up the balance. To learn more about the SEZ in Tomsk, please read the BISNIS report New Special Economic Zones in Russia: Focus on Tomsk and a recent report prepared by the Foreign Commercial Service, Russia: New SEZ Law.

In an effort to streamline the management of SEZs, the Russian Government has established the Federal Agency for the Management of Special Economic Zones, wh ich has posted several documents available in English about the Zones, including a Presentation on SEZs and SEZs and Investment Fund of Russia. The Russian SEZ project is a work in progress, so check for updates.

Software Outsourcing: Software outsourcing is a fastgrowing sector developing primarily in the regions. The main software development centers are located in Nizhny Novgorod, Novosibirsk, Tomsk and Moscow and St. Petersburg. According to the Ministry of Information Technology and Communications, Russia's IT exports amounted to $1 billion in 2009, a 250% increase compared to 2008. To promote software exports abroad, the Ministry is planning to create the Federal Agency for IT Export Assistance by the end of 2010.

Internet Development: The number of Internet users in the regions is also growing. In 2009, Internet access services increased by 55%. According to a poll conducted by the Public Opinion Foundation (FOM), Russia's Internet audience in the spring of 2010 was 21%, with the total number of Internet users estimated at 24.3 million. Industry insiders estimate PC ownership at 30 PCs per 100 households. In 2010, ADSL service providers expanded their regional customer base to include not only the corporate but also the consumer sectors as well. Initially, regional fixed line operators, (owning 87% of the fixed line bank) are expected to be the leaders in the regional ADSL market.

Dialup services are becoming less profitable. In 2009, the dialup share of Internet access service revenues declined 10 to 39%, prompting equipment manufacturers to reduce the production of modems and to focus on Ethernet, ADSL and wireless equipment. In 2003, the OMNI 56K modem generated half of ZyXEL's total sales in Russia. For 2010, the Taiwanese company reported sales of the OMNI 56K modems at 20% of company revenues.

Market Data

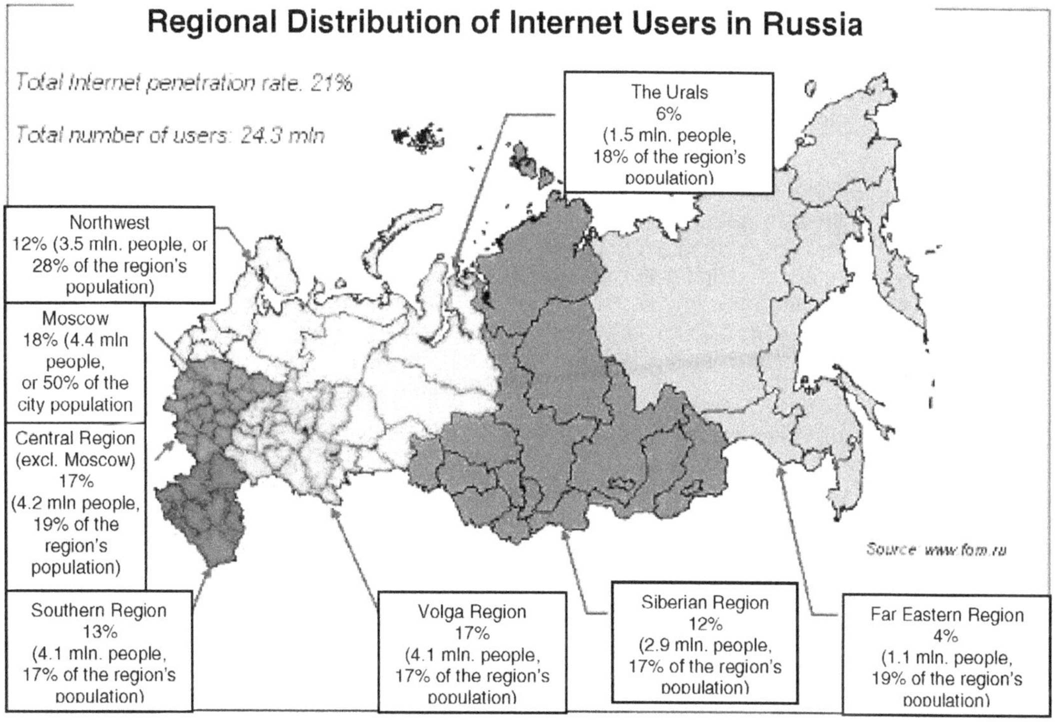

Hardware: According to estimates by IDC, a leading market research company, the Russian PC market grew 22% in 2009, reaching 6.3 million computers. Desktops make up 80% of all PC sales. The following Russian manufacturers lead the market in PC sales: Aquarius, DEPO Computers, Formoza, K3Systems, Kraftway. Foreign suppliers' share is 6%.

The notebook computer market, with its 84% growth in 2009, and a record 1.2 million units sold presents a different picture. Rover Computers (with 12.8% of the market share in the fourth quarter of 2008), is the only Russian company in the top ten notebook market player listing. Other leading foreign companies are Acer (28.2%), ASUS (16.6%), Samsung (8%), HP (7.5%), Fujitsu/Fujitsu Siemens (5.7%), Toshiba (4.1%), Dell (2.8%), Lenovo (2.1%) and Sony (1.9%). According to industry specialists, the notebook computer market accounted for 19% of the IT hardware market in 2009. In the notebook computer and server segments, foreign companies are gaining market share. Analysts expect a steady 17% annual growth of the PC segment, and desktops will outnumber notebook sales (in number of units sold) but will yield in market share due to declining prices.

The Russian server market is considered to be one of the most promising, projected to reach 120140 thousand units or about $4050 million in sales in 2010. Growth in the Intel architecture server segment surpassed the market average in 2009, where HP and IBM have secured 44% of the market share. IBM is targeting a vast array of potential customers, from small and medium enterprises to blade servers and hiend solutions. Sun is a leading supplier of UNIX systems focusing on the telecom, financial and government sectors. HP has been successful supplying hiend servers to the Russian government. Entrylevel servers are sold mostly to SMEs and account for half of the total number of units sold by HP. Active work with service partners, good support and spare parts depots has earned HP a solid customer base in the regions. Blade server sales are growing faster than others, with HP selling about 500 units every quarter. The blade server market is expected to double in 2010, estimated at 7,800 units.

Printers: There is growing interest in multifunction devices in the corporate sector, sales of highvolume and color laser printers is increasing. The near saturation in the market of the low price dot matrix, inkjet and laser devices affected sales in the second quarter of 2010. IDC noted that shipments were down by 20%, whereas shipments of network laser printers (priced at $400 per unit and up) continued to increase. Multi-function devices have increased 1.5 times.

Computer Monitors: In 2009, fifteen inch CRTs almost vanished from the Russian market, retaining only 25% of market sales, with 17" LCD monitors assuming the lead. In the regional markets, CRT sales to the corporate sector and government tenders retained their position to a certain extent. Professional desktop publishers and designers also remain faithful to large CRT screens, but sales volumes of DTPquality monitors had no significant influence on the overall market. Russian consumers are eying 19" LCD monitors, and as the price decreases (now at $300), sales are expected to increase. According to IT Research, the total volume of the Russian monitor market was 6.9 million units or $1.9 billion.

IT Services: CNews Analytics notes that in 2009, 13 to 15% of Russian IT expenditures were for auditing and consulting services, and 1% for IT training. The IT security industry in Russia has shown fast growth over the last couple of years, with over a 30% annual gain, exceeding the overall growth in the IT market. There has been a correspondingly significant development noted in IT securityrelated services. According to industry analysts, these services account for a 15 to 20% share of overall revenues of IT security companies, which is expected to reach 30 to 35% in the near future.

Software: U.S. software companies hold a dominant position in the Russian market. U.S. companies such as Microsoft, IBM, Sun Microsystems, and Oracle are universally recognized in Russia for their quality and sophistication. U.S. software products are available either directly or through representative offices or distributors. Imports from other countries are also growing, with U.S. software products facing increasing competition from European software vendors.

As in the rest of the world, localized language versions of U.S. software products – operating systems, word-processing software, and email applications can be found on most home and office computers in every region of Russia. The language localization of software is now moving further a field into regional languages. In Tatarstan recently, Microsoft unveiled the Tatarlanguage version of Microsoft Windows XP.

The sales of Microsoft products in Russia grew by 72% from June 2009 to July 2010. The percentage of regional sales reached 55%, compared with a 29% increase in 2001. Overall, regional sales have gone up by 76% over 2009. Windows OS sales accounted for 34% of Microsoft's total sales in Russia, Business Solutions (MS Office and MS Dynamics) 34%, Database, Server and ISA Server 2008based security solutions 26%. The sales of preloaded Windows XP increased 76% compared to the previous year with more than two million licensed copies of this operating system sold. Sales of corporate software to SME customers doubled.

On the enterprise front, the corporate database software market is clearly dominated by U.S. companies: Oracle, Microsoft and IBM.

Industry analysts estimate that in the ERP market SAP (39.7%), Oracle (21.7%), 1C (9.7%) and Microsoft Dynamics (9.4%) hold the largest market shares, followed by Russian company Galaktika (6.1%), Epicor Scala (3.7%) and Parus (2.8%). The raw materials industry, related continuous production industries and transportation remain the most active consumers of ERP systems. Many companies are thinking of going public and consider having an ERP system installed an advantage. Below is a snapshot of the largest Russian ERP projects, their locations, project costs and the IT vendor used.

Largest Russian Industrial Projects with ERP		
Company, location	$ In millions	Solution
Magnitogorsk Iron & Steel Works (Urals)	20	Oracle EBusiness Suite
Eurochem (multiregional, European part of Russia)	11.5	Oracle EBusiness Suite
The SiberianUrals Aluminum company *	8.4	mySAP Business Suite
Tactical Missiles Corporation JSC (Korolev, Central Region)*	7	mySAP ERP
Tiumentransgaz* (Siberian Region)	4.9	mySAP Business Suite
Uralkaliy (Potassium production, Urals)	4.2	Oracle EBusiness Suite
GMAvtovaz* (Togliatti, Volga Region)	2.1	SAP R/3
Voronezh Synthetic Rubber* (Central Region)	1.4	mySAP Business Suite
Mezhregiongaz* (Gazprom, multiregional)	1.2	1C Enterprise 8.0
Degtyaryov Plant* (Firearms and vehicles, Kovrov, Central Region)	1.2	Baan ERP5
Power Machines, (multiregional)	1	SAP NetWeaver
SeverstalMetiz* (Cherepovets, Central region)	0.9	BAAN IV
Urals Optical Mechanical Plant* (Urals)	0.5	IFS Applications

* -CNews Analytics Estimates Source: CNews Analytics, 2009

Best Prospects

There are good opportunities for U.S. companies in the following market segments:

Servers, Networking Equipment, and Data Center Solutions: The transition to 64bit server architecture is almost complete. Analysts note that Russian companies are moving away from the "patchup" approach to their IT policy, by building new complex infrastructures with highly productive data centers. This fuels the demand for highly reliable "heavy" server solutions, storage systems, networking equipment and power solutions.

ERP Solutions: As noted earlier, many companies in Russia are preparing to go public. The need to switch to transparent, international accounting standards drives the interest in ERP software. Government orders for enterprise automation solutions are also expected to grow. In 2009, the annual growth for ERP solutions was 21%, which is comparable to the overall growth in the IT sector.

Personal Computers and Software: Notebook sales continue to increase. IDC estimates notebooks represented 23% of the personal computer market in the 2nd quarter of 2010. Desktop PC computers are in constant demand. As for software, operating system and software application sales have increased due to the growing public awareness of IPR, and the efforts of developers to provide product support to licensed users only.

Regional Overview

St. Petersburg and North West Russia: Located 700 kilometers from Moscow and only 200 kilometers from Finland, St. Petersburg is the second largest city in Russia and was the capital for more than two centuries. St. Petersburg is ideally located for international cooperation, with easy access to European transport hubs. The city is home to the regional offices of Corning, Google, Intel, Lucent, Motorola, Sun Microsystems, and software outsourcing companies Quest Software, Reksoft, and DataArt. Because of the city's relative proximity to Moscow, many purchases of IT technology are made using Moscow sales channels, making it difficult to estimate the markets size. According to industry analysts, IT consumers in St. Petersburg are more price sensitive and the size of project budgets are smaller than in Moscow. The Russian government has been encouraging large companies to move their headquarters to St. Petersburg Russian conglomerate Gazprom, Vneshtorgbank, Sibur and Transnefteproduct, Sovkomflot and Transaero Airlines have recently registered their headquarters in St. Petersburg. The government will also relocate the Constitutional Court of the Russian Federation (from Moscow) to St. Petersburg. In addition, the growing SEZs in the Northwest of Russia, in combination with the above relocations significantly raise the importance and opportunities in this regional market.

Siberian Region: In 2008, the IT market in Siberia reached $1.51.8 billion, or 20% of the Russian IT market. Of that, IT equipment sales accounted for 49%, and services 38%. In 2009, the share of revenues generated by the services segment reached 44%, equipment 45%, software 3%, and telecommunications 8%.

Novosibirsk hosts the regional offices of Intel, Microsoft, Sun Microsystems, HewlettPackard, Siemens, Samsung, Shlumberger, Kraftway and others.

The Largest IT Companies in Siberia

Rating	Company Name	Location of Headquarters	$ Sales in 2009, Thousands	% Growth
1	NETA	Novosibirsk	$95,808	30,3%
2	CTGroup Group of Companies	Barnaul	$59,342	13,9%
3	Open Technologies 98	Moscow	$45,411	
4	SintezN Group of Companies	Krasnoyarsk	$16,978	39,4%
5	InsystAvtomatika	Omsk	$15,417	123,6%
6	NonoletComputers & Telecommunications	Novosibirsk	$14,261	22,9%
7	Utilex IT 2000	Novosibirsk	$13,059	164,4%
8	Sibintek Company	Moscow	$12,216	11,3%
9	Commed	Omsk	$8,337	73,4%
10	IT, Siberian Branch	Krasnoyarsk	$6,835	30,8%

Source: EkspertSiberia

The Urals: In 2009, the IT market in the Urals reached $1 billion, 10% of the overall Russian IT market, demonstrating steady growth over the last three years. Industry analysts expect that IT solutions will continue growing in the industrial, energy, banking and sales, retail and government sectors. Most of the larger IT companies are present in this region and many regional companies have gone national. As a result, customers in the Urals have the full spectrum of IT services available. The combination of regional government IT initiatives ("Electronic Russia", the implementation of electronic social security cards) and upgrades in local industries are driving the corporate consumption of IT hardware in the region. As the activity of national players rises due to largescale project experience gained in other regions, local players are expected to focus more on the region's SMEs.

Industry experts single out the following top 10 IT companies for equipment, services, and software in the Urals: Open Technologies 98, Arsenal+, Microtest, Triline, ASK, IVSSeti, Krok, Prognoz, SKB Kontur and Kloss.

Volga Region: According to the 2009 BISNIS report Electronic Hardware Sellers and IT Integrators in Nizhny Novgorod , the market in Nizhny Novgorod for system integration and electronic hardware distribution is estimated at $3035 million, with potential for further growth to $5060 million per year, which does not include consumer sales of electronic hardware.

Republic of Tatarstan (a constituent republic of the Russian Federation): The Ministry of Informatization and Telecommunications of Tatarstan has recently conducted an independent survey of Tatarstan's ICT sector. The survey concluded that Tatarstan does not have large private businesses, and that the government is heavily involved in controlling Tatarstan's economy. Moreover, until recently the government opposed outside financial and industrial entities from entering the Tatarstan market. The government of the Republic of Tatarstan has announced plans to enhance their ICT infrastructure, by implementing an eGovernment project, and a government electronic trading system, among other projects. In 2000, Vimpelcom, one of the major Russian cell operators attempted to invest in the local cell phone market without success. Not until the fall of 2002, was Vimpelcom finally successful in Tatarstan. Other cell phone providers, Megafon and SMARTS had similar problems getting started in Tatarstan. Notwithstanding the problems, these operators were finally successful doing business in Tatarstan.

In 2009, Tatarstan's ICT sector revenues amounted to $970 million, or approximately 3% of the overall ICT market volume in Russia. Hardware purchases were 70% of Tatarstan's IT budget, 30% was spent on software and services. The market for ITservices focuses on company IT infrastructure support. Depending on further efforts by the Tatarstan government to open the country for international business, this market may have potential for U.S. business. Several U.S. companies have achieved some success and according to KommersantDaily, Cisco Systems Regional Manager, Mr. Yuriy Kazantsev, stated that Cisco Systems ranks the Tatarstan market in their top three. In the last financial year Cisco's annual sales in Tatarstan grew by 47%, while their overall growth of sales in Russia increased 40%.

According Ms. Marina Savinova, the PR manager for Oracle CIS, Oracle also sees potential in Tatarstan. In the past two years Oracle's products have become instrumental in the development of the financial, telecommunication, power, chemical and oil sectors, as well as the Tatarstan government.

Key Suppliers

The following Russian companies have a wide network of offices affording them the opportunity to pursue leading projects, distribute hardware and software throughout Russia

№	Name	Turnover, $ thousands
Top 10 largest IT companies in Russia in 2009		
1	Merlion	$979,947
2	NKK	$800,655
3	IBS	$716,771
4	Lanit	$606,488
5	R-Style	$546,338
6	Technoserv A/S	$537,275
7	Ultra Electronic	$511,414
8	Kvazar-Micro	$491,014
9	Verysell	$415,942
10	Krok	$373,497

Source: Cnews, Turnover calculated at Rate: $1=R28.29

Prospective Buyers

In 2009, the principle prospective buyers for IT products and services were the telecom, government, financial transportation, oil & gas, and power engineering sectors. In 2008, the government of the Russian Federation increased use of IT technology twofold. In 2009, the government purchased over $212 million in IT technology, and has been the major IT service customer for the last two years.

In the regions with stronger concentrations of industrial IT users (oil & gas, machinery and metalworking), IT may play a pivotal role in the economic development of these economies. Case in point, there are more than 6,000 enterprises in the machinery and metalworking sector fueling a longterm need for IT technology.

Market Entry

Requirements for market entry are controlled centrally and are uniform for all of Russia. Computer hardware sold in Russia must conform to Russian standards of minimum safety and quality requirements, and must carry a conformity mark indicating that the product has been tested and approved for use in Russia. While the process can be timeconsuming, it is relatively transparent and the requirements are not especially onerous.

U.S. exporters generally experience few problems. Compliance testing is typically performed at commercially operated testing stations in Russia, and the results passed to GosStandart (the State Committee of the Russian Federation for Standardization and Metrology) who issue the certificates. Hardware and software operating in or interacting with a government entity may be subject to additional certifications. A detailed description of Russia's certification system and a list of U.S.based companies providing certification services for exports to Eurasian countries, is available at: http://www.bisnis.doc.gov/bisnis/bisdoc/cert_rf.htm

The U.S. Commercial service recommends the most effective way to operate in the Russian IT market is with a Russian partner. Some computer distributors have been in business for more than 10 years and have extensive experience and knowhow. Their detailed knowledge of the market and many business connections enable them to find both a buyer and a seller. Many distributors operate on an exclusive basis and may cover a large area of the country, allowing them to make a thorough analysis of sale possibilities, and to evaluate the product against competing products with regard to both price and quality.

MARKET ISSUES & OBSTACLES

There are barriers to U.S. exports of encrypted, commercialuse information technology products to Russia. They are of the nontariff nature, but costly nonetheless. In 2009, the Russian government proposed formalizing previously informal controls on imports and exports of products containing encryption. Currently this process requires a multistage inspection and permit process that includes an evaluation by the Federal Security Service (FSB) and import and activity licensing by Ministry of Economic Development and Trade (MEDT). These procedures are presently undergoing revision and it is hoped that with the recent signing of the U.S.Russia WTO Bilateral Market Access Agreement (a precursor to Russia's accession to the WTO), a more transparent system for import of encrypted electronic goods will be established. Also included in the Agreement are requests for actions to address piracy and counterfeiting, and to improve protection and enforcement of intellectual property rights before Russia completes its accession to the WTO.

The protection of intellectual property rights is a serious concern for U.S. companies in Russia. According to the Third Annual Piracy Study by Business Software Alliance and IDC Global Software released in May 2010, software piracy decreased 3% (down from 87% to 84%), in 2009. This could be due to the increase of laptop sales in the market, since most are purchased with preloaded licensed software. The Russian government is paying more attention to this issue, and is now conducting spotchecks in computer clubs and kiosks throughout Russia. According to the Russian Ministry of Interior, 6,432 criminal piracy cases were reported in the first ten months of 2010, with 3,082 individuals consequently sentenced. This is twice the number of cases initiated during the whole of 2009. In spite of these efforts, the impact on the availability of pirated computer software is still barely noticeable in the market. For companies whose business may be vulnerable to piracy, available on the U.S. Embassy website is has an IPR Toolkit, wh ich provides information on the conditions in Russia and how to take precautions.

Resources & Key Contacts

AmCham Moscow http://www.amcham.ru/
AmCham St. Petersburg http://www.amcham.ru/spb/
BISNIS. Information about Russian Federations' regions
http://www.bisnis.doc.gov/bisnis/country/rusfed.cfm
GosStandart, The Federal Agency for Technical Regulations and Metrology http://www.gost.ru/
Ministry of Information Technologies and Communications of the Russian Federation

http://english.minsvyaz.ru/enter.shtml Russian Center for Tests and Certification (Rostest)
http://www.rostest.ru Russian Standard, general representative of ROSTEST for North America
http://www.rosstandard.com

U.S. Embassy Russia http://www.usembassy.ru

For more information about this subject contact

Stefan Mizha Commercial Specialist

U.S. Commercial Service, U.S. Embassy Moscow Tel: 74957375017, Fax: 74957375033 Email: stefan.mizha@mail.doc.gov Website: http://buyusa.gov/russia

The U.S. Commercial Service — Your Global Business Partner

With its network of offices across the United States and in more than 80 countries, the U.S. Commercial Service of the U.S. Department of Commerce utilizes its global presence and international marketing expertise to help U.S. companies sell their products and services worldwide. Locate the U.S. Commercial Service trade specialist in the

U.S. nearest you by visiting http://www.export.gov/.

RUSSIA INSURANCE MARKET

The insurance sector in Russia is still underdeveloped in comparison to a majority of other European countries; however, it holds great potential for growth. The positive macroeconomic trends of the last few years and the improved investment climate, combined with the increased consumption capacity of the population have created conditions for significant insurance industry development.

The combination of weak competition, huge pentup demand, and the gradual liberalization of the market makes the Russian insurance market an attractive target for major foreign companies who bring new technology, experience, and professionalism. Both the Russian government and insurance industry show signs of greater acceptance of foreign competition and international best practices as Russian companies gain confidence and appreciate the potential of consumer acceptance of quality products. The implication for U.S. insurance companies is that there may be opportunities for entry and growth in the market despite the present restrictions.

Market Demand

Since the beginning of the economic reforms initiated by President Putin's Administration in 2000, significant progress has been made through structural reforms, which included debureaucratization, a new labor code, corporate governance policies, judicial reform, tax liberalization, pension reform, an opening of the land market, and a new customs code. These reforms, along with increased export earnings from the higher price of oil and gas, have brought about yearly improvements in the Russian economy. The resulting relative political stability has led to a reduction in macroeconomic risk factors.

From 2000 – 2009, the Russian insurance industry sharply increased sales in the midst of a growing economy, but the official figures were misleading as government mandated coverage and quasilifeinsurance schemes designed to conceal income and evade taxes constituted a large majority of premiums and contributed to the industry growth.

In 2009, however, the Russian Government's efforts to fight illegal schemes in the insurance industry started to bring results. The profile of insurance sales started shifting toward more voluntary and legitimate forms of insurance. This trend is reinforced by new Russian tax legislation, which reduces the incentive to use the more dubious forms of insurance. Corporate clients have started to seek more diversified insurance services and customers are buying more property, health, accident and other legitimate life insurance policies.

Other legislative and regulatory drivers include the introduction (in 2009) of obligatory automobile thirdparty liability insurance, a continuing boom in retail finance, and pension reforms. Gradual liberalization of the Russian economy for foreign investors and Russia's move towards WTO entry are opening the market for foreign companies who bring new business practices that in turn, create demand for classical forms of insurance.

As the Russian Government and the insurance industry show greater acceptance of foreign competition and international best practices more foreign insurers are entering the market, and those who are already in the market are increasing their presence. Russian companies are gaining confidence and appreciate the potential from greater consumer demand for quality products.

Market Data

In terms of total premiums/GDP or premiums/per capita ratio, the insurance industry in Russia is underdeveloped compared to other East European countries. However, during the past 10 years the growth has been significant. According to data released by the Federal Insurance Supervisory Service, as of March 2010, there were 1,061 insurance companies registered in Russia. The following table shows the financial results achieved by these companies in 2009.

Types of Insurance Collected Insurance Premiums	490.6	4%	471.6
Voluntary Insurance	291.1	10%	320.4
Life Insurance	25.3	75%	102.2
NonLife Insurance	265.8	22%	218.2
Personal Insurance (other than Life)	64.0	21%	52.9
Property Insurance (other than liability insurance)	185.6	21%	153.1
Liability Insurance	16.2	33%	12.2
Obligatory Insurance	199.5	32%	151.2
Obligatory Third Party Liability Insurance	53.7	9%	49.2
Obligatory Medical Insurance	140.7	45%	97.2

The data of the 1995 show a slow down of the insurance sector volume growth. In 2009, Russian insurance companies collected RR 490.6 billion of insurance premiums, which was a RR 19 billion increase in comparison to 2009.

2003	2009	2009	2010
RR 432.4 billion	RR 471.6 billion (+9%)	RR 490.6 billion (+4%)	N/A
USD 14.7 billion	USD 15.2 billion	USD 16.3 billion	N/A

At the same time, the total claims paid by the insurance companies in 2009 were RR 274.5 billion. For the first time in the history of the Russian insurance sector this figure had decreased in comparison with a previous year (RR 17.2 billion decrease).

This new negative trend has quite positive explanations. The decrease does not reflect lowered demand in insurance services, but indicates decrease of volumes of the socalled "serviceoriented" insurance transactions, i.e. schemes camouflaged in the form of "life" insurance services but tailored to conceal income and evade taxes.

Until recently, the life insurance market was growing dramatically, but in 2009 the Federal Government and the Federal Insurance Supervisory Service intensified measures aimed at fighting illegal schemes in insurance industry. A number of insurance companies most actively participating in the scheme had their licenses revoked. The supervision itself was tightened leaving less opportunities for tax avoidance schemes. As the result, many companies had to either significantly reduce these transactions or completely abandon this risky business, as they see more business opportunities in increasing demand for legal and classical insurance products. Due to the fact that fewer insurance companies offer these quasiinsurance schemes, the life insurance segment showed negative (75%) growth figures in 2009. Life insurance share in the total volume of insurance market decreased in 2009 from 21.7% to 5.2%.

However, the growth of the real life insurance market also has a negative trend. According to the analysis made by the United Financial Group (UFG), the growth rate of the real insurance market was slowly decreasing from 65% growth in 2003, to 28% in 2009. UFG predicts that by 2016, the real life insurance market may increase to $36.6 billion.

Key Suppliers

As mentioned before, there were 1,061 insurance companies in March of the 2010. According to figures announced at the "Russian Insurance Summit" in May 2009, U.S. capital is present in 12 insurance and reinsurance companies operating in Russia. U.S. insurance companies are becoming more interested in the Russian market and some wellknown insurers are considering the market entry. However, so far, only AIG and ACE have become visible players in the market.

Market Issues

The insurance market is subject to strict regulations and laws on the part of the state. On the one hand, certain regulatory restrictions can protect market players and their clients from the consequences of potential crises and economic downturns. On the other hand, the regulatory authorities' requirements represent a significant burden for insurance companies, increasing the cost of compliance. Due to the immense social significance of insurance, the Russian regulators introduced strict statutory capital requirements for insurance companies.
Due to new legislation, by 2012 the minimum charter capital for property insurance companies must not be less than RR 30 million (approx. USD 1 million), while insurance companies engaged in life/personal savingsbased insurance business and reinsurance companies must have a minimum charter capital of RR 60 million and RR 120 million respectively.

The Russian Government and the insurance industry show signs of greater acceptance of foreign competition and international best practices as Russian companies gain confidence and appreciate the potential for consumer acceptance of quality products.

In a law that applies to European insurers Russian legislators relaxed a ruling in place since 1992, that had limited foreign ownership of companies selling the most attractive products, such as life and obligatory types of insurance, to 49%. Although the law does not officially provide the same liberalization for U.S. insurers, according to unofficial comments made by highranking officials, the authorities will be treating European subsidiaries of U.S. insurers as European insurers. WTO accession, which is now being negotiated, is likely to speedup an opening of the market for other foreign insurers including U.S. insurers in the near term.

Taking into account the market potential, positive macroeconomic trends, continued economic reforms and gradual liberalization of market access for foreign capital, analysts forecast a significant growth in the industry.

The implication for U.S. insurance companies is that there may be opportunities for entry and growth in the market despite the present restrictions. A viable market economy has taken hold in Russia and the market will continue to grow as a consequence. In insurance, the combination of weak competition, huge pentup demand, and expected liberalization of the market offers an attractive target for major foreign companies who bring new technology, experience and professionalism.

AUTOMOTIVE INDUSTRY IN UPPER AND MIDDLE VOLGA[2]

The Volga valley has been a traditional location of automotive corporations in Russia for the last 40 years. The local automotive companies produced majority of Russian cars and a good lot of medium and heavy trucks in the Soviet Union, and then in the Russian Federation. The automotive profile of the region was unmistakably defined by Lada cars, produced at AVTOVAZ (Samara region, Middle Volga), UAZ sports utility vehicles (Ulyanovsk, Middle Volga), Volga sedans and GAZ trucks (Nizhny Novgorod, Upper Volga), , and KAMAZ heavy trucks (Naberezhnye Chelny, Republic of Tatarstan, Upper Volga). Under the centralized economic model, most components of the vehicles were produced either by the same companies or their subsidiaries, located close to a central conveyer department.

[2] **Roman Vvedensky, BISNIS representative in Nizhny Novgorod, Russia**

The historical monopoly of local automotive barons was broken over a decade ago, when Russian consumers began to change their preferences from new Russian cars to second hand models, imported from Europe and Japan, and then, after a national economic recovery in early 2000s, to new foreign cars, assembled in or imported to Russia. This new tendency covers, primarily, cars and sports utility vehicles (SUVs), and partly, light commercial vehicles (LCVs) and minivans. The local producers of medium and heavy trucks are in a better off position for they continue to control a vast niche in the national market, and steadily increase exports to CIS, and to some Asian and African countries.

Facing challenges from foreign car manufacturers and Russian consumers, the automotive corporations of Upper and Middle Volga have started to develop mediumand longterm strategies to retain their niches in the Russian market thru cooperation with foreign automotive companies (including car assembly and auto components production), considerable investments, improvement in quality management systems, and better use of their market advantages (sales channels, service and maintenance centers, cooperation with local governments).

The current report provides with a brief overview of major automotive corporations in the Upper Volga, and partly in the Middle Volga, and refers to the existing foreign projects in the automotive business. The report also includes a general forecast on potential development of the sector in the next 45 years, for it may be helpful for US companies, interested in this sector of the local economy.

MARKET OVERVIEW

The population of Russia, in general, and of the Upper and the Middle Volga region, in particular, has been demonstrating a steady growth in consumption of new cars since 2009, when local banks began to actively develop car loan programs. For the last three years, sales of new cars grew at minimum 15% per year in Russia. In 2009, sales were equally divided between Russian and foreign cars, but the balance was broken in favor of foreign cars, assembled or imported to Russia, in 2009.

The data on cars sales, provided by the Russian news agencies, differs to a certain extent, but all of them agree about positive dynamics in sales. Official statistics reported the following sales of new cars in Russia: 1.610 million cars in 2009, 1.834 million – in 2009, and a little over 2 million cars in 2010. The national economic magazine Expert evaluated the market of new cars in Russia at US$ 30 billion (or 790 billion Rubles) last year. The growth tendency would retain in the next four years, and the local experts forecast annual sales next to 3 million cars in 2010.

At the moment, there are six major plants in European Russia, which assemble foreign cars for the national market:

Avtotor (http://www.avtotor.ru), NorthWest of Russia, assembles KIA and BMW cars; Ford plant (http://www.ford.ru/ie/f_plant), NorthWest of Russia, assembles Focus models; TagAZ (http://www.tagaz.ru), South of Russia; assembles two models of Hyundai cars (Accent, Sonata), and one model of Hyundai light commercial vehicle (Porter);
GMAVTOVAZ (http://www.gmavtovaz.ru/new_ru/index.php), Middle Volga; assembles models of ChevroletNiva SUV (sports utility vehicle), and ChevroletViva car (production of this model may be suspended);

IzhAuto (http://www.izhauto.ru); Republic of Udmurtia, Upper Volga; assembles one KIA car model (Spektra); ZMA, Republic of Tatarstan, Upper Volga; assembles one FIAT car model (Albea), and two models of Ssang Yong SUV (Rexton, Kyron).

There are also a number of other assembly projects in Russia, focused on larger vehicles (e.g. assembly of Isuzu LCVs at UAZ plant, Middle Volga).

In early 2012, the share of foreign cars, assembled in Russia, has not exceeded 2527% of the total amount of foreign cars, sold in the national market. Still, the share of foreign cars, produced in Russia, would grow as there are more foreign assembly projects in the pipeline. Local experts forecast over a dozen of large foreign assembly projects in Russia by 2010. Some of these plants would be set as subsidiaries of multinational companies, some – as joint ventures with local manufacturers, and others organized as licensed production. Toyota, VW, Renault, and GM are the next four multinational companies to launch large scale assembly projects in Russia.

Assembly projects are encouraged by two decrees of the Russian federal government: Decree 166, issued in early 2009, and Decree 566, issued in late 2010. Decree 166 determines minimum customs duties on imported components for automotive assembly plants, when duties vary from 0 to maximum 15% depending on a category of an imported product. The first decree has set benefits for assembly projects, while the second decree (# 566) provides benefits for manufacturers of automotive components in Russia. The second decree has put down the customs duties on materials and basic units, necessary to produce automotive components. The list of car producers from the North America, Europe, and Asia, opening their plants in Russia, would be soon supplemented with a number of other foreign companies, leaders of the auto component market, which have already confirmed interest to open their plants in this country. Official statements have been made by Magna International Inc. (Canada), and a group of German companies, including Siemens AG, Robert Bosch AG, Linner, Zahnrad Fabrik Friedrichshafen AG. Some of the German companies have already launched their projects in Central Russia and in the Volga area.

Local assembly plants have contributed to rapidly growing sales of Ford and Hyundai cars in Russia. Ford Focus is assembled at the plant, opened next to StPetersburg in 2002. It has been a hit of sales with foreign cars in Russia for the last four years. In 2010, Ford sold almost 116,000 cars, SUVs and LCVs in the Russian market, where the sales of Ford Focus made 73,468 cars. Toyota has also high chances to increase sales in Russia after a launch of its plant close to StPetersburg. Last year, the company reported sales of 95,689 cars and SUVs in Russia, with a 32% share of Toyota Corolla models. Currently, the range of popular budget wise cars in Russia includes Ford Focus, Toyota Corolla, Mitsubishi Lancer, Hyundai Accent, and Daewoo Nexia. Recently, this budget car club has been joined by a new member Chevrolet with its Aveo, Lacetti, and Lanos models, assembled at GM plants in Korea. Production of these Chevrolet models may be launched in Russia within the next 1215 months.

MAJOR LOCAL PLAYERS

The Upper and the Middle Volga region is known for a high concentration of mechanical engineering companies, manufacturing a wide range of products for aerospace, shipping, and automotive sectors of the Russian economy. The local automotive plants generate nearly 65% of all revenues, reported by the industrial companies of the region. The regional automotive cluster is led by three local corporations:

AVTOVAZ (http://www.vaz.ru), Samara region, Middle Volga KAMAZ (http://www.kamaz.net/en), Republic of Tatarstan, Upper Volga GAZ group of companies (http://www.gaz.ru/about), Nihny Novgorod region, Upper Volga Last year, the major stake in AVTOVAZ went under control of RosOboronExport (http://www.roe.ru) from its previous owner SOK group of companies (http://www.sok.ru/en). RosOboronExport is the Russian state company, affiliated with the federal government. SOK group of companies retained another automotive assembly asset in the region IzhAuto plant (http://www.izhauto.ru), located in the Republic of Udmurtia, to the east of the Upper Volga region.

AVTOVAZ

AVTOVAZ is still the largest car manufacturer in Russia, although its niche narrowed from 38% in early 2010 to 31% in late 2010. The price range on old models of Lada cars vary from US$ 5,500 to US$ 9,500, which makes them attractive for local consumers, who are ready to put up with limited comfort and obsolete technical parameters of the cars because of an affordable price. The new models, developed by the company's experts, are priced higher, and they face a serious challenge from Korean cars, and Renault Logan car, assembled in Turkey.

Last year, AVTOVAZ produced 766,000 cars, where 99,000 cars were exported. This year, the company plans to produce 776,600 cars, including 110,000 cars for exports sales. The company's revenues in 2012 are forecast at US$ 6.3 billion. Lada Kalina is the latest model of a class B car, developed and produced by AVTOVAZ. The company plans to produce 145,000 Lada Kalina cars this year. Modest success of Lada Kalina sales motivated the company's management to look for a strategic partner among foreign companies, interested in the Russian market. In late December 2010, AVTOVAZ signed a MOU with Magna International Inc., to build a new plant at AVTOVAZ premises. The design production capacity of the new plant is 450,000 cars per year. The company plans to assemble a foreign car model (the name of the car brand is not disclosed), and a new local model under the brand name Lada. The production volume for two models is preliminary set at a 5050 ratio. In late 2010, the representatives of AVTOVAZ also announced plans to set a joint venture to assemble Renault Logan.

AVTOVAZ has got a recent experience of a joint project with a multinational company. GMAVTOVAZ produced 47,881 ChevroletNiva and ChevroletViva vehicles last year. The sports utility vehicle (SUV) ChevroletNiva, developed and designed by the U.S.Russian team of experts, is the main product of the joint venture, which has become rather popular in the Russian market due to its good technical characteristic and a reasonable price.

KAMAZ

KAMAZ is controlled by the company's management, although the list of its shareholders includes representatives of the local and federal government, and major national financial institutions. According to official statements, KAMAZ group of companies produced 43,344 trucks with a load capacity of 1440 tons in 2010. Traditionally, 25% of the output, including vehicles and assembly sets, was exported to other countries. KAMAZ has a number of assembly projects with foreign countries, including China, Kazakhstan, Ukraine, and Pakistan.

Alongside with AVTOVAZ, KAMAZ was the first to apply to the Russian government for the customs duty benefits on auto components, imported from foreign suppliers for KAMAZ trucks. Opposite to some large Russian corporations, which choose buying a license to assemble foreign vehicles in Russia, KAMAZ prefers to develop its own production and technology. To increase the quality of auto components, used in KAMAZ trucks, the corporation set joint ventures with leading foreign producers: a U.S.Russian JV CumminsKama, and a GermanRussian JV ZFKama, which supply KAMAZ with modern diesel motors and transmission systems, respectively. The management of KAMAZ has announced plans to invest over US$ 1 billion in a new reengineering program for the corporation. Currently, KAMAZ controls a 35% niche of medium and heavy trucks in the Russian market.

GAZ Group

GAZ group of companies is affiliated with the national holding group Bazovy Element (Basic Element, http://www.basel.ru/en), which controls a number of industrial, construction and financial assets in Russia. GAZ Group includes 18 enterprises, producing cars, buses, light, medium, heavy trucks, construction vehicles, diesel motors, and fuel systems in Russia. It controls a 50% niche in LCVs, and a 69% niche in buses, manufactured in Russia. The niche in cars is relatively small, and it does not exceed 57% of the total amount of cars, produced in this country. According to the official information of GAZ Group, its annual sales totaled US$ 3.37 billion in 2009 and US$ 4.4 billion in 2010.

GAZ automotive works, located in Nizhny Novgorod, is the largest company in GAZ Group, which generates over half of its total revenues. Last year, GAZ produced and sold 220,000 vehicles and assembly sets, where 20% were exported to other countries. Currently, the company's vehicles GAZelle and Sobol LCVs - are the most popular vehicles for small business in the Russian market. Still, the company's management intends to recapture the niche of Class C cars, lost by GAZ with a fading popularity of Volga sedans. Last April, Group GAZ bought a license and the equipment from DaimlerChrysler to produce restyled models of Chrysler Sebring and Dodge Stratus at its plant in Nizhny Novgorod. The design production capacity of a new plant is 65,000 cars per year.

GAZ Group made two more corporate purchases to level up its technology edge. Last year, it purchased the U.K. based company LDV (http://www.ldv.com), producing LCVs under the brand name Maxus. The Russian corporation plans to launch assembly of Maxus LCVs at GAZ plant late this year. Maxus commercial vehicles should enter the highend segment of the LCV family, produced at GAZ automotive works. GAZ Group also invested Euro 57 million in the diesel motor plant, purchased from Renault Trucks. The new plant will be located in the Yaroslavl region, Upper Volga, and it will produce annually 20,000 DCi11 medium and heavy diesel motors, complying with Euro3 ecological standards.

The experts of GAZ Group have also developed a heavy diesel motor with the Austrian company AVL (http://www.avl.com) to be mounted on heavy trucks and buses. Last November, GAZ Group announced signing of a MOU with Magna International Europe to set two joint ventures: one plant will produce plastic parts for exterior and interior components of vehicles (including bumpers), assembled by GAZ in Nizhny Novgorod , and another plant will produce pressed metal parts. Total investment of GAZ Group into the project with Magna International Europe is estimated at Euro 300 million.

SeverstalAuto

SeverstalAuto (http://www.severstalauto.ru/en) is another powerful national holding company, which is growing muscles in the regional automotive market. The company's automotive assets includes: UAZ plant (http://www.uaz.ru/eng), located in the Ulyanovsk region, Middle Volga, ZMZ motor plant (http://www.zmz.ru/eng/main.html), Nizhny Novgorod region, and ZMA plant (http://www.zma.ru) in the Republic of Tatarstan, Upper Volga.

The holding company gives a clear preference to cooperation with foreign car manufacturers. The company continued production only of two own SUV models (UAZ Patriot, and UAZ Hunter), where 30% of components for UAZ Patriot are foreign make. It ceased production of UAZ minivans and OKA midget cars, and concentrated on cooperation with Isuzu (Japan), FIAT (Italy) and SsangYong (Korea). The company announced a new car assembly project at the free economic zone Alabuga, Republic of Tatarstan, where it will assemble and, then, produce components for several FIAT car models: Albea, Paleo, Doblo, Grande Punto, and FIAT LCV Ducato. The design production capacity of the new plant is 150,000 cars per year. ZMA plant, another company's automotive asset in eastern Tatarstan, will also continue assembly of FIAT Cooperation with FIAT in the Russian market has also assisted SeverstalAuto to solve problems of ZMZ motor company, which traditionally supplied its motors to GAZ automotive works, mounted on Volga sedans, and GAZelle LCVs.

With the current production capacity of 240,000 motors per year, ZMZ may receive a maximum order of 179,000 gasoline motors or even less from GAZ this year. The joint project between ZMZ plant and FIAT Powertrain Technologies provides for assembly of a new diesel motor F1A, mounted on FIAT Ducato LCVs, and UAZ Patriot SUVs. The diesel motor will meet Euro3 ecological standards. The design production capacity of the project is 90,000 diesel motors per year. It will be launched in February 2008. Total investment in the project is estimated at US$ 100 million.

Foreign projects of auto component production in the Volga area

According to the info of the Russian magazine Expert, there are over a dozen of foreign projects, related to automotive component production in the Upper and the Middle Volga region. They include:

Stadco, a joint venture with SeverstalAuto, Tatarstan, metal press forming (the project is under development); Cummins, a joint venture with KAMAZ CumminsKama, Tatarstan, production of diesel engines; Robert Bosch AG, a joint venture BoschSaratov, Saratov region, production of ignition plugs and motor drive circuitry;

Robert Bosch AG, a joint project with Zahnrad Fabrik Friedrichshafen AG, Samara region, production of fuel systems and transmission components (the project to be launched in late 2012);

Zahnrad Fabrik Friedrichshafen AG, a joint venture with KAMAZ ZFKama, Tatarstan, production of transmission systems; LINNER, LINNER plant in the Volga area, production of grease filters (the project is under development); Hella Autotechnik, a joint project with AvtoSvet company (SOK Group), Vladimir region, production of front light lamp clusters; Delphi, a joint project with Samara Cable Company (SOK Group), Samara region, production of wire bundles; WOCO, WOCO plant, Samara region, production of industrial rubber and rubber metal articles; Tudor, a joint venture TuBor, Nizhny Novgorod region, production of batteries; - Autocomponent Engineering, a joint project with Plastic company, Samara region, production of steering wheels with safety cushions; Tenneco, Tenneco Automotive Volga plant, Samara region, production of dash pots and filters.

Nizhny Novgorod region also hosts ZAO InstrumRand (a joint venture of IngersollRand with Pavlovo mechanical engineering company, and GAZ automotive works), which produces electrical engineering tools, and OOO Lear, a subsidiary of Lear Corp., which produces car seats, and interior components for cars and LCVs. Bor Glassworks, the largest producer of glass in

Recommendations for U.S. companies

The U.S. companies, which take interest in the Russian automotive market, should closely monitor commercial news on the automotive projects, launched in the NorthWest of Russia, in Central Russia, in the Urals, and in the Volga area. There are also a number of new automotive projects, developed in Siberia and in the Far East, but they are likely to concentrate on assembly of Chinese vehicles, which may provide little business opportunity for a U.S. company.

Automotive projects, implemented in European Russia, and in the Urals, are often developed either directly or with involvement of wellknown multinational automotive companies, which are interested, in its turn, in reliable counterparts and subcontractors among North American, European or Japanese automotive firms. Local markets may come up with a good proposal on qualified labor for the new projects, and local suppliers of raw materials and logistics agents have already gained certain experience on how to work with foreign customers.

The new structure of the Russian automotive market will be set by 20092010, when foreign producers localize and launch their projects, and Russian companies reform their businesses. The current market situation pushes main players to actively communicate with potential partners, and to improve sales mechanisms. Now is the right time for a U.S. company, which has a business product to offer, to consider entry to the Russian automotive market. Growing competition among car producers and withdrawal of customs obstacles with an entry of Russia to World Trade Organization will make the market penetration harder after 2009.

A U.S. company, engaged in automotive production, may consider opening of a production site or a warehouse for its customers in Russia. Liberalization of customs duties on supplies of raw materials and units for automotive components production widens the range of customers from assembly plants to producers of auto components. A U.S. company may also offer its services in consulting and design to local car manufacturers, which continue production of their models, and which are interested to increase their attractiveness for a customer. It is little secret that local companies are also interested to improve their management systems and to optimize business processes, and a U.S. expertise may be highly demanded there. Preference will be given to U.S. experts or U.S. managers (the latter also get high salaries when hired by Russian companies), who have a good experience of competing with Asian car manufacturers. Development of the automotive industry in Russia will also create additional business opportunities for U.S. companies, which deal in aftermarket and sell equipment for automotive production as well as products for car service, repair and maintenance.

AVTOVAZ http://www.vaz.ru/

GMAVTOVAZ http://www.gmavtovaz.ru/new_ru/index.php

SOK group of companies http://www.sok.ru/en/

GAZ group of companies http://www.gaz.ru/about/

KAMAZ http://www.kamaz.net/en/

SeverstalAuto http://www.severstalauto.ru/en/

For more information on Upper Volga region, Russia, visit BISNIS online at

http://www.bisnis.doc.gov/bisnis/country/volga.cfm

TECHNOLOGIES MARKET OF RUSSIA

Russian mobile operators are moving to third-generation (3G) cellular technology, with GSM and NMT operators taking the lead. The auction of licenses and the launch of 3G commercial projects in the 1.9-2.1 GHz range are scheduled for the beginning of 2012. UMTS was chosen as the priority 3G standard increasing the demand for telecommunications equipment supporting GSM/UMTS standards. Based on the saturation of the cellular market and the demand for more services, 3G networks will be deployed in conjunction with other Broadband Wireless Access (BWA) technologies, to meet the growing demand for WiFi and WiMAX equipment.

MARKET DEMAND

By 2009, the cellular penetration rate in Russia was over 100% in seven regions: in the Moscow Licensed Area (MLA) the level of cellular penetration is over 151%, in St. Petersburg penetration is estimated at 133%, in the Krasnodar Territory, Kalmykiya, Astrakhan region, Samara region and the Khanty-Mansi Autonomous Area cellular penetration is over 100%. According to ACM Consulting (a management consulting and research agency specializing in telecommunications), the average level of cellular penetration in Russia reached 100% in August 2010. At the same time, the number of mobile subscribers in Russia reached 145 million, a 34 percent increase over 2009. According to the Ministry of Information Technologies and Communications, mobile operators' revenues reached $ 6.3 billion in the first 6 months of 2010.

On July 1 2010, amendment # 54 of the Federal Communications Law, known as O Svayzi, went into effect and cell phone users started paying for outbound calls only.

The current average revenue per user (ARPU) is $7, which is forcing mobile operators to look for new technology and, or add on services, as well as expanding into the regions and CIS countries to increase the revenues.

With the saturation of the cellular market and the demand for more services, the development of 3G networks in conjunction with other Broadband Wireless Access (BWA) technologies was selected by the Ministry of Information Technologies and Communications, as the best direction for the telecommunications industry in Russia.

In 2010, the Federal Agency for Networks started granting WiMAX licenses in the 2.5-2.7 GHz range. There are now several preWiMAX and WiMAX working networks, with major WiMax and preWiMax projects being launched in Moscow, St. Petersburg, Ekaterinburg, Chelyabinsk, Tyumen, Nizhnij Novgorod, and Samara.

Since 2009 the availability of Wi-Fi networks has shown steady growth across Russia, developing the fastest in Moscow, St. Petersburg and other large cities. There are now more than 650 hotspots in Russia and the number is expected to increase to 1000 by the end of 2010.

Market Data

The market for mobile network equipment is one of the biggest sectors of the telecommunications equipment market in Russia. Foreign producers from Europe (Nokia, Alcatel-Lucent, Sony Ericsson), Asia (Huawei, NEC, Avaya), and the US (Motorola, Nortel Networks, Cisco Systems) are the primary players. In 2009, sales of mobile network equipment reached $3.8 billion. Sales of mobile network equipment included mobile switching centers, base station controllers, base stations, radio relay links equipment, and multiplex equipment.

Three generations of mobile networks are currently represented in the Russian market (1st, 2nd and 2.5 generations). GSM (the standard) covers more than 90 % of the cellular market.

3G Technologies

The development of 3G technologies in Russia started in 1999, when the 3G Association (A3G) was founded by Russia's major mobile operators. Established to promote the development of third generation networks in Russia, in April2002, the Association created a working group to promote 3G services and to develop standards and a basic set of services for 3G networks. Currently the Association includes leading mobile operators, both domestic and foreign telecommunications companies, including U.S. companies, Motorola and Nortel Networks.

In 2001-2002, a pilot project of four trial 3G networks was initiated in Russia by MTS, VimpelCom (Beeline), North-West GSM (now MegaFon), and Sonik Duo (a 100% subsidiary of MegaFon), based on UMTS technology. Briefly, the four trial 3G networks (launched between October 2001 and April 2002) utilized foreign equipment to conduct coverage and capacity tests: 3G-3G, 3G-ISDN, 3G – GSM, 3G – PTSN interaction; tests for electro-magnetic compatibility/interference; Internet, multimedia, including web browsing, web-based games, Real Audio and Real Video data transmission, video conferencing within one city and long-distance, and video on demand. The equipment used in the projects (imported on temporary terms and supplied at no cost), was supplied by Alcatel, Ericsson, Siemens, and NEC. All four projects were successful, achieving their stated objectives, and were dismantled by the end of 2002. The Ministry of Communications and Information Technologies announced in 2002, after examining the test results of all four projects, that 3G was one of the best prospective developments for the telecom industry.

3G licenses -The launch of commercial 3G projects in Russia is planned for 2012. At present there has been only one 1.8-2.1 GHz license issued, granted in 2009 to Sky Link. According to the press, Sky Link is the largest CDMA operator in Russia. It was established in 2003 to consolidate regional NMT450 operators, and to form a federal IMT-MC-450 mobile network based on CDMA2000 1X technology in the 450 MHz spectrum. Sky Link has deployed networks in 21 regions and has licenses in 65 regions. Sky Link plans to modify their network based on CDMA2000 technology using Lucent Technologies' equipment. The company plans to develop a CDMA network in the 2.1 GHz spectrum (which is unusual for a CDMA standard). FYI – no tender was offered for this license. The press stated that Sky Link became a "fortunate owner of this license without any auction at all". According to Interfax Information Services Group, the Federal Telecommunications Agency Rossvyaz will announce a tender for 3G licenses in December 2010. The Ministry of Information Technologies and Communications reported that the State Radio Frequencies Commission announced their decision to "allocate radio frequency bands 1935-1980MHz, 2010-2025 MHz and 2125-2170MHz for the development of mobile IMT-2000/UMTS standard networks in Russia" on October 23, 2010. Three 3G licenses will be allocated through tender offerings in accordance with the commission's decision. It is possible that 3G licenses could be granted in early 2012.

The majority of Russian communications networks are based on GSM technology, the UMTS (18002100 MHz) frequency bands were chosen as the priority 3G standard for Russia. The A3G drafted the regulatory document, which is now being considered by the government of the Russian Federation. The number and specifications for 3G licenses are unknown at this time however, according to industry experts the licenses will be issued based on the following requirements:

 The licenses will be granted through tender offerings.
 The tender specifies that UMTS technology will be the standard in the 1.8-2.1 GHz range.
 The licenses will be valid for all of Russia; there will be no regional divisions.
 Three licenses will be issued.
 The license period is 25 years, with rights to extend.
 Each of three operators will be provided frequency band resources of not less than 35 MHz in

the 2GHz spectrum. The operator is to provide services not later than two years from the date of the frequency bands' assignment. The operators will cover the expenses for the conversion of frequency bands.

The big-3 Russian cellular operators -Mobile TeleSystems (MTS), VimpelCom and MegaFon -told Interfax that they are prepared to apply to bid on the 3G license tenders as soon as they are announced. All three companies will need to modify their networks from GSM to the UMTS standard. The implementation is expected to take about one year after licenses are issued. Commercial 3G networks are expected to start operating by the end of 2012.

The potential 3G subscribers' pool for the first half of 2012 is estimated at from 400,000 to 600,000. 3G operators expect profits of $50-70 million by the end of the first year. Further development will depend on the cost of voice services and what consumers are willing to pay.

Anticipating there will be four entrants (the big 3 and SkyLink) into the 3G market, the best prospects for

U.S. companies would be as suppliers of technology, equipment and solutions. MTS, VimpelCom, and MegaFon will focus on GSM/UMTS solutions and telecommunications equipment. Sky Link is expected to focus on CDMA2000 equipment. Regional providers are also interested in BWA development, and will be looking for WiMAX and WiFi equipment.

KEY SUPPLIERS

Major mobile operators and telecommunications companies prefer working with well known brand name products. Currently, the key suppliers in the telecommunications sector are Nokia, Ericsson, Motorola (in alliance with Huawei), NEC, Alcatel -Lucent, Nortel, ECI, Avaya, Cisco Systems, and Siemens.

These companies already have a strong presence in the Russian telecom market and are well positioned for the advance of 3G. According to our sources in Motorola, Motorola has recently built an alliance with Huawei to win 3G market power. Experts contend that the combination of low price Huawei equipment and high quality Motorola services is a winning combination.

Prospective buyers

The main players in the mobile network equipment market are the "big 3" operators, MTS, VimpelCom, and MegaFon.

Mobile Operators Market Share

MegaFon (3%), Smarts (2%), SibirTelecom (2%). **19%**

The "big 3" mobile operators represent 86% of the cellular market.

Vimpel Com 33%

Recently however, regional mobile operators have started to play a more active role in the industry. SMARTS, Uralsvyazinform, subsidiaries of Volgatelecom (Nizhegorodskaya sotovaya svyaz and other subsidiaries in the Volga Region), Sibirtelecom, and Dalsvyaz are all well positioned in the regions.

Other

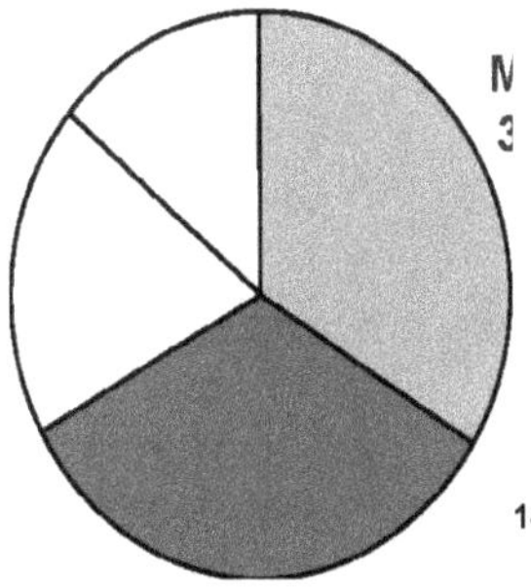

Among the leading mobile providers are
MTS (with a market share of 34%),
34% VimpelCom (33%), Megafon (19%), and others: UralSvyazInform (3%), Tele2

Top 10 Mobile Operators in Russia

Company Name MTS VimpelCom (Beeline) MegaFon Tele2 Uralsvyazinform	Market Share 34.20% 32.75% 18.93% 3.66% 2.92%	Subscribers-million 49.59 47.49 27.45 5.30 4.23
Novaya telefonnaya kompaniya (Vladivostok) SMARTS Sibirtelecom Motiv	0.47% 2.38% 1.86% 0.68%	0.68 3.45 2.70 0.99

Industry experts are predicting that WiMAX networks will be deployed by both regional mobile operators, and other telecommunication service providers. At least two operators, Sinterra and Komstar, have already received frequencies in 2.5-2.7 GHz range and have started developing WiMAX networks.

MARKET ENTRY

There are three basic ways to enter the market:

Via distributors – the majority of telecom equipment suppliers prefer working through local distributors. Some telecommunication equipment distributors have been in business for more than 7 years and have extensive experience and know-how. Their detailed knowledge of the market and many business connections enable them to find both a buyer and a seller for a wide range of equipment. They may operate on an exclusive basis or represent a number of companies, and may cover a large part of the country.

Through cooperative arrangements -developing one's expansion by cooperation with other telecom equipment vendors, who already have strong presence in the market, is a creative way to enter the market. The advantage for the vendors is being able to provide a wider range of equipment.

Work directly with operators and service providers -due to the way mobile businesses operate in Russia, working directly with mobile operators and other telecommunications service providers is another avenue for entering the market.

MARKET ISSUES AND OBSTACLES

Companies entering the market should be prepared to compete with major foreign telecommunications equipment manufacturers, especially Asian and European companies, who have a strong presence in the Russian market. Chinese manufacturers are pursuing opportunities, and their low prices remain their main competitive advantage.

Bureaucracy and lengthy decision-making processes are major problems that companies face in the Russian telecommunications market. Companies entering the market should be also aware of the complex regulatory environment. Laws governing the telecommunications sector, including the new communications law "O Svyazi", are open to varying degrees of interpretation. The law contains a huge number of requirements and procedures. Much work needs to be done to clarify and enhance the legislation governing the sector. The English version of the law is available on the website of the Ministry of Information Technologies and Communications of the Russian Federation at: http://english.minsvyaz.ru/docs/FED.doc.

Resources & Key Contacts

http://english.minsvyaz.ru/enter.shtml -the official website of the Ministry of Information Technologies and Communications of the Russian Federation.
English version of the website: yes

www.a3g.ru -the official website of The Third Generation Telecommunication Networks Operators Association (3G Association).
English version of the website: no

http://www.gsmrus.ru/en -the official website of the Association of GSM operators.
English version of the website: yes

http://www1.mtsgsm.com/ -the official website of MTS.
English version of the website: yes

www.vimpelcom.ru -the official website of VimpelCom (Beeline).
English version of the website: yes

http://eng.megafon.ru/ -the official website of MegaFon. English version of the website: yes

http://www.skylink.ru -the official website of Sky Link. English version of the website: no

RUSSIA: PACKAGING AND FOOD PROCESSING IN URALS

REGION.

1. General information.

Credit Suisse First Boston evaluates world's packaging market at $440 billion. The main markets are US (30% of world consumption), Western Europe and Asia. The share of Russia doesn't exceed 1,85% and equals to $8 billion. But according to the Russian Government's Statistic Committee growth rates of the market are more than 1012% annually, while Western market is growing by 45%. Packaging market in Russia becomes one of the most rapidly growing sectors of the economy. Experts predict increase in growth rates at least until 2010 and beyond until the market is fully saturated.

Development in Russia's packaging industry began with the country's economic reforms. During the years of the Soviet planned economy when there was a regular shortage of consumer goods and little market competition, the packaging industry was virtually nonexistent. After the disintegration of the Soviet Union and the beginning of market reforms, Russia was flooded with foreign packaged goods, which favorably differed from domestic products. While the local packaging industry suffered a dramatic shortage of basic materials for manufacturing quality packaging and labels, the attractive packaging and labeling of foreign goods created new expectations from Russian consumers, making these goods more competitive in the domestic market. Growing consumer welfare has resulted in a growing demand for packaged goods and a corresponding increase in sales of packaged goods.

Complete satisfaction of consumer demand for all main types of food products depends on the need for import of foreign products and for strengthening domestic products' positions. Increase in the competitiveness of domestic products continues to be one of the most important challenges in the development of the Russian food processing industry.

Growth in Russia's food industry has created favorable conditions for development of the packaging sector. It has also stimulated rapid growth in the domestic packaging industry. During recent years, the growth rate in this sector was much higher than the country's average economic growth. Moreover, rates of growth of packaging for consumer goods and food industry have higher rates than the market's average. The rapid growth of the packaging industry in Russia is a result of rapid growth in the overall variety and amount of goods available. There are changes in distribution practices and consumption patterns. New developments in retail trade infrastructure are proliferating. The acknowledgment of packaging as an important tool for preservation and safety of goods during transit and storage is increasing. The companies acknowledge the importance of packaging and labeling in products' marketing. Russian consumers become closer to European consumption culture, they consume more natural products with fastcooked products and concentrate their attention more on ecology.

The dynamics of the market are very attractive for both, local players and foreign companies. World's leaders, such as Alcan, Stora Enso, SCA, TetraPak, Amcor, Rexam, Sisecam, and OwensIllinois announced new projects in Russia. In general foreign companies have influenced the development of the packaging market in Russia. Companies such as Mars, Cadburry, BAT, Unilever, Nestle entered the market in the mid-90s and adopted western quality standards. Many of these companies are already ordering packaging in Russia, but domestic producers are often not able to meet their high standard requirements. There are still niches in the Russian market that are far from saturation and have great prospects for growth. US suppliers with highly sophisticated, accurate and reliable equipment have good market potential.

According to the evaluation of PRADO Marketing, European suppliers of packaging equipment dominate the market with 90% share. Among the leaders are Poland, Germany and Ukraine. Ukraine is listed here mainly because it serves as a corridor between Europe and Russia. In 2009 U.S. imports averaged 5.3% of all imports in the packaging market. As for the market of food processing equipment Germany and Italy have the strongest positions in Russia, they held 60% and 15% of the import respectively, while the market share of U.S. exporters is insignificant and is accounted for about 2% of the imports. U.S. equipment suppliers appear to be less willing to invest the time and the effort to sell to the Russian market through incountry representation or trade shows. However industry specialists believe that the market share for U.S. equipment could increase if U.S. companies expressed the same level of interest in entering the market as their European competitors do.

Furthermore, the market conditions have become more favorable for American goods as the dollar/ruble exchange continues to decrease. Consequently more Russian companies are showing interest in American products. Russian food processing companies are seeking a wide variety of equipment and materials including bakery, meat and poultry, milk, confectionery production, hard liquor, soft drinks bottling and packaging, fruit and vegetable processing and packaging, and regular and refrigeration storage facilities for food products.

A large number of international and federal retail chains entered the regional Urals market. Auchan, Metro, Obi, Ikea and others stimulated development of the packaging market. The role of the packaging materials is changing significantly and becomes an active element of marketing communications between manufacturers and customers.

Regional packaging enterprises are replacing their equipment with newer technology. The rapidly growing market lacks stateoftheart expensive machines as well as cheap and used equipment to meet the market needs.

FOOD INDUSTRY IN THE URALS REGIONS

2/1. Sverdlovsk Region

The food industry accounts for 6.5% of the total industrial output and is represented by a solid number of companies. The largest enterprises include: OAO Kalina Concern, OAO Fat Work, OAO Confectionary Association SladCo, OOO Pepsi International Bottlers (Yekaterinburg), OOO Meat Factory Yekaterinburgsky, MUP Yekaterinburg Bakery, OAO Yekaterinburg Flour Mill, OGUP Irbit Dairy, and OAO Yekaterinburg Vinshampankombinat.

As for the agricultural sector, demand in the Sverdlovsk Region for vegetables, potatoes, and poultry is fully covered by local production. Local output covers 70% of the region's dairy product consumption, 55% of meat, and 25% of grain. One of the top priority agricultural areas is poultry, with the Region accounting for some 13% of Russia's total poultry output.

One of the priorities in the economic growth projections of Sverdlovsk oblast is the structural reorganization of the agro industrial complex by increasing the investment in hightech and competitive enterprises.

2/2. Tyumen Region.

Because of the extreme climatic conditions and far northern location of the region farmland occupies only 3% of its territory. More favorable conditions in the southern districts allow the cultivation of grain, potatoes, vegetables, and feed crops. Livestock farms raise cattle, pigs, sheep, goats, horses, and poultry. More than 84% of the region's agricultural products are produced here.

Agricultural organizations in the autonomous districts specialize in the production of milk, eggs, and greenhouse vegetables. Fishing and reindeer herding are traditional occupations of the native people.

Per capita production is equal to 27 kg of meat (fattened beef and poultry), 163 kg of milk, and 326 eggs. Tyumen region leads the other regions of the Ural Federal District in per capita egg production.

The Region has 3.4 million hectares of agricultural lands. Annual gross output of grain ranges from 1.1 million to 1.6 million tons, vegetables – from 100,000 to 160,000 tons, and potatos – from 400,000 to

600,000 tons. Extensive hayfield and pasture areas provide favorable conditions for dairy and beef husbandry. The 2009 output of animal and poultry meat (live weight) was 141,000 tons, milk – 536,400 tons, and eggs – 1,252 million.

The agroindustrial sector, especially livestock breeding for meat, is developing very successfully in the region, but the industry lacks modern equipment. This fact explains the trend in the import by the Region, which include industrial equipment (65% of total imports), transportation vehicles, and agricultural equipment.

Chelyabinsk region.

Chelyabinsk Region is one of the major industrial regions of Russia. It ranks twelfth for the gross regional product and sixth for the industrial output. The Region possesses good scientific, labor, production, and natural resource potentials. It boasts successful metal, machine engineering, metal processing, fuel and energy, construction, and agricultural sectors. Agricultural production makes up only about 5% of the gross regional product, but the government is taking actions to increase this figure. One of the government's major economic growth projections is implemented in Agricultural sector and is aimed on raising productivity through implementation of energy saving technologies, deployment of new high yield crops and soil fertilizers, improvement of bloodstock, and better professional training for managers in the agricultural enterprises.

Tillage accounts for 43.9% of the output in the agricultural sector. Cattle breeding accounts for 56.1%. A total of 1,890,300 hectares were under tillage in 2009 and 823,100 tons of crops were harvested. In cattle breeding, meat production totaled 172,300 tons (live weight), milk – 605,000 tons, and eggs – 1,199,100 in 2009.

Also in 2009 Chelyabinsk enterprises involved in food sector, produced 183,500 tons of bread and bakery products, 190,200 tons of pasta products, 42,800 tons of confectionery, 626,100 tons of flour, and 27,900 tons of cereals. Meat and dairy product output increased by 8.9%.

In 2010 British Rexam, one of the world's top five consumer packaging companies, decided to build a plant to produce aluminum cans in the Argayash district of the region. The plant, which is being built at a cost of $73 million, will be operational in 2008 and will be equipped with a line to produce 800 million cans a year with a volume of 0.33 and 0.5 liters.

KhantyMansiysky Autonomous District – Yugra

Milk and meat cattle breeding

17 agricultural producers and 62 agricultural enterprises and farms are engaged in the milk and meat cattle breeding in the Okrug.

The total cattle breeding of all categories of farms comprises over 11 ths. heads, including 5.5 ths. cows.

Gross milk production amounts to 19.9 tons of milk, 5.5 tons of meat. Milk yield per 1 forage cow over the agricultural producers amounted to 3391 kg of milk. Most of the suburban farms have highgrade dairy herd, modern milk equipment, manufactories for meat processing. The processed milk is delivered to the social enterprises in the amount of 4090%. The assortment of the produced production consists of over 20 types.

Among the agro industrial enterprises and farms in the structure of the produced meat the quota of the cattlebreeding makes over 30%.

Swinebreeding

1 5 agricultural enterprises and over 70 agricultural enterprises and private farms are engaged in swine-breeding. The total swine number made 14805 heads on January 1, 2010.

Urban farms former economies of the industrial enterprises are engaged in swinebreeding. For the last years increase of the swine livestock is observed in the farms of the Okrug.

In the structure of meat production pork makes nearly 50%.

Poultry husbandry

On January 1, 2010 the total number of poultry of all kinds of farms comprised 148775 head. In 2009 37578 ths. eggs and 3695 centners of poultry were produced at the enterprises of all kinds. On the average 271 eggs were received from one henlayer over the Okrug.

Fish branch Over 160 enterprises of different kinds of property are engaged in fishing and fish-processing, including 20 fishing industry enterprises, 15 agricultural enterprises, over 125 national, tribal communities and businessmen without legal person formation.

Fish taking accounted for 8181 tons in the Okrug in 2009 or 115.1% to the level of 2009. 9732 tons of fish production were produced, it is by 1582 tons more than in the previous year.

2/5. YamaloNenetsky Autonomous District (Yamal)

Owing to the severe climate, agriculture in the region is limited to reindeer herding, hunting, fishing, and fur farming; reindeer herding accounts for 92.2% of all agricultural production. These sectors are the main occupations of the local native population, who are experiencing difficulty in the transition to market economy. However, in recent years, several dozen private farms and reindeerherding, furfarming, and hunting businesses have been registered in the area. The livestock farms are located in the Ob valley. At present, 13 state farms and new organizations and 34 private farms are involved in agriculture in the autonomous area. Projects are being worked out to set up companies to prepare raw fur materials from reindeer skins, rebuild the Salekhard Fish Canning Plant, and so on. Vacuumpacked reindeer and fish products and native craft items have received high marks from consumers at several AllRussian exhibitions and are in great demand.

The region is also known as a “delicious fish shop of Russia”. The rivers across the District have some one-third of the world’s total reserves of valuable whitefish species.

In 2009, the YamaloNenetsky Autonomous District produced 19,600 tons bread and bakery products.

Kurgan Region

The Kurgan Region ranks 18th in Russia for per capita grains and beans production, 14th for milk production, 12th for vegetables production, and 30th for meat, poultry, and potatoes production. The food industry is well developed here, with meatpacking plants, mills, creameries, and powderedmilk factories.

Metal processing, food and beverages together with machine engineering and metal processing account for a combined 85.4% of the Region's industrial output.

OAO Shadrinsk Canning Dairy Plant that is known allover Russia is the largest food and beverages company in the Kurgan Region, supplying the whole region with diary products.

In general, the agricultural sector is mainly focused on tillage (spring and winter wheat, fall rye, barley, and buckwheat), potatoes, vegetables, dairy breeding, beef farming, and pig and poultry breeding.

The Kurgan Region has a total land area of 7.1 million hectares: 3.9 million hectares (55%) of agricultural lands including 2.5 million hectares of arable lands and 1.8 million hectares (25%) of forests.

In 2009 Kurgan region produced: 5,900 tons of meat, 3,900 tons of sausages, 1,100 tons of butter, 62,100 tons of whole milk, 178,100 tons of flour, and 311,000 deciliters of vodka and liquors. The goods that were exported from the region include dairy products, edible fruit, and alcoholic and nonalcoholic beverages (16.3%of the region's total export). While main imports of the region, where food and food feedstock was accounted at 41% included vegetables and cereals.

Government officials of Kurgan region point out food processing and packaging industries as most attractive sectors for investment. That is development of high quality cereal production and livestock breeding, creation of agricultural companies for the production, procurement, processing, storage, and sale of agricultural products and food, and development of agriculture machinery maintenance infrastructure.

Republic of Bashkortostan.

Agricultural complex plays special role in Bashkortostan's life, where practically every third citizen lives in countryside. By the volume of agricultural production the Republic is found in the Top 3 of Russian regions, it holds the third place in gross grain harvest, the second in meat production and the first in potato and milk production.

Various forms of property and management are developing in Bashkir rural area, more than one thousand large and midscaled agricultural enterprises and about five thousands farms.

Bashkortostan practically completely supplies itself with grain and almost 6090% of foods in local shops are produced in the Republic. In 2009 the output of Republican agriculture was equal to 57,2 billion rubles and exceeded the level of 2009 by 1,6%. Production growth is anticipated by increase of gross harvests of agricultural cultures and cattlebreeding volumes on farms and in individual sector. The share of agricultural enterprises in production is equal to 34,5%, population 61,3% and farms 4,2%.

Harvest campaign2009 is completed in the Republic and 3.5 million tons of grain and oilbearing crops and 1.2 million tons of sugar beet have been harvested. Bashkortostan Republic is fully provided with highquality agricultural production of its own and Bashkir industry is supplied with raw material.

Bashkortostan is well known for its refinery, petrochemical, chemical, metal, and machine engineering enterprises, as well as for its modern agro industrial sector.

2/8. Republic of Udmurtia

The Republic's economy is multifaceted. Its leading sectors are machine engineering and metal processing, metals, oil, forestry and timber as well as beef stock and dairy farming, all of which offer a strong potential for cooperation. Especially because of the Republic's temperate climate and fertile soils there are great prospects to develop agro industrial sector

According to the Udmurtia Agricultural Ministry arable lands cover a total area of 1,865,100 hectares. The Republic grows fodder grain, potatoes, vegetables, and fiber flax. Cattle breeding accounts for 57.1% of the total agricultural output.

Main types of the Republic's agricultural output in 2009 included. 490,300 tons of grain, 576,800 tons of potatoes, 173,000 tons of vegetables, 4,900 tons of flax fiber, 605,800 tons of milk, and 604.6 million eggs.

The climate and nature of the Udmurtia Republic allow it to successfully develop multibranch agriculture, produce foodstuffs and agricultural raw materials for processing. Local topsoil is rather diverse but most of the arable lands are turf and podsoil.

The main agrarian crops grown in the republic are grain forage, potatoes and other vegetables, flaxfiber and forage grasses.

The production branch of agriculture is cattlebreeding. Its share in the gross volume of agricultural production amounts to 68%.

The food industry is represented by bakeries and macaroni plants, 8 meatpacking plants, 10 milk, butter and cheese factories, 15 factories producing liquor, soft drinks, beer, starch and syrup.

Perm territory*

One of the leading industries of Perm region are forestry and agriculture. These industries produce over 27% of GRP and employ around 30% of the economically active population.

Agriculture in the Region is represented by both tillage including winter rye, spring wheat, oats, buckwheat, long flax, potatoes, and vegetables, and meat and dairy cattle farming. Agricultural output was down 6.4% yearonyear in 2009.

In 2009 Food industry output of bread and bakery products totaled 151,800 tons, margarine products – 23,300 tons, butter – 3,724,000 tons, and whole milk – 192,400 tons.

As for The KomiPermyatsky Autonomous District* the leading industries are forestry, timber, and food and beverages, which account for 88% of the District's overall industrial production.

The food industry's share of total GRP is 31.8%. Food processing is mainly concentrated in the District's capital – Kudymkar. The bulk of local output (meat processing, dairy, and bakeries) is consumed within the District.

Agriculture is dominated by cattle breeding, mainly meatanddairy. Rye, oats, barley, soft wheat, potatoes, and vegetables are cultivated in the District.

In 2009 meat production was 1,200 tons, sausage – 1,100 tons, milk – 1,100 tons, butter – 600 tons, sour cream – 600 tons, and nonalcoholic beverages – 162,500 deciliters.

As for agricultural output in 2009, it was 25,300 tons of grain, 101,200 tons of potatoes, and 37,600 tons of vegetables.

** The Perm Territory was established on December 1, 2009, when two regions of Russia—the Perm Region* *and the KomiPermyatsky Autonomous District —united in accordance with the results of the referendum, which had taken place on December 7, 2003.*

USEFUL CONTACTS:

Sverdlovsk oblast:

Eduard Ergartovich Rossel, Governor Phone: (343) 370 5473 Fax: (343) 217 8777

Ministry of International and External Economic Relations of the Sverdlovsk Region 21/23, ul. Gorkogo, Yekaterinburg, Sverdlovsk Region, 620031 Phone: (343) 217 8672 Fax: (343) 217 8607

http://mvs.midural.ru/index/ru

Ministry of Agriculture of the Sverdlovsk Region 60, Rosi Luxemburg Street, Yekaterinburg, Sverdlovsk Region, 620026 Phone: (343) 3777800 Fax: (343) 3777800 Email: minsel@intermail.ru Website: http://www.midural.ru/selhoz/index.htm

Chelyabinsk

Petr Ivanovich Sumin, Governor of Chelyabinsk oblast 27, Cvillinga, Chelyabinsk, 454089 Phone: (351) 263-9241 Fax: (351) 2631283 Email: gubernator@chel.surnet.ru Website: http://www.uralchel.ru

KhantyMansiysky Autonomous District

Valery Timofeevich Bobylov, Acting Deputy Chairman of the Government of for the Agro Industrial Sector and Forestry.
Phone: (34671)92 028, 92 161
Fax: (34671) 92 028

YamaloNenetsky Autonomous District

Alexander Vasilievich Filipenko, Governor Email: FilipenkoAV@admhmao.ru

Website: http://www.admhmao.ru/governer/Guber_v/index.htm

Alexander Ivanovich Mazharov, Chief of the International and Interregional Relations.
Phone: (34922) 45 165, 45 167
Website: http://www.admhmao.ru

Kurgan Region

Nikolai Pavlovich Loginov, First Deputy Governor of the Region, Director of the Agriculture Department Phone: (3522) 43 3265 Fax: (3522)43 1520 Email: dsh@pp.kurgan.ru

Republic of Bashkortostan

Grigory Vasilievich Gorobec, Minister of Agriculture. 106, Pushkina Street, Ufa, 450008 Phone: (3472) 2346-45 Fax:(3472) 238766 Email:pochta@mshp.ufanet.ru Website: http://www.bashkortostan.ru

Boris Grigoryevich Kolbin, Minister of External Relations and Trade of the Republic of Bashkortostan

Phone: (3472) 79 9625 Fax: (3472) 79 9606 Email: mfrt@baskortostan.ru

Republic of Udmurtia

Nikolai Ivanovich Sobin, Minister of Agriculture and Food of the Republic of Udmurtia Phone: (3412) 70 7675, 78 6377 Fax: (3412) 78 7773 Email: msx@msx.udmnet.ru; http://www.msx.udmnet.ru

Perm territory

Mikhail Vyacheslavovich Antonov, Deputy Governor of the Perm Territory (ensures pursuing of the unified state policy in industry and nature resources, applied science, as well as state agriculture and food policy) Phone: (3422) 17 7164 Fax: (3422) 35 1667

For more information on Urals region, visit BISNIS online at

www.bisnis.doc.gov/bisnis/country/ural.cfm

BROADBAND MARKET

The rapid growth of the broadband market, especially for residential use, offers a wide range of opportunities for U.S. equipment and software suppliers. The best sales prospects are highspeed, broadband technologies, multiservice and multimedia solutions, including xDSL, Ethernet, BWA, and digital equipment. Currently, Ethernet and ADSL networks dominate the Russian broadband market, and the deployment of broadband wireless access networks via WiMAX also offers good opportunities for interested companies.

MARKET DEMAND

The Russian telecommunications market has continued to demonstrate notable growth driven by the Russian economy's consistent strong economic performance; the need to upgrade the country's telecommunications infrastructure; and the continued interest of investors in the telecommunications market. In 2009, the Russian telecommunications market was $23.9 billion, while in 2010, the market size was estimated at $28 billion. The annual growth of the sector continues at 2025% annually.

In the telecommunications sector, the broadband access sub sector is the best prospect for U.S. companies. The huge demand for Internet access is the stimulus for the growth of the sub sector. Since broadband technologies allow for the provision of a wide range of services including VoIP, IPTV, WiFi / WiMAX, etc., major telecom operators are actively developing this sub sector. The Russian market for broadband access now resembles the cellular market of five to seven years ago when the sector experienced tremendous growth. According to JeanPierre Vandromme, Chief Executive Officer of Golden Telecom, in four years the penetration level of broadband access in Russia will reach 5060%, approaching the average penetration level in Europe.

According to ComNews Publishing Group, the volume of the Russian broadband access market amounted to $458 million in the first half of 2010, and is expected to reach $1 billion by the end of the year. According to J'son&Partners (a consulting and research company specializing in telecommunications) in mid 2010, 1.8 million Russian households had broadband access to the Internet via ADSL, Ethernet or DOCSIS networks, and the demand is growing even faster than expected. According to market experts, 2.5 million households were using broadband services by the end of 2010. By 2008, the number of households using broadband is expected to exceed 6 million. According to LAN (a Russian telecom periodical) in 2010, the growth of the Moscow region broadband market was estimated at 50% and the regional broadband market almost doubled. The amount of broadband subscribers in 2009 grew by 200% in Moscow and 320% in the regions.

Residential broadband accounts for 30% of the market, with an estimated volume of $380 million, which is expected to reach $500 million in 2012. Although the availability of broadband access in the regions is lagging behind that of the Moscow region, demand remains strong and is expected to continue it's rapid growth in many of the Russian regions in 2012. With a consequent decrease in the Moscow market share from 55% to 35% over the next two years.

The corporate broadband market is well developed. Although 5.5 million Russians use broadband access services regularly, over 80% of them use these services at work, not at home. Therefore residential broadband is where the greatest potential for U.S. companies lies for providers, integrators, and equipment producers.

MARKET DATA

The distribution of broadband connections remains extremely unequal. According to J'son&Partners, Moscow occupies 45% of the broadband connections, the Moscow region another 10% of total connections; St. Petersburg 5%, and the balance of all connections (40%) are used by the regions. According to market experts, the broadband penetration in Moscow is currently 25% and will reach 50% by 2009. Two thirds of all new connections are executed in the regions, where the demand for broadband access services remains highest.

In 2009, Comstar, one of the leading telecom providers in Russia launched the STREAM project, which initiated the boom in the broadband industry. STREAM is an Internet access provider using ADSL technology, becoming the market leader in Moscow after only two years of operation.

BROADBAND TECHNOLOGIES

The market for broadband access in Russia is characterized by a strong competition of technologies. Since the technology in the regions is highly differentiated, the selection of the technology is based on the telecom infrastructure in place. At present, ADSL and Ethernet dominate, representing 90% of the market. In addition, many new services and solutions (using converging technologies) are being introduced.

Ethernet – Ethernet is very prominent in the national broadband market. All major global software suppliers support this technology. Ethernet revenues are 65% of the market.

ADSL ADSL increased 27% to 36% last year and is expected to continue showing strong growth in 2012. A contributing factor to this growth is due to the entry of Svyazinvest (the largest telecom holding company with subsidiaries in many of the regions); tariff restructuring and better territory coverage in comparison to Ethernet. The competition between ADSL and Ethernet will increase, especially in the larger cities where better telephone networks are available. In the first half of 2010, provider revenue from ADSL services amounted to $102 million, 50% higher than a year ago, or 22% of the market share. The structure of the ADSL market is similar in most regions of the country: within each region there is a strong ADSL operator who dominates. St. Petersburg is the only exception, where there are three big players leading the market (Web Plus, PeterStar, and North West Telecom).

Cable TV This category includes broadband access via DOCSIS and HFC (Hybrid FiberCoaxial) technologies. Cable TV networks are being actively developed and are showing steady growth, although not significant as yet, (estimated at 57%). Currently operators begin by providing payTV services and then expanding their services range.

BWA The market for broadband wireless access (BWA) is primarily represented by two technologies: WiMAx and WiFi. Although the BWA segment is comparatively low (7 to 9%), it is one of the most promising sub sectors for broadband in Russia.

WiMAX There are several preWiMAX and WiMAX operating networks in Russia, with major projects being launched in Moscow, St. Petersburg, Ekaterinburg, Chelyabinsk, Tyumen, Nizhnij Novgorod, and Samara. Moreover, industry experts expect regional mobile operators and other telecommunication service providers to actively develop *WiMAX* networks. The lack of available frequencies is the primary obstacle to *WiMAX* network development. At present, 70% of the 2.52.7 GHz frequency band is occupied by special services leaving little room for growth. Nevertheless, at least two operators, Sinterra and Comstar have already received licenses and started deploying *WiMAX* networks.

WiFi Since 2009 the availability of WiFi networks has shown steady growth across Russia, developing fastest in Moscow, St. Petersburg and other large cities. There are now more than 650 hotspots in Russia with an estimated 1000 by the end of 2010.

KEY SUPPLIERS

Major telecommunications providers and integrators prefer working with wellknown brand name products. Currently, the key suppliers in the broadband sector are (listed in alphabetical order) Aperto Networks, Cisco Systems, Huawei, Lucent, Motorola, Nortel, Siemens, and WiLAN. These companies already have a strong presence in the Russian telecom market.

National manufacturers are also well positioned for the advance of the broadband market. Such companies as Zelax, Nateks, NSG, Lightcom and others are well positioned in the market.

PROSPECTIVE BUYERS

In 2010, about 1,200 companies provided broadband services in Russia. The top 20 providers account for 60% of the market share. The key players (which are at the same time key consumers of related equipment and software) can be divided into two groups:

1. **Established operators** This group includes Svyazinvest; MGTS (Moscow city telephone network); telecom companies under the Ministry of Telecommunications of the Tatarstan Republic; Bashinformsvyaz; Dasgsvyazinform, Rossvyazinform of the Tyva Republic; and Sakhatelecom of Sakha Republic. These networks cover the whole of Russia and make up over 90% of the country's capacity. Svyazinvest's subsidiaries have licenses for the provision of local, domestic longdistance and international telephone services, data transmission, etc. They also provide ISDN services, wireless subscriber access and mobile services. Regional operators own the core telecom infrastructure providing services to all groups of the population. Their activity is regulated by federal authorities.

Top 4 Broadband Access Providers in Moscow

Company Name	Market Share	Technology	Subscribers, thousands
Comstar-OTS/STREAM	34%	ADSL	359,8
Corbina Telecom	9.5%	Ethernet	100
Comcor-TV/Akado	9.3%	Cable TV	98
Central Telegraph/QWERTY	7%	Ethernet	75

2. **Independent telecom services providers** This group includes independent fixedline, mobile and other telecom services providers.

The strong positions of the established operators (MGTS, Rostelecom, etc.) are based on their existing infrastructure and interregional coverage. Though the fixedline market is still dominated by established operators, independent operators are starting to gain position. New operators have already conquered 56% of the local and long distance market in Moscow. At present, four private companies hold 60% of the Moscow broadband access market: ComstarOTS (STREAM), Corbina

MARKET ENTRY

There are three basic ways to enter the market:

- Via distributors – The majority of telecom equipment suppliers prefer working through local distributors. Some telecommunication equipment distributors have been in business for more than 8 years and have extensive experience and knowhow. Their detailed knowledge of the market and many business connections enable them to find both a buyer and a seller for a wide range of equipment. They may operate on an exclusive basis or represent a number of companies, and may cover a large part of the country.
- Through cooperative arrangements – Expanding by cooperating with other telecom equipment vendors, who already have a strong presence in the market, is a creative way to enter the market. The advantage for the vendors is being able to provide a wider range of equipment.
- Work directly with operators and service providers – Major telecom service providers often prefer working with equipment manufacturers directly, which facilitates meeting their complex needs more efficiently.

MARKET ISSUES AND OBSTACLES

Companies entering the market should be prepared to compete with major foreign and local telecommunications equipment manufacturers, who have a strong presence in the Russian market.

Companies entering the market should also be aware of the complex regulatory environment. Bureaucracy and lengthy decisionmaking processes are major problems in the Russian telecommunications market. Laws governing the telecommunications sector, including the new communications law "O Svyazi", are open to varying degrees of interpretation. The law contains a huge number of requirements and procedures, and much work needs to be done to clarify and enhance the legislation governing the sector. The English version of the law is available on the website of the Ministry of Information Technologies and Communications of the Russian Federation at: http://english.minsvyaz.ru/docs/FED.doc.

RESOURCES & KEY CONTACTS

http://minsvyaz.ru/ the official website of the Ministry of Information Technologies and Communications of the Russian Federation.
English version of the website: yes

http://www.svyazinvest.ru/ the official website of SvyazInvest. English version of the website: yes
http://en.json.ru/ the official website of J'son&Partners. English version of the website: yes

HEALTHCARE EQUIPMENT MARKET

On January 1, 2010, the Russian government launched a number of reforms to address critical problems in their health care system. The reforms started with an implementation of the Federal Drug Reimbursement Program known as Additional Drug Supply Program (DLO) for select categories of the population. President Putin has proclaimed health care reform as one of four national priority projects, which represented significant increases in public spending (along with projects focused on education, agriculture and housing). These reforms together represent an important breakthrough in the development of the health care system and offer longer-term opportunities for advanced U.S. drugs, medical equipment and services. While this report is focused broadly on the effects of the reforms, it pays special attention to the positive impact the reforms are having on the Russian market for U.S. medical equipment and supplies.

THE HEALTHCARE SYSTEM

Until 2009, health care occupied a relatively low position among the government's priorities. The promise of free health care for all citizens that was stipulated in article 41 of Russia's Constitution was in name only. Generally, health care system was inefficient and very expensive, precluding investment into its modernization and development. Even today, total health care spending in Russia at all levels, according to different estimates, is now only about 4 percent of the GDP in comparison to 9-11 percent in developed countries. The World Health Organization said that in 2003, the state spent $167on health care for every Russian citizen. The United States spent $5,711 per capita; Germany, $3,204; and France, $2,981. The average Russian citizen's out-of-pocket expenses for pharmaceuticals, medical devices and services are equally low: from 9 to 12 times lower than in Western countries. Recently published statistics show that insufficient health care funding in the country has led to high mortality rates and low average life expectancy: 59.1 years for men and 72.5 for women. The country's population has been sliding by 700,000 annually in the past decade: from 150 million in the early nineties to about 142 million today. Russian men live 15-19 years less than men in leading European countries, USA and Japan. For Russian women the difference is 7-13 years. Forty years ago, the difference was only 2-3 years.

It is currently estimated that only one fifth of the Russian population of 142.4 million has access to quality health care. This is especially problematic since Russia's health care network is already enormous, including 9,663 inpatient hospitals, 16,615 outpatient polyclinics, and 3,252 emergency stations. Further, Russia has 608,588 doctors and 1,388,349 paramedics. The majority of hospitals and polyclinics are public and belong to federal, regional or local governments. There is also a number of so-called agency health care establishments to serve specific large governmental entities such as the Ministry of Transportation, Ministry of Economic Development and Trade, Ministry of Defense, etc.

Though Russia does possess significant numbers of highly qualified doctors and health care professionals, medical equipment in the majority of clinics and hospitals is archaic and hygienic conditions do not even meet domestic standards, let alone established Western practices. Other chronic problems of the Russian health care system include undeveloped health care infrastructure, low wages and inadequate training for physicians and paramedics, especially in the primary-care segment, lack of attention to preventive care and resulting unnecessary shift to hospital-based care.

The country lacks clear-cut standards of medical assistance to citizens, which is guaranteed and paid for by the state. Mandatory medical care insurance and public programs can only support a small portion of medical services as well as related drugs and medical supplies. In reality, only a very limited number of medical procedures and operations are provided free of charge. Usually patients have to pay for medical devices used during surgeries and operations themselves officially, based on prices set up by each hospital. Patients continue the practice of paying for formally free surgeries and procedures unofficially, with the proceeds going directly to the doctors. Moreover, the majority of medicines and supplies necessary for in-patient treatment have to be paid for by patients out of their pockets. As for high-tech treatments, only a small percentage of the population gets them for free. Long lines for free high-end operations and procedures preclude patients from having them in a timely manner and diminish their effects for patients. Therefore, those who can afford such operations pay for them to speed up the process.

It has become obvious that the imbalances in the health care system are very deep rooted; the current system of mandatory medical insurance has failed to raise health care standards. State guarantees for free medical health care for citizens is now little more than rhetoric; and that unless significant efforts were undertaken to expedite reforms, mortality rates would increase while life expectancy would continue to diminish.

HEALTH CARE FUNDING, REIMBURSEMENT AND MEDICAL INSURANCE

At the moment, the two major sources of public health care funding - mandatory medical insurance funds (30 percent) and spending supported by federal and regional budgets (70 percent) do not cover all healthcare expenses. As a result, one-fifth of overall (public and private) health care spending is covered out of patients' pockets. Voluntary health care insurance programs account for approximately one third of the total private health care expenditures. According to long-term reform plans, the county will move to a one-source funding model when mandatory medical insurance funds will serve as the only source of public health care funding, providing transparency and control over cash flow within the system.

At the moment the medical insurance market in general is underdeveloped. There are a few private insurance companies that have access to servicing public mandatory medical insurance funds, such as

Maks-M, Rosno, Spasskiye Vorota, and Gasprommedstrakh. However this market segment cannot be characterized as open. The level of competition is restricted due to the lack of appropriate funds and regulations, high level of centralization and corruption. Most of private insurance companies predominantly work with private money through voluntary medical insurance programs. The basic principals of insurance-based health care system – the healthy pays for the sick and a patient has a right to choose a health care provider – are practically not working.

Implementation of DLO Program has been a first step to establishing a healthcare insurance system covering purchases of drugs and providing access to quality medicines. DLO is only accessible for various groups of disabled (pensioners and children with disabilities, disabled soldiers, invalids from trauma at work, etc.). The participants of DLO received a right to choose between getting 450 rubles in monetary compensation or giving it up and becoming part of the DLO program and thus getting access to free drugs which they needed. In fact, the cost of drugs (which a significant portion of invalids get for free under DLO) significantly exceeds the 450 rubles. There are about 14 million invalids and other categories of population on the federal level that are eligible for participation in DLO, yet only about half of them participated in the program in 2009. There are also about 35 million disabled people who receive subsidies for drugs from local budgets. Due to the DLO Program about $1.4 billion of federal budget money was pumped into the country's pharmaceutical market (planned allocations for the Program were $1.8 billion). The government intended to spend an additional $ 1.1 billion on DLO in 2010 and $1.5 in 2012.

Despite all positive effects of DLO program on the size of the Russian pharmaceutical market (in 2010 it increased by 35 percent mostly as a result of DLO), it only covers a portion of population and pertains primarily to drug supply. However the issue of provision of medical devices and services to population is untouched by this system and urgently needs reforming. According to Nelli Naigovzina, Deputy Head of the Expert Department of the Administration of the President and member of the Presidential Multi-Agency Task Force on the National Priority Project "Health", the mandatory health care insurance system from its very creation in early 1990s had some fundamental flaws. The major drawbacks are as follows. The unified social tax, which is the main source of financing of the mandatory health care insurance, is too low to meet the demands and scale of the system. Another major obstacle is lack of clear-cut standards for medical assistance guaranteed by the state. In other words, there is no unified description of basic package of medical services, which are provided by the government free of charge to each citizen. According Ms. Naigovzina, the main goal is to develop detailed and concrete standards for medical assistance guaranteed by the state. At the moment it is very difficult to tell what the government guarantees in terms of medical assistance are. Ordinary people have little guidance and do not understand for what type of assistance they should pay and to what extent their participation in sharing costs should be.

Business community and specifically insurance companies and private clinics offer their view on the reform in health care insurance. One of such proposals is as follows. The government together with the doctors' community and the public develops a basic package of medical services guaranteed by the state for every citizen. The cost of the basic package is the same for everybody. This basic package is financed through health care social tax on income of the working population. For low-income citizens, children and non-working pensioners the basic health package is financed out of the state budget funds. All the collections are channeled to one insurance fund and from there transferred to public and private insurance companies. Under such a system, the insurance companies become a real driving force of the health care system. They control the transfer of health care funds within the system, are responsible for selecting clinics and hospitals of different specialization, which are able to provide a wide range of services to patients. Thus, the basic principal of the system is that a patient has a right to choose a medical service provider and insurance company at his/her discretion.

The new system is supposed to encourage competition among insurance companies in order to attract the maximum number of patients, it will stimulate them to work with the clinics and hospitals which provide the best service. They will further strictly control the doctors and invest their own funds in improving the clinics and hospitals they work with. Insurance companies will also be able to provide additional services to patients at a fee, which the patients will bear themselves or with support of their employers. As a result, voluntary insurance costs can be significantly reduced.

Despite significant attractiveness of the above proposals, international practices show that health care insurance systems based on dominant control of insurance companies over the entire process lead to many flaws and imbalances, economical factors start to outweigh effective medical treatment goals. Insurance companies in many cases are interested in offering less expensive treatments, technologies and drugs, which may be detrimental to patients. However it is not the only and the most important obstacle. Many best ideas in Russia are implemented differently from those in the Western countries because of the Soviet times inertia and mentality as well as red tape. One more important factor is the structure of economy characterized as state capitalism, the current high level of centralization and corruption. There is a threat that a small group of insurance companies having strong connection to the government will do their best to eliminate competition in the industry leading to mediocre or low service and uncontrolled growth of health care costs to the population.

PRIVATE HEALTH CARE SERVICES

Strong demand for private health care services has led to a significant growth in the number and size of private clinics as well as the volume of paid medical services. This trend started back in the beginning of 1990s. The total volume of paid medical services is currently estimated at $6.5 billion, which accounts for one-fifth of the overall financial resources spent on health care in the country. The paid medical services market is growing by 20-30 percent every year. The paid medical services market includes three major parts: so called pure commercial medical services, medical services covered by voluntary health insurance programs and so called shadow market.

Most of the purely commercial health services are represented by private dental clinics. Other private health care establishments specialize in such areas as ophthalmology, cosmetology, urology, gynecology, and physiotherapy. The current specialization breakdown is due to such clinics not requiring enormous investment (normally from $100 thousand to $500 thousand), or large premises with overly expensive equipment. The secondary factor is the demand for such specialties from the population. Treatment of socially important diseases such as cardio-vascular, for example, and transplant logy of organs cannot be treated without significant government subsidies and strict control. Since expenses necessary to establish a sound private multi-profile clinic are high (they include high cost of advanced medical equipment, rents, decent wages for doctors), serious investors are slow to invest into such private clinics. The profitability rates are still low, ranging from 10 to 20 percent. It will take some 8-10 years and significant improvement in the management before such investment start to flow.

There are only a few large multi-profile private clinics in the country. Moscow has only three such clinics: AO Meditsina, Center for End surgery and Lithography and Family Doctor Clinic. Small and medium-size specialized private clinics are located not only in Moscow and St. Petersburg. They are spread all over key Russian regions, including Volga region, Urals, Siberia and Far East. Private clinics are completely self-financed, they do not get any access to budget funds which are used by state clinics to pay for equipment, communal services, rents, wages, etc.

Most of the owners of such clinics believe the system is still flawed since private clinics do not have access to any of the budget or voluntary health care insurance funds. They hold that both the quality of health care and the accessibility to modern treatments would much improve if private clinics were part of the voluntary medical insurance system. Patients could use voluntary medical insurance policies to cover part of their expenses in private clinics and pay for the rest out of their personal funds. Currently private clinics do not have access to mandatory state health care insurance programs. Moreover, Regional Health Care Committees (regional health care authorities) are impeding their participation in such programs fearing that unprofitable territorial clinics and hospitals operating under their auspices will lose competition and eventually leave the market. The so-called state funded maternity certificates, which women could use to pay for obstetrics expenses are only valid in public clinics. Private clinics are not reimbursed for such services. Currently proclaimed right of a patient to choose a clinic will remain nothing but a declaration until private clinics have equal access to mandatory insurance funds.

The most dynamic, high technology and transparent segment of the paid medical services market are services covered by voluntary insurance policies. The voluntary medical insurance market has been growing by 25-30 percent annually in the last five years. Its share in the total volume of paid medical services, including the shadow market, is estimated at 20-30 percent. The overwhelming majority participants of the voluntary health care insurance system are represented by corporate clients. The share of private individuals is still very low. Despite all advantages of voluntary health care insurance programs (quality care, modern clinics and hospitals, access to advanced medical equipment and latest technologies, there is still a vivid conflict between doctors who tend to prescribe the most expensive medicines and treatments and insurance companies which tend to offer the most economical solutions. Another drawback of voluntary health insurance is the fact that insurance companies usually work with a same group of clinics and hospitals, which belong to the top category in terms of equipment, service and conditions. However they do not cover federal and regional clinics, which do not meet the top category position, but have the best specialists in a particular field. Therefore, many patients prefer to choose clinics based on the criteria of the best specialist in the certain field. Voluntary insurance programs are not always able to meet this requirement.

Solvent citizens usually prefer neither private clinics nor state clinics, which in the recent years have been allowed to provide paid service causing double standards and vicious practice of faster medical assistance to those who pay. They prefer qualified specialists regardless of which clinic or hospital he/she works for. Such specialists are usually chosen based on the recommendations of relatives, colleagues and friends. Professionals as more efficient also accept this approach since doctors get their payments directly from the patient without official bookkeeping or taxes. Thus, a key reason for the current imbalances is the fundamental lack of free medical assistance standards and strict norms. Many experts agree that the reform of the healthcare insurance system should start from developing basic medical assistance packages guaranteed by the state and developing clear-cut standards for medical assistance strictly observed by all players.

KEY MEDICAL EQUIPMENT MARKET INDICATORS

The major goals of the National Priority Project "Health" as currently implemented are the re-equipping of hospitals and clinics with advanced medical equipment, building new medical centers, and improving basis for high-end medical assistance. These goals cannot be achieved without significant improvements in the state of the domestic medical equipment market.

A significant portion of the medical equipment and devices used in public clinics and hospitals is obsolete and needs replacement. Russia does not produce many types of high-end medical equipment and relies exclusively on imports of such equipment. While the resulting opportunities in the market are vast, financing remains insufficient to address the needs of the medical industry despite recent health care reforms and significant increase in federal and regional budgets allocations for health care.

The Russian Medical Equipment Market is one of the fastest growing sectors of the economy. Currently, the total volume of medical equipment market in Russia is estimated at $2 billion. The average annual growth of the market is 15-16 percent. Imports of medical equipment have recently played a significant role accounting for approximately 65-70 percent of the total market. The top five foreign suppliers to the Russian healthcare market are Germany (29%), United States (20%), Japan (15%), Italy (6%), and Switzerland (4%).

Some 90 percent of Russia's domestic production of medical equipment and devices is manufactured at 660 enterprises having federal licenses for the production of medical equipment and devices, including 220 plants which are primarily dedicated to the defense industry. The Ministry of Health has approved over 20,000 medical products and devices for use in treatment but only 12,000 of those are represented among the list of locally made products. According to market research company TSMI Pharmexpert, in the next three years the Russian medical market will increase three times mainly due to significant improvement of local manufacturing basis and growth in domestic output.

The Russian government allocates significant resources to support local manufacturing of medical equipment and devices. However many times those resources are used inefficiently. For example, according to Profil magazine #40 of October 30, 2010, the federal government has recently allocated $200 million to build a plasma processing plant in the city of Kirov. However there is no technical basis and plasma available for such production facility in Kirov. Alternatively, such technical basis and raw materials exist in Ivanovo. According to Profil, estimated expenses for constructing a plasma processing plant in Ivanovo are only $2 million which is 100 times less than in Kirov. Despite that fact, government bureaucrats decided that it would be more appropriate to build a plant in Kirov and buy raw materials for that plant abroad. It is evident that they count to get a notoriously known commission (or simply kickback) from the suppliers of plasma calculated as a percentage of the transaction (imported raw materials are usually several time more expensive than locally made ones).

Main components of the National Priority Project "Health" and their effects on the medical equipment sector

The National Priority Project "Health" was designed to significantly improve the Russian health care sector by pumping in significant funds and improving medical infrastructure. One of the first steps of the project was focused on upgrading the nation's primary health care sector by raising wages for general practitioners and nurses in regional and municipal polyclinics whose job is to tend to day-to-day crisis. Further initial steps included providing new equipment and ambulances to regional and municipal clinics and hospitals, and supporting nationwide vaccination campaigns and checkups. Starting in 2012, the Ministry of Health wants to concentrate efforts on building a number of high-tech medical centers and devotes mote attention to high-end medical assistance. The government allocated $2.2 billion under the priority project "Health" in 2010. For 2012 this figure is estimated at $4 billion. According to Minister of Health and Social Development Zurabov, in 2008 the total funding for health care from all sources, including the national priority project funds, will amount to $37 billion.

The implementation of the Project is supposed to be supported by enacting laws and regulations, which will modify the health care system structure in the long run. The key such laws and regulations include New Law on State Guarantees for Medical Assistance, New Law on Mandatory Health Insurance, Law on Standards of Medical Assistance and others. The work on the laws has not been finished and other laws have been stalled by legislative infighting. One positive change in the health care system restructuring is the fact that starting 2012 the government is launching a series of 'pilot health care management and funding projects' in 17 regions of Russia. The projects include development of most efficient health care funding models, and replacing the old, redundant and inefficient multi-channel health funding system by funding health care from one source.

Following are two major areas of the Project, which directly impact the medical equipment and supplies market:

- re-equipping federal clinics and hospitals with new diagnostic equipment and ambulances ($1,050 billion);

- building ten high-tech multi-profile medical centers as well as a number of regional less invasive cardiovascular surgery centers; and significantly improving and enhancing high technology medical assistance to population, such as open heart operations, transplantology of key organs, neuro-surgical brain operations and other complex surgeries, treating severe forms of endocrinology diseases and others ($1,717 billion).

First Vice Prime Minister Dmitry Medvedev, who personally oversees implementation of the four national priority projects, has given several interviews and published articles on the results of these projects in the past few months. In an article published in the January 25, 2012 edition of Kommersant Daily, a leading business daily publication in Russia, Medvedev mentioned that, due to wage increases under the National Priority Project "Health," the number of district general practitioners increased in 2010 by 3.5 thousand. Within the framework of the project 5.5 thousand health care establishments were re-equipped with new medical equipment and ambulances. The fleet of ambulances equipped with all necessary state of the art equipment increased by 6.7 thousand cars. He also admitted that the first steps of the project were not free of mistakes. Raising salaries for general practitioners and certain categories of nurses and aids while leaving them untouched for doctors-specialists and other categories of nurses has led to interoffice tension within clinics, increases in bribe-taking among specialists, and a general deterioration of the workplace atmosphere.

Many aspects of the National Priority "Health" reflect traditional bureaucratic interest in limiting open tenders stipulated by law and assigning large government construction and procurement contracts to those 'court providers and suppliers' who are recognized for their guaranteed kick-backs. The latest example is the decision of the government to build ten brand new large multi-profile medical centers. The cost of the construction is estimated to be 1.5-2 times higher than of that of an ordinary modern medical center. Many leading doctors and heads of key medical centers are confident that such large-scale investment into construction is not necessary. They argue it would be much more economical to designate a top medical center in each field of medicine among the existing medical centers and invest into improving their technical and technological basis. These top centers have significant experience in providing high-end medical assistance, which can be used as a pattern for replicating in their affiliates located in different parts of the country.

At the moment only 15-25 percent of total need for high technology medical assistance is satisfied. The unsatisfied demand for high-technology medical assistance could be met by private and so-called 'agency clinics' which currently do not have access to mandatory insurance funds and thus cannot service the treatments and technologies which could be used for the benefit of the entire population. Modern treatments and technologies help to solve a fundamental conceptual problem of the Russian health care: over-emphasis on hospital care at the expense of outpatient diagnostics and early prevention. The duration of hospital stay in such clinics is two-three days while treatment of the same disease in an old style municipal clinic requires at least two weeks.

What is taking place with the National Priority Project "Health" now is an attempt to make up for years of neglect following the 1991 Soviet collapse. In the past 15 years, disease and death have skyrocketed while the money for combating them has steadily waned. However, according to the Moscow Times of December 4, 2010, one of the most serious problems facing policy-makers as they seek to improve the nation's health care system is the firmly ingrained nature of off-record payments and bribe-taking that has come to permeate the current medical system.

Corruption scandals

Russian authorities are working fight the perception and to demonstrate decisiveness during the most recent corruption scandals in the Federal Mandatory Medical Insurance Fund. One of the factors, which led to investigation by the Prosecutor General' Office over the Federal Mandatory Medical Insurance Fund, was the enormous debt for drug deliveries under DLO Program that the Federal government had incurred. The investigation showed that contracts to deliver drugs under DLO were purportedly awarded without tenders to companies close to senior levels of the Ministry of Health. Drugs and equipment were supplied at inflated prices with further splitting profits with government officials. The management of the fund was arrested and accused of taking bribes from pharmaceutical distributors in exchange for favoritism in granting government contracts for purchases of drugs.

The toughest criticism of the corruption scandal was given by the first Vice Premier Dmitry Medvedev whose opinion was published on the Kremlin's official web site at: http://www.kreml.org/news/135133257. Medvedev expressed overall dissatisfaction with the work of the Ministry of Health and Social Development and characterized the DLO system as cheating. According to Medvedev, some swindlers make medicines; others sell them, and a third group act as middlemen using government program funds to their benefit.

Opportunities for U.S. Medical Equipment Manufacturers

Despite inefficiency and corruption related to spending of additional resources under the priority project, there was a significant increase in the level of health care spending in the country. Foreign suppliers, including U.S, actively participated in procuring medical equipment under the priority project, especially the most advance types of such equipment and newest technologies. Foreign medical equipment suppliers through their authorized local representatives continue working with Roszdrav (www.roszdravrf.ru) on participation in tenders. Roszdrav is the main government agency responsible for organizing tenders to procure drugs and medical devices for federal clinics and hospitals.

Foreign medical equipment suppliers, including U.S., continue procuring equipment to both public and private clinics and hospitals through their authorized local distributors/agents. Despite rapid growth of private clinics and private health care services, the Russian health care system remains hyper centralized and overly regulated by the state. Private clinics can solve a lot of country's problems in health care and are considered as more suitable partners for U.S. companies. However since the overwhelming majority of funds goes to public clinics, U.S. companies should consider cooperation with such clinics as a strong factor.

Russian government agencies, including the Ministry of Health and Social Development, have recently made some progress in publishing its laws, regulations, judicial decisions and administrative rulings on transparency is missing, especially with respect to countries mechanisms for healthcare financing; tenders for state purchases and decisions on government reimbursement and price registration.

Conclusion

Reforming the Russian health care system is a challenging task. It is evident that it will take more than one or two years. The authorities have started the reforms by changing those things that are either highly visible or are easier to handle. First of all, additional money was pumped into the system to fund drug reimbursement programs and increase wages for district physicians (general practioners) and paramedics, which was made possible thanks to the Country's windfall profits from high oil prices. Secondly, they have invested into construction of new medical centers using the considerable experience of extensive development models accumulated during the Soviet time. However the basic element of the health care system – health care insurance – remains under reformed. Russia still has to build a functional and solid system which will take into account and balance the interests of major players: patients, the state, insurance companies and medical centers. Government officials have identified that, in the future, special attention must be given to creating independent controlling bodies that will oversee spending and ensure the efficiency of the system. Another identified next step will be encouraging investments into fundamental medical research and the commercialization of medical technologies.

ENERGY AND POWER GENERATION MARKET

In 2002, the Russian government began reforming the power generation industry. The main goal was, and remains, to upgrade the aging and outdated heating and electricity infrastructure. RAO UES (Russian Open Stock Company Unified Energy System), the national utility company, hopes to raise $118 billion in the next five years. To meet this goal, it will have to attract foreign investment. The current strategy assumes that RAO UES will close its doors as a holding company in 2008, with much of its power generation assets privatized. This report summarizes the key elements of the reform project in order to alert U.S. companies to the changing market and potential opportunities in Russia.

MARKET DEMAND

The Russian electric power market is the fourth largest in the world, producing 5.5% of the world's electricity. In the late 1990s, an analysis of the power industry's performance in Russia indicated that the sector was losing competitiveness and investment appeal. From 19911998, Russian electricity consumption steadily declined due to general economic stagnation and low purchasing power of the population. But since 1999, as a result of a healthier economy, electricity consumption has steadily increased and grew 4.2% yearon-year from 2009 to 2010. This growth rate is expected to continue for the next several years, in line with general economic growth.

The Russian Ministry of Industry and Energy reports that in the first half of 2010, power plants produced 66.8% of energy, hydro stations 17.4%, and nuclear plants 15.7%. Thermal power plants produced 382.52 billion kWthr (7.5% more than in 2009), hydro stations generated 99.55 billion kWthr (5.6% less than 2009), nuclear plants produced 89.98 billion kWthr (5.9% more than 2009). The production of electrical energy in JanuaryJuly, 2010 totaled 572.29 billion kWthr (4.7% up from the 2009 period).

Russia now finds itself needing to modernize a large portion of its power generation facilities and RAO UES hopes to attract more than $100 billion investment in the industry in the next five years. It plans to increase capacity by 40.9 Mwatts in the coming four years. RAO UES estimates it needs 100 gas and 67 steam turbines, 125 waste heat boilers and about 70 turbines for coalfired stations. It is quite likely that purchase orders for power generation equipment may grow to tens of billions of dollars. According to industry sources, last year local manufacturers produced only $2 billion worth of this equipment type, creating a promising market for foreign vendors.

REFORM PROCESS

RAO UES Plan Update Approved. The original reform plan projected that by the end of 2010, the electricity sector of Russia would be demonopolized. Some significant achievements have been made, one of which is the launch of a competitive electricity pricing system in September 2010. However, because of the size and complexity of the reform process, the deadline for reform has now been extended to 2010.

RAO UES has made the strategic decision to sharply increase investments since some developing regions, such as St. Petersburg and the Urals, underestimated the growth in power usage and suffer from severe supply shortages that are constraining economic growth. The plan for building new facilities and power grids and replacing outdated equipment has been revised upward a number of times. These updates were included in the overall development scheme and in February 2012, RAO UES announced its new investment and modernization program for the electric power industry. A fiveyear investment plan totaling $118 billion was approved. These investment funds will be used to build and upgrade power generating facilities. In 2012, the first year of the updated plan, UES plans to attract $15 billion. No other Russian corporation has requested such a large investment. In spite of these challenges restructuring of the power sector is considered to be one of the most successful reforms in the Russian economy in the last decade.

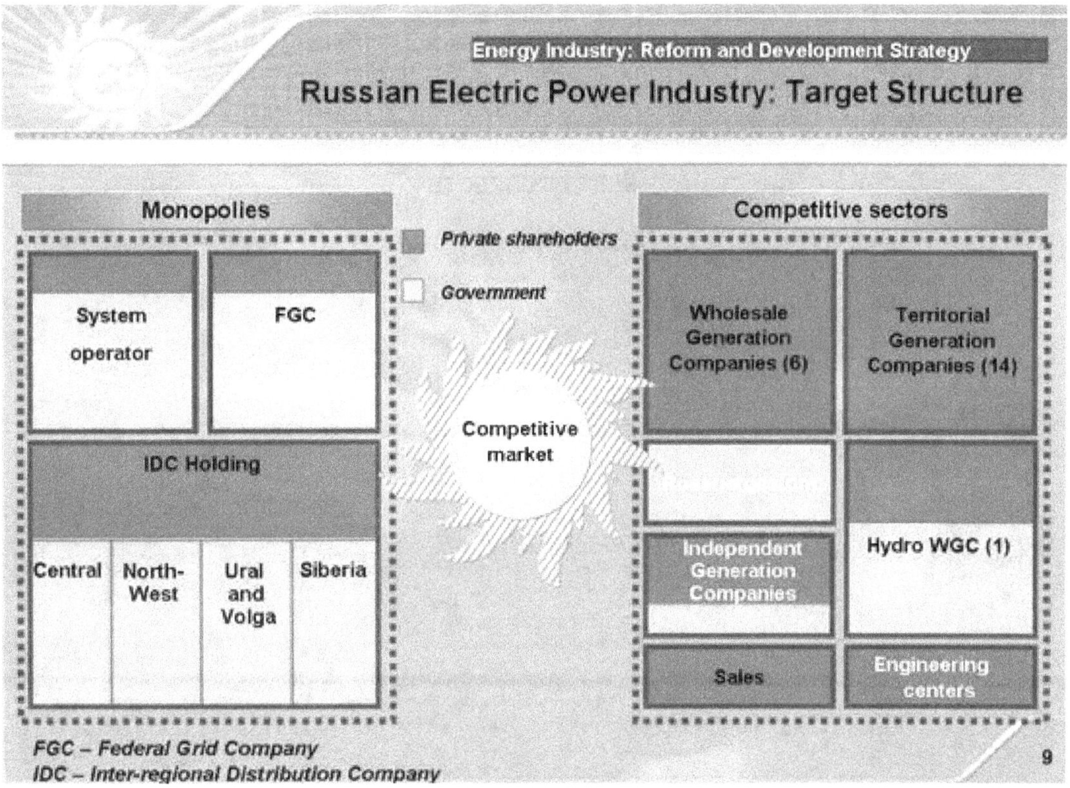

Reform Goals: The main goals of the reform project are to increase the efficiency of the power industry and make the sector attractive to private investors. The updated plan is expected to improve the national power generation infrastructure, bring power supply to every building in Russia and help the industry meet the growing market demand for power generation, which has grown between 4% and 5% annually since 1999, according to official statistics. For example, power generation currently held by the natural monopoly are to be separated and privatized. New entities responsible for distinct activities are to be created in place of the former vertically integrated companies, with highvoltage transmission and dispatch functions remaining stateowned. Sales and repair companies are also to be privatized.

Market Participants: As illustrated in the following chart, 6 Wholesale Generating Companies (OGKs), 14 Territorial Generation Companies (TGKs), HydroOGK, Rosenergoatom and independent generating companies were formed as part of the industry privatization. The government will retain ownership of: System Operator (SO), Federal Grid Company (FGC), and Interregional Distribution Companies (IDC).

Additional information in English about OGKs and TGKs, their structure, lists of power plants included in each entity, and contact information may be found at:

http://www.raoees.ru/en/reforming/WGCs/show.cgi?WGCs.htm

Private Investments: According to "FCNovosti Information Agency Daily" the Russian government has approved RAO UES' plan for placing additional shares for wholesale and regional power generating companies as a means to attract private investment. It is expected to attract about $8 billion of private investments in 20122010. Additional shares placements are planned for OGK3 and OGK5 and TGK3 and TGK5 in 2012; for OGK4, TGK1, TGK9 and TGK10 in 2008; and for TGK8, OGK1, OGK2 and OGK6 in 20092010.

The following examples illustrate that large multibillion corporations are very interested in obtaining shares in the Russian power sector. In January 2012, Norilsk Nickel, a Russian metal giant, bought shares of OGK3 for $3 billion. Moscowbased Mosenergo, Russia's largest regional power generating company, which supplies 80% of Moscow's heating needs, found Gazprom, the Russian energy giant as its main investor. According to Russian government officials, the acquisition of a controlling stake in Mosenergo is crucial for the development of Mosenergo as a gas and energy corporation taking into consideration the fact that natural gas exceeds 92% in Mosenergo's fuel balance.

BEST PROSPECTS

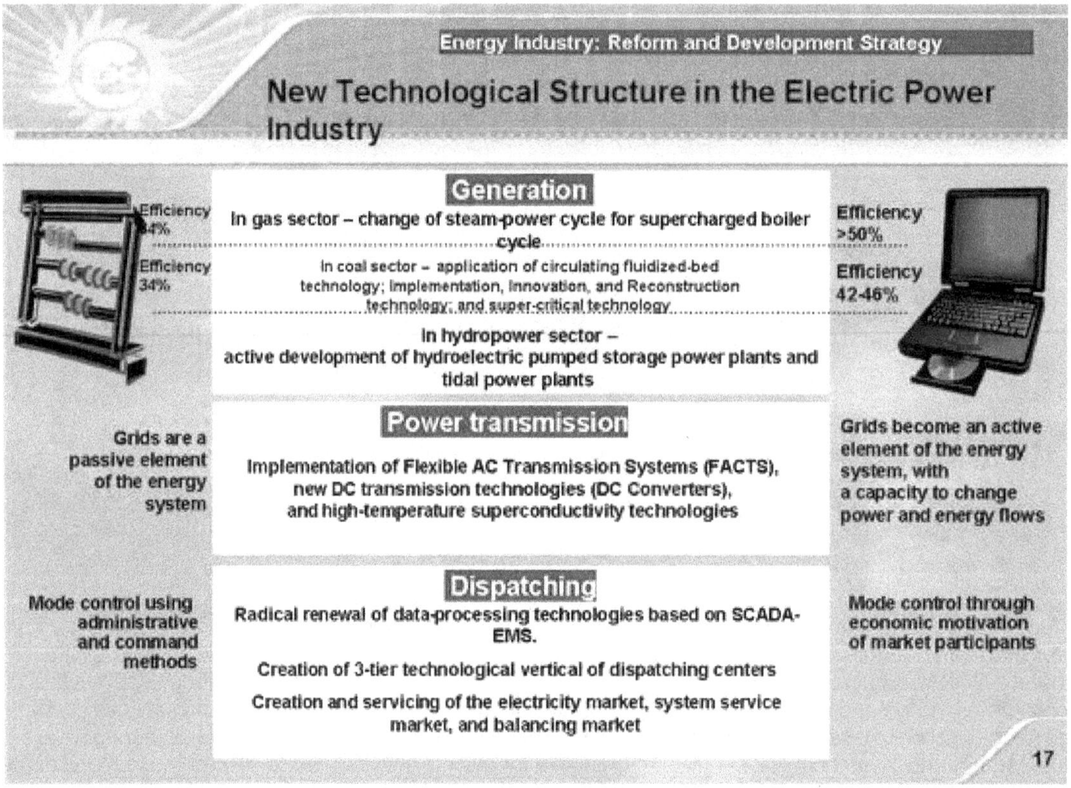

"New Investment Program of RAO UES of Russia Holding Company" (Moscow, February 13, 2012)

Industry experts estimate that 60% of Russia's existing power capacity is scheduled for retirement or rehabilitation by the year 2010, including both gas and coal fired units. The principal items for rehabilitation or retrofitting will be turbine units and boilers. As part of this rehabilitation program, greater attention will be paid to environmental and energy efficiency at power generation facilities. Among the most significant equipment needs for the power generation sector will be for thermal power plant modernization, fuel switching, conversion, plant construction and life extension of existing equipment. As for hydroelectric plants, plans include the rehabilitation, modernization and expansion of existing plants and the construction of new plants. The Russia power sector also presents specific opportunities for developing and installing small generating capacities (under 30Mwatts).

In terms of additional equipment and technology, the industry is interested in buying advanced, computer-based, energy management systems for internal power plant operations and system level control; environmental control equipment for coal and gas fired power plants; and process control equipment.

The updated reform plan stipulates changes to the entire technical structure of the power industry. The following slide from CEO Chubais' presentation (cited above) illustrates the planned changes in generation, power transmission and dispatching technologies.

KEY SUPPLIERS

The ambitious plan for restructuring the power industry is having a great impact on equipment manufacturers, both domestic and foreign. Domestic suppliers produce a wide range of basic electric power generation equipment, which dominate the market. However, because Russian engineering firms do not currently compete in the market for large turbines there is a demand for imported hardware in the large and midrange segment. Currently, the major players in the Russian market are: Power Machines (Siloviye Mashiny), Siemens, OMZ, Alstom, General Electric, ABB, AoZ Podolsk, M Alliance, and others.

Demand in the Russian market is extremely price sensitive. While the quality and performance of such equipment is generally below that of cuttingedge western equipment, Russian power equipment manufacturers enjoy a very substantial price advantage over western equivalents. The lower costs of domestic producers, in comparison to imports, are forcing importers to lower their prices. For this reason, the most aggressive foreign companies seeking to supply the Russian market with power generation equipment are attempting to do so via local manufacturing with Russian joint venture partners.

Integration Between Local and Foreign Manufacturers: There are some positive examples of integration of Russian and Western technologies. In 2009, Siemens bought 25% plus one share in Siloviye Mashiny, or Power Machines, a large turbine maker in Russia. The joint venture targets to produce and sell gas turbines using German technology and to conduct turbine operation and maintenance (O&M) work. In this example of integration between local and foreign manufacturers, participation of a foreign company assists the JV build consumer confidence in the quality of Russian equipment and also helps Russian manufacturers market their equipment more successfully. With the help of Siemens, Silovye Mashiny started producing gas turbines of 160 Mwatts, while earlier produced turbines of 90 Mwatts.

The United States is considered one of the leading suppliers of electric power hardware to Russia and also a major player in the market for engineering solutions, turnkey projects and consulting services. Russia is very receptive to U.S. products. Companies such as General Electric, Dresser, Compressor Controls Corporation, Pratt and Whitney, and Black and Veatch are present in the Russian market and their products are available either directly or through representatives or distributors.

Imports from third countries are also growing. U.S. firms are encountering increasing competition in the Russian market from European and Chinese manufacturers.

Under the reform plan, Russian managers are currently focused on improving the operational efficiency of their assets and are increasingly receptive to turnkey engineering solutions to enhance their competitiveness. In 2002, RAO UES started purchasing equipment and services through a system of open tenders. Approximately 17,000 tenders for energy projects were processed through the world's largest marketplace for power generation equipment online at www.b2benergo.ru. Most of the Wholesale and

Territorial Generating Companies have their own marketplaces on their websites. A foreign vendor needs to keep in mind that all paper documentation for tenders should be submitted in the Russian language. Current information about new tenders, application procedures and other participation requirements may be found at: http://tenderenergo.ru. The website is in Russian and intended for local representatives of

U.S. companies working with Russian power supply firms.

MARKET ENTRY

There are several ways to approach the Russian energy market including participation in trade fairs specializing in electric power products, advertising in professional trade journals and direct mail. Complete information about the products, including specifications, prices and delivery conditions is essential to stimulating interest.

The U.S. Commercial Service believes that the most effective way to operate in the Russian electric power market is to find an appropriate Russian partner. Some distributors have been in business for more than 15 years and therefore have extensive experience and knowhow. Their detailed knowledge of the market and many business connections enable them to find both a buyer and a seller. Many distributors may operate on an exclusive basis and may cover a large area of the country, allowing them to do a thorough analysis of sale possibilities, and to evaluate products against competitors with regard to both price and quality.

Major foreign manufacturers of power supply equipment, including GE, Honeywell, Pratt and Whitney, Siemens, Mitsubishi and others, have opened representative offices in Russia. Some

U.S. EPCM contractors have opened their own offices as well. Several procurement officers have expressed their strong preference for suppliers to be locally based as it enhances the service element of their offering. A number of engineering and construction services sold in Russia must conform to Russian standards including Health, Safety and Environment (HSE) requirements and must be licensed according to the Russian laws.

An important factor that American companies must consider is language. English language penetration in Russia is rather low, around 5%. Many decisionmakers in this sector know enough English to communicate but Russian is necessary for negotiations and communication with lower level employees in large domestic companies where English is not their working language.

MARKET ISSUES AND OBSTACLES

U.S. exporters often experience problems with government bureaucracy, poorly established rule of law and corruption in the areas such as establishing a business, tax collection, dispute settlement, property rights, product certification and standards, as well as Russian Customs clearance. Import tariffs for power sector equipment range from 520%, plus VAT of 18% (local suppliers are also subject to the same VAT tax on domestic deliveries). Imported power equipment must be certified as conforming to Russian safety and operating standards by the Russian standards agency, the Federal Agency for Technical Regulations (www.gost.ru) or one of its accredited testing bodies. U.S. companies in many industry sectors have noted that certification of imported equipment in Russia can be difficult, timeconsuming and expensive.

RUSSIA CHEMICAL INDUSTRY

The chemical industry plays an important role in the Russian economy. It accounts for about 5.5% of the country's industrial production and about 5.4% of total hard currency earnings. It reflected 10.6% growth as sales of petrochemicals become more prevalent in Russian business. The main trends in the chemical industry in 2012 are: stable growth in chemical industry output and increased investments in new projects. The development of technological infrastructure and the growth of chemical products sales present good opportunities for U.S. firms, especially for those with a reliable Russian partner.

CHEMICAL INDUSTRY OVERVIEW

The reasons most often cited for the positive outlook on the Russian chemical sector stem from the economic reforms being implemented. These reforms are credited with the overall increase in output and a wider distribution of business activities. The chemical sector in 20092010 was estimated to be approximately $30 billion, and the volume of imported chemical products was 13%. The domestic Russian chemical industry is composed of approximately 800 firms specializing in a broad range of activities including plastics, synthetic rubber, tires, paint materials, chemical fiber and thread, petrochemicals and synthetic resin and plastics. Leading Russian chemical companies include: LukoilNeftekhim, Sibur Holding, TatneftNeftekhim, Nizhnekamskmeftekhim, EuroChem, PhosAgro, Akron, Uralkaliy, Silvinit, Novomoskovkaya Stock Company Azot, Schekinoazot, Tomskneftekhim, and Kazanorgsyntez.

The evolving Russian economy, new technologies and global market fluctuations have resulted in the following sector trends in 2012:

- Growth of Russian industrial output
- Rapid increase of endusers
- Sharp competition among chemical suppliers
- Increased investment
- New project development
- High demand for new/updated equipment

Beyond 2012, the Russian chemical industry is expected to trend toward an export–oriented industry with over 40% of domestic production sold abroad. According to the Ministry of Industry and Energy Russia's share of world carbamide and ammonia production is 15%. In 2009, the Russian export of chemical products was around $11.5 billion. Chemical and petrochemical products account for 6.5% of Russia's total exports including mineral fertilizers, rubber, plastics and raw petrochemicals products. Interfax (Chemical report of November 2009) reported that in 2009 export of mineral fertilizers accounted for about 26% of all chemical exports, synthetic rubber for 7%, ammonia for 4.8% and methanol for 2.2%.

Domestic Production In the first half of 2012, Russian manufacturers doubled polypropylene production, synthetic resins grew 22,3%, polyethylene grew 12.8% and production of truck tires grew 7.4%. New production facilities for polystyrol and polypropylene were launched by Nizhnekamskneftekhim and Stavrolen (part of Lukoil). According to an RBC daily report from April 2012, Sibur Holding (majority owned by Gazprom) plans to start production of polyvinylchloride with a capacity of 300 thousand tons in the Nizhny Novgorod Region.

Nevertheless, over the last few years the local chemical market has been evolving. According to the Russian Ministry of Industry and Energy, most of the industry's capital assets are outdated, the depreciation exceeds 60%, and there is a high demand for new equipment in all sectors.

Industry experts of the Russian Chemists Union assume that an initiative of the Russian Government to create Special Economic Zones (SEZs) will stimulate the development of chemical manufacturing. Companies seeking to invest in the SEZs will benefit from lower taxes and duties. The most advanced plans in the chemical and petrochemical sectors are for SEZs in Central Russia, at Tomsk and Elabuga. In Tomsk, a project to produce titaniummagnesium was developed by experts at Tomskneftekhim, Sibur, and a local catalysts institute, and a plant to produce PS film from raw materials has been established at the Elabuga SEZ.

Due to the development of new projects, the chemical market in Russia has grown geographically; but various estimates still have up to 60% of the demand for the chemical industry concentrated in Central Russia in the Moscow and Leningrad Regions, in Nizhny Novgorod and in theTatarstan Republic, all considered to be the most promising regional markets for chemical industry development.

Imports According to a recent Interfax Chemical Industry report (November 2009) the highest demand for chemicals to be imported into Russia is for pharmaceuticals, which account for about 19% of Russia's total chemical imports, plastics, fiber and thread, synthetic dyes, polystyrene and painting materials, synthetic detergents and pesticides.

Russia is very receptive to U.S. chemical products, and companies such as Dow Chemical, Dupont, Procter & Gamble are brands universally recognized for their quality and sophistication. Leading western companies are present in the Russian market and their products are available either directly, through representatives or through distributors. Some local industry experts expect at least 20% growth in U.S. imports by the end of 2012, although this prediction rests on an acceleration of Russia's overall economic growth and continuation of aggressive marketing efforts by U.S. suppliers.

Imports from third countries are also growing and U.S. firms meet increasing competition from European chemical vendors in the Russian market. German, Dutch and Scandinavian suppliers have gained market share through direct distribution or by establishing local subsidiaries. Brand awareness in the Russian market and a well organized distribution network make it possible to compete with such chemical manufacturers as: Unilever, Akzo Nobel, BASF, Bayer and more. As additional foreign companies enter the Russian chemical market, the use of joint ventures to set up local production facilities is expected to grow.

MARKET ISSUES

An import duty is applied to the declared cost of chemical products or equipment physically crossing the board of the Russian Federation, plus 18% VAT. The necessary documentation for the tangible imports of chemicals and equipment is an original invoice. Upon arrival, however, it is necessary to complete a number of forms, which are usually handled by a customs broker. According to the Russian Ministry of Economic Development and Trade import duties for 70% of all chemical products are close to WTO (World Trade Organization) requirements now. However, when Russia accedes to WTO, import duties for a number of chemical products will be lowered from 1020% to 6.5%.

Russia has a satisfactory network of highly qualified distributors ranging from the very large broadliners and those with a large dealer network to the small highly specialized resellers. Most Americanorigin chemical products are sold through this channel. In addition, many U.S. chemical companies have their own subsidiary in Russia and a welestablished distribution network throughout the country. A list of chemical companies operating in Russia may be found at: http://rccnews.ru/Eng/?ID=384&Search_String=&Search_Group=2

Chemical products and equipment sold in Russia must conform to minimum safety standards and quality requirements and must carry a conformity mark, indicating that the product has been tested and approved for use in Russia. While the process can be timeconsuming, it is relatively transparent and the requirements are not especially onerous. U.S. exporters generally experience few problems. Compliance testing is typically performed at commercially operated testing stations in Russia, and the results passed to the State Standards Agency (www.gost.ru) who issues the certificate.

An important factor that American companies must consider is language flexibility. English language penetration is rather low, though there are language classes in all secondary schools. It is expected that English will expand with time. Some distributors of chemical products and equipment have been in existence for more than 10 years and therefore have extensive experience and knowhow. Their detailed knowledge of the market and many business connections enable them to find both a buyer and a seller for all products in their offering. They may operate on an exclusive basis and cover a large part of the country enabling them to make a thorough analysis of sales possibilities and to evaluate a product against competing products.

Useful Links

http://www.ruschemunion.ru http://www.amcham.ru/

IRKUTSK FOREST COMPLEX

GENERAL DESCRIPTION OF INDUSTRY

East Siberia is the taiga land, and the Irkutsk region is one of the most virgin territories in Russia, with nearly 92% of its area covered with forest. The Irkutsk region occupies the second place in Russia after Krasnoyarsk by timber resources, estimated on the level over 9 billion cubic meters 25% of the entire timber resources in Siberia, or 12% of Russian reserves. The region is ranked first in Russia by volume of timber harvesting.

Coniferous woods larches, pines, Siberian pines and firs prevail in the Irkutsk region (more than 75% of forests). Angara pine growing in the basins of the Angara and the Yenisey rivers is most widely spread species (about 25% of all forests) and considered most important source of valuable timber. Average reserve of timber per one hectare in the Irkutsk region equals 130 cubic meters, compared to about 110 cubic meters in Russia in general. The space of mature forest that could be put into industrial use equals 11.7 million hectares, or about 20% of forest areas. Calculated periodic yield in 2010 amounted to 53 million cubic meters of timber but the actual exploitation equals about 40% of this area. Nearly all forests, with the exception of urban parks, are owned by the state.

Unique resource potential of this territory allowed development of the forest industry since mid 1950s; large enterprises Baikalsk Pulp and Paper Combine, Bratsk and Ustllimsk Timber Combines were established; now they provide about 70% of total forest industry output in the Irkutsk region. At present Irkutsk forestry is represented by timber harvesting, processing, pulp and paper and woodchemical sectors. After the economic recession of 1990s, the industry has demonstrated sustainable growth since 1997:

Forest complex now occupies one of the leading positions in the economy of the Irkutsk region and provides more than 20% of industrial output in the region. About 150 large and medium enterprises, more than 1,500 small companies and nearly 70,000 employees work in lumbering, processing and exporting of timber. The output of the Irkutsk forest complex provides about 10% of total timber harvested in Russia, 12% or Russian sawn timber, 6.1% of chipboard, 7.3% of fiberboard, 53.5% of cellulose and about 7% of cardboard.

The region exports more than 6 million cubic meters of log and 1.7 million cubic meters of sawn timber per annum. Southeast Asian and Pacific counties constitute the main market for the wood products of the East Siberia. China (about 82% of export of round timber) and Japan (12%) are the major consumers of Siberian wood. Export of round timber to China is in most cases carried out by individual entrepreneurs and small companies, while Japanese companies prefer to deal with large Russian producers. Steady growth of volume of export transactions is demonstrated by the region from USD 551 million in 2000 to USD 1.32 billion in 2009; at present the share of forest products in total exports of The Irkutsk region reach 31%.

Corporation Ilim Pulp Enterprise, Ltd. is the largest producer in Irkutsk forest industry. The company headquartered in St.Petersburg was established in 1992. Ilim Pulp is ranked among world's top ten producers of market cellulose, and occupies 6th place by the total area of leased forest areas and volume-produced timber. Ilim Pulp employs more than 44,000 people, and produces 60% of market cellulose and 85% of boxboard in Russia. In 2010 the enterprises of Ilim Pulp in the Irkutsk region harvested 5.07 million cubic meters of wood. Investments of Ilim Pulp into maintenance and development of its facilities in the Irkutsk region in 2010 amounted to USD 40 million.

Several regional agencies and associations were established to support development of forest industry, they can provide considerable facilitation to western companies interested in establishing economic presence in the Irkutsk region.

Union of Wood Producers and Wood Exporters of The Irkutsk region was established in 1994, and includes more than a hundred wood producing companies, including Bratskcomplexholding, JSC, Ustllimsky LPK, JSC, Baikalsky Pulp and Paper Compine, JSC, Irkutsklesprom, JSC, IgirmaTairiku, JSC and many other organizations. Its main tasks aim at support of entrepreneurship and development of external economic collaboration of local wood producers, and coordination of foreign trade activities and price policy. The Union is also engaged in facilitation of attracting the investments in Irkutsk forest complex. Association of Small CompaniesTimber Producers and Exporters of the Irkutsk region uniting companies with annual production of less than 20,000 cubic meters of timber was established in 2009 and incorporated into the regional Union of Wood Producers. However, the majority of more than 1,500 individual entrepreneurs and small companies engaged in timber industry does not belong to any professional unions.

Irkutsk Scientific and Research Institute of Wood Industry is engaged in design and development of projects in wood harvesting and processing, workplace safety and accident prevention measures, as well as engineering design for new equipment. It prepares programs and business plans for local wood producers, provides consulting and facilitation to import transactions of equipment for wood industry. The Institute coordinates with Russian and foreign financial institutions the documents related to investment loans and leasing operations; provides assistance in assembly and operation of specialized equipment for timber harvesting and processing.

The Irkutsk regional Innovation and Service Center for Timber Industry was established in 2009 as a structural division of Irkutsk State Technical University, in order to facilitate technical reequipment and proper personnel training for Irkutsk wood producers. The Center maintains contacts with a large number of enterprises of wood complex, providing educational, analytical and consulting services. As a dealer, this agency represents many Russian and Western producers of woodprocessing equipment; the Center has a representative office in the U.S., providing search for equipment suppliers in the U.S. and Canada, and is interested in establishing new contacts with U.S. suppliers of equipment and technologies related to deep processing of wood (sawing, drying, wood waste processing equipment).

To implement the development of regional forest industry plans a special Committee on Forestry and Forest Industry was established in 2009 in the Administration of the Irkutsk region; activities of the Committee are mostly associated with attracting investments and general coordination of the branch's economic performance.

MAIN CHALLENGES AND TRENDS OF IRKUTSK FOREST INDUSTRY

The local government emphasizes that forestry development is one of the priorities for local economy. Presence of several transportation trunks, sources of cheap power and well trained specialists make Irkutsk quite capable of becoming a center of forest industry in Russia. However, the branch faces several major problems.

Considerable deterioration of equipment is one of the main constraints for Russian forest industry. The age of equipment is about 25 years on average, deterioration of capital assets equals 59%, and on some wood processing enterprises reaches even 80%. These factors stipulate necessity of investments in reequipment of forest complex as a primary task. Modern woodprocessing equipment, tools and technologies for deep processing of wood and wood waste reprocessing are in high demand. Dozens of local companies and several agencies promote and distribute advanced forest machinery and equipment (felling, skidding, sawing, dry kiln), as well as auxiliary devices and goods (hoisting equipment, antiseptics etc).

Insufficient transportation infrastructure is another serious challenge. According to estimation of experts, more than 70% of Irkutsk wood reserves are actually inaccessible to timber producers. Distance is another depressing factor 500600 km transportation of timber by railroad or 200 to 300 km by truck make the delivery inefficient. Development of road infrastructure in the Irkutsk region is observed at present but it is insufficient and does not exceed 1% per year.

Many of local timber producers presently implement diversified investment programs, as several following examples should illustrate. New plant providing deep processing of wood was launched in 2012 in Mogotuy village, nearly USD 3 million coming from various sources were invested into this project. Sibexportles, LLC, affiliate of Russian Forest Holding, actively introduces modern technologies; the investment plan of the company envisages more than USD 230 million of investments, and in the next few years the company expects to have one of the leading positions in the region. Investment program of I lim Pulp is primarily oriented to replacement of obsolete equipment with advanced western machinery; the company plans to invest about USD 130 million to reach 82% share of imported equipment used in felling by 2010, as compared to 11% in 2010. The company also pays proper attention to environment protection and spends several million of dollars every year for natureconservative measures on its pulp and paper enterprises.

Russia still keeps the leading position by volume of export of nonprocessed wood; the share of round logs in export of timber in the Irkutsk region reaches 44%. The efforts of state power are now oriented to reduction of export of round timber, development of domestic wood processing and production with high added value. Local government offers support to foreign companies tending to establish joint ventures in the region.

The Concept of the Irkutsk region Forest Complex Development in the period 20122015 adopted in late 2010 implies priority development of deep mechanical and chemical processing of wood, as well as processing of low quality soft timber. In addition to that, such issues as development and optimization of logistics, ensuring business transparency and small business support are emphasized by the Concept. According to forecasts, by 2015 export of round timber will be reduced to minimum; production of sawn timber will reach 7 million cubic meters per annum, cellulose 2.5 million cubic meters (construction of 2 pulp and paper plants is envisaged). Implementation of the project implies nearly 1.5 billion of investments.

Illegal harvesting and export of timber is one of the major problems of Irkutsk forest complex, too. In 2009, only about a half of exporters could officially prove the origin of shipped timber. The experts estimate shadow trafficking of timber on the level of 11.5 million cubic meters per annum. With more than a thousand harvesting companies working in the region, it has been very difficult to track legitimacy of all felling operations and shipments of timber. To prevent unauthorized felling that causes millions dollars of damage to the regional economy, monitoring system was I ntroduced in 2009, ensuring total control over timber harvesting.

Voluntary certification also prevents illegal trade of timber. Since October 2010 Japan has suspended import of noncertified timber; similar protection measures will be implemented in Europe in 2008. Only several enterprises in the Irkutsk region conducted certification so far, and Regional Administration and Forest Stewardship Council (FSC) presently undertake many efforts to introduce certification to local forest producing enterprises.

To regulate export shipments of wood, the Administration of The Irkutsk region established a number of timber terminals based in the facilities of large wood processing enterprises. In such sites, working as brokerage agencies, collection, sorting, marking, customs clearance and shipment of timber are performed. At present, shipments of round logs are made from 80 points in The Irkutsk region, 47 of them have the status of terminals. In addition to wood terminals, first Russian timber exchange was established in 2009. With the general goal of regulating and optimizing the trade in timber in the region, the exchange is supposed to develop unified trade rules and fix fair export prices. As a result of these measures, export price of round timber raised by 40% by 2012. In the nearest future, work of terminals will be stopped, while exchange trade in wood will be developed further.

In late 2010 regional authorities also announced the idea of developing wood processing clusters, i.e. establishing production cooperation of large companies and SMEs working in forest industry.

There is another development that seriously affects the regional budget: while forest industry ensures more than 20% of industrial output in the Irkutsk region, it provides only about 5% of tax proceeds in the regional budget. Previously, however, before coming of vertically integrated holdings headquartered in Moscow and St.Petersburg, the branch provided up to 30% of collected taxes.

The issue of rational forest management starts to receive due attention at present. Local forest operators presently harvest not only the selected valuable species, but increase harvesting and processing of less valuable and softwood forests, too. Firefighting and reforestation technologies and equipment are actively introduced in the industry now, too.

COOPERATION WITH WESTERN COMPANIES

Irkutsk forest complex possesses high potential and attracts many foreign companies. Two out of about ten joint JapaneseRussian companies operating in The Irkutsk region IgirmaTairiku (the oldest JV established in 1987) and TMBaikal are among the flagships of local timber industry; they success is associated with application of advanced technologies in deep processing of wood. In 2009 joint RussianSwiss company Royal Wood launched a USD 18 million worth processing plant, equipped with wood processing machinery produced by leading European manufacturers. One of the most recent examples a pulp and paper plant, to be constructed with China in UstKut City; the cost of this project is two billion dollars.

In October 2010, Ilim Pulp signed a memorandum of understanding with the US International Paper (www.internationalpaper.com, largest pulp and paper company in the world, and the largest private owner of timberland in the United States; in the US it operates 18 pulp, paper and packaging mills, 94 converting and packaging plants, and five wood products facilities). The MOU states that, by means of purchase of 50% of Ilim Holding's shares worth about USD 1.3 billion by International Paper, in 2012 the parties will establish a joint venture Ilim Group, JSC, with the headquarters in St.Petersburg. The new company will be mostly focused on products with high added value such as office paper, bleached board and cardboard.

Longterm joint investment program of the new joint venture, unique in the scale of Russia, envisages about USD 770 million (according to other sources up to 1.2 billion) of investments by 2011. Largest part of funds will be invested into further development of pulp and paper production, and about 200 million into Ilim Pulp's affiliates engaged in logging operations. Implementation of this program will allow the company to seriously increase production capacity (increase of output by 39% by 2011 is predicted) and improve the product quality. In addition to further increase in production of market cellulose and cardboard by Ust'Ilimsk LPK production facilities to manufacture new types of products will be established on Bratsk Cellulose Combine. Ilim Pulp also plans about USD 100 millions of investment into development of timber processing enterprises not covered under JV agreement.

Chinese, Japanese, Thai, Malaysian, Belgian companies also demonstrate strong interest in establishing new wood processing companies for joint production in the Irkutsk region.

The World Bank delegation visited Irkutsk in 2009. Irkutsk was among several other Russian regions where the pilot project of sustainable forest exploitation developed by the World Bank might be implemented. In addition, the World Bank together with the International Finance Corporation was among the main sources of borrowed funds allocated for modernization of Ilim Pulp. It is worth noting that Ilim Pulp is a regular recipient of millions of loans from other western financial institutions, e.g. BNP Paribas and HSH Nordbank AG.

In summer of 2009 US R.E. Taylor & Associates and Winrock International arranged a prolonged tour in Eastern Siberia for a group of representatives of western wood products manufacturing companies, including several US producers (USNR Corporation, Global Forest Partners, Woodgrain Millwork). The visitors met with twenty major forestry and wood processing plants in the Krasnoyarsk and Irkutsk regions, and came to the conclusion that most of local wood processing companies were in the process of implementation new investment projects (starting of new sawmills, upgrading operations etc), or planned production expansion. Members of the delegation also made several other important observations: "Local producers usually prefer European woodprocessing equipment. The funds used in new mill construction and upgrade projects usually originate from log and lumber export profits, ... or from loans of Siberian banks. Foreign investments in Siberian forestry are still rather limited, and in Irkutsk are presented mainly in the form of several JapaneseRussian JVs. However, many local companies search for sources of capital to invest in modernizing and expanding their manufacturing plants. The experts also pointed that log and lumber production in Siberia would increase further as more capital is invested in the forestry and manufacturing industry".

In September, 2009 several highranked officers of USDA Forest Service visited the Irkutsk region. A Memorandum of Understanding was signed between the Forest Service and the Russian Federal Agency of Forestry several days before their visit to Irkutsk; the MOU implies cooperation in the spheres of forest management, protection and reforestation , forest legislation, voluntary certification, science and research etc. The Irkutsk region might be an appropriate site for implementation of pilot projects of forest monitoring, sustainable exploitation of forest resources and greenhouse gas sorption envisaged by this document.

In 2010 the US companies made several large transactions to Bratsk Pulp and Cardboard Combine, JSC, affiliate of Ilim Pulp in The Irkutsk region. Cranston Machinery won the tender for supply of equipment for packaging of cellulose and supplied equipment for the amount of 1 million dollars. The same combine purchased equipment worth USD 600,000 produced by US Morbark, applied in processing of bark wastes and heat generation (in the early 2001 Morbark Sales Corporation also supplied ecologically friendly pulp chips producing equipment worth 1 million dollars to Baikalsk Pulp and Paper Combine). Affiliates of Ilim Pulp regularly purchase timber harvesting and road construction machinery produced by Caterpillar and John Deere (a harvesting complex worth 1,140,000 euro was purchased by Ilimsibles in 2010, several others will be procured in 2012 in terms of more than 100 million worth contract signed with John Deere in 2009).

The exhibition Forest Utilization and Wood Processing in Siberia, held annually by the exhibition company Sibexpocenter, attracts tens of western companies dealing with wood processing equipment and technologies (mostly from Italy, Germany, Sweden, Finland, China, the Czech Republic). This exhibition is a good way to promote equipment and services related to forestation, harvesting, deep mechanical and chemical processing of timber.

OPPORTUNITIES FOR US COMPANIES

Forest industry of the Irkutsk region possesses large potential for further development and provides following opportunities for investments and international partnership development:

Investments in wood processing. According to expert estimations, Russian wood industry needs about 2 billion dollars of investments per annum, and demand for investments reaches a billion dollars in the Irkutsk region only. Irkutsk producers lack access to financing; largest players tend to borrow relatively cheap funds abroad. Investments in deep processing of wood meet hearty welcome and miscellaneous facilitation of local authorities. The Administration of the Irkutsk region and several agencies dealing with forest industry keep the databases of projects/business plans worth from less then a million to a billion dollars, received from companies interested in attracting investments and establishing joint ventures.

Supplies of equipment for harvesting and deep processing of wood, pulp and paper production, monitoring of forest resources, firefighting, miscellaneous auxiliary devices and equipment. Contacts with potential dealers or final consumers can be established using contact information indicated in the webregisters of Russian wood producers indicated below.

Consulting and management support in forest monitoring, reforestation, environment protection, quality management. For example, in 2009 Ilim Pulp launched automated control system, and since 2010 started introduction of integrated management system covering the main business processes, production planning, budgeting, technical maintenance and repair, investments, human resources, sales and supply chain management.

Forests along the main transportation routes in the Irkutsk region are mostly depleted, while considerable reserves of valuable timber are preserved in large woodlands located in distant and hardtoreach districts of this vast region. Further development of forest industry in the regions is closely associated with road construction and development of transportation infrastructure. Some local producers, e.g. JV Igirma Tairiku, already invested large amounts in construction of timber-carrying roads, and cost efficient technologies might be in demand.

Lowrise wood house construction. The President of Russia gave development of lowrise construction the status of a national project, and regional authorities in Irkutsk presently pay much attention to establishing favorable conditions to investments in this sector. The US is the leader in residential wood construction; various types of carcass, panel and modular technologies in wooden construction are broadly used in the US, and such experience and technologies provide much interest to Russia.

Annual exhibition **Forest utilization and wood processing in Siberia** September 0407, 2012 Exhibition company SibExpoCenter, JSC 253a, Baikalskaya st., Irkutsk, 664050, Russia Tel./fax +73952353139, 352239, 358223, 352900 Email: sibexpo@mail.ru URL: www.sibexpo.ru (contains English version)

Administration of The Irkutsk region

Department of Timber Industry and Forestry

1a, Lenina st., Irkutsk, 664027, Russia Tel. +73952256287, 256291

Committee on Forestry and Timber Industry

1a, Lenina st., Irkutsk, 664027, Russia Tel. +73952256270, 256247, 256294 Fax +73952256284, 256291

Union of Wood Producers and Wood Exporters of The Irkutsk region

122, Piskunova st., Irkutsk, 664023, Russia Tel. +73952534065

Irkutsk Scientific and Research Institute of Wood Industry, JSC

122, Piskunova st., 664023, Irkutsk, Russia Tel. +73952224591, 233044, 230639 Fax +73952229650 URL: www.niilp.irks.ru

The Irkutsk regional Innovation and Service Center for Timber Industry

83, Lermontova st., Irkutsk, 664074, Russia Tel. +73952405146 Fax +73952405100 Email: tpwood@rambler.ru, tpwoodlpk@gmail.com URL: http://www.istu.edu/technopark/region/woodinnov-center.html

Irkutskgiprolestrans, JSC

(prepares design and estimate documentation, design of timber industry facilities) 125, Dekabrskih Sobytiy st., 664007, Irkutsk, Russia Tel. +73952271028 Fax +73952273434

Sibgiprobum

(performs S&R, project and design activities in the sphere of timber and pulp and paper industries) 6, Stepana Razina st., Irkutsk, 664000, Russia Tel./fax +73952242281 URL: www.sgb.irk.ru

Forestry Agency in The Irkutsk region

(deals with forest utilization, regeneration measures, fire protection, state accounting of forest resources, forest auctions) 31, Gorkogo st., Irkutsk, 664003, Russia Tel./fax +73952335981, 243155 Email: baikal@les.irk.ru

East Siberian Chamber of Commerce and Industry

16, SukheBator St., Irkutsk, 664003, Russia Tel. +73952335060, 335128 Tel./fax +73952335116 Email: info@ccies.ru URL: http://ccies.ru/en

Web resources:

www.forest.ru Russian forest industry descriptions, legislation etc.; in English.
www.lesprom.com electronic marketplace (incl. wishtobuy leads), forest industry news, search for partners; in English.
www.wood.ru diversified portal of Russian wood industry; in Russian (slightly developed English version www.wood.ru/en).
www.ruswood.ru electronic marketplace, register of producers, legislation, forest industry news etc.; in Russian.
www.fsc.ru Forest Stewardship Council; Russian; www.fsc.org international site of FSC.
www.drevesina.com daily news, market reviews, analysis, register of wood producers; in Russian.
http://catalog.wood.ru registry of Russian organizations engaged in forest industry, contains contacts of 150 Irkutsk companies; in Russian
www.woodbusiness.ru diversified forest industry portal, in Russian.
www.spindle.ru specialized electronic magazine devoted to wood processing and furniture production; in Russian.
www.woodpages.ru Russian timber and woodprocessing portal, register of producers of wood processing and auxiliary equipment; in Russian.
http://timberindustry.report.ru compilation of links to wood industry related sources; in Russian.
www.paperindustry.ru register of Russian pulp and paper producers; in Russian.

Illustrative sites of several Irkutsk companies, working in the sphere of wood processing:

www.papermills.ru English version of the site of Ilim Pulp Enterprise, Ltd http://igt.irtel.ru JV Igirma Tairiku, LLC www.woodexport.ru Lespromexport, JSC www.sibrw.ru JV Royal Wood, JSC www.irkmebel.ru Irkutsk Furniture http://avgustsib.irkutsk.ru New House, LLC http://lph.irtel.ru Zhdanovskiy Timber Industry Enterprise. http://bratskles.ru JV IcebergSiberia, LLC www.baikalwood.narod.ru BaikalWood, Ltd www.sibterema.ru Siberian Terema (Towers) http://dakolesprom.irk.ru DakoLesprom, JSC www.ooonb.ru NB, LLC http://bagin.angara.ru individual entrepreneur Bagin

OPPORTUNITIES IN TRAVEL AND TOURISM

Overall, Russian outbound travel to foreign countries continues to grow with the number of Russian tourists traveling abroad during the last ten years almost doubling. Growth in travel to the U.S. decreased as a result of the Russian financial crisis of 1998 and the events of 9/11, but has rebounded since 2003. Stronger economic ties, a rise in the ruble value and mutual interest in cultural and educational exchanges drive outbound travel to the U.S. This report presents an overview of Russian travel and tourism trends with particular attention to outbound travel of Russian tourists to the U.S.

MARKET DEMAND

Russia has experienced stable economic growth and financial prosperity for the last eight years under President Putin's administration. Growth of the domestic market, along with increased export earnings from oil and gas has contributed to yearly improvements in the Russian economy. A major construction boom and continued growth in consumer spending is contributing to overall economic growth. This dramatic growth shows signs of spreading beyond Moscow and St. Petersburg into the vast "regional areas" of Russia – a total of 11 time zones.

According to the International Monetary Fund[1], Russia's GDP grew 7.4% in 2010, and 8.1% in 2012, reaching $1.29 trillion. Per capita GDP is estimated to have reached $9,075 in 2012, as compared to $4,039 in 2009. Real disposable incomes continue to outpace GDP growth. Eight years of economic and political stability, rising revenues from export trade, appreciation of the domestic currency and continuing growth of disposable income at the annual rate of over 10% has stimulated consumer spending.

These economic factors are creating a strong market demand for travel – both tourist and business, both domestic and foreign.

Market Data

The number of Russian tourists traveling abroad grew 22% from 7.75 million in 2010, to 9.37 million in 2012. The strong growth in travel abroad is based on a number of factors:

- Increased disposable income and consumer spending
- Increased prices for domestic travel destinations has dulled their cost advantage
- Increased business, educational and cultural exchanges
- Development of outbound travel services
- Appreciation of the ruble against the dollar

OVERALL OUTBOUND TRAVEL

Statistics show that travel to CIS (Commonwealth of Independent States, or the former Soviet Union) countries constitutes 53% of the total travel in 2012. However, the overwhelming majority of Russian tourist travel was to nonCIS destinations. This is explained by the fact that many visits to the former Soviet republics were for reasons other than tourism, i.e. business, personal, emigration, services and military duty.

ALL OUTBOUND TRAVEL OUTBOUND TOURIST TRAVEL

NonCIS Countries CIS Countries

CIS Countries 0.5 million

16.3 million 18.0 million

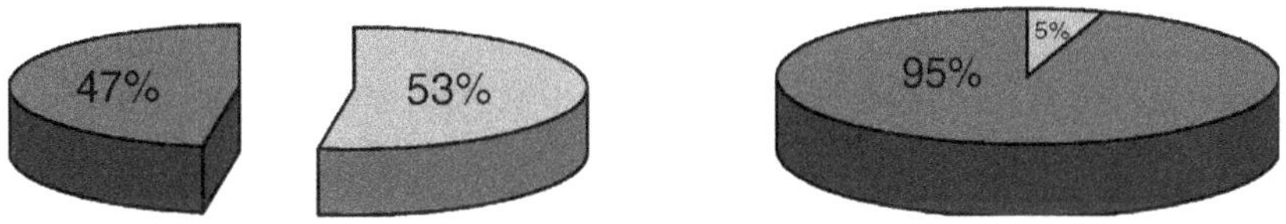

NonCIS Countries 8.9 million

Source: Rosstat

According to Rosstat, (http://www.gks.ru) 34.3 million Russians traveled abroad in 2012, 18%

more than in 2010. The growth rate for tourist travel is slightly higher at 21% (9.4 million travelers), while business travel decreased 8%. Turkey has held first place in the total number of Russian tourists for the past several years. Turkish travel operators market their destinations at all trade shows and maintain an overall aggressive marketing campaign in Russia. Because of proximity to Russia and the readily available goods that can be carried back to Russia, China holds second place, and Egypt is third. The top three markets by growth rate are Thailand (60%), Austria (44%), and Tunisia and Egypt (39%). These impressive growth rates illustrate a large and growing market for foreign destinations. Outbound traffic statistics indicate that in addition to traditional warm and seaside destinations more Russians choose countries where time on the beach may be supplemented by other activities such as cultural and sporting events, shopping and recreation.

Travel to the United States

A Russian financial crisis in 1998, and the events of 9/11resulted in a downward trend in Russian tourist travel to the U.S. until 2003. Since that time, the number of tourists has grown annually and the growth rate is accelerating. According to the Office of Travel and Tourism at the U.S. Department of Commerce, the number of Russians traveling to the U.S. on tourist visas totaled 113,000 in 2012, up 20% from 2010.

There are four major reasons attributed to this increase:

1. Visa processing has improved significantly and Russian tour operators are educating travelers to this fact.

The U.S. Embassy (Moscow) and Consulates (St. Petersburg, Ekaterinburg and Vladivostok) have made great progress in streamlining the visa application process in the face of a rapidly growing number of applications; instructions, documents, and fees are described online at the Embassy's website:

http://moscow.usembassy.gov/consular/consular.php?record_id=visas

The availability of this information online has made it possible to counter the market's impression that U.S. visas are expensive, difficult to obtain, and take a long time to process. The information is available in the Russian language, making it easy for a Russian tour operator to point potential travelers to a single source of information on the process, timeframe and cost to obtain a visa.

The U.S. Department of State website offers information on the average wait times for visas anywhere in the world at:

http://travel.state.gov/visa/temp/wait/tempvisitors_wait_result.php?post=Moscow&x=66&y=18

2. The ruble has strengthened against the U.S. dollar.

The falling value of the dollar is a financial incentive for tourists to look to the U.S. for economical tour packages and destinations. A tour package priced at $2700 in April 2012 cost a Russian buyer RUR 70,090. A year later, in April 2008 that same package price cost RUR 63,577, a decrease of 9%.

3. There is a growing preference for U.S. tour packages in relation to European destinations.

As the market becomes more educated about U.S. destinations, visa processing, and purchase value, the Russian market increasingly looks to the U.S. for destinations. The most requested destinations include New York City, ski and winter sports resorts, national parks, gambling destinations, and entertainment destinations such as Disney properties.

4. Travelers who have been to other destinations are interested in U.S. destinations for their next trip.

Russian tourists who have traveled to Asia and Europe in the past are willing to look for destinations that are different from those they have already visited. The activity may be similar, but a different destination is appealing. For example, skiers who have visited Austria and Switzerland because it is close are looking to Colorado, Utah and Vermont for their next trip.

In a survey conducted by the Foreign Commercial Service Moscow Office, participating Russian tour operators reported the following observations regarding Russian tourist travel to the U.S.:

- The average trip duration is 1214 days.
- A typical trip includes more than one destination and at least two major cities.
- The most popular activities include historic sights, shopping, recreational activities and sports,
entertainment, visits to natural landmarks, and beach leisure.

- The busiest points of entry are New York, Atlanta, Los Angeles and Miami.
- The percentage of families traveling with children is 3035%.
- Accommodation preferences – Delux/5 Star (40%), Superior/4 Star (40%) and First Class/3 Star
(20%).

BUYING TRENDS

There are a number of ways in which Russians purchase tours to the U.S. Most tourists go to travel agencies to make their selection and order their entire travel package from an agent. Though payments via the Internet are not yet the norm, some more advanced Internet users make their selection and reservations online and then go to a travel agency to purchase their selection. As high speed internet access becomes more readily available in homes and the workplace, and as credit card usage increases it is expected that online purchasing will grow. Some travelers are sent by their employers to agencies in order to purchase corporate travel packages.

Visit USA Committee

Responding to a growing interest in developing inbound travel to the United States from Russia, the U.S. Commercial Service has promoted the establishment of a Visit USA Committee, uniting local tour operators, air carriers, U.S. suppliers and government organizations. The Russian Visit USA Committee will become a major instrument for promoting inbound travel to the United States by facilitating information exchange and formation of business ties between travel firms and professionals in the two countries.

An informal Visit USA Committee was formed immediately following International Pow Wow in 2012. The Committee consists of Moscowbased travel and tour operators that combined book approximately 80% of U.S.bound tourist travel. The Committee meets on an informal but regular basis and offers a forum for U.S. vendors to come to Moscow and present their destinations.

Based on data gathered from the Visit USA Committee and recent trade show visitors, the most promising destinations in the U.S. include:

- Cities: New York City, Miami and Las Vegas
- National Parks
- Ski and Winter Resorts

• Leisure and Entertainment Complexes

New York City has been and will likely remain the most popular city destination for Russian tourists in the near future. Personal and business travel to NYC are often combined. Russians have family, historic and cultural ties to this city putting NYC on the top of any list for brand awareness, following by Miami and Las Vegas. Interest in the U.S. National Parks is growing as there are no such parks in Russia. Ski and winter sports resorts have become more popular in recent years as they provide a unique travel experience in variety, beauty and quality of service. Because of the falling dollar they have become more economical than European destinations. Other specific destinations of interest include various locations in Florida famous for their comfort and opportunities for different forms of leisure, and Las Vegas, considered by many Russians to be the gambling and entertainment capital of the world.

Prospective Buyers

American Best Getaways, Inc.

Margarita Polyakova, General Representative 149 Madison Ave, Suite 202, New York, NY 10016 Tel. (212) 5325130 Fax: (212) 5325127 Email: contact@americanbestgetaways.ru

Vista Tour

Liudmila Vakhrusheva, Director VIP and Corporate Travel 54/1 Prospect Lenina, Yekaterinburg, Russia Tel. +7 (343) 350 0302

http://www.vistatour.ru

Geont

Margarita Odinokova, Manager 11 Novy Arbat, Office 804, Moscow, Russia Tel: +7 (495) 291 7161

http://www.geont.ru Email: geont@aha.ru

Roza Vetrov

Lidia Sladkova, Head of VIP and Individual Travel 17 B. Kommunisticheskaya Ulitsa, Bldg. 1A, Moscow, Russia Tel: +7 (495) 967 6868 Fax: +7 (495) 911 2208

http://www.rozav.ru Email: sweet@rozav.ru

NYC & Co.

Valeri Ishunkin, Account Manager 39 Prospect Mira, Bldg. 2, Moscow, Russia Tel: +7 (495) 937 5950 (ext. 124) Fax: +7 (495) 937 5951

http://www.nycvisit.com Email: vishunkin@aviareps.com

Euro Business Tour

Alexander Chiburaev, Executive Manager 25 Mozhaiskoe Shosse, Office 318/319 Tel: +7 (495) 105 6533 Fax: +7 (495) 440 7997

http://www.viptravel.ru Email: alexandre@businesstour.ru

America Travel

Margarita Babayan, General Director 16 Ulitsa Dm. Ulyanov, Bldg. 2, Office 88, Moscow, Russia Tel: +7 (495) 935 7925 Fax: +7 (495) 935 7926

http://www.americatravel.ru Email: pktours@online.ru

Centra (Central Travel Agency)

Galina Redkina, President 15 1st Brestskaya Ulitsa, Moscow, Russia

http://www.centra.ru Email: gal@centra.ru

Agency 001

Daryana Boyarintseva, Head Manager 12 Posledny Per., Moscow, Russia Tel: +7 (495) 730 5899 Fax: +7 (495) 207 0357

http://www.agency001.ru Email: dasha@agency001.ru

International Exchange Center

Armen Karapetyan, General Director 4 B. Devyatinsky Per., Moscow, Russia Tel: +7 (495) 252 0067 Fax: +7 (495) 255 4958 Email: armen@iec.ru

Vegas USA Club

Vitaly Kuznetsov, General Director 2 Smolensky Per., Moscow, Russia Tel: +7 (916) 301 0083 Fax: +7 (495) 649 0083 Email: vk@vegasusaclub.com

INNA Tour

Svetlana Kurkovich, Deputy Director Business Development 13 Kalanchevskaya Ulitsa, Moscow, Russia Tel: +7 (495) 983 3039 Fax: +7 (495) 983 3036

http://www.inna.ru Email: s.kourkovich@inna.ru

Lanta Tour

Oksana Perepechina, Deputy Director USA and Individual Travel Dept.
14/23 M. Vlasyevsky Per., Moscow, Russia
Tel: +7 (495) 638 5262 Fax: +7 (495) 638 5261

http://www.lantatur.ru
Email: Perepechina@lantatur.ru

MARKET ENTRY

The Russian travel and tourism market is competitive, and relatively transparent. Between 70% and 80% of all tour companies are small and mediumsize enterprises. However, newcomers to the market may be exposed to unexpected hidden barriers to entry ranging from additional charges and fees to flaws in legislation and corruption. For that reason, it is recommended that new arrivals to the market establish contacts with local firms and work with them in the form of partnership or a subsidiary.

Market Issues and Obstacles

A growing demand for new destinations generated by rising personal incomes and ruble appreciation will stimulate further diversification of the tourist market. Apart from new destinations, demand for new services and new forms of travel are to be expected.

On January 1, 2012 Russian tour operators are no longer required to undergo mandatory licensing.

On June 1, 2012, the Federal law "On the principles of business activity in the tourist sector of the Russian Federation" came into effect. According to this law, tour operators selling tour packages for travel outside the CIS are required to provide liability insurance for up to RUR 5 million per traveler. The insurance will protect travelers from financial insolvency of their tour operators. The law came as a reaction to numerous cases of financial insolvency and fraud among Russian travel agencies.

Some in the Russian travel industry believe that the law does not account for the broad interest of the travel and tourism business community. Smaller companies may be at a disadvantage as banks and insurance companies may give better terms to large volume vendors and drive small and mediumsized companies out of the market. Industry experts believe this situation could gradually force as many as 7,000 to 8,000 small and mediumsize companies out of business as independent tour operators and cause market consolidation. This may create opportunities for U.S. companies seeking to establish direct presence on the Russian travel and tourism market.

Airlines

Aeroflot Russian Airlines
37 Leningradsky Prospect, bldg. 9, Moscow
Phone: +7 495 223 5555 Fax: +7 495 155 6647
www.aeroflot.ru
Delta Airlines
11 Gogolevsky Blvd., 2 floor, Moscow
Phone: +7 495 937 9090 Fax: +7 495 937 9091
www.delta.com
American Airlines
20, Sadovaya Kudrinskaya, office 207
Phone: +7 495 234 40 74
www.aa.com
Singapore Airlines
Hotel Renaissance, 18/1, Olympisky Prospect, Moscow Phone: +7 495 937 5920 Fax: +7 495 931 9067
www.singaporeair.com
Travel Industry Association (TIA)
Luiz De Moura, Jr., Senior Director, International Marketing 1100 New York Avenue, NW Suite 450 Washington, DC 200053934 Tel: +1 202 408 2151
http://www.tia.org
International Trade Administration Office of Travel & Tourism Industries
U.S. Department of Commerce
http://tinet.ita.doc.gov
R
U.S. Department of Homeland Security, USVisit Program
Cynthia Obas, Office of Outreach and Public Liaison 1616 N. Fort Myer Drive Arlington, VA 22209 Tel: +1 202 298 5023 Email: www.dhs.gov
BFOR International

Bjorn Bieneck, President & CEO 805 Princess Anne Street, Suite 1 Fredericksburg, VA 22401 Tel: +1 540 373 9935

Russian Travel Industry Union
Sergey Shpilko, President 11, Stoleshnikov per., office 426 Moscow, 107031 Russia Tel: +7 495 692 2464
http://www.ratanews.ru Email: rata@rata.ru

Russian Association of Tour Operators
Svetlana Fedorova, Head of Public Relations 23/2, B. Molchanovka, office 4 Tel: +7 495 203 0064
http://www.ator.biz Email: ator@ator.biz

For More Information

The U.S. Commercial Service in Moscow, Russian Federation can be contacted via email at: Vladimir.Goryachev@mail.doc.gov; Phone: +7 495 737 5034; Fax: +7 495 737 5033; or visit our website: http://www.buyusa.gov/russia

The U.S. Commercial Service — Your Global Business Partner

With its network of offices across the United States and in more than 80 countries, the U.S. Commercial Service of the U.S. Department of Commerce utilizes its global presence and international marketing expertise to help U.S. companies sell their products and services worldwide. Locate the U.S. Commercial Service trade specialist in the

U.S. nearest you by visiting http://www.export.gov/.

OPPORTUNITIES IN OIL AND GAS INDUSTRY

The Russian oil and gas industry is a strategic sector of the Russian and accounts for 61% of Russian exports. The industry has demonstrated strong performance in the last 18 months and is concentrated on about a dozen development projects. This report provides an overview of the most important upcoming projects, including major transport projects and refining upgrades. These projects are expected to result in significant sales opportunities for U.S. equipment and services suppliers, including oil and gas equipment, design, engineering, surveying, service equipment, heavy and light construction, transportation, catering, housing, shipping, medical suppliers and others.

MARKET OVERVIEW

Russia's oil and gas industry continues to prosper from sustained high prices and increasing exports. According to various industry reports oil and gas production in Russia grew 2.5% in 2010, oil and gas exports were up 2%, refining was up 5.5% and estimates for growth in 2012 are 2-4%. Recent mergers and acquisitions by industry giants Gazprom, Rosneft and Lukoil indicate the industry is consolidating and maturing, and is emerging as the driver of growth within the energy sector in terms of operation, service, equipment and technology.

The following Russian companies posted the highest oil and gas condensate extraction volumes: Rosneft, Lukoil, TNK-BP, Surgutneftegaz, and Gazprom Neft. Among foreign players operating in the market Chevron, ExxonMobil, ConocoPhillips, Hydro and Sibir Energy enjoyed the largest growth.

Major trends in the Russian oil and gas market include the following:

Consolidation: Where 20 different companies might have been found on the market in 2000, today one might find no more than 6-8. In other words, the market has become more structured and stable with fewer and larger players.

Increasing activity of domestic companies and their strengthening positions: They currently command more than 70% of the market and their share continues to grow. While most activity is taking place in Western Siberia, Sakhalin distributors have begun to show the desire and incentive to put resources into other regions for more modest projects.

High depreciation of fixed assets: Depreciation exceeds 60% as of January 2012, with the figure for the main gas pipelines being 59%, for compressor stations 90%, and for other equipment 62%.

Growth of gas export contracts: High export prices are resulting in accelerated construction of pipelines, rather than in the modernization of fixed assets.

At present, this sector incorporates more than 15,000 enterprises in Russia. Locally produced oil and gas equipment enjoys a price advantage, particularly in transportation and pipeline segments, although their technology is often old and their manufacturing facilities are outdated like a whole complex of machine-building enterprises in the Urals region. However, competition among importers has also intensified as evidenced by an increase in the number of tenders.

U.S. equipment, technological solutions and products for the industry are recognized for their excellent quality and after-sales service and oil and gas field machinery, oil recovery, exploration and field management services are expected to remain in first place for U.S. exports to Russia.

The oilfield services market experienced a major boost during 2010, rising to $12 billion. Growing demand has been reported for work-over, rehabilitation/reconditioning equipment/services as well as drilling and well tools and products. The largest oilfield services companies operating in Russia include: Integra, Baker Hughes, Bentec GmbH Drilling and Oilfield Systems, Parker Drilling, PetroAlliance, Schlumberger Oilfield Services, Halliburton, M-I Swaco, BJ Services, Weatherford, and Pride International.

PROJECTS

Industry experts anticipate that major oil and gas development projects in the Yamal Peninsular, multiple Sakhalin projects and Timan-Pechora areas in Western Siberia, as well as Arctic shelf will catalyze technological upgrades as well as construction, infrastructure and other services for oil and gas field development on a large scale. Russia has the longest sea shelf in the world and about 85% of it is located in the Arctic region. According to the government program for oil and gas offshore development gas suppliers should reach more than 170 billion cubic meters and more than 10 million tons of oil annually by 2030. The main greenfields are in the Barents Sea, and the Obskaya and Tazovskaya offshore zones.

Major oil and gas projects in Russia:

1. Sakhalin –1
2. Sakhalin –2
3. Timan-Pechora - Lukoil/ConocoPhilips
4. Shtokman gas fields – Gazprom
5. Yamal Peninsula - Gazprom
6. Nord Stream – Gazprom
7. Caspian Pipeline Consortium - Chevron, Lukoil, and others
8. Kharyaga (Nenets Autonomy Region) – Total, Norsk Hydro
9. Vankor oil and gas field – Rosneft

10. Priobsky Oil Field – Rosneft
11. Khanty-Mansijsk Oilfields – Rosneft
12. Kovykta gas field (east Siberia) - Gazprom, TNK-BP

According to industry experts and numerous news reports gas production in Russia should grow to 742-754 billion cubic meters by 2015 compared to 638 billion cubic meters in 2009. The bulk of the increase is expected in Northwest Russia (up 38 billion cubic meters) due to the development of Shtokman offshore deposit in the Barents Sea, and in East Siberia (up 33 billion cubic meters) due to the Kovykta deposit in the Irkutsk Region Russia is moving ahead on prospective new gas export routes to Europe, particularly for LNG. A feasibility study for a project to transport natural gas to Europe and the U.S. from the giant Shtokman gas field across the Baltic Sea is underway. The pipeline is expected to be able to deliver up to 30 billion cubic meters of gas per year. In autumn 2010, Gazprom said it would go ahead on its own with this gas field development. But currently the state gas monopoly is actively attracting foreign partners to its $20 billion project.

According to the FC-Novosti Information Agency, by 2015, gas exports may reach 274-281 billion cubic meters compared to 207 billion cubic meters in 2009, with export-oriented gas production growing at a priority pace. As much as 30 billion cubic meters of gas will be delivered to China annually along a new Trans-Altai pipeline. Gas deliveries to Europe will grow from 154 billion cubic meters to 175 billion cubic meters, with due account for supplies along Nord Stream and the prolongation of the Blue Stream pipeline to Italy and Central Europe.

Russian gas exports to the former Soviet republics will be gradually replaced with Central Asian gas, which has been historically cheaper than Russian one. The share of the former Soviet republics in Russia's gas export will go down to 6%.

Other recent developments include the construction of the **East Siberia–Pacific Ocean** (ESPO) oil pipeline (Taishet – Ust-Kut – Talakan – Aldan – Skovorodino). Transneft, a state-owned oil transportation company, is taking a lead on it. Earlier, Russian President Vladimir Putin insisted that the route should be moved away from the pristine and unique Lake Baikal. This made the pipeline 20% longer. Currently, the projected cost of the pipeline, with consideration of route changes, inflation and growing prices of pipes and construction materials, is $13.1 billion. However, according to preliminary estimates Russia's exports will increase by some 30%, reaching the level of both the Japanese and Korean markets. Interfax reports that in the first phase, 15 million tons of oil from ESPO will be delivered through a branch to China to be completed by the end of 2012 and 15 million tons by rail to Primorye for further delivery through Kozmino. The pipeline is expected to be commissioned in October-December 2008. The second stage will be built from Skovorodino to Kozmino. Branches will also be built to oil refineries in Khabarovsk and Komsomolsk-on-Amur. Oil deliveries along ESPO may reach 7 million tons a year to the Komsomolsk refinery and 5 million tons to Khabarovsk. A new refinery with an annual capacity of 10-20 million tons is being designed for the ultimate destination of ESPO. It is estimated that the final stage of the project will be commissioned in 2015-2017.

REFINERIES

High oil export duties lead the companies to refine more oil and sell fuel to the domestic market and export more products with lower export duties. To meet the growing demand for fuel and other oil products in the Russian Northwest, Surgutneftegaz is planning to build a $6 billion refinery in the Leningrad Region by 2011, according to The Moscow Times (September 28, 2012 "Surgut to Build Refinery"). The new plant, Kirishi-2, will be able to process 12 million tons of oil a year, which will boost the company's refining capacity by 50%. Surgutneftegaz will invest at least $2.8 billion to build a catalytic cracking unit in 2009 to produce more light products at Kirishinefteorgsintez.

Tatneft, one of the biggest Russian oil producers will build the $5 billion refinery in Nizhnekamsk by 2009.

The company has contracted Fluor Corporation to implement the project. Other oil quality of shipment to European standards as the country's crude-export taxes make sales of refined products more attractive.

Russian projects to upgrade refineries in 2009-2010:

Company	Refinery Upgrades	Investment (millions)
Lukoil	Permnefteorgsintez	$139
	Volgogradneftepererabotka	$302
	Nizhegorodnefteorgsintez	$375
TNK-BP	Ryazanksy Refinery Plant	$407
	Saratovsky Refinery Plant	$ 54
Slavneft	Yaroslavsky Refinery Plant	$211
Rosneft	Komsomolsky Refinery Plant	$727
	Tuapse Refinery Plant	$784
TAIF	Nizhnekamsky Refinery Plant	$550

BEST PROSPECTS

Some local experts on oil and gas equipment expect at least 20% growth in U.S. imports in 2012-08 and beyond, a prediction which assumes that Russia's economic growth will continue at its current healthy rate, and that U.S. suppliers will continue to market aggressively. The best prospects for U.S. equipment and services are oil recovery, well optimization, horizontal drilling, hydro-fracturing equipment and services, offshore development technologies and equipment, work-over, rehabilitation/reconditioning equipment/services as well as drilling and well tools and products, and idle well re-commissioning services. The most lucrative prospects for U.S. equipment exports are for greenfield and transportation projects. The market for brownfields is also generally good, although more price sensitive.

Market Entry

Russia has a wide network of highly qualified oil and gas equipment distributors ranging from the very large broad-liners and those with large dealer networks to the small highly specialized resellers. Most U.S. products are sold through this channel. In addition, a number of U.S. companies have their own subsidiaries and well-established distribution networks throughout the country. Russian distributors tend to believe that it is not always cost effective for a manufacturer to maintain a representative office in Russia, until sales volumes become substantial. Leading U.S. companies, such as Halliburton, Schlumberger, JB Services, M-I Swaco, Parker Drilling, Baker Hughes, as well as other foreign players from Germany, Norway, and France, are well represented in the Russian market and their products are available either directly or through representatives or distributors.

Recently, additional channels have become available, such as independent sales agents and e-commerce services. Some oil and gas equipment distributors have been in existence for more than 20 years. They have substantial experience and have developed extensive business connections, putting them in a position to fully service the needs of U.S. exporters. They will also be able to provide a thorough analysis of sale possibilities and evaluate products against their competitors in terms of both price and quality.

The U.S. Department of Commerce recommends that the Russian market for oil and gas equipment be approached recognizing the difficulties which can be encountered, but also with an appreciation for the significant sales potential. Russia's unclear, often parallel, lines of governmental and commercial authority, convoluted management-shareholder relations, selectively and sporadically enforced commercial legislation, and instances of corruption make this a difficult market. To succeed in this challenging business environment, a company should cultivate strong connections with Russian industry and with other Western companies with complementary interests; maintain a physical company presence in Russia; enter the market with a long-term strategy; exercise thorough due diligence and be persistent.

Another way for American companies to participate in the market is by partnering with Russian design and engineering firms, which still have limited ability to exercise strict quality control over manufacturers. Flexibility in approaching project development is important and companies need to adapt rapidly and often cooperate with other firms.

MARKET ISSUES

There are very few trade barriers to the marketing and sale of oil and gas equipment in Russia. Although it is the importer who pays the duties, levies and taxes, it ultimately is factored into the final sales price. As such, it is an important factor, which determines the competitiveness of the exporter. Russia's tariff system is based on F.O.B. prices. The customs duty rate on imported business equipment into Russia is 10-15%. To this an additional 18% "import VAT" is charged. Importers must obtain certificates showing that their products meet Russian standards. Few U.S. exporters experience problems in obtaining certification, but the process can take time and involve additional expense. Compliance testing is typically performed at commercially operated testing stations in Russia or abroad, and the results passed to GosStandart of Russia (State Agency of the Russian Federation for Standardization and Metrology) who issues the certificate. Information on the procedure can be obtained from the importer or from the U.S. and Foreign Commercial Service in Moscow.

RESOURCES & KEY CONTACTS

AmCham Moscow http://www.amcham.ru/
AmCham St. Petersburg http://www.amcham.ru/spb/
GosStandart, The Federal Agency for Technical Regulations and Metrology http://www.gost.ru/
Ministry of Energy and Industry of the RF
http://www.minprom.gov.ru/

Ministry of Natural Resources of the RF
http://www.mnr.gov.ru/
Russian Center for Tests and Certification (Rostest) http://www.rostest.ru
Russian Standard, general representative of ROSTEST for North America

http://www.rosstandard.com

U.S. Embassy Russia http://www.usembassy.ru
U.S. Department of Energy, Energy Information Administration:

http://www.eia.doe.gov/emeu/cabs/Russia/Background.html

For more information about this subject contact the U.S. Commercial Service in Moscow, Russia at: Moscow.Office.Box@mail.doc.gov; Phone: 7-495-737-5030; Fax: 7-495-737-5033; or visit our website: http://www.buyusa.gov/russia/en/

AEROSPACE AND DEFENSE MARKET

This report provides information about the current status of the Russian market for aviation equipment and services. The report features the market size, a discussion of the ongoing consolidation of the domestic Russian aviation industry, and opportunities that exist for U.S.

exporters of aircraft, parts and equipment, and services.

Background

The Russian Government views aviation as one of the strategic national industries and maintains strict oversight of foreign investment in the sector. Indeed, the military and civilian aircraft industries are inseparably joined, relying on the same producers and employing the same factories and employees. Last year, Russia set a new record with exports of military equipment reaching $6.1 billion, over half of that figure representing aircraft and related equipment. The industry is also vital to the continued economic wellbeing of many Russian cities. While officially, some 450,000 personnel are directly related to the aircraft manufacturing sector (¼ of all the employed in the defense sector, the number of those in related industries would likely double that number.

The Russian aviation industry was seriously afflicted by the market reforms of the last decade. Starting in 1990, government subsidies to the industry were slashed and the procurement of new aircraft, equipment and spares were drastically reduced, this left factories operating at only a fraction of their capacity. The stateowned airline Aeroflot was divided into the International carrier and numerous local airlines (currently about 200). Decentralization generally had a detrimental effect on the industry. Many local airlines chased for shortterm gains at the expense of fleet modernization. Human factor is another dimension of the problem. Brain drain from the leading research facilities has reached tremendous proportions: from 1991 approximately 2000 scientists and researchers have left the country annually. On the average Russian scientific community has lost over 40% of its scientific potential, and the aviation industry was one of the most affected.

The Russian Government is taking active steps to consolidate the industry in order to deal with disintegration in the industry and to build up its competitive advantage. In February 2010, President Putin signed the decree on formation of the Unified Aviation Building Corporation (UAC). In November 2010, Russia's Defense Minister Sergey Ivanov was appointed Chairman of the UAC board. UAC, with an estimated asset value of about $3.6 billion, will unite about 20 Russian major aviation enterprises, including 7 aircraftbuilding plants and 5 design bureaus. Among others, UAC will include Sukhoi, MiG, Illyushin, Irkut, Yakovlev and Tupolev – most famous Russian aircraftbuilding plants.

The longerterm goal of the UAC, according to the Ministry of Energy and Industry, is to become one of the world's leading players, to reach a minimum return of $6 billion and, by 2015, to match the sales volume of Airbus, Boeing, Bombardier and Embraer.

UAC will have four structural divisions, including Military Aviation, Civil Aviation, Transport and Specialized Aviation, Parts and Components. It is planned that UAC will initially manufacture 30% civil and 70% military aircraft. The state will hold 75% of the new structure's military business, 51% in transport and specialized sector and 25% in the civil aviation. Eventually, UAC will switch 50% civil aircraft output.

Consolidation is also under way among airlines and manufacturers of aviation supply equipment. By consolidating the industry, the Russian Government plans to at least double the production within the next 10 years, according to Viktor Khristenko, Minister Industry and Energy.

International cooperation is an important area of Russia's aerospace sector development. Sukhoi Superjet100 (RRJ) is Russia's most dynamic and ambitious national project, designed to replace aging Russian airplanes and intended to compete worldwide with those made by Bombardier and Embraer. The SuperJet project is a family of mediumrange passenger aircraft, designed to seat 75 to 95 passengers. Sukhoi plans to produce at least 700 Superjet planes, and intends to sell 35% of them to North America, 25% to Europe, 10% to Latin American, and 7% to Russian and China. The first planes will be completed in 2012. The RRJ project includes participation of many major U.S. and European aviation corporations, including Boeing, Honeywell, B/E Aerospace

(U.S.), Snecma, Thales, Messier Dowty (France), Liebherr Aerospace (Switzerland) and others. Boeing acts as a minority investor and consultant in such areas as project management, market planning, certification and customer support.

SIZE OF THE MARKET

The Russian air transportation market is expected to grow in the near future. According to data released by the Russian Ministry of Transportation, in 2009, Russian airlines transported 35 million travelers, an increase of 3.9% compared to 2009. By 2010, it is expected to exceed 50 million travelers per year. Airbus experts say that for the next 20 years, the volume of passenger transportation in Russia is expected to grow faster than globally. The Russian market will grow 6% on the average annually, whereas the rest of the world will have only 5.3% annual growth.

To accommodate this growing demand, airlines will require 200 long haul aircraft and 300 regional aircraft. Other statistics from the Ministry of Industry and Energy indicate that the need for regional aircraft will amount to 320350 units up to year 2022, which is approximately $6 billion. According to Airbus estimates, the Russian industry will require more that 600 aircraft at the total cost of $45 billion. Another 80 freight aircraft will be needed to meet the growing cargo transportation needs. The above statistics makes the Russian market one of the most attractive national markets for manufacturers and suppliers of aircraft and related aviation equipment.

Smaller regional aircraft (both for chartered VIP flights and for public flights) is another important market segment of the industry. According to reports from the Ministry of Economic Development and Trade, air transport will remain the single way of transportation in the Eastern regions of Russia. The average distances among inhabited areas in Siberia and the Russian Far East are about 600700 kilometers. Roads are in poor condition and ground transportation can take several days. The number of inhabitants in Siberian towns and settlements is fairly small and planes with 1520 seats would work best to meet their needs. No information is available about the exact size of this market.

Challenges faced by the industry

The Russian aviation industry is currently not able to supply sufficient number of quality aircraft to meet the internal growing demand. The following factors have a role to play:

Aging of the Russian fleet. According to the Federal Agency of Air Transport (2010 statistics), the Russian fleet is comprised of 5,385 planes and helicopters, with most aircraft operating since Soviet times. Only 2,481 aircraft are currently in service (46.07%). Among this operating fleet, 761 aircraft (about 30%) have been in service for more than 25 years. In total, up to 95% of the current fleet needs replacement and upgrading. According to reports from Boeing released in 2009, practically all the planes used today must be decommissioned until 2024.

Operational inefficiencies of domestic aircraft. The Russian aircraft is 1040% less effective compared to Airbus and Boeing in terms of fuel efficiency, weight, after sale service, and noise reduction capacity, according to Mr. Sergey Koltovich, Head of the Aeroflot Planning Service.

Slow aircraft renewal by the domestic industry. In 2009, the Russian industry produced the maximum of 12 aircraft, according to Reuters. That same year, Airbus and Boeing produced 378 and 290 planes, respectively. In 2009, the domestic aircraft factories were operating only at about 30% of their capacity. Scaling down of aircraft production comes as a result of reduced government funding and insufficient R&D investment, following the market reforms in the early 1990s.

Need to comply with new ICAO standards. Most Russian aircraft in service do not comply with existing ICAO noise standards. Only a few types of the existing Russian aircraft (TU204, TU0214 and IL96300) meet

Stage3 noise standards currently in effect in EU countries and the United States. Further introduction of the Stage4 noise standards will require heavy expenses by airlines to comply. Cost is a major delaying factor cited by Russian carriers. For example, the cost of fitting a ground collision system to a Russian aircraft (TU-154 or IL96) is estimated at $50,000100,000 per aircraft. However, if this replacement does not take place quickly enough, Russia may lose a significant share of the European market ($ 30 million), which is 3 million passengers annually.

Export orientation of major aviation manufacturers. Since foreign markets offer more lucrative gains to major domestic aviation manufacturers (Sukhoi, MiG, Irkut, etc.), they try to promote their products outside of Russia. Out of 94 helicopters produced in Russia in 2009, only 3 helicopters went to the Russian internal market, according to the Ministry of Industry and Energy. The recent growth in production of aircraft tends to benefit export oriented transactions, rather than Russia's internal market.

Substandard aircraft parts crisis

Recent crashes in Russia have drawn increasing attention to the use of substandard and counterfeit parts by some Russian airlines. Russian officials have also identified this as a serious problem for ensuring the operational safety of the nation's air transport system. The demand for substandard parts tends to be generated by numerous small airlines that do have not sufficient funds to purchase quality parts and try to get cheaper deals at the expense of travelers' safety. Russian prosecutors and officials with the Transportation Ministry have discovered many violations of safety regulations in the work of air carriers, and serious drawbacks in the activities of regulatory bodies. According to the Prosecutor General's Office, airplane parts produced by unofficial sources were used in a number of aircraft, possibly leading to inflight emergencies.

In September 2010, the Russian Federal Agency for Supervision on Transport initiated revision of the entire parts supply chain in Russia in an effort to identify dealers of counterfeit parts. The Russian market of aircraft parts includes 600 independent suppliers, 300 parts manufacturers and 48 repair factories, according to Mr. Igor Kirpichev, Director of the Center for certification of aircraft equipment.

OPPORTUNITIES

The growing air transportation market in Russia and the challenges faced by the domestic industry listed above offer opportunities for U.S. exports and U.S.Russian cooperation projects.

• Exports of aircraft and parts

Foreign airplanes are viewed by Russian airlines as an opportunity to modernize their aging fleets and to strengthen their flight safety and dependability. For example, Aeroflot plans to give up using older Soviet planes, such as IL86, TU135 and TU154, in favor of Boeing 787 and Airbus A320. New Russian models, RRJ and IL96, will also become part of the Aeroflot modernized fleet. By 2010, Aeroflot plans to acquire 110 foreign aircraft, 30 new RRJ and 6 IL96300.

As of August 2010, Russian airlines use 116 foreign passenger planes (long haul and regional), capturing airplanes in 2009, that number could rise from 50 to 70 per year in 20102010, according to International Lease Finance Corporation.

Western avionics and engines are another business opportunity for U.S. exporters, as Russian aircraft manufacturers are seeking to make their domestically produced aircraft competitive and attractive to Russian and foreign carriers by bringing them in compliance with international noise, emissions, navigation, and other requirements.

In 2010, the Russian Government has made some significant moves to reduce import tariffs in order to facilitate procurement of foreign aircraft and parts.

Following the signing of the bilateral U.S. – Russia market access agreement in November 2010 that is an important element in Russia's WTO accession, Russia's import tariff concessions will yield significant market access opportunities for the U.S. civil aircraft industry. Tariffs on wide body aircraft will be reduced from 20% to 7.5% over 4 years following accession. Civil aircraft parts, including engines, will be reduced to an average of 5%. Leased aircraft will also enjoy reduced tariffs. Effective immediately, Russia will dramatically reduce tariffs on leased narrow body aircraft with less than 50 seats and with between 115 and 160 seats. Such aircraft can be made available under leasing agreements entered into between now and January1, 2011.

The Russian Government has also temporarily lifted import duties on parts and materials used in the production of aviation engines. The decree, which will come into force in mid December 2010, is part of government efforts to assist the joint Saturn/Snecma SaM146 engine program for the Sukhoi Super Jet100. The decree will also allow other engine producers benefit from the concession for a period of nine months.

• International cooperation projects

The aerospace sector is one of the most promising areas for U.S.Russian commercial partnerships, especially for hightechnology investments that support skilled jobs in both countries. Joint projects that are most likely to succeed are those that combine the advantages of Russia's aerospace – especially expertise of Russian aerospace experts, Russian airframe manufacturing experience, with U.S. strengths in aircraft engines, avionics, and other onboard systems. Boeing operates the Boeing Design Center in Moscow, employing Russian engineers to work in research, materials, design, information technology, and modification work on the 777, the 787, and other commercial aircraft models.

Russia is also a key supply of raw materials – especially titanium – used in Western aerospace production. In August 2010, Boeing signed off on a joint venture with VSMPOAvisma to supply titanium for its airplanes. Boeing will purchase $18 billionworth of VSMPO's titanium products.

The Russian Government and industry representatives are looking for broader cooperation with foreign firms in order to revitalize their domestic industry and integrate it into the global aviation industry. In October 2010, the Russian Government passed a decree for greater foreign ownership in aerospace ventures, making changes to the 1998 law that confined foreign ownership to only 25%. The new decree will allow foreign companies to own stakes of up to 49% with Presidential approval. The decree does not represent a wholesale opening of the Russian aerospace industry, as the government will retain the blocking interest in joint ventures. It is, however, indicative of the general trend to attract muchneeded foreign investment in this strategic industry.

TRAVEL AND TOURISM RUSSIA TO THE US

Overall, Russian outbound travel to foreign countries continues to grow with the number of Russian tourists traveling abroad during the last ten years almost doubling. Growth in travel to the U.S. decreased during a financial crisis in the 1990's and after the events of 9/11, but has rebounded since 2003. Stronger economic ties, business activities and mutual interest in cultural and educational exchanges drive outbound travel to the U.S. This report presents an overview of Russian travel and tourism trends with particular attention to outbound travel of Russian nationals to nonCIS (Commonwealth of Independent States) countries, including the U.S.

MARKET DEMAND

Since the start of the economic reforms initiated by President Putin's Administration in 2000, significant progress has been made through structural reforms and liberalization of the economy. These reforms, along with increased export earnings from oil and gas have brought about yearly improvements in the Russian economy. In 2010, the Russian economy continues its sustained steady growth. In 2009, GDP grew by 6.4% to $765.5 billion. According to the Ministry of Economic Development and Trade (MEDT), in 2010, the GDP growth for JanuaryAugust reached 6.7% yearonyear and in JulyAugust it exceeded 7%.

Adding to overall economic development, the year 2010 continues a multiyear trend of strong consumer spending and a construction boom.

MARKET DATA

Business Monitor International (BMI) in its "Russia Tourism Report" (2010)[1] states that the number of Russian tourists traveling abroad continues to grow. The Russian population's propensity to travel abroad is based by a number of factors, such as:

Growth in spending capacity
Growth of price levels inside Russia (many tourists in the past preferred less expensive domestic destinations)

Increasing business, educational and cultural exchanges
Development of outbound travel services

[1] Russia Tourism Report Q3 2010, (London, Business Monitor International, Ltd., 2010), page 8.

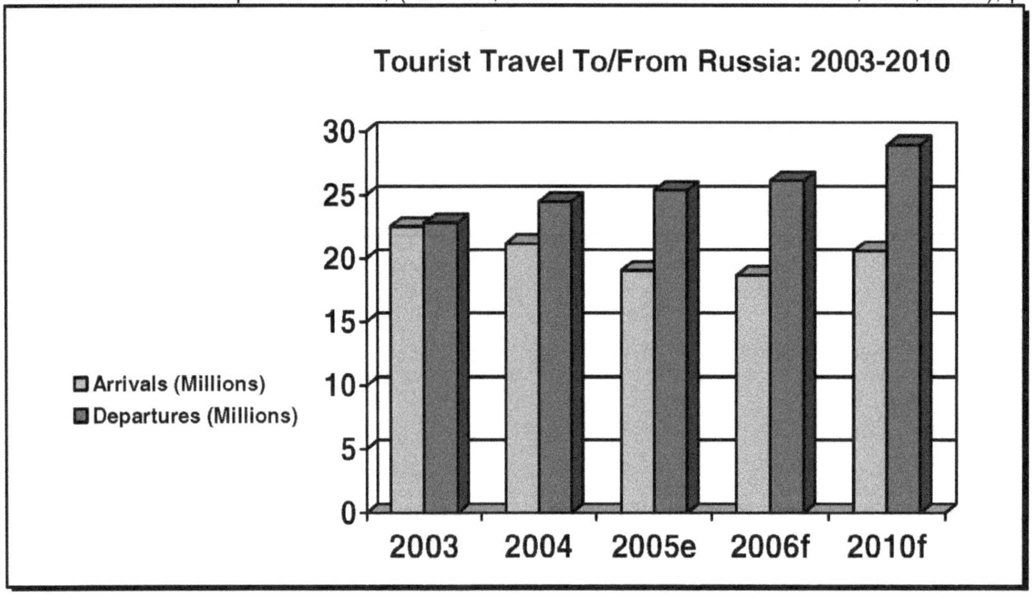

Source: Russia Tourism Report Q2 2010, BMI

Outbound travel can be divided into two main categories: CIS and nonCIS countries. According to the Russian Association of Travel Agencies' (RATA) statistics, despite the close economic and cultural ties that still exist between Russia and other countries of the former Soviet Union, the prevailing number of Russian nationals traveling abroad in 2009 visited nonCIS countries. The figures, however, do not reflect travel by immigrants and military personnel.

Source: Russian Association of Travel Agencies, 2010 (http://www.ratanews.ru/)

RATA recently reported that the number of Russian tourists traveling abroad during the last ten years increased 80% from 1995 to 2009. The last five years contributed to the most growth as a financial crisis in 1998 and events of 9/11 negatively affected the T&T industry. In 2000, outbound travel revived and continues to grow.

Outbound travel can be divided into four main categories: services (military and transport personnel), visits to relatives, tourism and business. Logically, because the CIS countries were united as one country (Soviet Union) in the recent past, travel to visit relatives is a prevailing portion of the outbound travel. However, if we look only at nonCIS countries, tourism remains the

The following table shows the statistics of outbound travel from Russia to the most popular destinations outside the CIS. The table includes only those countries that were visited by more than 100,000 Russian travelers in 2009.

Number of Russian Travelers by Destination (Thousands)

Country	1995	2000	2009
Total	8,396	9,819	14,838
1. China	343	997	2170
2. Finland	641	1585	2100
3. Turkey	764	733	1903
4. Estonia	1752	1040	1204
5. Germany	443	450	815
6. Poland	479	1075	803
7. Lithuania	1081	1156	793
8. Egypt	55	136	770
9. France	127	136	335
10. Italy	145	167	308
11. Spain	135	232	279
12. United Arab Emirates	211	118	222
13. Great Britain	117	110	218
14. Greece	130	89	200
15. Czech Republic	57	90	183
16. Bulgaria	125	104	179
17. Japan	152	146	164
18. Cyprus	109	137	143
19. USA	165	114	120
20. Switzerland	49	77	120
21. Austria	47	48	108

Source: Russian Association of Travel Agencies, 2010 (http://www.ratanews.ru/)

Outbound Travel to the United States

The aforementioned statistics reflect the fact that fewer (37.5% decrease) Russians travel to the U.S. today than ten years ago. In 1995, the number of Russian travelers visiting the U.S. was 165,000 and the country was in the list of top10 most popular nonCIS destinations. During the last decade the U.S. moved from 9th to

19th place in the ranking of the most visited nonCIS travel destinations.

Since 1995 outbound travel from Russia to the U.S. has steadily decreased until 2003, when 99,000 Russian travelers visited the U.S. In 2009, the trend changed to a positive rate (14% growth in comparison with 2003), and in 2009, the absolute number of travelers to the U.S. increased from 113,000 to 120,000, a 6% growth in comparison with 2009.

Source: Russian Association of Travel Agencies, 2010 (http://www.ratanews.ru/)

According to data released by RATA, a majority of departures from Russia to the U.S. is related to personal trips or business. Tourism is the third most popular purpose. The fourth category of travel purpose to the U.S. is service – travel by transport personnel traveling to the U.S. as part of their duties.

. The four major reasons attributed to this increase are: a more favorable visa situation, weakening of the dollar, preference for U.S. tour packages over those offered to European destinations, and those who have traveled to Europe and warm climate destinations in the past are selecting tours to the U.S. as their next travel destination.

Key Suppliers

The number of Russian travel agencies that promote travel to the U.S. is limited: Croc Travel Agency, Holiday Time, Roza Vetrov, Progress Tour, Lanta Tour Voyage and other agencies. There are also U.S.owned corporations that provide outbound travel services, mainly for corporate clients, include American Express International Services Ltd. and Carlson Wagonlit.

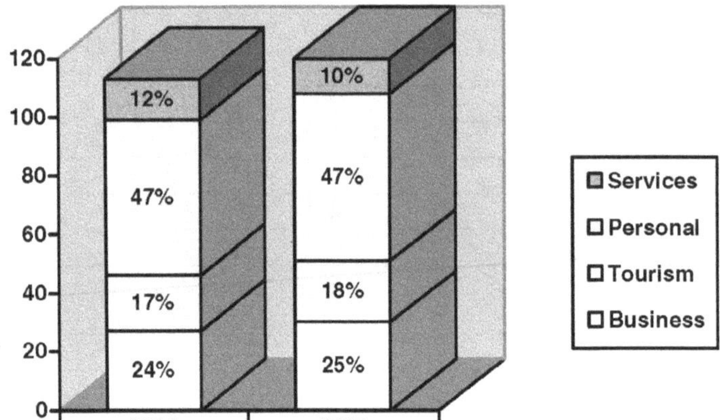

	2004	2005
Services	14	12
Personal	53	57
Tourism	19	21
Business	27	30

(Thousand of Travelers)

Source: Russian Association of Travel Agencies, 2010 (http://www.ratanews.ru/)

First half 2010 data from RATA shows a 15.6% increase over the first half of 2009 in tourist travel

Prospective Buyers

RATA completed a survey of Russian travel agencies regarding local demand for outbound travel. Based on the results of the survey RATA came to the following conclusions:

A continuing growth of clients traveling to foreign countries for the first time is making a significant contribution to the T&T market growth.
Repeat outbound travel to the same locations is growing. (In Moscow the share is 45%.)
Russian nationals are starting to seek a wider range of destinations, i.e., foreign countries.

There are a number of ways in which Russians purchase tours to the U.S. Most people go to travel agencies to make their selection and order their entire travel package from an agent. Though payments via the Internet are not the norm, some more advanced Internet users make their selection and reservations online and then go to a travel agency to purchase their selection. Some travelers are sent by their employers to agencies in order to purchase corporate travel packages.

Russian Association of Travel Agencies

Mr. Gennadiy Pavlovich Shpilko, President Phone: 7 (495) 9611370/71 Fax: 7 (495) 6922759 Email: rata@rata.ru Web Site: http://www.rata.ru

Russian Business Travel Association

Ms. Elena Anatolievna Suvorova, President Phone: 7 (495) 250 6815/16/31 Fax: 7 (095) 2506532 Email: info@btw.ru Chayanova St., 15/5, Office 1104 Moscow, 125267 info@btw.ru Web Site: http://www.rbta.ru

Russian Hotel Association

Mr. Gennadiy Andreevich Lamshin, Executive Director Phone: 7 (495) 2341203/1170/1328 Fax: 7 (495) 2341170/1328 Email: info@rha.ru 150, Prospect Mira, KosmosHotel, Office 0982 Moscow, 129366 info@rha.ru Web Site: http://www.rha.ru

INVESTMENT FUNDS AND OPPORTUNITIES

This report provides brief information about the investment priorities of the Russian Investment Fund (RIF) and resulting Public Private Partnership (PPP) opportunities for U.S. Engineering and Project Management firms. The Investment Fund was set by the Russian Government in 2009 to support projects of national importance. The emphasis is on infrastructure development projects and PPP will be a key component of the implementation strategy.

About the Investment Fund

Most of the Investment Fund's resources are to come from transfers from the Stabilization Fund via an increase in the cut-off oil price for the latter by $1 bbl. Another source will be the forecasted gain due to reduced interest payments in case of early repayment of Russia's debt. Budget-2010 allocates 69.8 billion Rubles to the Investment Fund, with financing in 2012-2008 set to exceed 70 billion Rubles per year (according to August 2009 reports, 72.9 billion rubles in 2012 and 73.2 billion rubles in 2008).

The Ministry of Economic Development and Trade (MEDT) has the authority to sign investment project agreements to be implemented through the Investment Fund. Proposals will be taken from Russian regions, municipalities, private companies, including foreign investors and firms that already have foreign investment.

Overview of investment projects

In December 2009, German Gref, MEDT Minister, listed some of the projects to be financed through the Investment Fund, saying that in 2010 preference would be given to several infrastructure projects including:

-About two dozen projects in road construction, including projects to build a highway and railroad to link Moscow and St Petersburg, a logistics center near the Black Sea port of Novorosiisk, and beltways around Moscow and the city of Sochi (the Black Sea coast).

-A project to create a network of transit airport hubs – about five or six hubs will cost no more than $2 billion to build, but may bring Russia as much as 3.5 –4 billion euros in annual revenue.

-Infrastructure development of the lower Angara River area in Siberia. Viewed as the most ambitious project in Russia for the past 30 years, this project will include construction of the Boguchanskaya hydroelectric plant, an aluminum smelter, two paper & pulp factories, and the development of three oil fields with a combined estimated output of 3 million metric tons.

List of projects to be funded

St. Petersburg: construction of a toll highway "Western Rapid Diameter"

Project period: 2009-2010
Size of investment: $3.1 billion
Contribution of the Investment Fund: $1 billion
Payback period: 25 years (from the start of construction)
Project description: the toll highway will consist of 3 segments -Southern (10,99 km), Central (9,55 km) and Northern (26,06 km). The highway will have 14 intersections with city roads. Projected traffic load for 2025: 97.3 -120.5 thousand vehicles in Southern segment (per 24 hours), 105 -131 thousand in Central segment and 21.6 -64.6 thousand in Northern segment. Key advantages of the project: connecting St. Petersburg transport hub with a network of federal highway and highways leading to Finland, Estonia, Ukraine, Byelorussia and neighboring regions; greater efficiency of intra-city transportation, including transportation flows to North-western, Central and Southern areas of St. Petersburg.

St. Petersburg: construction of Orlovsky Tunnel under Neva River

Project period: 2010-2010
Size of investment: $989 million
Contribution of the Investment Fund: $330 million
Projected description: the tunnel will provide 24-hour connection of the Neva River banks.
Key advantages of the project: increasing cargo transportation, reducing shipping downtime, connecting central part of the city directly with federal highways and the city beltway road.

Leningrad Oblast: Ust-Luga Seaport Complex

Project period: 2010-2008
Size of investment: $315 million
Contribution of the Investment Fund: $91 million
Payback period (discounted): 12.9 years
Projected description: the complex will be expanded to include another 97.8 hectares.
Construction of berths and purchase of handling equipment.
Key advantages of the project: expand the loading and the cargo handcomplex.

Moscow Oblast: Moscow-St.Petersburg toll road

Size of investment: $2 billion
Contribution of the Investment Fund: $966 million

Payback period (discounted): 18 years ling capacity of the seaport
Projected description: development of modernized road network for integration in international transport corridors. Third quarter of 2010 will include conducting a bid for concession agreements for construction and use of the Rapid Auto Highway Moscow – St. Petersburg.
Key advantages of the project: optimization of transport communications, expanding the transport infrastructure.

Moscow Oblast: Moscow-Minsk interchange onto MKAD

Size of investment: $646 million
Contribution of the Investment Fund: $374 million
Payback period (discounted): 12 years
Projected description: re-form transportation flows, take the transportation load off the Roublevo-Uspenskoye, Podushkinskoye and Skolkovskoye highways. Third quarter of 2010 will include conducting a bid for concession agreements for construction and use of Moscow-Minsk interchange onto MKAD.
Key advantages of the project: optimization of transport communications, creation of 2 000 jobs.

Don Highway

* Size of investment: $745 million
* Projected description: the project will cover four Russian regions – Moscow Oblast, Lipetsk Oblast, Voronezh Oblast and Krasnodar Region. It will build up the transport capacity of the highway linking Southern and Northern parts of Russia.
* Key advantages of the project: optimization of transport communications among important Russian regions, integration into the international transport networks.

Rostov Oblast: Water Supply System Construction

* Project period: 2010-2020
* Size of investment: $374 million
* Contribution of the Investment Fund: $192 million
* Private investment: $538
* Payback period (discounted): 15 years
* Projected description: creation of 87 mainstream and distributing water supply networks to provide 700 thousand square meters of drinking water and 460 thousand square meters of sewage drain daily.
* Key advantages of the project: improvement of living conditions, compliance with international requirements to prevent transboundary pollution of the Azov and the Black seas.

Krasnodar Region: Krasnodar – Abinsk – Kabardinka Toll Road

* Size of investment: $4.2 billion
* Contribution of the Investment Fund: $2.2 billion
* Payback period (discounted): 8 years
* Projected description: enhance the transport capacity of A146 Highway.
* Key advantages of the project: optimization of transport communications.

Krasnodar Region: Development of "Taman" Seaport Infrastructure

* Size of investment: $2.3 billion
* Contribution of the Investment Fund: $883 million
* Payback period (discounted): 11 years
* Projected description: creation of a new transportation corridor for shipment of additional 30 million of cargo in Southern Russia.

* Key advantages of the project: increase trade turnover, creation of 1 900 jobs, increase transit capacity of the region.

Republic of Tatarstan: Construction of Petrochemical Complex in Nizhnekamsk

* Size of investment: $4.9 billion
* Contribution of the Investment Fund: $618 million
* Payback period: 6.6 years
* Projected description: construction of a complex of oil-processing and petrochemical plants to process hydrocarbon materials. Plans are to increase volume of oil processing from 7 to 14 million tons per year.
* Key advantages of the project: promote processed oil materials instead of raw materials.

Omsk: Restoration of Omsk Water Supply System

* Project period: 2010-2030
* Size of investment: $580 million
* Contribution of the Investment Fund: $202 million
* Payback period: 23 years
* Projected description: construction and restoration of 380 kilometers of mainstream and distributing networks for water supply and sewage. The project will modernize facilities and equipment to provide 600 thousand square meters of drinking water and 580 thousand square meters of sewage drain daily.
* Key advantages of the project: creation of additional infrastructure resources for water supply and sewage to support construction of 10 million square meters of communal housing (for 640 thousand inhabitants).

Krasnyarsk Region: Transport Infrastructure for the Lower Priangarye

* Size of investment: $13.4 billion
* Contribution of the Investment Fund: $1.3 billion
* Projected description: creation of a new industrial area in the Krasnoyarsk Region powered by the Boguchanskaya hydroelectric power station and supported by other regional resources.
* Key advantages of the project: expand opportunities for companies to invest in businesses related to metallurgy, forest processing, petrochemical industry and other.

Republic of Tuva: Rail Line Kyzyl – Kuragino

* Size of investment: $2.8 billion
* Contribution of the Investment Fund: $2 billion
* Payback period: 13 years
* Projected description: construction of the rail line will facilitate development of the Elegestsky coking coal deposits.
* Key advantages of the project: economic and social development of the region. Development of the coking coal deposits will provide more than 3 000 jobs, construction of the rail line – 18 000 jobs and rail line use – 8 000 jobs. The project will drive earning for the regional budget.

Chitinskaya Oblast: Transport Infrastructure to develop local mineral deposits

* Project period: 2012-2015
* Size of investment: $5.3 billion
* Contribution of the Investment Fund: $1.5 billion
* Payback period: 14 years
* Projected description: development of regional deposits of copper, gold, silver, molybdenum, iron and other "hard" minerals.

* Key advantages of the project: creation of additional 71 000 jobs in the region, economic development of the Chita region.

For More Information

For more information on these and other infrastructure investments, please contact the U.S. Commercial Service in Moscow, Russia via e-mail at: vladislav.borodulin@mail.doc.gov; Phone: +7(495) 737-5036; Fax: +7(495) 7375033 or visit our website: www.buyusa.gov/russia. Contact person: Vladislav Borodulin, Commercial Specialist.

The U.S. Commercial Service — Your Global Business Partner

With its network of offices across the United States and in more than 80 countries, the U.S. Commercial Service of the U.S. Department of Commerce utilizes its global presence and international marketing expertise to help U.S. companies sell their products and services worldwide. Locate the U.S. Commercial Service trade specialist in the

U.S. nearest you by visiting http://www.export.gov/.

ENVIRONMENT MARKET

The Russian government has for years neglected environmental protection. As a result, the environmental situation in the country has been aggravating and in many cases is out of control. Burning environmental problems, including low quality of water in rivers and lakes, poor water sanitation, incidence of oil spills, polluted air and soil, have forced the government to place more emphasis on the environment. The government adopted a number of laws and regulations stipulating introduction of water and waste water management technologies, stricter emissions controls as well effective solid waste recycling systems in major cities such as Moscow and St. Petersburg and a number of other regions. Russia has a legislative framework aimed at protection of the environment, some of the norms and regulations are even stricter than in Europe. However the problem is enforcement.

Another important problem is the fact that many of these norms are obsolete and do not comply with modern Western requirements. This report focuses on the municipal solid waste management equipment and technologies market. It discusses current regulations and rules governing that market and analyses opportunities for U.S. companies.

CURRENT STATE OF ENVIRONMENTAL PROTECTION IN RUSSIA: FACTS AND FIGURES

In the Soviet Union and then Russia manufacturing industries have always generated huge amounts of waste, however authorities never cared about it given the country's vast territory and abundant natural resources. Due to the Russia's enormous environmental capacity, the concept of environmental protection was considered as a problem for future generations.

Currently, about 80 billion tons of hard metallurgical, machinebuilding, mineral resource, chemical and energy and fuel industries waste has been accumulated in the dumps and deposits of Russia. Growing oil and gas production as well as expansion of other extraction industries exact a heavy cost to the health of the land and people. It is estimated that annual volumes of chemical reagents in contaminated industrial wastewaters ejected into surface water streams reach 17 million tons. These reagents contaminate 25 million cubic meters of topsoil. Complete utilization of coextracted gas in oil extraction does not exceed 80 percent in Russia. Up to 17 billion cubic meters of nonutilized gas extracted alongside with oil is burned annually in gas torches. As a result, more than 400,000 tons of hazardous substances are released into the atmosphere each year. In addition, 560 million tons of methane is estimated to leak annually into atmosphere from oil and gas extraction facilities, not counting accidental outbursts and pipe leakage. There are numerous other examples of lack of federal environmental control measures in extraction and manufacturing industries. Decades of neglect of environmentally safe technologies, inadequate attention to protecting nature and health created double impact on wasted resources and environment.

Air pollution levels in major cities are very high. According to Roshydromet (Federal Service for Hydrometeorology and Environmental Monitoring, in 2009 the level of air contamination in 22 Russian of air contamination was estimated as high or very high. It means that half of Russia's population breathes polluted air. All inhabitants of Moscow and St. Petersburg breathe polluted air.

Environment has not been priority for municipal governments for decades as well. A few following examples prove how serious the problems are nowadays. St. Petersburg, which is considered one of the most advanced areas in the country in terms of water sanitation, has poor quality drinking water due to the city's antiquated iron pipes. Kaliningrad, a Baltic Sea gateway of Russia, pumps 70 million cubic meters of untreated, heavily polluted water into the Baltic Sea annually. Industrial pollution in the Urals casts a dark shadow, affecting a number of cities and their population. In some cases the rivers are dead, in others water is undrinkable. The Techa River in Chlyabinsk is the worst case, polluted with radioactive waste from the Mayak nuclear plant.

The recent analysis of water quality in the Moskva River and its confluents, the results of which have been published in July 28, 2010 edition of Rossiyskaya Gazeta daily newspaper, shows that level of contamination ranges from medium to very high. The main threat comes from high presence of biogenic products in the water caused by untreated sewage and waste dumped into the rivers.

The situation with waste collection and processing is painful too. According to May 4, 2012 edition of Rossiyskaya Gazeta, annually inspectors of Gostechnadzor (Federal Service for Ecological, Technological and Atomic Control), a government agency overlooking waste collection and processing, reveal 600 unauthorized disposal tips and about 2,000 disposal bulks in the Moscow region only. The total sum of fines, which they collect amounts to $6.000. However these measures do not help to radically improve the situation because the fines imposed on legal entities for unauthorized waste disposal are ridiculously small, only less than 2 dollars. At the same time fines imposed for similar violations on physical persons vary from $18 to 180. Therefore, many enterprises prefer to pay fines for unauthorized dumping of their waste instead of investing into collection and processing.

MARKET DEMAND AND MARKET DATA

According to different estimates, the total market for environmental technologies and products is estimated at $7001,000 million. Current rates of the growth of the market are 2025 percent a year. At the same time waste management capacity is not fully used. The key components of the market include: solid waste management, water treatment and air purification.

In the last several decades Russia's waste output has been growing faster than industrial production. To date Russia has accumulated 80 billion tons of solid waste, including industrial and residential. Russia generates around 3.5 billion tons of waste annually, including 36 million tons of municipal solid waste. According to the Ministry of Natural Resources of the Russian Federation only 30 percent of total waste is recycled or processed. For industrial waste, the percentage of processed waste is 35 percent of the total volume. As for municipal solid waste, it is only 5 percent, except for Moscow where the percentage reaches 27 percent.

Analysts believe that using existing technologies and equipment Russia could recycle 50 percent of its industrial waste and 10 percent of its municipal waste. The main reason for underexploitation of existing recycling capacities is undeveloped environmental protection concept, lack of uptodate waste sorting rules and technologies, low environmental culture and education of population as well as Municipal solid waste market consists of two parts, which are being financed from different sources:

- Residential Waste (financed by municipalities and population)
- Commercial and Public Waste (financed by enterprises and institutions)

Waste market covers five main areas:
• Collection
• Storing
• Transportation
• Landfilling
• Processing and management

Waste management is becoming more attractive for private investment despite a number of obstacles. First of all, there are no tax breaks for providers of waste management services. Secondly, waste collection and transportation costs are generally high due to the country's large territory and significant distances between waste management facilities and industrial plants producing waste. Thirdly, unlike European countries, no recycling fee is built into the final cost of packaging. Therefore, foreign investors planning to build recycling facilities in Russia have to think about financing sources for collection and transportation of waste.

Lastly, wasteprocessing industry does not produce finished products; it produces raw materials, which are further used in production of finished goods. Often times, these recycled raw materials are not cost effective in comparison to original raw materials. Cost effective recycled raw materials include aluminum, mercury from mercury lamps and other metals, as well as glass and cardboard. However less cost effective types of recycled waste such as tin, tire, plastic waste, including polyethylenetereftalin (PET), polythene, polypropylene, etc. are getting more and more attention from investors.

Examples of environmentally safe behaviors by manufacturing facilities are still few. However there are positive examples. It is reported that in April 2012 Metallurgical Industrial Complex of Nizhniy Tagil, part of Evraz Group, won the first place in the European Quality Gold Medal contest. The company competed with more than 150 other companies involved in conservation, pollution control and waste recycling activities and was the winner in the Russia's TOP 100 Enterprises in the Environment and Environmental Management category.

Another positive example is the completion of the Environmental Protection Program for the city of Lipetsk, which was started in 2009. The corner stone of the program was emission control on the major roads by arranging traffic lights in such a way that allows uninterrupted passage of the traffic lights. It was discovered in the course of air monitoring that major emissions happen during breakaway and braking. By reducing those, where possible, the city's authorities managed to reduce the atmospheric pollution index from 24.4 to 8.6. As a result Lipetsk was removed from the list of highly polluted cities.

A significant number of industrial enterprises and cottage villages around Moscow have started using waste pressing and shredding equipment to significantly reduce waste transportation costs. Mayor of Kaliningrand in North West Russia has formed an administrative and technical inspection responsible for garbage collection in the city. The inspection has installed about 1,000 garbage containers in the city.

BEST PROSPECTS

Best selling products include:

Waste sorting, pressing, crushing and washing equipment;
Plastic and steel waste containers;
Special containers for dangerous waste;
Refuse collecting vehicles and litter bins;
Waste incineration plants;
Hydraulic presses for packing paper, cardboard, plastic and other kinds of waste;
Recycling equipment for production of plastic packaging;
Food waste processing equipment;
Polymeric, plastic and paper waste processing equipment.

REGULATORY ENVIRONMENT, MARKET ISSUES AND OBSTACLES

At the moment there are key seven laws governing environmental protection. They contain conflicting and exclusionary clauses, lack appropriate detailed elaboration. The Russian Ministry of Natural Resources has started to develop an Environmental Code, which will include all aspects of environmental protection. The corner stone of the Code will be incentives for introduction of the bestknown world environmentally safe technologies. Those enterprises, which will not introduce the best technologies, will have to pay significant taxes. These taxes will be used to develop environmentally safe technologies. Currently from 80 to 90 percent of all industrial enterprises use obsolete and unsafe environmental technologies. In 2010 Rostechnadzor conducted an environmental examination of business plans for construction of 297 new enterprises. The approval was received by 268, 19 projects were rejected. The Environmental Code will also stipulate high fines for environmentally unsafe enterprises and tax incentives for waste management projects. However until this Code is adopted as a law Russia will continue to rely upon an undeveloped legislative environmental framework.

Currently there are no welldefined norms for recycling of certain types of waste, for example, for utilization of batteries containing lead as well as mercury lamps. Similar legislative gaps relate to tire and used cars processing.

Sorting of waste by the population and use of separate containers for different types of waste are still not developed in Russia. Some of the cities are introducing these new garbage collection technologies as pilot projects. For example, such project is currently implemented in the city of Dubna, Moscow region. However, generally there are no laws and regulations stipulating participation of population in waste separation. The majority of citizens do not contribute in any way to sorting solid waste, leaving this job to a small group of people; this way the issue remains outside the cultural and educational mainstream. However waste management cannot succeed without citizens' participation on a mass scale.

Generally regulatory environment for solid waste management activities has been significantly improving in the last several years. A number of key Russian cities and regions have been adopting laws and regulations creating incentives for waste collection by population, private investment into the sector, developing publicprivate partnerships and attracting foreign investment. A significant number of solid waste management projects are under preparation for launching or have been launched in such cities as Kazan, Novosibirsk, Krasnoyarsk, Bryansk, Kursk, Tyumen and several others. According to the February 16, 2012 edition of Rossiyskaya Gazeta, in the last several years 16 modern solid waste management complexes have been built or modernized in the Moscow Region. The Moscow region has a purpose sampling program for utilization of waste for the years 20092010 according to which the Moscow region authorities plan to spend more than $230 million on waste management.

Responding to aggravating situation with garbage disposal in the Moscow region, authorities have been establishing paid garbage containers on the key roads and highways, which could be used by passing by cars. Currently, free containers, which are put on a number of Moscow region highways are only eligible for longrange drivers and tourist buses. "Dachniki", owners of small cottages and summerhouses around Moscow, do not have right to use free garbage cans on the roads.

On November 30, 2009, the Moscow City Duma (municipal legislative organ) passed a Law #68 on Production and Consumption of Waste in the City of Moscow. The Law draws distinction between recyclable material resources and recycled raw materials. According to the law, recyclable material resources are not identical to recycled raw materials. Recyclable material resources are extrapolated from the waste mass directly, they can be reused after additional processing. Recyclable material resources are turned into recycled raw materials after recycling. The law stipulates that municipal authorities are financially responsible for extracting recyclable raw materials from the waste mass. However, the government will not take full financial responsibility for further processing, or recycling. It actually should be responsibility of private business. In other words, the Moscow government will pay for sorting out waste out of municipal solid waste flow, but not for recycling waste. The law also provides for certain government support for private recycling activities.

According to Professor Adam Gonopolsky, Deputy Director of Ecotechprom State Enterprise (a waste recycling company), the new law boosts the development of recycled materials market. However it encourages recycling of only a few, selective types of waste with relatively high level of profitability. Such types of waste include cardboard, glass and aluminum, while the components that are harder to collect or sell, i.e. tin, plastic and Tetra Pak packages, are less attractive to recycling facilities.

Another important clause of the law is new requirements towards dangerous waste. Specifically the law stipulates that dangerous and extremely dangerous medical waste created by hospitals and clinics must undergo mandatory disinfection before warehousing and transportation to places where it is incinerated.

The law also provides for budget subsidies and low interest loans to legal entities and individual entrepreneurs who introduce effective lowwaste technologies, use recycled materials in production. Budget funding is also provided for research and development activities in the area of waste management and recycling.

There are certain administrative and management barriers, which hamper development of solid waste have to pay fees for waste collection to their respective local budgets, despite of the fact that waste processing facilities which they use might be located outside the territory they belong to. For example, Moscow processes most of its waste outside the city in the Moscow region. For example, 70 percent of all solid waste processed in the Moscow region comes from Moscow. However the waste management fees, which are paid by Moscow companies, go the city budget with negligible funds being received by the regional budgets. This situation is an obstacle to developing modern solid waste management plants in the Moscow region. Moscow city authorities plan to solve the problem by building waste incineration plants on the borders with the Moscow region. However this approach led to a lot of discussion about the effects of these plants on the health of population of both the Moscow city and the Moscow region. Regional authorities declared that they would do their best to prevent construction of such plants.

KEY SUPPLIERS

Foreign suppliers solid waste management equipment dominate the market. Imported equipment and products account for over 60 percent of the total market. Following are the shares of different types of domestically manufactured environmental equipment and products in the total market volume for each category:

waste management – 29 percent;

water treatment – 45 percent;

air purification equipment – 15 percent.

The main foreign supplier of environmental equipment, including solid waste management equipment, is Germany, which accounts for 20 percent of all imports. Germany is followed by Italy, Sweden, USA, UK, Finland and Switzerland. Success of German companies in Russia can be attributed to the German government support for financing environmental projects through Hermes credit lines. German companies also widely use leasing arrangements.

There is a number of significant number of Russian manufacturers of solid waste management equipment, which specialize in such areas as metal scrap and chips processing (KEMET); hydraulic and other presses for different types of waste, including scrap paper and cardboard (Tochnaya Mechanika), defective apparel, footware and electronics articles (STATICO Group); vibrocompression equipment for recycling ironcarbon containing waste into briquettes (EcoMashGeo); waste transfer stations, household waste containers, wastelifting equipment (Ecopress); complex plants for disinfection of medical waste (Obninsk Center for Science and Technologies); solid waste sorting equipment, automatic briquette producing lines (OAO “Stankoagregat”); solid waste transportation vehicles (Mechanical plant Spetstrans); thermal processing of medical, biological and oil containing liquid waste (ZAO “Bezopasnye Technologii”); solid waste containers (Spetsmechanizatsia); waste incinerating plants (ZAO Turmalin), treatment of medical biological and veterinary waste (CISNatural Resources); equipment for collection, compaction and transportation of waste (Waste Systems).

However many types of the most advanced and efficient solid waste management equipment are imported because local manufacturers cannot meet the domestic demand for such equipment. (Please see the Best Prospects Section for the types of modern equipment, which is in high demand).

2. Department for Industrial and Domestic Waste Neutralization, Management and Processing of the City of Moscow

19 Porspekt Mira
Moscow 129090
Tel.: 74956813645

Fax: 74956889989 3. Federal Service for Environmental, Technological and Atomic Control of the Russian Federation

Mr. Konstantin Borisovich Kulikovskiy, Head
4 Lukyanova Street, Building 8
Moscow, Moskva 105066
Phone: 74959116435 /3084
Fax: 74959113084, 2616043
www.rostehnadzor.ruF

4. Federal Service for Hydrometeorology and Environmental Monitoring

Mr. Aleksander Ivanovich Berditskiy, Head

12 Novovagankovskiy Per.

Moscow, Moskva D242, GSP5, 123995
Phone: 74952521486 Fax: 74952525504/9484/2434
Email: media@mecom.ru
Web Site: www.meteorf.ru

SAFETY AND SECURITY EQUIPMENT

The Russian safety and security market is constantly growing and innovating, thus providing U.S. exporters excellent opportunities. With 20% annual growth for the past two years, its value was approximately $1.7 billion in 2012. This report provides an overview of the safety and security equipment market, best prospects, and information about Russian industryrelated exhibitions.

MARKET DEMAND

The Russian market for safety and security systems is developing rapidly, offering great potential for U.S. companies. Industry specialists note that one recent trend is the convergence of IT and safety and security technologies, which creates more opportunities for high quality U.S. technology exports. For example, the IPbased CCTV segment exceeded 100% growth in 2010 and color CCTV cameras will soon outnumber monochrome units. The best opportunities for U.S. manufactured hardware sales are in wireless and IPbased solutions in various equipment segments, access control systems, intruder alarm systems, integrated control systems, biometric equipment, and identifiers and readers. The strength of the safety and security systems market is its constant innovation and price competitiveness. New concepts and products may open new opportunities.

MARKET DATA

In 2010, the total value of Russia's safety and security services and equipment market was $5.6 billion. Demand is expected to grow 21% and reach $6.8 billion in 2012, with services totaling $5.1 billion, or 75% of the market, and safety and security equipment amounting to $1.7 billion. Regarding regional segments, 60% of the market is concentrated in Moscow and St. Petersburg, 23% in the Urals Federal District, 11% in the Siberian Federal District, and 6% in the Northwest Federal District. The rest of the market is divided between the Volga, Far East and Southern Regions.

Annual market growth in the equipment segment is 12% to 30% depending on the product category. In 2010, the Russian CCTV and video surveillance segment totaled $420 million, or 30% of the equipment market, with 30% annual growth. It is considered the most developed and competitive segment. The size of the security and fire alarm segment was around $320 million (23% of the equipment market), increasing 12-15% annually. The intruder alarm and perimeter protection segment was also worth $320 million, growing 1215% per year as well. Access control systems reached $225 million, a 16% share of this market, with current annual growth of 1516%. Other more minor product categories account for the remaining $115 million of the 2010 equipment segment.

According to market experts, two sectors, CCTV and access control systems, will dominate the market over next three years because they demonstrated the highest growth rates and largest sales volumes during past several years.

SAFETY AND SECURITY EQUIPMENT MARKET: KEY SEGMENTS

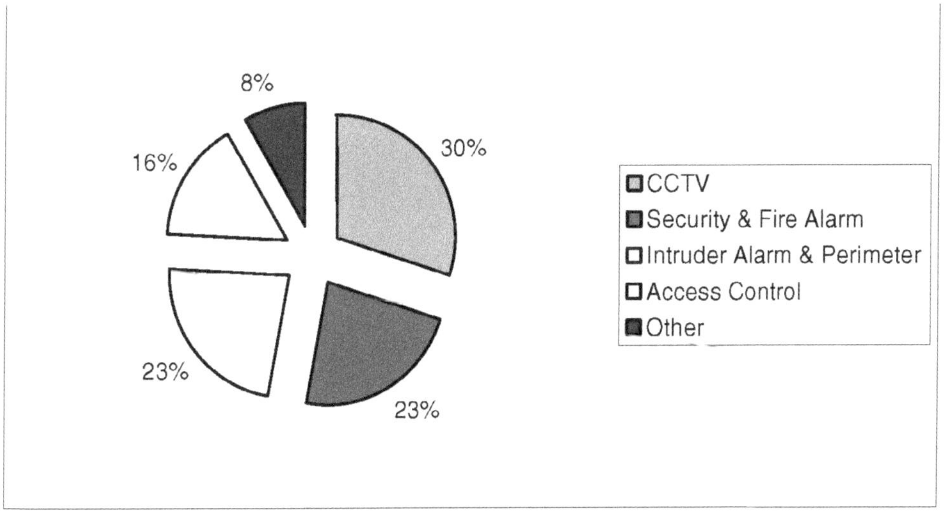

Source: US Commercial Service Moscow.

Depending on the segment, the share of imported products ranges from 50% to 80%. Experts estimate that up to 80% of access control, about 50% of intruder and fire alarms, and more than 80% of CCTV systems are imported. Even locally manufactured equipment contains 60% to 80% imported components.

KEY SUPPLIERS

Suppliers are global companies but they are differentiated by region of manufacture and by equipment pricing. Depending on the market segment, lowcost solutions usually come from China, Taiwan, and Korea. Premium systems are imported from the U.S., Western Europe (Great Britain, Germany, France, Italy), Eastern Europe (Poland, Czech Republic), Japan, and Israel.

Prospective Buyers

Market participants can be divided into two groups, state enterprises and agencies, on the one hand, and nongovernmental organizations on the other. State agencies are represented in the security service market by the security agency of the Ministry of the Interior of the Russian Federation; security agencies of other Federal Ministries and Agencies; and federal unitary enterprises. Federal unitary enterprises in most cases would fulfill the purchasing and installation functions for the state agencies. All purchases by the state must be performed through tenders.

Nongovernmental market participants include private security agencies; security services of private companies; equipment distributors; specialized trade companies; and systems integrators that participate in security and safety equipment integration projects. Currently, there are over 300 distribution companies working in the Russian security market, although the channels are becoming concentrated and often smaller firms are simply resellers for the major distributors. Among the leading distributors are SatroPalladin, Luis+, and Ultra Star.

MAJOR SAFETY AND SECURITY END USERS SEGMENTS

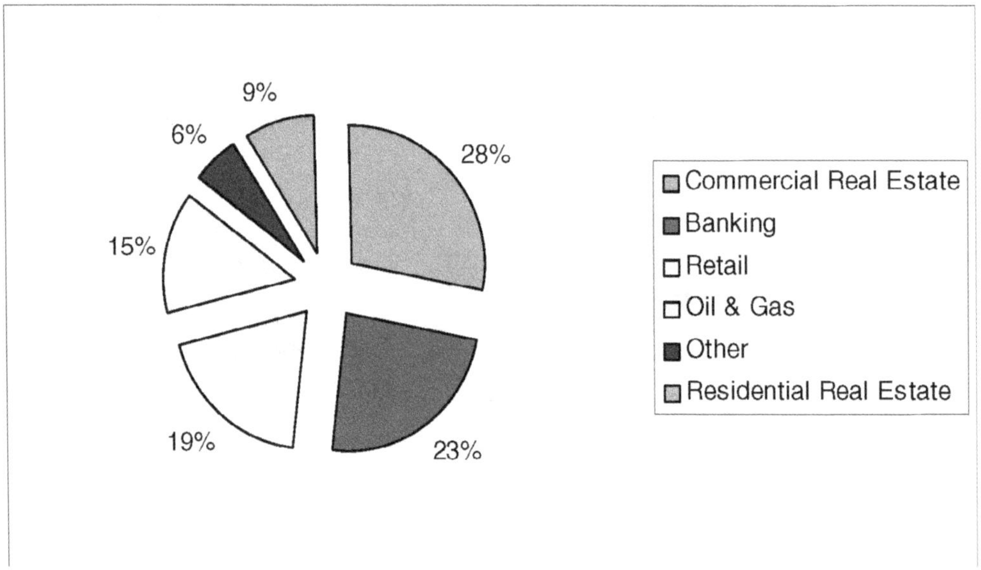

Source: Annual Report by the Russian Security Industry Association.

Regarding safety and security equipment "consumers", there are several major industries that generate demand. According to the GMT Plus Marketing Agency, commercial real estate, banking, retail, and oil and gas are major endusers of this equipment. One of the current trends in this market is the increasing purchase of equipment and services by the residential real estate sector.

MARKET ENTRY

There are three basic ways to enter this Russian market:

Distributors – the majority of safety and security equipment buyers prefer working through local distributors. Some safety and security equipment distributors have been in business for more than eight years and have extensive experience. More importantly for this industry, they have established connections in the government. Their detailed knowledge of the market and their multiple business connections enable them to find both buyers and sellers for a wide range of equipment. They often represent a number of companies, and may cover a large part of the country.
Cooperative arrangements – cooperating with other equipment vendors that already have a strong presence is a creative way to enter the market. The advantage for vendors is being able to provide a wider range of equipment.
Working directly with security agencies and service providers – service providers sometimes prefer working with equipment manufacturers directly, which facilitates meeting their complex needs more efficiently. In this case the most advantageous way is to work with large systems integrators.

Finding a local partner knowledgeable in the industry and with experience in participating in procurement tenders would be the most effective path to entering the Russian market.

MARKET ISSUES AND OBSTACLES

Companies entering the market should be prepared to compete with foreign and local safety and security equipment manufacturers that have a strong presence in the Russian market. They should also be aware of the complex regulatory environment, bureaucracy and lengthy decisionmaking processes that are major problems in the Russian market. Safety and security equipment requires mandatory certification by government agencies. Depending on the equipment type, the Ministry of Interior, the Federal Security Service, and the Ministry of Information Technology and Communications might all be involved.

Organizations

Russian Security Industry Association

http://www.rasi.ru/index_eng.php

SIA – the U.S. Security Industry Association

http://www.siaonline.org/

Groteck Co., Ltd **http://groteck.net/security**

VNIIPO, AllRussian ScientificResearch Institute for Fire Prevention (Fire security equipment certification body) **http://www.vniipo.ru/**

Publications

Sec.ru – Industry Online Periodical **http://www.sec.ru/**

CCTV Focus Magazine – Industry Periodical **http://www.cctvfocus.ru/**

Russian Security Media & Exhibitions Brand Awareness 2010 report by GMT Plus **http://www.gmtplus.com/publications.php?id=9**

POWER GENERATION MARKET

A window of opportunity has opened in the Russian Federation for U.S. companies in the power generation market. During Soviet rule, the USSR had a single power company that supplied both heat and electricity across the largest country in the world. Russia urgently needs to modernize its power grids, transformers and other electric power generating equipment, of which only 30% currently meets market standards. Power usage is growing 4% annually, but the emerging power companies, despite aggressive refurbishment and building plans, are unable to keep pace with the growth in demand.

To attract foreign investment and create the commercial benefits of a free market, the national electric company (RAO Unified Electric System) has embarked on an aggressive restructuring plan that will result in the privatization of the system. More than 400 power companies will be spun off, starting with 20 wholesale and territorial generating companies. A stream of IPOs started in 2010 with two wholesale generating companies and will continue over the next few years; 15 IPOs are scheduled for 2012. Funds raised from private and public placements will be used to refurbish and convert existing plants and to build new ones.

This reform and restructuring of the former single power entity responsible for both electricity and heat has created the need for foreign investment, expertise and products. The power sector is increasing its capital expenditures on technology development and refurbishment and estimates the investment through 2012 will be approximately $190 billion. According to Russian Government officials, investment in power generation will triple from 2012 to 2008. A total of about $26 billion will be invested in thermal power generation, more than $9 billion in hydropower, $14 billion in power grids, nearly $24 billion in distribution, and nearly $13 billion in nuclear power generation. RAO UES intends to build 20.9 GW of generating facilities, or about 13% of the current capacity of all of its facilities.

POWER GENERATION REFORM PLAN

RAO UES is the holding company that controls the vast majority of assets that were once part of the single power system in the USSR. Some regional power companies have already been spun off and are acting independently or have majority investment partners from other Russian companies. RAO UES is a holding company that owns controlling stakes (49%100%) in 73 regional vertically integrated energy companies and 44 federal power plants (of which 8 are under construction), 100% in OAO Federal Grid Company and 100% in OAO System Operator Centralized Dispatching Administration.

RAO UES generates 69% (635.8 billion kWh) of general electricity output and 32.4% (468,8 million Gcal) of general heat production in Russia. The company owns 96% of the highvoltage grids (2,496.9 Tkm) and 77% of the distribution network (1,747.416 Tkm) in Russia. It employs 578,000 people.

The reform process will result in major changes. For example, power transmission and dispatching functions held by the former monopoly will be separated from noncore activities, such as production, supply and repair services. New entities responsible for distinct activities will be created in place of the former vertically integrated companies. A similar process within the generation, sales and repair entities will result in companies focused on core activities. In 2010, RAO UES endorsed projects to spin off 60 regional energy jointstock companies, including wholesale generating companies (OGKs) and territorial generating companies (TGKs). According to RAO UES management, starting in 2012, the independent sector's share of the wholesale electricity market will grow by 15% annually, to reach 50% by 2009.

RAO UES will retain control of the federal grid as well as the rights to sell electricity abroad.

OPPORTUNITIES

Engineering/Procurement/Construction/Management (EPCM and ECM) Contracts

Power companies and large industrial companies that are building their own power plants recognize the need for, and are seeking foreign expertise in engineering, construction and management of their refurbishment and greenfield projects. *Power companies and their EPCM contractors are required to obtain multiple bids for all projects and some have indicated they have difficulty obtaining the required 3 bids for each tender.* Foreign ECM and EPCM contractors have been successful in winning tenders.

A few power companies have their own inhouse engineering and construction capabilities and need ECM contractors for specific equipment purchases while most of them offer EPCM contracts, especially for greenfield projects. In order to obtain reliable and costefficient electricity, large industrial companies (domestic and foreign) are seeking EPCM contractors to build power plants (greenfield projects) near their factories.

Equipment and Engineering Services

Power companies and large industrials seek the equipment and engineering services required to refurbish existing plants, convert existing plants from one fuel type to another, and build new plants. Engineering design skills are in particularly short supply. Large turbines (>250 megawatts) are not produced in Russia and must be sourced from foreign manufacturers. EPCM contractors seek suppliers of compressors, pumps, instrumentation, controls, and much more.

Investment

The Russian Government and the power companies have stated publicly that foreign direct investment is welcome and some foreign investments have been made. Though majority ownership of power generating companies by foreign entities requires Russian Government approval, opportunities for minority equity ownership are abundant. Long term relationship building is key to any strategy for large equity stakes in this market.

Market Issues

It is recommended that vendors interested in the Russian power generation market establish an office in the Russian Federation in order to maintain ongoing communication with RAO UES and the generating companies that emerge from the restructuring process. The most effective channel of entering the Russian power equipment market is through a Russian agent or distributor, which has previous experience in this field. These companies are familiar with the local market and also have exhibition and sale/demonstration sites, as well as service facilities.

The most successful approach to the market for U.S. firms is to engage a local representative who is thoroughly trained about the specific product advantages and capabilities. Some major American and foreign manufacturers of power supply equipment, including GE, Honeywell, Pratt and Whitney, Siemens, Mitsubishi and others, have opened representative offices in Russia. Some U.S. EPCM contractors have opened their own offices as well. Several procurement officers have expressed their strong preference for suppliers to be locally based as it enhances the service element of their offering. A number of engineering and construction services sold in Russia must conform to Russian standards including Health, Safety and Environment (HSE) requirements and must be licensed according to the Russian laws.

An important factor that American companies must consider is language. English language penetration in Russia is rather low, around 5%. It is expected that the use of English will expand with time. Many decisionmakers in this subsector know enough English to communicate but Russian will be preferred for negotiations and in communication with lower level employees in large domestic companies where English is not their working language.

Problems with government bureaucracy, poorly established rule of law, corruption in areas such as establishing a business, tax collection, dispute settlement, property rights, product certification and standards, and customs clearance are general problems experienced by U.S. exporters.

Competition from foreign vendors exists in the power sector, including Siemens and E.On (Germany), Enel (Italy), Alstom (Switzerland) and Mitsubishi (Japan).

Useful Links

http://www.raoees.ru/en/

http://www.mosenergo.ru/eng/

http://www.eurosib.ru/eng/

http://www.ebrd.com/new/stories/2010/20100908.htm

http://www.eia.doe.gov/emeu/cabs/Russia/Electricity.html

http://www.amcham.ru/

For More Information

The U.S. Commercial Service in Russia can be contacted via email at: Moscow.Office.Box@mail.doc.gov;

Phone: 74957375030; Fax: 74957375033 or visit our website: http://www.buyusa.gov/russia/en/

AUTOMOTIVE INDUSTRY OPPORTUNITIES

Russia remains the fastest growing market for new car sales in Europe and one of the most dynamic markets in the world. The sales of cars in Russia in 2010 reached $38 billion, a 27 percent increase over 2009 (and a six-fold increase since 2001). While domestic car sales did see a small increase in sales over 2009, they are rapidly losing overall market share to imported vehicles as well as domestically produced foreign makes. Another key important trend is that the import of used imports also continues the decline of the last couple years. Number-wise, the market in 2010 grew 16% over 2009, from 1.77 million vehicles in 2009 to over 2 million last year with the share of vehicles from Russian brand manufacturers decreasing from 47.5% down to 37%. Most market analysts believe these trends will continue in 2012.

Due to growing household incomes, the structure of the market has changed. Consumer preferences are shifting from the "below $10,000" range to the "between $10,000 – $20,000" range for automobiles. Even more dramatic, the high-end car market niche demonstrated 70% growth over previous year.

The trends are illustrated in the following tables and charts:

Table 1 and Chart 1. Car sales in Russia (thousand units):

	2003	2008	2009	2010
Domestic	870	880	840	800
Domestic assembly of foreign makes	54	128	155	280
New imports	164	279	459	720

Used imports	400	317	312	260

Table 2 and Chart 4. Car sales in Russia (million US Dollars):

	2002	2003	2008	2009	2010
Domestic	3,700	4,300	5,200	6,000	7,000
Domestic assembly of foreign makes	100	600	1,500	2,000	4,000
New imports	2,700	3,500	7,600	14,200	19,000
Used imports	4,200	4,000	3,700	3,600	3,000

Table 3 Best Selling Imported Cars in the Russian Market Sold Through Official Dealers in 2010 and Growth Rates (by Major Manufacturers)

Manufacturer/Brand	2008(units)	2009 (units)	2010 (units)	Growth rate of 2010 over 2009 (percent)
Ford	36,082	60,564	115,985	92
Hyundai	50,686	87,500	100,685	15
Toyota	43,867	60,638	95,689	58
Nissan	28,434	46,485	75,529	62
Renault	16,126	29,177	72,484	148
Chevrolet*	56,514	66,532	70,307	6
Mitsubishi	30,097	55,148	68,845	25
Daewoo	35,398	48,600	66,717	37
Kia	18,759	25,000	59,993	143
Mazda	8,565	21,100	32,290	53
Opel	9,153	9,139	19,983	113
Volkswagen	7,588	13,911	19,186	60
Suzuki	6,685	9,803	16,118	64
Honda	6,009	8,906	15,723	77
Peugeot	8,782	9,251	15,287	65
Skoda	5,428	7,535	14,835	97
Citroen	4,345	6,922	11,934	72
Volvo	5,048	5,713	10,801	89
Lexus	3,559	5,369	10,065	87
Audi	4,100	6,115	10,050	64
Mercedes-Benz	4,029	4,848	9,316	92
BMW	4,807	6,678	9,031	42
Subaru	3,733	4,160	6,604	83
Land Rover	2,436	4,075	6,299	55
Great Wall	-	4,070	4,788	18

Iran Khodro	-	-	4,534	-
Total	409,119	564,711	1,008,826	79

* - including 47,908 locally-manufactured Chevrolet-Niva and Chevrolet-Viva

The best-selling models include Ford Focus, Renault Logan, Mitsubishi Lancer, Daewoo Nexia and Matiz, Hyundai Accent, Getz and Tucson, Toyota Corolla and Camry, Chevrolet Niva, Lacetti and Lanos; and Nissan Almera.

SUV MARKET

The Russian SUV market has grown to become the largest SUV market in Europe with the total count of 185,000 new vehicles sold and tremendous growth of 45% over the last year sales result. By far, the best-seller in the SUV sector was the low-cost Chevrolet Niva, a joint project of GM and AutoVAZ, at a base cost of just over to $15,000. The Niva, and its many 'tuned' derivatives, finished the year with 41,000 sold vehicles (a 10% decrease below the previous year due in large part to the highly publicized management takeover of GM's domestic partner AvtoVAZ by federal authorities). The next most popular were the imported Hyundai Tucson and Toyota RAV4 selling in Russia at over $30,000 (sales result is over 12,000 vehicles of each model). The SUV market will continue to grow at an annual speed of 20-25% in the next 3-5 years due to growing incomes of Russian consumers.

DOMESTIC CAR PRODUCTION

Domestic automotive manufacturing continues to suffer from management difficulties, obsolete technologies and equipment, and a lack of financial resources. However, 2010 saw much needed investments by all major domestic car manufacturers and several agreements and partnerships with well-known Western manufacturers have resulted in the past year. AutoVAZ just signed a preliminary agreement with Magna involving cooperation in developing new vehicles at the AutoVAZ facilities. Russkie Machiny (Russian Vehicles - former RusPromAuto), owner of GAZ, also successfully purchased the assembly line to manufacture Dodge Stratus and Chrysler Sebring, and acquired the leading British producer of light commercial vehicles, LDV Holdings. Severstal Auto has cooperated with Korean Ssang Yong to assemble Rexton, Kyron and Actyon SUVs and Italian Fiat Group to assemble Albea and Doblo models. SOK Group partnered with Korean Kia Motors to assemble Spectra cars. Thus, all major domestic car and LCV manufacturers have focused on cooperation with international automotive firms in their efforts to secure their positions in the Russian market. Now that competition is getting tougher, Russian automotive companies plan to invest in modernization of their facilities and increase the import of components and technologies from the world automotive market leaders.

the Russian government took the decision (Decree 166) to drastically reduce import taxes for automotive components imported by OEMs. The import taxes have either been abolished (engines, power trains, exhaust systems, and body parts) or cut to as low as three percent (starters and spark plugs) for components supplied to assembly projects. In 2010, the government extended this incentive to include tier-1 component manufacturers (Decree 566).

Local Assembly of Foreign Makes

The local assembly of foreign makes continues to show good results. In 2010, this sub-sector grew faster than imports, and exceeded even the most favorable forecasts. There are several new assembly projects on the way. Toyota is building a plant in St. Petersburg, which is supposed to be put into operation in the end of 2012 to assemble initially 25,000 Camry for the local market. General Motors, Nissan and Volkswagen announced multi-million investments in assembly facilities that are supposed to be put into operation in 2008-2009. GM and Nissan plants are already under construction in the suburbs of St. Petersburg.

Tier-1 Component Projects

Although major international automotive manufacturing companies are already active in the Russian market, international component manufacturers are remain cautious to establishing manufacturing operations. So far, only a few international component manufacturers have set up facilities or announced their plans to establish manufacturing in Russia. The most well-known companies in this list include Johnson Controls, Tenneco, Cummins, Bosch, ZF, VDO, Magna, Siemens, Nokia, Michelin, etc. The major obstacle to rapid development in this sector remains insufficient demand for quality components. However with the obvious fast growth in the market for locally-assembled foreign vehicles, opportunities in this sector will be increasing. The Russian government is taking further efforts to attract international component manufacturers in Russia

PRACTICAL INFORMATION FOR BUSINESS AND INVESTMENTS

DOING BUSINESS IN RUSSIA

MARKET OVERVIEW

With over 140 million consumers, a growing middle class, and almost unlimited infrastructure needs, Russia remains one of the most promising markets for U.S. exporters.

Russia is the world's 11th largest economy and has the highest per capita GDP ($15,900) of the BRIC countries. It is an upper middle income country, with a highly educated workforce and sophisticated, discerning consumers.

Russia's economy has begun to recover from the economic crisis that started in 2008, with GDP growth at 4.0% for 2010. This growth was slightly less than anticipated due to drought and wildfires, which disrupted agriculture, commerce and industry. Economists forecast real GDP growth of 4.3% in 2011.

Russia was the U.S.'s 37th largest export market and the 17th largest exporter to the U.S. in 2010. U.S. exports to Russia were $5.97 billion, a 12% increase from 2009. Russian exports to the U.S. were $26.5 billion, up 41% from 2009. Russian sources list the country's leading trade partners as: Netherlands, China, Germany, Italy, Ukraine and Turkey.

U.S. accumulated investment in Russia is approximately $21.3 billion. According to Russian data, the U.S. is Russia's 10th largest foreign investor.

Russia anticipates joining the WTO in 2011, which would liberalize trade with the rest of the world and create opportunities for U.S. exports and investments.

MARKET CHALLENGES

Russia is a geographically vast market, spanning nine time zones and encompassing over 17 million square miles.

Seriously underdeveloped infrastructure poses logistical challenges, especially accessing markets outside of major cities.

An incomplete transition from central planning has led to an insufficiently integrated economy and disparities in wealth distribution, geographically and demographically.

Conducting business may be impeded by: burdensome regulatory regimes; inadequate IPR protection; extensive corruption and lack of rule of law, inconsistent application of laws and regulations; lack of transparency; and excessive government interference in business matters.

Recent reforms make it easier for companies to hire expatriate employees, but the Russian immigration and visa system requires time and patience for business travelers to obtain necessary permissions to do business in Russia.

English is not widely spoken, although knowledge of the language is expanding, especially in the major cities.

MARKET OPPORTUNITIES

In alphabetical order:

Apparel
Automotive Parts & Service Equipment / Accessories
Aviation
Construction / Greenbuild
Consumer Electronics
Cosmetics / Toiletries
Electric Power Generation & Transmission Equipment
Medical Equipment
Refinery Equipment
Safety & Security Equipment
Travel & Tourism to the U.S.

MARKET ENTRY STRATEGY

Developing business in Russia is resource intensive, requiring serious commitments of time, personnel and capital.

Conduct market research, such as with the U.S. Commercial Service's Gold Key or International Partner Search services, to identify opportunities and potential Russian business partners.

Conduct due diligence, such as with the U.S. Commercial Service's International Company Profile service, to ascertain the reliability of business partners.

Consult with U.S. companies already in the market, as well as with the U.S. Commercial Service and business organizations, such as the American Chamber of Commerce and U.S. - Russia Business Council.

Communicate regularly with Russian business partners to ensure common understanding of expectations.

Frequent travel to Russia is strongly recommended to establish and maintain relationships with business partners and to understand changing market conditions.

Maintain a long-term timeframe to implement plans and achieve positive results.

Abide by all Russian laws and regulations (taxes, customs, labor, etc.) – retaining local tax, legal and government relations advisors is strongly recommended.

Conduct business in accordance with all applicable U.S. laws, as well as standard U.S. and international business practices.

Utilize letters of credit or other secure financing vehicles, avoid sales on open account.

Explore use of U.S. government financing, such as the Export-Import Bank (Ex-Im Bank) and Overseas Private Investment Corporation (OPIC), as well as multilateral development banks, such as the European Bank for Reconstruction and Development (EBRD).

Develop working relationships with national, regional and/or local governments and consider implementing corporate social responsibility programs.

Patience, perseverance and perspective are keys to success in Russia.

SELLING U.S. PRODUCTS AND SERVICES

USING AN AGENT OR DISTRIBUTOR

Encompassing nine time zones, Russia is the largest country in the world by landmass. Therefore, many businesses tend to approach the Russian market on a regional basis. Most new entrants start in Moscow and then move into the regions either through an existing distributor or by seeking new distributors in those locales. As both Moscow and St. Petersburg are major population and business centers, many Western firms have representatives there. Some companies have successfully entered the Russian market by starting distribution in other key regions first because of market features and industry sector concentrations (e.g., woodworking in northwest Russia, energy projects in Sakhalin and western Siberia) and then expanding elsewhere. Well-organized distribution channels are established in western Russia, especially in Moscow and St. Petersburg, and continue to develop rapidly in southern Russia, the Volga region, Urals, Siberia and Russian Far East. To succeed in Russia, it is important to choose sales targets and distributors carefully.

U.S. companies have four basic options when choosing a distribution channel:

1) Agents

It is not a common practice in Russia for foreign companies to rely solely upon the services of an agent. Distributors and representative offices, however, often employ agents in the Russian regions in order to promote their products.

2) Distributors

The most common market entry strategy is to select a good distributor or several distributors (depending on the product). U.S. companies can consider a variety of national, regional and local distribution alternatives. In some product categories (e.g.,

apparel, cosmetics, packaged foods, alcoholic beverages, consumer electronics, and household appliances), foreign suppliers can choose from a growing number of established distributors. A good distributor will typically sell and deliver foreign suppliers' products to end-users and/or the retail market and provide a wide range of logistical support, i.e., customs clearance, warehousing, inventory management, etc. However, handling promotion and advertising campaigns exclusively through independent distributors can often produce disappointing results. Russian distributors normally handle products from multiple suppliers and are not typically dedicated to promoting a specific company's product unless the supplier provides substantial support for promotion and advertising. Russia's retail law also limits some types of promotional activities.

3) Representative/Branch Offices

Some foreign manufacturers, in addition to using distributors, have established their own representative offices. The major advantage of opening a representative office is that foreign companies have more direct contact with their end-users and control over the promotion and distribution of their products. However, under the Russian Civil Code, such offices cannot be directly involved in commercial activity. Instead, they typically oversee a network of distributors and/or agents that perform commercial functions. This approach affords greater control by the foreign supplier over the distribution process and helps to reduce risks.

As Representative Offices may not take part in commercial activities, Branch Offices have become increasingly more popular. According to a 1999 foreign investment law, foreign companies may engage in commercial activities through their legally established branches. Branches are accredited for five years and must be registered with tax authorities and other state organizations.

Both Representative and Branch Offices can be attractive to foreign businesses wishing to operate in the Russian market because there are fewer tax and other administrative burdens and currency control restrictions may not apply.

4) Foreign Subsidiaries

Some foreign manufacturers, particularly in the cosmetics, pharmaceuticals, consumer appliances, durables and industrial products sectors, have registered their wholly owned subsidiaries in Russia. They then sell directly to their own companies registered in Russia who import for their own account. This approach affords full control of the supplier over distribution and helps to further reduce possible risks from false invoicing and other irregularities sometimes committed by independent importers and distributors. For more information on registering a company in Russia, please refer to the "Establishing an Office" section below.

U.S. exporters are advised to cultivate personal relationships with their Russian representatives and clients, to proceed gradually, and to ensure they have a contingency plan should problems arise. Since it is often difficult to find information on Russian companies, it is strongly recommended that U.S. firms consider using the International Company Profile service to validate potential partners. The U.S. Commercial Service strongly advises against the risky practice of a company representative simply visiting Russia once or twice, selecting a representative, granting exclusive representation, and then moving quickly to consignment or credit sales without first establishing a payment and performance history. In addition, exporters are cautioned to take primary responsibility for registering their brand names in Russia and not to rely on a partner to do this. Finally, it is important to provide a Russian partner with Russian language product information and marketing materials. These can be prepared in the United States or done jointly with a Russian partner.

The U.S. Commercial Service provides assistance to U.S. companies in finding local partners through the Gold Key Service, Pre-Service Market Assessment, International Partner Search, International Company Profile, Customized Market Research, Platinum Key and other products and services. Information about these services can be found at http://www.buyusa.gov/russia/en/products_services.html .

ESTABLISHING AN OFFICE

The U.S. Commercial Service can provide basic counseling on registration requirements and procedures. However, it is strongly recommended that interested U.S. companies seek legal advice on business registration. U.S. Commercial staff can provide contact information for U.S. and Russian consulting firms that offer professional legal advice in this area.

REGISTRATION OPTIONS

The following basic laws and government resolutions regulate business registration in Russia:

The 1999 Federal Law "On Foreign Investment in the Russian Federation"

The 1994 Part I of the Civil Code

The 2001 Federal Law "On State Registration of Legal Entities"

Russian Government Resolution No. 319 "On Authorized Federal Entity of the Executive Power, Providing State Registration of Legal Entities" of May 17, 2002, and a number of legal acts.

Conducting business without registration is illegal. Although the federal law governing the process is uniform throughout Russia, it is often subject to local interpretation.

Russian law offers several commonly used structures to conduct business:

Representative or branch office of a foreign company

Registration as an individual private entrepreneur

Companies:

- Limited Liability Company (OOO)
- Privately held, closed joint stock company (ZAO)

o Publicly held, open joint stock company (OAO)

Branch offices and accredited representative offices are both legally distinct from Russian corporations, which may be established by foreign firms either as joint stock companies with partial Russian ownership, or as wholly owned subsidiaries of a foreign firm. Foreign ownership can be as high as 100%, with some exceptions. For example, foreign investment is limited in industries defined by the "Strategic Sectors Law" (discussed in this chapter under "Joint Ventures/Licensing").

BRANCH OFFICES

Branches are not considered independent legal entities, though they may negotiate, market or provide other business support on behalf of firms based outside Russia. Setting up a branch may be worthwhile if a foreign company is starting to pursue business in Russia and is exploring opportunities. Many large U.S. firms began their Russian operations as locally established branches.

Branches of foreign firms must register with the State Registration Chamber, which is part of the Ministry of Justice of the Russian Federation. Branches will incur the following fees for accreditation: RR 120,000 (State duty) plus RR 15,000 for one year; RR 30,000 for two years; RR 45,000 for three years; and RR 60,000 for five years.

ACCREDITED REPRESENTATIVE OFFICES

Like branches, accredited representative offices are not independent legal entities; they may not be involved in commercial activities. After accreditation is obtained, the office should register with the local or regional registration chambers, located in many Russian cities. Advantages of an accredited office include annual/quarter (rather than monthly) reporting requirements for some activities (including some tax payments), and the ability to issue invitations for U.S. partners to visit Russia on business visas. Up to five foreign employees may work with an accredited office of a foreign company. Offices are usually accredited for one to three year terms.

Accredited representative offices must register with the State Registration Chamber or the Russian Chamber of Commerce and Industry in order to be included in the State Register of Accredited Representative Offices of Foreign Legal Entities in the Russian Federation. Certain specific businesses must register with appropriate state organizations, depending on their industry. Such agencies include the Central Bank, Ministry of Economic Development Ministry of Finance, Ministry of Transportation, Ministry of Industry and Trade, Ministry of Energy and others. According to internal procedures, accreditation of a representative office or branch should take 21 business days (for registration with the State Registration Chamber) starting from the day the full set of required documents are provided.

Representative offices will incur the following fees for accreditation: (1) USD 1,500 for one year, USD 2,500 for two years and USD 3,500 for three years for the accreditation with the Russian Chamber of Commerce and Industry plus RR 3,000 payment or (2) RR 30,000 for one year, RR 60,000 for two years and RR 75,000 for three years for the accreditation with the State Registration Chamber. An additional fee of RR 15,000 may be paid for expedited accreditation within seven days.

Further information is available on the State Registration Chamber website at http://www.palata.ru .

COMPANIES AND TAXATION

Companies are required to register with the local Tax Inspectorate (the tax registration will also include registration with the Russian Social Security Funds). Documents for state registration should be prepared and submitted to the local Tax Inspectorate in accordance with Chapter 12 of the August 8, 2001 Federal Law "On State Registration of Legal Entities." An authorized legal entity, the Moscow Department of the Ministry of Finance of the Russian Federation (15, Tulskaya Street, Moscow) provides counseling to business people on registration procedures and registration documents.

Further information on company registration, including the list of documents to be submitted, as well as contact information for local tax authorities can be obtained from the following website: http://www.nalog.ru

TAX CODE

Major revisions of Russia's tax code took place from 1999 to 2003. The resulting tax legislation more closely matches the needs of a growing market economy, and many of the provisions of previous legislation that distorted the business environment and kept many businesses in the shadow economy have been removed.

The most fundamental changes were reflected in the new chapters of the Tax Code Part II and affected the value added tax, excise taxes, individual income tax and profits tax. Also affected was the Federal Law "On the Introduction of Amendments and Additions to Part II of the Russian Federation Tax Code and to Separate Russian Federation Legislative Acts." These changes aimed at improving Part II of the Russian Tax Code were passed by the Duma and enacted into law in 2003. The ongoing tax reform has further improved procedural rules and reduced the overall tax burden in the country.

Implementing numerous changes in the Russian Tax Code has resulted in some confusion. A general overview of Russian taxes follows, but companies operating in Russia should consult with a professional tax advisor to learn about the latest developments.

Profits Tax

The profits tax is levied on net profits. Effective January 2009, the profit tax rate was reduced from 24% to 20% (18% of this amount is allocated to Regional Russian authorities and 2% to Federal) to address the economic downturn. The regional authorities may, at their discretion, reduce their regional profits tax rate to as low as 13.5%. Thus, the overall tax rate can vary from 15.5% to 20%. Depreciation provisions were improved with the introduction of a 30% initial lump sum depreciation deduction and revision of non-linear depreciation rules. The tax rate was reduced in tandem with the introduction of more realistic interpretations of deductible expenses, the combined effect of which is to significantly reduce the profit tax burden and support the Russian economy during the financial downturn.

The provisions on profit taxation enable foreign companies operating in Russia to benefit from the reduced withholding tax rates and exemptions under Russia's double taxation treaties (the U.S. and Russia have had a double taxation treaty in place since 1992), which in certain cases could result in advantages to U.S. companies. For example, representative offices are permitted to deduct expenses incurred on their behalf by a parent company located abroad.

Value Added Tax (VAT) and Import Duties

VAT is designed as a tax to be borne ultimately by consumers, but is collected on a basis similar to the European Union model. VAT is calculated on sales value and is applied at a uniform rate of 18%, except for certain foodstuffs, pharmaceuticals and children's clothes, which are taxed at 10%. Some products, such as certain financial services and medical equipment, are entirely exempt from VAT. As of January 1, 2008, in an attempt to bolster R&D and investment in technology, intangibles such as inventions, software, industrial designs and production know-how are exempt from the VAT.

Imports are also subject to VAT, calculated based on the customs value of the item plus customs duties and fees. In addition, import duties are assessed at specified rates, ranging from 5% to 30% (as of January 1, 2010, import duty rates for some goods increased with the introduction of the Customs Union between Russia, Belarus and Kazakhstan). They are assessed according to classification and are applied to the customs value of the imported goods, including shipping charges and insurance. Goods imported by foreign partners as in-kind contributions to the charter capital of a new enterprise may be exempt from import duties during a period specified in the charter documents and import VAT under certain conditions (e.g., the goods qualify as technological equipment which has no analogues manufactured in Russia).

In general, goods manufactured or assembled in Russia, whether by a Russian or foreign company, and then exported out of Russia, are not subject to VAT. If these goods are exported before payment is received, then no VAT should be collected. On the other hand, if payment is received before shipment, the exporter must pay the applicable VAT and then request a refund from the tax authorities. Changes in the method of VAT collection for certain entities such as diplomatic missions, effective January 1, 2010, have resulted in some confusion as businesses and government offices make the needed adjustments to the revised system.

Social Welfare Taxes

As of January 1, 2010, the Unified Social Tax was replaced by social security (payroll) contributions to the State Pension Fund, Social Security Fund, Federal Medical Insurance Fund and Territorial Medical Insurance Fund. A business is liable for the entire amount of social security contributions and no amount is withheld from employees. The recent implementation of the change in social welfare taxes has resulted in some confusion, as businesses and government offices make the needed adjustments to the new system.

The social security contributions apply at the aggregate rate of 34% on an employee's annual salary of up to RR 415,000 (the threshold may be adjusted in the future by the Russian Government); the portion of an employee's annual salary in excess of this threshold is exempt from the social security contributions. Social security contributions are payable as follows: 26% to the State Pension Fund, 2.9% to the Social Security Fund, 2.1% to the Federal Medical Insurance Fund, and 3% to the Territorial Medical Insurance Fund. The social security contributions apply to all payments to individuals (including individuals applying a simplified system of taxation) even if made from net income. Importantly, salary or other payments to foreign citizens temporarily present in Russia (i.e., not having a permanent resident permit) are not subject to social security contributions. Social security contributions are paid on a monthly basis and the calculations of the social security contributions are filed with the State Pension Fund and the Social Security Fund on a quarterly basis.

Reduced social security contribution rates apply to certain business categories, including agricultural producers (20.2% in 2011-2012 and 27.1% in 2013-2014), software and high-tech companies (14% in 2011-2017), certain mass media companies (26% in 2011 and 27% in 2012) and companies engaged in special innovation projects (14%).

Workplace accident insurance is paid by the employer in addition to social security contributions. Rates vary from 0.2% to 8.5% depending on the established class of professional risk.

Withholding on Dividends, Interest and Royalties

Foreign legal entities without a business presence in Russia are subject to a withholding tax of 10% on freight services provided in Russia. Dividends are taxed at a rate of 15%, interest and royalties at a rate of 20%. These rates are often reduced pursuant to an applicable relevant double taxation treaty (the U.S.-Russia tax treaty potentially may reduce the dividends rate as low as 5%, depending on whether certain ownership and investment criteria are met, as well as lower the tax on interest and royalties to 0%). Lease payments and other income are subject to a 20% withholding rate.

Land, Property and Personal Income Taxes

Local authorities may impose a tax on land according to its type and location. The rate is higher in Moscow and St. Petersburg than in some other cities and rural areas.

The personal income tax rate for Russian tax residents is a flat 13% imposed on worldwide income (non-residents are taxed at 30% on Russian-source income).

Franchising

Franchising as a business model only came to Russia in the early 1990s. The first foreign franchises were primarily American and Italian restaurant chains. Franchise legislation was formally adopted in 1994 by the Russian Civil Code, specifically in Chapter 54, where franchising is defined as a "commercial concession." Since then the number of franchise companies has steadily grown. While foreign franchises dominated the market for the first decade, a number of Russian retailers, restaurant and drugstore chains began to expand using the franchise model. Currently, there are more Russian than foreign franchise organizations. It is difficult to estimate the number of franchises currently working in Russia because some are registered under other legal forms, such as through licensing agreements or sales contracts. The franchising business model has developed mainly in the restaurant and fast food, retail, and other consumer-service areas. Most franchisers choose to establish partnerships with franchisees in Moscow or St. Petersburg; however, there are several other cities with million-plus populations, which can provide excellent opportunities for expansion.

There are still some gaps in Russian franchising legislation, but local franchising entrepreneurs, with the help of the Russian Franchise Association, formed in 1997, are actively working to create a more favorable legal and business environment for the expansion of franchising in Russia, and to support and protect the interests of its members.

According to the Russian Civil Code amendments as of January 1, 2008, the subject matter of the franchising agreement currently includes the rights to use a trademark, service mark and any other objects of exclusive rights, in particular commercial designation and know-how, which cannot be granted free-of-charge. Also, for a franchising agreement to be valid, it has to be executed in written form and registered with the Federal Service for Intellectual Property, Patents and Trademarks (Rospatent).

The annual BuyBrand International Franchise Exhibition (www.buybrand.ru), held annually in Moscow in September, is a good way to make contacts and become acquainted with the market.

DIRECT MARKETING

Given the relatively underdeveloped state of some distribution channels in Russia, direct marketing has become an effective and profitable alternative, especially outside of Moscow and St. Petersburg. Telemarketing and fax marketing to business customers is common in Russian cities, but it is not particularly effective. Other direct marketing channels (catalogs and e-commerce) are developing quickly.

Direct selling (for example, for health and beauty products) works well and is cost effective for the distributor, since it develops an effective distribution network. For a large number of under-employed workers and pensioners in Russia, the option of supplementing their income through working in direct sales is quite attractive. World Direct Selling Association statistics revealed that direct sales in Russia in 2010 amounted to $3.06 billion and that almost 4.9 million salespeople Russia-wide were engaged in direct selling.

Leading direct sales companies such as Amway, Avon, Mary Kay and Tupperware are active in Russia. According to Russian law, companies may not use direct sales for such products as biologically active food additives and vitamins. At present, these products can only be sold through pharmacies, kiosks, and health stores. For more information on the direct selling industry in Russia, visit the Russian Direct Selling Association website at: www.rdsa.ru.

JOINT VENTURES/LICENSING

U.S. companies may become strategic partners with Russian firms by taking an equity position in Russian joint stock companies and thus establishing joint ventures (JV). Establishing a JV in Russia demands meticulous planning and sustained commitment. In most cases, it is advisable for the U.S. partner to retain managerial and voting control. JVs in which foreign partners hold minority stakes are dependent on the good intentions of their Russian majority owners. Experience shows that foreign minority shareholders may face serious difficulty in protecting their interests in Russian courts.

One advantage of a JV is that it helps a U.S. firm gain a measure of Russian identity, which can be useful in a culture where many still view foreigners with suspicion. The May 2008 Strategic Sectors Law identified 42 industry sectors requiring the Russian government's pre-approval of a foreign firm's purchase of controlling interest. Additionally, political pressure is mounting in Russia for domestic content mandates in key sectors or for large-scale procurements. For example, some foreign investments in the oil industry may be required to source 70% of their goods and services from Russian providers. Firms that creatively help oil producers meet these requirements will have an advantage in this industry.

Russian and U.S. partners often view JVs differently. U.S. companies, especially smaller ones, often view JVs as a means of securing a local partner with experience in the Russian market. On the other hand, many Russian managers view a foreign partner chiefly as a source of working capital and these managers may place a low priority on local market development. While there are many examples of successful JVs, a U.S. investor invites trouble when it cedes oversight of any aspect of a JV to a Russian partner which does not share the same objectives. Before making financial or legal commitments, U.S. firms should thoroughly explore whether a potential partner shares their priorities and expectations. Any firm that forms a JV in Russia should be ready to invest the constant personal attention of U.S. managerial staff to keep the business on course, both before and after the venture has achieved commercial success.

U.S. technology is sometimes licensed for Russian production outside the context of a joint venture. Major hurdles that must be overcome include quality levels attainable by Russian facilities in the absence of significant retooling, uncertain intellectual property protection and difficulty in receiving regular and prompt payments. In the opposite direction, Russian companies generally are eager to license their technologies to foreign companies in exchange for the cash infusion.

SELLING TO THE GOVERNMENT

Government procurement has always been a powerful incentive for the development of the SME sector in Russia. Given the amount of post-Soviet government property, the market for state procurement is quite impressive in value. The term "government procurement" includes all state agencies, ministries, state non-budget funds, state-owned plants and factories, high schools, hospitals, companies operating infrastructural facilities such as Mosvodokanal-company operating the water and sewage system of Moscow or GorMost Company, operating all Moscow bridges, parks and lawns. These entities buy a large range of products from stationary to complex road building or construction equipment, and from food to drugs and medical equipment.

The Ministry for Economic Development (MED) and Treasury are responsible for developing Russian procurement policy. All the legal initiatives are developed by this Ministry and sometimes jointly with Ministry of Industry and Trade; however, MED is always the lead in any joint projects.

On the other hand, it has always been a challenging issue for SMEs to apply and start supplying government agencies or affiliated structures. Until 2005 there was no proper legislation regulating procurement operations, which led to some corrupt practices. Companies close to the management of the state-owned public organizations have often pre-negotiated the results of the tenders leaving no place for fair market competition.

Many companies have encountered the problem that, despite being a major producer of the commodity and offering the best price, they still could not win. It is possible that the commission will find a minor fault in the tender application or its specifications and thus reject the bid and give preference to another bidder.

Russian Federal Law N94-Ф3 of July 21, 2005, requires all federal, regional and municipal government customers to publish all information about government tenders, auctions and other purchase procedures on the Internet. Other laws that regulate government procurement in Russia are: Federal Law 218-Ф3, 53-Ф3, 142-Ф3, 207-Ф3, 229-P (about the ecommerce platform www.zakupki.gov.ru), and 94-Ф3 (anti-corruption act for government procurement). The business community as well as many public organizations admit that the law in its existing form allows for much corruption. Therefore, President Medvedev ordered MED to revise the law and apply anti-corruption amendments. On Novermber 11, 2010, the new wording of the law was approved by the State Duma (Russian Parliament). These laws stipulate new government procurement policies and are directed at transforming them into transparent business practices with equal rules and opportunities for all participants.

If a US company considers entering the Russian market and becoming a government supplier it must consider whether its equipment or products compete with any similar goods produced in Russia. Federal law states that the preference should be granted to the local manufacturer. The law also states that in case foreign goods outbid the local good for some reason, an additional discount of 10-15% is to be granted by the seller.

The potential for the success of US producers to sell to the government often depends on the US company identifying the right partner in this market. The direct sales model (B2G) does not fit the Russian market first because the government needs the goods that are tendered to be available for a spot deal and this is only possible when the company runs its own operations or has a partner, and second because the bidder must be a Russia-based legal entity. The second key to success is to spot the unique opportunities where Russian companies have no competitive edge or offer solutions that can outbid the local supplier, using either logistical or financial advantages.

The government decree dated December 5, 2008 (№427), states that Russia manufactured goods will enjoy a 15% preference if any foreign manufactured goods are offered for the tender and that, if a company offering foreign goods wins the tender, the contract is to be signed with a 15% discount. This decree is not valid if the sought products or services have no competing analogues in Russia. For these reasons, it is advisable to enter the Russian government procurement market either with a unique portfolio of products or to start operations aimed at launching manufacturing units within Russia.

Federal law 94-Ф3 on government procurement is not valid for natural monopolists such as Gazprom or Russian Railways or Rosneft. However, work is now ongoing to reconsider the current status of procurement policies at these state-owned companies and to make them dependent on federal law to enhance the structure of spending and to cut excessive costs. Such a change in the procurement policies at state-owned corporations will be a step forward toward the elimination of corruption in these companies. The main regulators who consider complaints about companies and agencies infringing on the procurement law are the Federal Antimonopoly Service, MED, and the Ministry of the Interior (when there is a criminal case).

To see the list of tenders, one can enter the government website www.zakupki.gov.ru, which is available only in the Russian language. State-owned companies like Russian Railways or Gazprom have English versions of their websites where they also place information on their tenders.

DISTRIBUTION AND SALES CHANNELS

Well-organized distribution channels have developed significantly over the last few years, particularly in the major population centers, such as Moscow and St. Petersburg, and have begun to expand to the regions. In the consumer sector, some large-scale retail stores have recently emerged in Moscow that are able to buy in bulk and negotiate relatively long-term commitments. Large shopping malls have opened up on the Ring Road circling the capital and are giving the Moscow retail environment more of the characteristics of other European cities. Shopping malls and big box stores are common sights in St. Petersburg, Moscow and many other Russian cities.

By utilizing these domestic distribution organizations, the task of bringing goods to market in Russia has been greatly eased. However, their geographic coverage can be limited, and accessing markets in some of the regions can still be problematic. In these regions, U.S. firms may encounter erratic distribution, unpredictable and tough competition, and word-of-mouth marketing. Although Russia boasts increasing numbers of western-style stores in major cities, much distribution and retailing still takes place through such informal channels as kiosks and open markets. Those who succeed do so through a combination of improvisation and innovation, combined with a substantial investment of time and a tolerance for early mistakes. U.S. companies with a long-term market development strategy may find regional markets well worth exploring.

St. Petersburg remains the main port of entry for a variety of consumer and industrial products for European Russia (Russia west of the Urals). Vladivostok is the main port of entry for the Russian Far East. In general, the transportation infrastructure in this vast country is still underdeveloped and in need of major upgrades. The majority of cargo moves by rail and the road network is in need of expansion. Major western freight forwarders and express couriers are active in Russia.

SELLING FACTORS/TECHNIQUES

As with any country, successfully marketing and selling goods and services in Russia requires adaptation to its commercial climate and business practices. Market research is required to identify opportunities and potential Russian business partners. The choice of a partner is key and should be done only after conducting sufficient due diligence to determine its reputation and reliability. The U.S. Commercial Service has services to assist with market research, identifying partners and conducting due diligence (http://www.buyusa.gov/russia/en/products_services.html).

Both before and after launching operations, travel to Russia is strongly recommended to establish and maintain relationships with business partners and to understand market attributes. Marketing in Russia requires patience: exporters should maintain a long-term perspective and not expect immediate results. It can be helpful to network with companies already in the market, as well as business organizations, such as the American Chamber of Commerce in Russia and the U.S.-Russia Business Council.

Business planning should include advertising, market promotion and regular visits to Russia. When recruiting personnel or identifying business partners, local talent should be utilized, especially for government relations, which can be of critical importance, and professional services of all kinds, whether law, accounting or engineering, etc. Absentee management should be avoided; it is important to communicate regularly with Russian business partners to ensure common understanding of expectations. Partners can assist with required testing and certification, after-sales service, customs clearance, warehousing and preparation of Russian-language marketing and instruction materials.

Business should always be conducted in compliance with all Russian laws and regulations (taxes, customs, labor, etc.), as well as applicable U.S. laws and standard business practices, including corporate governance and accounting practices.

Companies that undertake corporate social responsibility programs in the U.S. should consider developing a similar approach for the Russian market.

Exporters should avoid selling on open account until they have developed a well-established track record with buyers; letters of credit and other secure financing vehicles are available. Another option may be U.S. government or multilateral development bank financing, such as the U.S. Export-Import Bank (Ex-Im Bank), the U.S. Overseas Private Investment Corporation (OPIC) or the European Bank for Reconstruction and Development (EBRD). Exporters should be prepared to adjust prices according to currency fluctuations.

Russian purchasers are generally sophisticated and highly educated. They are likely to be internet users and receptive to imported goods. Russian purchasers may be price sensitive, but are frequently willing to pay for quality, especially for recognized and reliable imported brands – another reason to invest in advertising.

ELECTRONIC COMMERCE

In 2010, e-commerce in Russia reached the $9 billion mark in sales. The business-tobusiness segment increased to $3 billion. The Internet advertising market reached $400 million in 2010, with Yandex Direct, Google Adwords and Rambler Begun among the key players.

The number of Russian Internet users has increased dramatically over the past five years, and varies from 32 to 50 million people according to different sources or 30-40% of the population nationwide. Internet penetration is estimated at 43.6% with an installed base of 69.1 million personal computers. Over 75% of these users are consolidated in the European part of the country. Future growth in Internet usage is expected to be significant.

Payment mechanisms are developing quickly and offer a wide range of payment methods - SMS, credit card, payment aggregators, web-money and cash payments. The number of online shops in the Russian market has reached 20,000, selling almost $4 billion worth of goods in 2010. Home appliances and electronics accounted for 50% of sales, with the fastest growing subsectors being electronics and household goods. Many companies buy products from foreign E-commerce platforms, such as Yahoo Auctions, Ebay and Alibaba, and resell them in Russia, offering escrow services like PayPal.

Although the number of consumers with credit and debit cards is increasing rapidly, many Internet businesses in Russia still do not accept online payments but rather use their websites as a front end for the buyer to select goods and place an order to be delivered. Businesses offering goods or services that can be accessed immediately (electronic downloads and service account top-ups, for instance) offer credit card payment options most frequently. E-currency payments are also an option. The number of consumers with credit cards who are willing to use them online is constantly increasing and banks have begun offering various E-commerce payment products. Sales through these channels are sustaining a current rapid growth.

The Russian government's "E-Russia" program is intended to stimulate the growth of E-commerce throughout the country, using federal and local E-government initiatives as a catalyst. Another government initiative is the launch of the E-commerce platform www.zakupki.gov.ru and accreditation of several private e-commerce platforms such as Sberbank Ast, MMVB Information technologies and RTS Tender, which is aimed at centralizing government and municipal purchases and making them transparent. These sites consolidate all procurement inquiries from government agencies, thus providing qualified suppliers the opportunity to sell products and services directly to the government.

TRADE PROMOTION AND ADVERTISING

Television, radio, print, and billboard media are ubiquitous in the Russian market. Most international advertising agencies are active in Russia; domestic agencies are present in the market as well. Strong economic growth and increasing incomes have resulted in growth in the advertising industry, although enforcement of some advertising laws has been inconsistent, leading to situations where already purchased advertising is then disallowed by local government officials. Advertising clients include successful Russian manufacturers of consumer goods, particularly of processed foods and beverages, as well as foreign producers.

In response to the economic crisis, many companies cut their advertising budgets. However, in 2010 the market started to recover rapidly and companies are now actively increasing their media and marketing budgets. Though traditional forms of advertising are still prominent in Russia, in the context of the crisis, advertising agencies reconsidered their approach to the communication mix and increased their share of nonstandard communication methods, including "below the line" (BTL), trade programs, ambient media, and flash mobs (publicity stunts). Advertising on the internet continues to be a growth industry.

The following is a list of media outlets and print publications listed from highest to lowest penetration in Moscow[1]:

TV Channels

ORT http://www.1tv.ru NTV http://www.ntv.ru Russia 1 http://www.rutv.ru TNT http://tnt-online.ru STS http://www.ctc-tv.ru

Radio stations

Avtoradio http://www.avtoradio.ru Russian Radio http://www.rusradio.ru Shanson http://www.chanson.ru Europa Plus http://www.europaplus.ru Retro FM http://www.retrofm.ru Yumor FM http://www.veseloeradio.ru

[1] Source:TNS statistics

Press

Daily newspapers

Metro http://www.metronews.ru/msk Moskovsky komsomolets http://www.mk.ru Iz ruk v ruki http://www.irr.ru Sovetskiy Sport http://www.sovsport.ru Rossiskaya Gazeta ("Russian newspaper") http://www.rg.ru

Weekly newspapers

Teleprogramma http://www.kp.ru/daily/tv Arguments and facts http://www.aif.ru Extra M http://www.extra-m.ru Komsomolskaya Pravda Tolstushka http://kp.ru/daily/friday

Weekly magazines

7 Days http://www.7days.ru Antenna – Telesem http://www.antenna-telesem.ru Teleweek http://teleweek.ru Teshin Yazik http://trisemerki.ru/izdaniya/jurnaly/Teschin-Yazyk/index.htm TV – 7 http://www.tv7.ru

Monthly magazines

Caravan of stories http://www.karavan.ru Za rulem http://www.zr.ru Vokrug Sveta http://www.vokrugveta.ru Cosmopolitan http://www.cosmo.ru Lyubimaya Dacha http://ldacha.ru

PRICING

Russian consumers are attracted to bargains, but are increasingly able and willing to pay for quality merchandise. U.S. companies exporting to Russia should be prepared to offer competitive prices for their goods, knowing that in many areas they face inexpensive Russian, Asian and strong European and other third-country competition. With a few exceptions, all goods and services sold in Russia are subject to a value-added tax (VAT) of 18%. Imports into Russia are subject to VAT, which is assessed on the CIF value of an imported shipment plus applicable duty. In addition, in many sectors with strong local and third-country competition, it will be necessary to spend money on advertising and brand promotion. All these costs should be figured into the U.S. exporter's pricing structure and become part of a long-term marketing and sales program.

SALES SERVICE/CUSTOMER SUPPORT

Good after-sales service, training and customer support can be a major competitive advantage for U.S. firms entering the Russian market, as Russian manufacturers are known for inadequate post-sale service.

Similarly, buyers of sophisticated equipment of all types - from computers and process controls to medical and mining equipment - are keenly interested in training, as their employees may never have used particular products or brands. U.S. firms able and willing to offer training and support for products, particularly in remote sites, can gain a significant advantage over competitors. Conversely, companies unwilling to make this commitment may find themselves at a distinct disadvantage to European or Asian companies, whose proximity facilitates training and service. After-sales service is also often an important component in leasing arrangements in Russia, and will play a larger role in the decision process as leasing continues to develop. Leasing in Russia is covered in Chapter 7.

PROTECTING INTELLECTUAL PROPERTY

IPR Climate in Russia

Several general principles are important for effective management of intellectual property rights in Russia. First, it is important to have an overall strategy to protect IPR. Second, IPR is protected differently in Russia than in the United States. Third, rights must be registered and enforced in Russia, under local laws.

U.S. firms should proactively take steps to protect their intellectual property in Russia, including registering their trademarks with the Federal Service for Intellectual Property, Patents and Trademarks (Rospatent) and the Russian Federal Customs Service. It is vital that companies understand that intellectual property is primarily a private right and that the U.S. government generally cannot enforce rights on behalf of private individuals in Russia. While the U.S. government is willing to assist, there is little it can do if the rights holder has not taken the fundamental steps necessary to secure and enforce his IPR in a timely fashion. The U.S. Commercial Service can provide a list of law firms based in Russia, which can provide advice on registering intellectual property and enforcing rights.

A good business partner is an important ally in protecting intellectual property rights. Legal counsel familiar with Russian laws can assist to reinforce the partners' IPR obligations by drafting a contract that includes non-compete clauses and confidentiality/non-disclosure provisions.

It is also recommended that small and medium-sized companies work with trade associations and organizations to support efforts to protect IPR and stop counterfeiting. There are a number of these organizations, both Russia-and U.S.-based. These include:

-American Chamber of Commerce in Russia (AmCham) -National Association of Manufacturers (NAM) -International Intellectual Property Alliance (IIPA) -International Trademark Association (INTA) -Coalition Against Counterfeiting and Piracy -International Anti-Counterfeiting Coalition (IACC) -Pharmaceutical Research and Manufacturers of America (PhRMA) -Biotechnology Industry Organization (BIO) -Coalition for Intellectual Property Rights (offices in the United States and Moscow)

- Russian Anti-Piracy Organization (RAPO) (represents the Motion Picture

Association of America) -Business Software Alliance (represented by Baltic Law Offices in Russia) -Association of Branded Goods Manufacturers in Russia (RusBrand) -Federal Service for Intellectual Property, Patents and Trademarks (Rospatent) -Russian Federal Customs Service -Russian Ministry of the Interior, Economic Security Department

More detailed information on IPR issues in Russia is provided in Chapter 6 (Investment Climate). Contact information is provided in Chapter 9.

IP Resources

A wealth of information on protecting IPR is freely available to U.S. rights holders. Some excellent resources for companies include the following:

-For information about patent, trademark, or copyright issues -- including enforcement issues in the U.S. and other countries -- call the STOP! Hotline: 1-866999-HALT or register at www.StopFakes.gov .

-For more information about registering trademarks and patents (both in the United States as well as in foreign countries), contact the U.S. Patent and Trademark Office (USPTO) at: 1-800-786-9199; www.uspto.gov

-For more information about registering for copyright protection in the United States, contact the U.S. Copyright Office at: 1-202-707-5959; www.copyright.gov.

-For U.S. small and medium-size companies, the Department of Commerce offers an "International SME IPR Advisory Program" available through the American Bar Association that provides one hour of free IPR legal advice for companies with concerns in Brazil, China, Egypt, India, Russia, and Thailand. For details and to register, visit: http://www.abanet.org/intlaw/intlproj/iprprogram_consultation.html

-For information on obtaining and enforcing intellectual property rights and market-specific IP Toolkits visit: www.StopFakes.gov. This site is linked to the USPTO website for registering trademarks and patents (both in the United States as well as in foreign countries), the U.S. Customs & Border Protection website to record registered trademarks and copyrighted works (to assist customs in blocking imports of IPR-infringing products) and allows you to register for Webinars on protecting IPR.

o For an in-depth examination of IPR requirements in specific markets, toolkits are currently available in the following countries/territories: Brazil, Brunei, China, Egypt, European Union, India, Italy, Malaysia, Mexico, Paraguay, Peru, Russia, Taiwan, Thailand, and Vietnam.

o For assistance in developing a strategy for evaluating, protecting, and enforcing IPR, use the free Online IPR Training Module on

www.stopfakes.gov

-The U.S. Commerce Department has positioned IP Attachés in key markets around the world. Contact information for the IP Attaché who covers Russia is available at: http://www.buyusa.gov/russia/en/pto.html or by emailing *RussiaUSPTO@trade.gov* .

Due Diligence

As previously noted, Russia can be a challenging market fraught with obstacles for the

U.S. company that does not take the time to learn about the business environment and choose local partners wisely. Taking shortcuts in evaluating business opportunities and in selecting local partners is not advisable. Complicating these efforts is the fact that the Russian economy continues the transition from a closed, centrally planned economy to a more open, market economy. This means that basic business information about regulations, company ownership and credit worthiness are not always easy to find, and the regulatory framework continues to evolve requiring companies to stay up-to-date with changes. The U.S. Commercial Service offers the International Company Profile service as a way to evaluate potential partners. For more information on this and other services, visit https://www.buyusa.gov/russia/en. Noted below are additional resources.

Local Professional Services

While professional services in Russia are expensive, attempts to avoid such expenditures could be perilous. In Russia's unsettled commercial environment, early and ongoing advice on tax and legal issues will ultimately save both aggravation and money. Russian commercial regulations are contained in thousands of presidential, governmental and ministerial decrees. Often, these decrees and laws overlap or conflict. Determining tax obligations is a complex task. Furthermore, Russian accounting practices differ markedly from Western standards. Although the Russian government has officially stated that conversion to international accounting standards is a priority, the process is still far from complete.

In Moscow and St. Petersburg, there are many offices of major western accounting, legal and consulting firms blending the skills of Russian and foreign professionals. Competent smaller firms also operate under Russian or western management. U.S. firms should avail themselves of locally based specialists familiar with issues confronting western firms in Russia. The U.S. Commercial Service offices throughout Russia maintain lists of local attorneys and accounting firms. The American Chamber of Commerce in Russia is also a good source.

Web Resources

U.S.Commercial Service in Russia: http://www.buyusa.gov/russia/en

U.S.Department of Agriculture: http://www.fas.usda.gov ; http://eng.usda.ru

U.S.Embassy in Russia: http://moscow.usembassy.gov State Registration Chamber: http://www.palata.ru/en Company Registration: http://www.nalog.ru Russian Direct Selling Association: http://eng.rdsa.ru American Chamber of Commerce in Russia: http://www.amcham.ru

LEADING SECTORS FOR U.S. EXPORT AND INVESTMENT

APPAREL

Unit: USD thousands

	2009	2010	2011 (estimate)	2012 (estimate)
Total Market Size	49,320,000	51,790,000	55,410,000	59,460,000
Total Local Production	3,350,000	3,640,000	3,910,000	4,090,000
Total Exports	1,380,000	1,500,000	1,530,000	1,550,000
Total Imports	47,350,000	49,640,000	53,030,000	56,910,000
Imports from the U.S.	189,000	159,000	202,000	244,000

Note: Estimates from Esper Group and Russian Ministry of Industry and Commerce.

Overall, experts believe the Russian apparel market to be untapped and low risk, making it an attractive growth area for companies. According to research conducted by the Esper Group, a fashion industry consulting organization, the Russian apparel market grew by 57% in the first quarter of 2010 compared to the same period in 2009. However, since some segments of the market are close to saturation, experts predict the total annual market growth at the level of about 10% for 2010.

The apparel market had been booming for the last few years but was slowed down by the economic crisis in late 2008. In 2009, the market experienced only a 5% growth rate. Many consumers switched to the lower priced segment which allowed mass market retailers like Zara and H&M to actually grow (Zara's sales grew by 20% and H&M's by 24%; GAP sales in Moscow, however, have not fared as well and fell by over 5% in the first nine months of 2010.)[2] The first quarter of 2010 appeared promising and indicated a recovery with sales exceeding the previous year's first quarter by 57%.

Women's apparel is the largest segment of the market. Its share is about 60% while men's clothes hold 24% of the market. According to the Esper Group, men's apparel will stagnate with 2010 growth only at 1-2%. Meanwhile, women's and children's apparel are expected to grow by approximately 10%.

Analysts also expected the Russian luxury market to grow by 12 % in 2010. This would be the first signs of growth after the serious economic downturn in 2008-2009 when a number of luxury distributors went out of business and some companies including Diesel, Alexander McQueen and Stella McCartney left the market. With improvements in the economy, such international brands are now planning to return to the market (Diesel has already signed a contract with a Russian show room that is planning to open thirty Diesel shops all over Russia by 2014. It has been reported that Alexander McQueen and Stella McCartney are also negotiating the opening of their boutique shops). U.S. brands such as Ralph Lauren, Coach and others are also present in the market and operate through local distributors and licensing agreements.

[2] Source: www.bsmarket.ru and www.rbcdaily.ru; GAP information from Esper Group

Outdoor markets still remain the most popular apparel distribution channel in Russia. According to BSMarket, the share of this channel is about 75%. This type of distribution is mostly typical in the regions, while the situation in the larger Russian cities is very different. Of the population that lives in larger cities, 11% to 22% shop in single-brand boutiques; up to 45% prefer shopping malls. Discount centers are also a popular format for the larger cities.

Apparel is divided into three major categories based on price:

Structure of the Russian apparel market based on the pricing

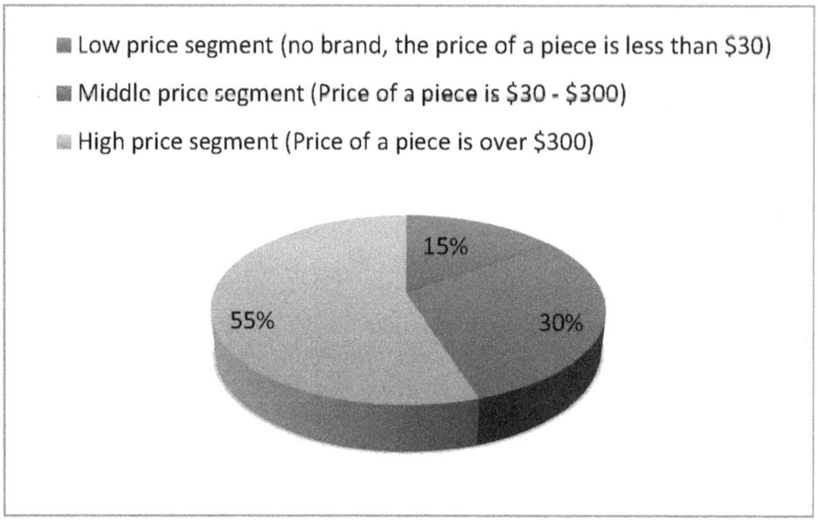

Market insiders remain very optimistic about the prospects of the Russian apparel market. Companies have resumed building new shopping malls in large cities. The number of new shopping centers has led to a decrease in rental rates and lower barriers to market entry. The more stable economic situation has encouraged people to spend more on apparel and accessories.

Sub-Sector Best Prospects

Casual apparel

Children's apparel

Active wear

Evening wear

Luxury apparel

Opportunities

Despite the fact that many well-known brands have already entered the market, the sector still has a great deal of potential. Opportunities remain in mid-priced apparel and the premium segment that is quickly recovering after the economic crisis.

For U.S. firms interested in the Russian apparel market, exhibiting at one of the key Russian apparel trade shows is advised. These trade shows are a powerful marketing tool and reassure Russian buyers that the U.S. company is committed to establishing and maintaining its presence in the Russian market.

Web Resources

Organizations

Russian Ministry of Industry and Commerce Moscow, Russia, http://www.minprom.gov.ru

Commercial Service Contact Oksana Prokofieva, Commercial Specialist Tel: +7 (495) 728-5529
Oksana.Prokofieva@trade.gov

AUTO PARTS & SERVICE EQUIPMENT / ACCESSORIES

Unit: USD Thousands

	2009	2010	2011 (estimate)	2012 (estimate)

Total Market Size	15,200,000	18,800,000	20,800,000	24,100,000
Total Local Production	9,900,000	11,500,000	12,000,000	13,000,000
Total Exports	200,000	200,000	200,000	400,000
Total Imports	5,500,000	7,500,000	9,000,000	11,500,000
Imports from the U.S.	800,000	850,000	900,000	1,000,000

Source: U.S. Commercial Service estimates

Russia represents a large potential market for the U.S. automotive industry. Currently, the rate of car ownership in Russia is only 30% of the U.S. rate. The total Russian motor vehicle fleet is estimated at 38 million units, including 28 million cars.

Russia is the largest and fastest growing automobile market in Europe. From 2001-2008, the Russian automotive market grew at an annual rate of 20-25% per year , and included a robust sales of imported used cars and trucks. The world financial crisis that started in 2008 put a damper on the Russian car market. Sales of new cars dropped 49% in 2009, while sales of trucks fell even more, by 70%. . Used vehicle sales ceased as a result of the crisis and new, increased import duties.

In 2010, Russia's car and LCV market started to recover, demonstrating 30% market growth and reaching sales of 1.9 million vehicles, including 1.4 locally manufactured units. Industry experts expect the vehicle market to continue to grow in 2011 and achieve 2.2 million vehicles. The number of domestically assembled foreign makes is expected to be 800,000 units. Overall, Russia's automotive market is expected to continue to recover, growing 15% per year through 2015.

As part of the automotive industry, the supply chain and market for components, including aftermarket replacement parts and accessories was also greatly affected by in the 2008 financial crisis. However, since Russian domestic manufacturers are not capable of producing the quality parts, accessories and equipment required for modern cars and trucks, the imported parts market was not hurt as badly as the vehicle market.

The Russian auto industry is one of the major sectors ofthe domestic economy. The Russian Government is taking measures to support the industry. Nonetheless Russian vehicle assembly and component manufacturing factories remain crippled by outdated equipment, lack of modern technologies and inadequate management. The major local automotive market players include: GAZ Group, a subsidiary of Basic Element, the largest Russian aluminum manufacturer; Sollers, a former subsidiary of the leading Russian steel producer Severstal, and AutoVAZ, currently controlled by the state owned Rostechnologies Corporation and Renault (25% equity). The majority of component manufacturing assets are owned by a number of independent manufacturers.

There are several projects underway to assemble foreign cars in Russia, including those of Ford, GM, Toyota, VW, Nissan, Renault, PSA, Mitsubishi and Hyundai. Ford's plant began operation in July 2002 in a suburb of St. Petersburg. The high demand for the new Focus model made Ford one of the sales leaders in 2002-2010. GM has two ventures in Russia: the GM-AvtoVAZ joint venture has manufactured the Chevrolet-Niva SUV since September 2002, and a new assembly plant in St. Petersburg projected to make 70,000 Chevrolet and Opel crossovers annually. In 2005, Renault started manufacturing its low-cost Logan vehicle at a Moscow-based facility, the factory's current turnover is about 70,000 vehicles. In December 2007, Toyota launched an assembly facility in St. Petersburg to manufacture 50,000 Camry vehicles annually. Nissan opened its plant in St. Petersburg in 2009 to produce the Teana and X-Trail. Volkswagen/PSA opened its plant in Kaluga in 2008. Hyundai began operation a new plant in St. Petersburg in 2010 that will manufacture 150,000 low-cost sedan vehicles – the Hyundai Solaris – developed specifically for the Russian market. There are also several other lesser known projects: Sollers set up Ssang Yong SUV assembly and Fiat low-cost sedans in Yelabuga and another Ssang Yong assembly facility in the far-east region of Russia.

There are also truck and bus assembly projects in Russia being developed by Volvo and Scania. The major obstacle to successful development of foreign assembly projects in Russia is the lack of local component suppliers.

Sub-Sector Best Prospects

Engine and engine components, steering components, brake system components, powertrain components, seats, tires, interior components, specialty equipment for cars, automotive aftermarket service and maintenance, and new car dealerships.

Opportunities

The best opportunities for U.S. firms are in the establishment of local manufacturing facilities or the formation of joint ventures with Russian firms and the supply of components to foreign vehicle assembly projects in Russia. Those projects' operators are so interested in developing component supplier bases that they are ready to financially support interesting projects. International financing institutions, such as the EBRD (European Bank for Reconstruction and Development), are also inclined to provide financing for automotive projects in Russia. Although the Russian automotive industry was significantly affected by the 2008-2009 recession, industry analysts believe that the growth demonstrated in 2010 will continue in the mid-to-near future, since the demand is still considerable.

Another good prospect is to supply upgraded equipment and technology to Russian manufacturers. Opportunities also exist in the licensing and transferring of modern technology to Russian component manufacturers.

Aftermarket sales of replacement parts and accessories are dynamic, with high customer receptivity to U.S. products. Many U.S. brand names are very well known and sell strongly in Russia. Some of the "Made in the USA" products that Russian motorists seem to favor are lubricants, automotive chemicals and off-road accessories. There are no known trade barriers affecting imports of U.S. automotive products; tariffs for many imported spare parts are a relatively low 5%. The most important factor affecting growth of sales of U.S. aftermarket products in Russia is the U.S. exporters' lack of interest in sharing brand building risks with local distributors. In the crisis-affected market, the small and mid-size suppliers of specialty equipment for cars will be competitive if they are aggressive in their market entry, brand-building and promotion actions.

Finally, Russia lacks a well-developed network, even in the largest cities, of high quality aftermarket maintenance and service centers. Many of the first foreign car brands introduced to Russia are now coming to the end of their manufacturers' warranty period, creating opportunities for U.S. companies to partner with Russian automotive businesses to meet increasing demand for quality, independent aftermarket maintenance and repair services.

Web Resources

Organizations

National Association of Automotive Component Manufacturers 5 Sushchevsky Val, bldg 2 Moscow 127018 Russia Tel: +7-495-974-8772, 73, 74 napak@napak.ru

St. Petersburg Association of Automotive Component Manufacturers 16 Bolshaya Monetnaya Str. St. Petersburg 197101 Russia Tel. +7-812-313-8254 apac@spbapac.ru

Publications and market research

Autobusiness Market Research Agency and Magazine http://www.abiz.ru/en

Autostat Market Research Agency http://www.autostat.ru/Default_Eng.asp

Commercial Service Contact Alexander Kansky, Commercial Specialist Office Tel: +7 (812) 331-2881 or +7 (812) 331-2600 **Alexander.Kansky@trade.gov**

AVIATION RUSSIAN AIRCRAFT AND PARTS MARKET

Unit: USD thousands

	2009	2010	2011 (estimate)	2012 (estimate)
Total Market Size	4,406,000	5,887,000	7,938,000	10,838.000

Total Local Production*	3,777,000	5,500,000	7,975,000	11,564,000
Total Exports*	2,300,000	3,133,000	4,261,000	5,795,000
Total Imports+	2,929,000	3,520,000	4,224,000	5,069,000
Imports from the U.S.+	419,000	275,000	294,000	314,000

* Based on official data from the United Aircraft Corporation - reflects sales of military and civil aircraft, excluding aircraft parts (data not available)

+ HTS Code 88 (Aircraft, Spacecraft, and Parts of Thereof), from Global Trade Atlas.

The Russian aviation industry remains an important strategic industry and a promising market for foreign suppliers of aircraft equipment. In 2010, the Russian Ministry of Industry and Trade reported positive growth dynamics in aircraft production (an increase of 114.9%), helicopter building (+153.6%), aircraft engine-making (+128.5%), and air instrument-making (+135.3%). These positive trends are attributed to financial support from the Russian government under the 2008-2015 Aircraft Industry Federal Program.

The following investment projects in the aircraft industry are underway:

Regional Sukhoi Superjet-100: Certification is almost complete and the delivery of the first Superjet-100 is scheduled for February 2011 (Armenian Armavia Airlines). The total aircraft orders have reached 170, with more regional airlines expected to line up as customers.

MS-21 short-to-medium range aircraft: Project design is under way. The Irkut Aviation Plant is currently modernizing its production facilities to prepare for manufacturing.

New Mi-38 utility transport and Ka-62 multipurpose helicopters: Prototypes are in construction and flight certification tests are currently under way. Production is expected to being in 2013-2014.

In 2011, the Russian government plans to allocate more than 70 billion Rubles (USD 2.3 billion) to support the aircraft industry through a number of support measures including: 1) direct financial contributions to key industry holding companies (UAC, Oboronprom, United Engine-Making Corporation); 2) subsidies to selected plants to support modernization of production facilities; and 3) subsidies to selected plants to prevent bankruptcy. As the Russian aircraft industry re-vitalizes, civil aircraft production in 2010 remained relatively low. Only 7 aircraft were produced by the United Aircraft Corporation (4 An-148, 2 Tu-204 and 1 Tu-214) and were sold mainly to Russian state agencies.

At the same time, the Russian aviation market experienced a significant increase in passenger turnover in 2010. According to Russia's Federal Air Transportation Agency, Rosaviatsyia, the number of passengers on Russian domestic and international flights rose from 24 million to 31.2 million in the first seven months of 2010, an increase of 30%. The agency also announced that Russia's top four airlines (Aeroflot, S7, Transaero, UTair) are economically stable. Aeroflot, the market leader in the Russian industry, carried 6.3 million passengers between January and July 2010, a 33% increase over the same period in 2009. The increase in the industry was attributed to low costs of oil, competitive flight prices and the rebound of consumer confidence in the Russian economy.

Boeing forecasts that air carriers in Russia and Commonwealth of Independent States (CIS) will take delivery of about 960 new airplanes over the next 20 years at a cost of $90 billion. New airplane deliveries will be driven largely by the need to retire older, less fuel-efficient single-aisle airplanes and regional jets, as airlines replace them with new-generation, more fuel-efficient models.

In September 2010, Boeing and the Russian Technologies State Corporation (Rostekhnologii) signed a $3 billion definitive agreement for 50 Next-Generation 737 airliners. The agreement includes purchase rights for an additional 35 Next-Generation 737s. Industry experts believe that the economic benefits and operating efficiencies demonstrated by the Next-Generation 737 directly support the corporation's plan to provide Russian airlines with efficient and reliable airplanes that will help them profitably grow their domestic and international operations.

Because of low domestic aircraft production and the increased need for new efficient airplanes for Russian airlines, the Russian government has been gradually easing protectionist barriers that restrict imports of foreign aircraft and aircraft parts. In November 2008, Russia abolished a 20% import duty on aircraft having more than 300 passenger seats, covering such western aircraft as B747, B777, B767-700, A340-500 and A340-600. In June 2010, the Russian Government approved a proposal to zero-out the duties for civilian planes with a passenger capacity of 250-300 passengers, covering A310, A330, A340, B767, B787, and some modifications of A350. Twenty-percent duties on aircraft having 50-111 and 160-219 passenger seats remain. Experts believe that the import duties in these categories are preserved to protect Russia's regional aircraft (Superjet100 and An-148) and short-to-medium aircraft (MS-21 and Tu-204/214).

Sub-Sector Best Prospects

Avionics and Aircraft Systems

The two major Russian aircraft projects – the Sukhoi Superjet-100 and MS-21 – are examples of continued interest by Russian airframe manufacturers in complete on-board systems from western suppliers. The following types of western systems were used to support these two projects: hydraulics, cabin interior, integrated air management and fly-by-wire flight control, wheels and braking systems, landing gear systems, auxiliary power systems, etc. Suppliers for these designs have already been determined by Russian airframe manufacturers but additional projects are underway. Some opportunities may be available in the aftermarket segment, as Russian manufacturers of aircraft and helicopters as well as some airlines strive to upgrade and modernize their existing fleets using western systems. In the helicopter segment, it is reported that some foreign customers require that Russian helicopters be equipped with certain western systems (avionics, for example).

Aircraft Engines

Many Russian airframe manufacturers prefer western aircraft engines as the Russian engine-building industry is still developing. Several European aircraft engine makers have established a presence in Russia to support their market expansion. For many of them, the goal is not simply the sale of engines but also the creation of joint ventures, production localization and joint programs in the market. Opportunities for collaboration may be available both for new projects (SaM146 aircraft engines for the Superjet-100) and in the modernization segment (CFM56 aircraft engines for leading airlines such as Aeroflot, S7 and Transaero).

Smaller Aircraft Components

Smaller items such as amplifiers, control units, accessories, miscellaneous components, and subsystems may be in demand both by Russian OEMs and tier suppliers. In addition, Russian distributors are another target market for such items. Working with distributors may facilitate entry not only into the aviation industry, but also into associated industries, such as electronics, defense, telecommunications, and others.

Machine Tools

The market for machine tools in the aviation industry is growing due to increasing state funding and the need for modernization of production facilities by airframe manufacturers and tier suppliers. In March 2010, MAG Industrial Automation Systems, the world's largest U.S.-based machine tool company, signed a more than $9 million contract to supply the Russian aviation's first automated composites processing system consisting of three machines: a composite fiber placement system and two of MAG's HyperMach Vertical Profilers. The advanced composites equipment will support United Aircraft Corporation's MS-21 series of commercial airliners.

Software

The Russian aviation industry continues to primarily utilize western software solutions. Siemens PLM Software solutions have been successfully used in many UAC projects and key programs, such as the SSJ-100, to enhance collaboration and optimize workflow. In October 2010, VISTAGY Inc., a leading provider of industry-specific engineering software and services, announced the sale of FiberSIM composites engineering software to Solver company that will be using FiberSIM for the first time in conjunction with the Viper 1200 fiber placement system from MAG to design and manufacture composite parts on behalf of Voronezh Aircraft Plant (VASO) for various projects.

Opportunities

The current trend in the Russian aviation industry is to decrease its reliance on imports of complete western air systems and instead to emphasize the development of capabilities to manufacture similar products locally. For example, a tender for MS-21 avionics resulted in a cooperative agreement between Rockwell Collins and Russian company Avionica to develop a special avionics system for this aircraft. Further down the value chain, market opportunities are expected to arise for western manufacturers of high-tech machine tools and smaller aircraft components, as the Russian industry continues to build its capacity to produce locally. In the interim, however, western avionics, navigation systems and other large integrated components will continue to be in demand by Russian manufacturers of aircraft and helicopters to meet their current needs, especially in the modernization and the aftermarket segments.

Most Russian OEMs, tier suppliers, and distributors that are active in the aviation industry also manufacture and supply products for other associated industries, such as military and defense, automotive, electronics, and energy. U.S. suppliers may benefit from these synergies.

The links between the defense and aviation sectors are especially strong. Modernization of the Russian military is becoming an important national priority and the state order for arms is expected to grow in the near future. Between 2007 and 2015, the Russian government plans to allocate 4.9 trillion rubles ($162 billion)[3] to support modernization of the army. The same enterprises active in the aviation industry (OEMs and tier suppliers) will receive additional state

[3] Exchange rate used: $1 = 30.18 rubles

funding and support under this program allowing them to reinforce their ability to modernize and procure new machine tools and other equipment.

Web Resources

Participating in trade events remains a critical element in a successful business development strategy for Russia. U.S. companies can meet prospective Russian partners not only at major Russian trade shows, but also at international shows, especially in Europe. Examples include the Farnborough International Air Show, Paris Air Show, and the ILA Berlin Air Show. Besides these major aerospace shows, there are also a large number of specialized exhibitions on such topics as machine tools and aerospace testing. Major Russian and international shows are listed below:

Internet Resources

http://www.avia.ru/english : Russian Aviation News & Information Server http://www.aviaport.ru : Aviation News Agency "Aviaport" (only in Russian)

Commercial Service Contact Vladislav Borodulin, Commercial Specialist Tel: 7 (495) 728-5235
Vladislav.Borodulin@trade.gov

CONSTRUCTION / GREENBUILD

Unit: USD thousands

Value of Housing Units	2009	2010	2011 (estimate)	2012 (estimate)
Total Market Size	14,500,000	14,700,000	15,000,000	15,300,000
Total Local Production	7,000,000	8,500,000	9,000,000	9,300,000
Total Exports	-	-	-	-
Total Imports	7,500,000	6,200,000	6,000,000	6,000,000
Imports from the U.S.	800,000	900,000	1000,000	1,100,000

Data Sources: 1) Rosstat http://www.gks.ru/bgd/regl/b10_12/Main.htm ; 2) Interviews with industry experts

The Russian construction sector suffered a severe slowdown in late 2008, losing almost 45% of its volume. At the time, sector growth was driven by extensive residential and commercial construction across Russia, infrastructure projects and, to some extent, planning for the Sochi Olympics. Experts were forecasting a construction boom to continue through 2009 and 2010.

The economic slowdown impacted many sectors of the economy, including construction, as it is highly dependent on the banking sector and available financing. Many developers had to postpone ongoing projects because of a lack of financing.

Overall, construction activity in most Russian cities (St. Petersburg, Krasnodar, Nizhny Novgorod, Kazan, Samara, Rostov, etc.) contracted significantly. Specifically, residential housing construction, a key indicator in the sector, has been declining for the last two years at the rate of 5.5% in 2010 and 8% in 2009, in volume terms totaling 33 million square meters. [4]

Despite the slowdown, many developers remain optimistic and continue to look at this market as a tremendous opportunity. Many in the industry already see an increase in projects and expect market growth in 2011 and 2012. Some of the increase may be attributable to the development of infrastructure needed for the Sochi Olympics.

Additional market growth may be fueled by private residences construction and country home (dachya) construction. This sector is expected to experience growth given the high cost of apartments in city centers. Many people prefer to build their own homes rather than finance expensive apartments with mortgage financing.

The construction of sports facilities, hotels, and transportation systems has already begun in Sochi and the Krasnodar region and will continue for the next four years, creating opportunities for suppliers. Russian companies will continue to demand construction equipment and building materials. Given the reliability of foreign-manufactured equipment and building materials, Russian companies tend to prefer to purchase from Western manufacturers.

The construction equipment market is characterized by a shortage of inventory and a high degree of equipment wear and tear (45%-75% of equipment). Local manufacturers suffer from insufficient investment in R&D; the result is a lack of modern technology, poor management and the absence of government support. These factors contribute to the growth of construction machinery imports; about 50% of the equipment used by construction companies is foreign,

[4] Source: Rosstat publications

either new or used. The main players in the Russian market are Caterpillar (United States), Volvo (Sweden), JCB (U.K.), Komatsu (Japan) and Hitachi (Japan). Asian producers, especially Chinese are very aggressively entering the market, thus intensifying competition for all suppliers.

Price is an important factor but one mainly considered by small construction companies or minor subcontractors. Nowadays large companies employing more than 1000 people prefer leasing equipment rather than buying it. Leasing companies prefer working with top manufacturers, whose products have higher residual value. U.S. and European equipment can serve up to three-five years of intensive use without costly repairs, while Chinese products often last much less.

Up to 95% of apartments and homes in Russia are sold without interior finishes; therefore, demand for such products will continue to grow. Although 80% of building materials are sold in open markets, the “Do it yourself” (DIY) segment continues to expand as demonstrated by growing consumer purchases at such stores as OBI, Castorama and IKEA.

Basic products that are used for the primary finishing such as cement, concrete mixes, plasterboards, and plastic windows are manufactured locally using mostly German technologies. Technology leaders such as Knauf (Germany) have numerous plants in the country.

Greenbuilding

Green building is a nascent sector in the Russian economy, though it is increasing in popularity as domestic consumer energy prices rise and people and organizations become more conscious of spending and the positive effects of a healthier environment. Green industry experts believe that 2010 marked a significant rise of green building activity in Russia. Following approval of the new Federal Law “On Energy Savings and Improving Energy Efficiency” in November 2009, the nascent Russian green building community has been playing an increasingly active role in promoting awareness of green building concepts in the traditional construction sector, and supporting expansion of green standards.

The Russian Green Building Council (RuGBC) created in November 2009 is the key catalyst and is playing a leading role in green standards implementation for the industry. Russia's Ministry of Natural Resources plans long-term collaboration with RuGBC and intends to develop a program of joint events and courses.

Over the past year, the RuGBC has built a strong membership base (120 members) on a philosophy of 'standard neutrality' and offers equal support for the rating tools relevant to the Russian market – LEED, BREEAM, DGNB and the emerging Russian National Standard. RuGBC has also supported the development of green standards and sustainable design and construction methods for the Sochi 2014 Winter Olympic Games, resulting in several international fact-finding missions and seminars, as well as the adoption of BREEAM and LEED as standards for top venues.

In 2010, the first two Russia 'green" buildings received internationally accepted certifications – Ducat Palace, an A class office building and retail complex, developed by Hines, received BREEAM "very good," and the Swedish SKF bearing factory in the Tver Region received LEED NC v.2.2 Gold. Another 14 buildings are registered for BREEAM certification, 6 are registered for LEED and several pilots are being considered for DGNB.

In addition to certified buildings, there is the emergence of buildings with "green features". In 2010, the first "Green Awards" competition took place in St. Petersburg as part of the ProEstate Investment Forum. The top award went to the headquarters of WWF Russia – Panda House. The emergence of these initial projects is an important milestone in Russian green market transformation.

Some of the perceived drivers of sustainable property development in Russia include:

The increasing perception by investors that green certification (BREEAM, LEED or DGNB) represents lower investment risk based on evidence of lower voids in these buildings;

Demand from international corporations for green offices due to international policies and standards;

Increasing government-led initiatives towards sustainability – energy efficiency and innovation;

The attractive prospect of higher rental and sales levels in green certified buildings due to a growing demand, following increased awareness of green building concepts and anticipated increases in energy prices. The upcoming deregulation of energy prices in Russia is expected to increase costs for end-users by up to 200% in 2011.

Sub-Sector Best Prospects

Construction equipment: Tractors, bulldozers, mobile cranes, concrete pumps and mixers, excavators, compaction rollers, front loaders and crushers, metal cutting equipment, fast building technologies and equipment.

Building materials: Roofing materials, wall building materials, energy efficient materials, construction additives and interior decoration materials and sanitary products.

Green building: Green building includes products ranging from green architecture to energy-conserving materials and fixtures (toilets, light bulbs, appliances). Possibilities for future growth areas include insulation and heating systems. Non-toxic building products will likely gain popularity. "Smart home" technology should also attract a great deal of interest from Russian consumers.

Prospective buyers are in fact all construction firms, contractors, and any business whose plans include construction or renovation of a local facility. Non-Russian companies are more likely to use energy-efficient construction than Russian companies. Many foreign investors, especially European investors, will lend money for construction only if it meets certain environmental requirements, particularly sustainability and efficiency. European and American companies are also more likely to undertake green projects than Russian firms. For these reasons, non-Russian companies located in Russia offer opportunities to providers of energy-efficient and environmentally responsible building supplies and services.

Opportunities

U.S. construction equipment is well known in Russia for its excellent quality and reliability. U.S. manufacturers can further improve their market share by offering state-of-the-art technology and products, and by employing reputable agents and/or distributors. Price, reliability, availability of sales financing and after-sale service continue to be the main competitive criteria for equipment exports to Russia. Given the current value of the U.S. dollar to the Euro, used construction equipment from the United States may become popular among Russian companies that want to minimize their costs.

Opportunities also exist for licensing and transfer of modern U.S. technology to Russian equipment and component manufacturers.

Provided the right price is established, U.S. building products can compete against those from European suppliers. Because DIY chains have become much more active in the Russian market, U.S. companies can also be competitive in retail sales of DIY products in these chains.

Green building: Opportunities for green construction in Russia are dependent upon overall construction nationwide. In the wake of the global financial crisis, construction is expected to see real growth again in 2011, as the economy improves after two years of contraction, the country prepares for the 2012 APEC Summit in Vladivostok, the 2014 Olympic Games in Sochi, and the 2018 FIFA World Cup, and as President Medvedev moves along with the Skolkovo technology park project.

Among future projects, the technology park at Skolkovo in particular should prove to be fertile ground for green building and technology, as it will be an opportunity for Russia to showcase its modernization efforts.

Sochi Olympic Games construction is another excellent opportunity for American suppliers of green building materials and services to showcase their products. Specifically, the International Olympic Committee has mandated that certain standards be met. Ten of the 202 planned Olympic buildings will be either LEED or BREEM certified, and 150 objects will be certified by Olympstroy corporate standards for energy efficiency.

In December 2010, Russia won its bid with FIFA to host the 2018 World Cup tournament and is planning the construction of 16 state-of-the-art stadiums in 13 cities, mostly in Western Russia. Each stadium will have a price-tag between $70- $300 million.

Further, there are several large-scale green sustainable projects that will be soon built in Russia and may present some opportunities for U.S. exporters:

NCC (http://www.ncc-spb.ru/en) is building a housing development in St. Petersburg called Swedish Krona (to be completed in Q4, 2014). This will be an apartment block area with a park, playgrounds, sport facilities, shops and parking. NCC is planning to use various new construction technologies, including energy efficient materials, to build a comfortable city living place that meets European standards.

BTK (www.btkdevelopment.ru) is in the process of developing a project for an energy efficient office building in the center of St. Petersburg (2000 sq. meters). The company is planning to build this project according to LEED standards and receive the appropriate certification.

Setl City (www.setlcity.ru) is beginning to develop a project called Sem Stolits (www.7stolic.ru), which will utilize the principles of energy efficiency including a collector heating and water supply system, specially designed sanitation facilities and energy-efficient insulation and windows (to be completed within 15-17 years).

Organizations

Federal Construction and Housing Agency www.gosstroy.gov.ru

Builders Association of Russia www.a-s-r.ru

Construction World: The Associate Board of Architecture, Construction, Development and Reconstruction of Moscow www.stroi.ru

Ecostandard Ecological services and expertise - 1st organization certified by U.S. Green Building Council http://www.ecostandard.ru/en

Green Building Council Russia http://www.rugbc.org/lang/en

Ministry of Energy and Industry of the RF http://www.minprom.gov.ru

Integrated Body for Urban Design Policy and Development of Moscow http://www.stroi.ru

New Law on Energy Efficiency
http://www.bakermckenzie.com/ALRussiaNewDevelopmentsSavingEnergyJan10
Publications

Construction http://www.ianc.ru

Spec-Technika http://www.spec-technika.ru

Rosstat Publications http://www.gks.ru/bgd/regl/b10_12/Main.htm

Zhilaya Sreda http://www.finestreet.ru/magazine/home

Beautiful Houses http://www.houses.ru

Tepliy Dom http://www.teplydom.com

Commercial Service Contact (Construction and Building Materials) Timur Uddin, Commercial Specialist
Timur.Uddin@trade.gov
Tel: 7 (495) 728 5526 (direct)
Commercial Service Contact (Green Building)
Vladislav Borodulin, Commercial Specialist Tel: 7 (495) 728-5235
Vladislav.Borodulin@trade.gov

CONSUMER ELECTRONICS

USD thousands

	2009	2010	2011 (estimate)	2012 (estimate)
Total Market Size	18,500,000	20,370,000	22,500,000	25,000,000
Total Local Production	3,000,000	4,000,000	5,000,000	6,200,000
Total Exports	1,500,000	1,630,000	2,000,000	2,200,00
Total Imports	17,000,000	18,000,000	19,500,000	21,000,000
Imports from the U.S.	1,200,000	1,800,000	2,500,000	3,500,000

The Russian consumer electronics market includes telephones, MP3 players, home and automotive audio/video equipment, personal computers, TV sets, calculators, GPS automotive navigation systems, home security and automation products, products for playback and recording of digital video and audio media, digital cameras and camcorders, and other products for entertainment and communications.

Before the recent economic crisis, the consumer electronics market was one of Russia's most developed and most competitive retail sectors with annual growth rates ranging from 10% to 25%, depending on the product. According to data published by GFK-Russia (a subsidiary company of the German GFK-Group), the size of the combined consumer electronics and household appliances markets in Russia was $36.8 billion in 2007 and $40.6 billion in 2008.

In 2009, Russia's consumer electronics market drastically declined. Industry experts evaluated market at $18.5 billion (a 35% decrease compared to 2008). However, starting 2nd quarter of 2010 the consumer electronics market started to show the signs of recovery.

Based on expert evaluations, including GFK-Russia research, the U.S. Commercial Service estimates the following 2010 sales volumes for key product groups:

Product Category	2010 $ Million	% change from 2009
Audio/video equipment	5,300	8
Personal computers, components, and accessories	6,800	3
Mobile, radio phones and other telecommunication devices	5,500	25
Photo equipment	1,250	25
Home office equipment and consumables	1,520	-5
Total	20,370	10

In 2010, sales growth in the audio/video industry subsector was mostly generated by the demand for flat panel TVs, including Full HD, LED, 3D, and Slimline models. The most sought after products in the IT subsector were mobile computers, including notebooks, netbooks, and tablet PCs. Desktop computers continued to lose their share of the market. The market for telecom products was mostly driven by sales of mobile smart phones with touch-screen technology and mobile phone accessories. The digital photo market showed strong signs of recovery mostly because of increased sales of compact digital cameras providing higher resolution and advanced features at affordable prices. The market for office equipment continued to recover, but did not show positive dynamics compared to 2009.

Accurate figures for the consumer electronics market in Russia are difficult to determine due to a large number of so-called “grey market products” imported into the market. However, with the growth of the largest retail chains, whose market share will increase, a corresponding decrease in “grey market” goods is expected.

Imports

The major portion of the consumer electronics market is occupied by products imported from Asia, Europe, and the United States. All major global brands are represented in Russia and have wide recognition. The U.S. consumer electronics share of the Russian market is mostly represented by IT products, high-end audio products, automotive audio and navigation products, home security and automation products, and mobile phones.

Domestic production

Local production is mostly represented by a big number of small and medium size Russian IT companies, and several telecom manufacturers. An example of foreign investment in domestic IT industry is the $50 million HP and Foxconn joint venture, which started production of HP desktop computers in St. Petersburg in April 2010.

Other local manufacturers include ODMs (original design manufacturers) providing EMS (electronics manufacturing services) for contract manufacturing of CRT, PDP, and LCD TVs, as well as DVD players under the Sony, Panasonic, Akai and other well-known brand names.

Distribution

Consumer electronics products are imported and distributed in Russia by a big number of distributors. All major international brands have their representative offices or authorized distributors as well. About 50% of consumer electronics marketed in Russia are sold by several of the largest retail chains that have hypermarkets and stores located in Moscow, St. Petersburg and other large cities. Another 25% are sold by regional chains, while the rest is sold by small retail companies and through the internet. However, recently the share of products sold via the Internet significantly increased. According to Citibank Russia's analytical department, the volume of products sold through the Russian Internet in 2012 will increase by 33% and will reach $27 billion.

Participation in local trade shows/conferences and international events focused on Russia is very important for promotion of new products and establishing contacts with key industry people.

Sub-Sector Best Prospects

Audio/video equipment
Automotive audio and navigation products
Home security and automation products
Multi-media
Wireless and networking products
Mobile computers

Opportunities

The Russian market, with its 140 million population, has huge potential size and it offers continued growth potential due to the relatively low penetration in product groups, such as computers and Hi-End digital products, especially in the remote regions.

Prior to the impact of the global economic crisis on the Russian market that began in late 2008, the consumer electronics sector was recognized as one of the fastest growing in Europe. During the crisis, however, customers started to save on purchases of consumer electronics, which are discretionary items for Russians. However, industry analysts believe that following industry recovery in 2010, the Russian market will continue to grow in 2011.

Computers will continue to be the main growth driver of Russia's consumer electronics industry, with increasing sales of notebooks, netbooks, and tablet PCs. According to expert estimates, local PC assemblers control about 80% of the PC market. Therefore, computer components will also continue to be in a strong demand.

High-end mobile phones, particularly the latest smart phones and 3G handsets, are highly sought-after status symbols for Russian consumers. According to Business Monitor International, it is expected that by the end of 2013, more than 50% of handset sales will be of 3G models, from around 10% in 2009. However foreign suppliers will be concerned by apparent Russian government threats to ban imports of handsets that do not have a Russian GPS system.

Quality, functionality and uniqueness should be competitive advantages for all products imported to Russia. New highly advanced products are in constant demand and their sales show continuing growth. As most of these products are imported and there is always strong demand for the latest and most technological categories, solid opportunities exist for U.S. companies, particularly in high quality electronics gear and modern digital electronic products. Therefore, Russia remains a significant international market for U.S. consumer electronics.

Organizations

Russian Association of Trading Companies and Manufacturers of Consumer Electronics (RATEK) http://www.ratek.org

Commercial Service Contact Mikhail Minkevitch, Commercial Specialist Tel: 7 (812) 326-2582
Misha.Minkevitch@trade.gov

COSMETICS/TOILETRIES

Unit: USD thousands

	2009	2010	2011 (estimate)	2012 (estimate)
Total Market Size	9,700,000	10,300,000	11,200,000	12,208,000
Total Local Production	4,752,000	5,049,000	5,474,000	5,967,000
Total Exports	193,000	208,000	210,000	229,000
Total Imports	5,141,000	5,459,000	5,936,000	6,470,000
Imports from the U.S.	101,000	131,000	135,000	147,000

Source: Estimates by industry experts and U.S. department of commerce databases.

The Russian cosmetics and toiletries market has been experiencing steady growth and has been one of the fastest growing industry sectors in Russia during the last decade, with growth of 10-15% prior to 2008. According to Staraya Krepost, in 2009, the total value of the Russian cosmetics and toiletries market was approximately $9.7 billion, and increased approximately 8% in 2010. Fifty-three percent of the market consists of imported products.

Key market segments are: make-up, hair care; skin care products; and toiletries. Spa, pedicure, and manicure products are also fast growing subsectors in the cosmetics industry. Russians spend a significantly higher portion of their income (12%) on cosmetic products than do their overseas counterparts.

Domestic manufacturers have a 47% share of the mass-market and middle market brands. Major manufacturers like Kalina, Nevskaya Kosmetika, Svoboda and Faberlic produce both mass-market and higher-end skin care products, which are considered on par with western luxury market quality standards. The competition between foreign and local manufacturers in the mass-market and middle market segments is intense. Generally, foreign producers outpace local ones with the use of new technologies in the manufacturing process and larger marketing and advertising budgets.

The market recently experienced profound changes in distribution with retailers becoming the key players in the market versus distributors. According to L'Agence de Lux, cosmetics and toiletries distribution channels include:

Cosmetic retail chains (30%)
Department stores (25%)
Direct sales (20%)
Pharmacies (10%)
Outdoor markets (10%)
Internet-sales, concept-stores (5%)

Distributors are shifting their business from developing wholesale trade to expanding retail chains. Specialized retail chains such as L'Etoile, Ile de Beaute and Yves Rocher, with outlets in all major Russian cities, are showing the fastest growth rates.

The assortment of products in retail chains has changed too with middle-market and mass-market brands complementing exclusive products. The share of mass-market products in retail chains has grown to 20%. An additional channel for mass-market and middle-market brands, as well as curative cosmetics, is pharmacies, especially pharmacy chains. Russian consumers perceive cosmetics sold through pharmacies to be safer and more effective.

A new and recent trend in market development is a shift in the overall market share from Moscow to the Russian regions. Currently, the ratio between large cities and regional cities is 50/50. This is especially true in cities with a population of over one million and where there are a substantial number of people with high purchasing power.

The last several years have been characterized by a rapidly growing demand for high quality and customized cosmetic products. Both foreign and local manufacturers have succeeded in creating awareness and educating consumers about different skin and hair types, as well as the advantages of using a full range of skin and hair products.

Sub-Sector Best Prospects

The best sales prospects for U.S. export include the following categories: make-up, skin and hair care products in all market segments, professional skin care products for home use, spa products and treatments, beauty and hair salon products and equipment, anti-aging cosmetics, natural cosmetics, curative and professional products, manicure and pedicure products, and cosmetics for men and children.

Opportunities

Russian consumers traditionally trust foreign brands more than local ones because they are perceived to guarantee consistent quality. According to industry specialists, the future of the Russian cosmetics and toiletries market is in niche marketing and narrow customization. Given intense competition between foreign and local manufacturers, especially in the mass-market and middle-market market segments, the cost of entering and developing the market is now higher.

Success will depend on larger investments in advertising, marketing and promotion, including participation in specialized trade shows. U.S. manufacturers can improve their market visibility by offering exclusive cosmetic products and by employing qualified agents/distributors. Price continues to be the most competitive factor limiting export opportunities. U.S. producers may consider opening a representative office to conclude agreements with retailers directly or establishing manufacturing facilities in Russia and partnering with local companies to make their products more competitive.

Web Resources

Organizations

Cosmetics-Perfumery Russian Association
http://www.pcar.ru/index.php?lang=eng&PHPSESSID=8c7dfc8dbf7d9c6085dcffe648ed0531

Expo Media Group Staraya Krepost (organizer of specialized events and publisher)
http://www.cosmopress.ru/eng

National Alliance of Cosmetologists and Dermatologists http://www.nadc.ru

Publications

Salon-expert (specialized edition for spa and beauty salons owners) http://www.salon-expert.ru

Kosmetika optom (cosmetics portal) http://kosmetikaoptom.ru

Intercharm (perfumery and cosmetics portal) http://www.intercharm.net/eng

Kosmetik International (magazine) http://www.ki-online.ru/en

Cosmetics and Perfumery (magazine) http://kosmetika.potrebitel.ru

Cosmetics and Medicine (magazine) http://www.cmjournal.ru

Make-up portal http://www.make-up.ru

Cosmomir (perfumery and cosmetics portal) http://www.cosmomir.ru

Cosmetics in Russia (perfumery and cosmetics portal in English) http://www.cosmeticsinrussia.com

Commercial Service Contact Irina Podsushnaya, Commercial Specialist Tel: 7 (4232) 499-381
Irina.Podsushnaya@trade.gov

ELECTRIC POWER GENERATION & TRANSMISSION EQUIPMENT

(billion Kwh)	2009	2010	2011 (estimate)	2012 (estimate)
Electricity Generation	978.6	1025.0	1058.0	1090
Electricity Consumption	964.4	1009.2	1045.0	1075
Electricity Exports	14.2	15.8	13.0	15.0

Source: Russia System Operator; *Federal Tax Service.*

Russia holds the world's largest natural gas reserves, second largest coal reserves, and eighth largest oil reserves. It is the fourth largest generator and consumer of electricity in the world; its 440 power stations (77 coal-fired) have an installed generation capacity of 220 GW. The grid links over two million miles of power lines, 93,000 miles of which are high voltage cables over 220 kV. Electricity generation is based largely on thermal (gas - 46%, coal - 18%), hydro (18%), and nuclear (17%) power. 60% of thermal generation is from combined heat and power plants (CHP). Russia operates 31 nuclear power reactors in 10 locations, with an installed capacity of 21 GW. Despite considerable geothermal, wind and wave resources, renewable energy production accounts for less than one percent.

In 2002, the Russian government began reforming the power sector. The main goal was, and remains, to upgrade the aging and outdated heating and electricity infrastructure. The restructuring involved the separation and privatization of the generation, transmission and sales companies. The grids were brought under regulatory supervision. Power generation was divided up into seven wholesale generating companies (OGK) – including RusHydro, 14 territorial generating companies (TGK), independents and state owned entities. OGKs contain power plants and specialize mainly in electric power generation. TGKs contain predominantly combined heat and power plants (CHPs). The gradual liberalization of the wholesale electricity market, completed in January 2011, now allows producers to charge market prices. The transmission grid remains mostly under state control.

As a result of the reorganization, Inter RAO UES became a major generating company in Russia in the field of export and import of electric power. The total installed capacity of the power plants owned or managed by the company is around 18,000 MW. The company's main types of activities are generation of electric and thermal power, sales of electric and thermal power to consumers, and export and import of electric power.

Foreign and domestic companies have invested about $27 billion in the power sector; as a condition of their investment, they committed to create 186 GW of new capacity by 2020. As Russia emerged from the crisis, some investment plans were resumed, with strong growth anticipated. According to the International Energy Agency, the Russian power sector will require a $440 billion investment by 2030 to avoid regional blackouts and meet future demand. This will include installing new generating capacity and significantly modernizing what is currently installed.

The European Bank for Reconstruction and Development has invested in many of the new power generating companies. In addition, as part of its crisis response actions in its Russia strategy for 2009-2012, EBRD states it will provide support to both private and state-owned power companies, with balance sheet restructuring, refinancing, liquidity support or financing of investment shortfall for priority projects with high energy efficiency parameters. In June 2010, EBRD also laid the groundwork for a strategic partnership with the Federal Grid Company.

Russian equipment producers are also modernizing their production. Power Machines (Siloviye Mashiny) is the market leader with a share of over 50%. It unites production, supply, construction, maintenance and modernization of equipment for thermal, nuclear, hydraulic and gas turbine power plants. The following big international energy equipment holdings are well established and have joint ventures or their own production facilities in Russia: General Electric, Siemens, Alstrom, ABB, Skoda Power, Mitsubishi Heavy Industries, Ansaldo Energia, and Areva.

Sub-Sector Best Prospects

The development of the energy sector has led to an increasing demand for highly technological equipment that is efficient and environmentally friendly. The Russian power engineering industry, well developed before the fall of the Soviet Union, can no longer supply all of Russia's energy sector needs.

Opportunities

The most competitive markets are concentrated around the cities of Moscow and St. Petersburg, whereas the regions are considered growing markets. Western equipment is usually installed in newly built infrastructure, while existing equipment is mainly maintained with locally produced equipment and to a lesser extent upgraded with Western devices.

According to the Energy Strategy of Russia for the period up to 2030, the priorities in the electric energy industry are:

developing gas turbines with a capacity of 300-350 MW and highly efficient condensation combined cycle gas turbine units with a capacity of 500-1000 MW and a performance index exceeding 60%;

designing standard modular combined cycle co-generation units with a capacity of 100 and 170 MW and a performance index amounting to 53-55% for heat and power plants;

developing environmentally friendly coal condensation units on ultra supercritical steam conditions with a capacity of 660-800 MW, as well as combined cycle units on solid fuel gasification (200-600MW) and coal synthesis gas;

introducing technological energy complexes working on gas and solid fuel for combined production of electricity and synthetic liquid fuel;

developing highly integrated intelligent transmission and distribution networks (Smart Grid) in Russia's Unified Energy System;

developing power electronics, especially various types of network control devices (flexible alternating current transmission systems), automated electricity demand control systems; and hydroelectric equipment for tidal power plants.

Russia is generally very receptive to U.S. products. Companies such as General Electric, Dresser-Rand, and Compressor Controls Corporation are present in the Russian market and their products are available either directly or through representatives or distributors. Imports from third countries are also growing. U.S. firms encounter increasing competition in the Russian market from European and Chinese manufacturers. Companies with production capacities in Russia tend to have an advantage over those that produce equipment abroad. This is the main motivation for foreign companies to form joint ventures and start production in Russia.

Tenders for energy projects are processed through the world's largest marketplace for power generation equipment online at www.b2b-energo.ru. Most of the OGKs and TGKs also have their own marketplaces on their websites. A foreign vendor needs to keep in mind that paper documentation for tenders is generally required in the Russian language. The power stations officially publish tenders for some renovation tasks. For major projects, they work with specialized engineering, procurement and construction companies (EPCs). Current information about new tenders, analytical materials, regulatory documents, application procedures and other participation requirements may be found at http://tenderenergo.ru . The website is in Russian and intended for local representatives of foreign companies and Russian power supply firms. Information on state procurement (government purchases) can also be found at http://www.b2b-energo.ru/?lang=eng .

The Russian government has stated that it intends to expand the role of nuclear and hydropower generation in the future, to allow for greater export of fossil fuels, with a plan to increase nuclear generation to twice its current level. However, many nuclear plants are due for decommissioning, some of the older reactors will likely be replaced in the near future (ten nuclear units currently under construction), and meeting such a target will require billions of dollars of investment per year over the next decade.

Web Resources

Russian Ministry of Energy http://www.minenergo.gov.ru Rosatom - Federal Agency for Nuclear Energy http://www.rosatom.ru/en Rosenergoatom http://www.rosenergoatom.ru/eng Press Center of Nuclear Energy and Industry http://www.minatom.ru/en System Operator http://www.so-cdu.ru Federal Grid Company http://fsk-ees.ru/eng Inter RAO UES http://www.interrao.ru/eng

The OGK and TGK websites (many also in English) may also contain information about each company's investment, procurement and production plans.

OGK-1 http://www.ogk1.com/en OGK-2 http://www.ogk2.ru/eng OGK-3 http://www.ogk3.ru/en-main OGK-4 http://www.eng.ogk-4.ru Enel OGK-5 http://www.ogk-5.com/en OGK-6 http://www.ogk6.ru/en RusHydro http://www.eng.rushydro.ru TGK-1 http://eng.tgc1.ru TGK-2 http://www.tgc-2.ru/en Mosenergo/TGK-3 http://www.mosenergo.ru Quadra/TGK-4 http://www.quadra.ru

TGK-5 http://www.tgc5.ru/eng.html TGK-6 http://www.tgc6.ru/index.php?id=news&L=1 Volzhskaya TGK/TGK-7 http://www.en.votgk.ru Southern Generation Comp/TGK-8 http://www.tgk-8.ru TGK-9 http://www.tgk9.ru/eng.html Fortum/TGK-10 http://www.fortum.ru TGK-11 http://www.eng.tgk11.com Kuzbassenergo/TGK-12 http://www.kuzbassenergo.ru/eng Yenisei TGK/TGK-13 http://eng.tgk13.ru TGK-14 http://www.tgk-14.com

Commercial Service Contact Anna Avetisyan, Commercial Specialist Tel: 7 (495) 728-5398
Anna.Avetisyan@trade.gov

MEDICAL EQUIPMENT

Unit: USD Thousands

	2009	2010	2011 (estimate)	2012 (estimate)
Total Market Size	3,300,000	3,500,000	3,700,000	3,800,000
Total Local Production	510,000	530,000	600,000	620,000
Total Exports	70,000	90,000	120,000	140,000
Total Imports	2,860,000	3,060,000	3,220,000	3,320,000
Imports from the U.S.*	137,000	170,000	190,000	200,000

Source: Remedium and industry experts; Global Trade Atlas

Russia has instituted a comprehensive reform of its healthcare system and healthcare is "Priority #1" in the government's new national priority projects. Russia's healthcare system is evolving rapidly and this is creating many promising areas for U.S. medical equipment exports. It is currently estimated that only 20% of the Russian population of 142 million has access to quality healthcare. The majority of hospitals and polyclinics are public and belong to federal, regional or local governments.

At the moment, the two major sources of public healthcare funding - mandatory insurance funds (30%) and spending supported by federal and regional budgets (70%) - do not cover all healthcare expenses. As a result, a significant portion of overall (public and private) health care spending (about 20%) is covered out of patients' pockets. Voluntary healthcare insurance programs account for approximately one-third of the total private healthcare expenditures. According to long-term reform plans, mandatory insurance funds will serve as the main source of healthcare funding, providing transparency and control over cash flow within the system. However, despite the ongoing healthcare reforms and significant increases in federal and regional budget allocations for healthcare, financing remains insufficient to address the needs of the industry.

On January 1, 2011, the new law "About Mandatory Healthcare Insurance" was adopted. This law makes the patient the most important segment of healthcare. Money will "follow" the patient and the government will finance the medical procedures, not the healthcare facility. This law allows the patient to choose the healthcare insurance company, medical facility and doctor. According to this law a patient can choose both state and private medical facilities. Those rights will be supported by the mandatory healthcare insurance card, which will be valid throughout Russia. As a result, the quality of medical services will improve because the government will pay the medical facility for the full cost of every medical procedure.

The Ministry of Health and Social Development has developed a document called "Health Care Through 2020." According to Health Minister Golikova, this document will be incorporated into a long-term strategy of social and economic development.

The Russian medical equipment and supply market is one of the fastest growing sectors of the economy. Despite the severe economic downturn that began in 2008, in 2009 the total volume of medical equipment and supplies in Russia grew 38% to reach $3.3 billion. This puts the market among the 20 fastest growing markets in the world, yet annual per capita spending is a very low $23. Industry experts predict that the market will grow at a rate of 5.5% per year, reaching $4.3 billion by 2014 or $31 per capita.

Almost two-thirds of the medical equipment and devices used in public clinics and hospitals are obsolete and need replacement. Russia itself does not produce much high-end medical equipment and must rely almost exclusively on imports. The Federal Service on Surveillance in Healthcare and Social Development of the Russian Federation (Rosdravnadzor) has approved over 20,000 medical products and devices for use in treatments, 60% of which are locally manufactured (appliances - 3,000; equipment - 1,000; instruments - 7,000; glass and polymer medical products - 700). About 1200 Russian enterprises, 90% privately held, manufacture an array of medical devices, including apparatus and appliances (45%), medical instruments (10%), medical equipment (9%), glass and polymer medical products (10%), other medical products (26%).

According to various sources, imported medical devices constitute 60% of the Russian market. The statistical data show that 40-45% of imports come from Germany, 20-25% from the U.S., 10% from Japan and 5% each from Italy and France. For the last three years, a growing number of cheap analogues from China and Pakistan have entered the Russian market in large volumes.

Russian medical equipment manufacturers are making some progress in several traditional and developing segments. First, most routine X-ray diagnostic procedures are done on Russian-made equipment. Apart from that, the Russian medical device market is well represented by monitors for various uses, including those for intensive therapy, surgical operations, pregnancy and at the patient's bedside. Also, Russian companies manufacture certain models of electrocardiographs, encephalographs and rheographs.

A particular focus of Russian manufacturers (usually 15% of the products made at any given plant) is on producing surgical tables, lighting systems, sterilization equipment, cameras for disinfection, beds and medical furniture. The Russian manufacturer KB Vzlet developed the "Kosmea" apparatus used for cardiac artery bypass surgery that works without an artificial blood-circulation apparatus. "Trekpor Technology" Holdings developed an industrial magnetic-resonance accelerator for the production of membranes.

Sub-Sector Best Prospects

Despite recent breakthroughs and the fact that locally made medical equipment is two to four times cheaper than imported equipment, Russian production still lags behind the majority of developed countries. Thus, Russia is still dependent on imports for a significant number of medical equipment industry sub-sectors, especially those requiring large investments in R&D, innovative technologies and automation. The best prospects for medical equipment include:

Computer tomographs
Blood pressure instruments and equipment
Respirators
Endoscopes
Ultrasound scanning equipment
Syringes, catheters, dental disposables, ophthalmological equipment
X-ray equipment for general medicine, surgery and veterinary
Artificial kidney complex components (oxygenators and dialysis machines)

Due to the aspiration of the Russian government to increase domestic capacity, there is a developing trend of cooperation between Russian and U.S. medical equipment firms. For example, at the end of 2008, GE Healthcare and one of the leading local manufacturers, Medical Technologies Limited (MTL), announced a strategic partnership to make diagnostic imaging equipment in Russia. The Ural Optical and Mechanical plant bought a license from the German company Siemens to produce a computer tomograph (CT). Cooperation between the JSC Ural Priborostroitelny plant and Italian manufacturers resulted in production of an ultrasound scanning instrument that won one of the tenders for the National Health Project. Finally, the Izomed company successfully manufactures another ultrasound diagnostic instrument in cooperation with a Japanese company. Such joint cooperation can bring accessible, innovative and modern healthcare technologies to support Russian government projects modernizing healthcare in various disease areas.

Opportunities

Recent reforms in healthcare have created opportunities for U.S. medical equipment suppliers. In September 2005, President Putin announced that healthcare would be one of four key national projects, along with education, housing and agriculture. President Dmitry Medvedev (first Deputy Prime Minister beginning in November of that year) was in charge of these projects. The total federal budget allocated under the National Health Project in 2006 was $4 billion (excluding loans and state guarantees) and nearly $5 billion in each of the following years.

The National Health Project is designed to significantly improve the Russian healthcare sector, giving impetus to both the pharmaceutical and medical equipment markets. The implementation of the project is supported by laws and regulations, which will modify the healthcare system structure over the long term. Key laws and regulations include laws on state guarantees for medical assistance, mandatory health insurance, and standards of medical assistance. In 2010 the National Health Project was financed at $4.8 billion. In 2011 the financing will be $3.9 billion, in 2012 - $3.8, in 2013 – $2.6. The significant decline in the figures does not mean that the healthcare spending will decrease, because the numbers mentioned above will be only taken from the federal budget, the rest of the money, intended for providing mandatory healthcare insurance will be drawn from the Mandatory Healthcare Insurance fund. Since contribution payments of all working people to the Mandatory Healthcare Insurance Fund increased by 2%, in 20112012 this Fund will receive additional $15.3 billion. In 2010 each region developed its own program of healthcare development.

Organizations

Ministry of Health and Social Development http://www.minzdravsoc.ru

Russian Federal Service on Surveillance in Healthcare and Social Development http://www.roszdravnadzor.ru

Commercial Service Contact Yuliya Vinogradova, Commercial Specialist Yuliya.Vinogradova@trade.gov Tel: 7 (495) 728-5586

REFINERY EQUIPMENT

Unit: USD thousands

	2009	2010	2011 (estimate)	2012 (estimate)
Total Market Size	6,000,000	9,000,000	11,000,000	11,000,000
Total Local Production	3,000,000	5,500,000	6,000,000	6,000,000
Total Imports	3,000,000	3,500,000	5,000,000	5,000,000
Imports from the U.S.	1,200,000	1,600,000	2,300,000	2,300,000

Source: CS Russia estimates

Russia ranks among the top ten countries in proven oil reserves, and is the world's largest exporter of oil and natural gas. Proceeds from the oil and gas industry account for almost half of Russian federal budget revenues, most of it coming from exports of crude oil and natural gas. Lately, however, a strong emphasis has been placed on the necessity to develop the Russian oil and gas refining and petrochemical industry, which should reduce Russia's dependence on global crude oil and gas prices. The plan is not only to fully employ existing domestic refining capacities, but also to gradually build up and upgrade existing refineries and build new ones. In perspective, this strategy should lead Russian companies to focus on the export of processed petroleum products rather than crude oil and gas, and to meet the increasing domestic need for high quality petroleum and petrochemical products.

One of the major incentives for the rapid technological upgrade of Russian refineries is the official ban on the production of low-quality fuels. Production of Euro-2 gasoline must cease on December 31, 2010; of Euro-3 gasoline on December 31, 2011; of Euro4 on December 31, 2014. Similarly, production of class 2 and 3 diesel fuels is to cease on December 31, 2011, and class 4 on December 31, 2014. As a result, most of the Russian oil majors have been actively investing in the upgrade of their refining facilities, creating new opportunities for US manufacturers of refining technologies and equipment.

Thus, Russia remains one of the few regions that continue to look at major investment programs in the downstream sector. A reason for this trend is the relatively small investments made in the sector over the past decades. According to varying assessments, a total technical upgrade of the Russian refining industry requires $30 to 50 billion.

Sub-Sector Best Prospects

The following general areas can be identified as most promising:

Emphasis on secondary refining upgrades to increase the depth of refining, from current levels of 60% up to 80% and above, including development and installation of new visbreakers and introduction of delayed coking processes;

Upgrade of primary (top) refining units with the objective of increasing light-end product bleeding and reducing electricity consumption;

Optimization of commercial motor gasoline production, and upgrade of catalytic reformers to produce high-octane components of motor gasoline;

Introduction and/or upgrade of low-sulfur diesel fuel production units;

Upgrade of catalytic cracking units to increase the yield and RONC of gasoline and improve energy-efficiency in this process;

Transfer of certain types of fuel hydrogenation units to light hydrocracking technology, in order to increase diesel fuel output;

Transfer of decommissioned catalytic reformers to isomerization processes of C5-C6 hydrocarbons to produce high-octane components of motor gasoline;

Adaptation of atmospheric distillation and thermal cracking units to visbreakers;

Optimization of internal refinery energy systems, including installation of energy-efficient, stand-alone gas-turbine and diesel power plants where appropriate to lower refineries' power consumption costs;

Upgrade of storage and intermediate reservoirs;

Cogeneration of refinery heavy bottoms into steam and electricity, or other relevant utilization technologies; and

Introduction of modern integrated process control and accounting systems, including Distributed Control Systems (DCS).

Smaller oil producing companies are looking for opportunities to process crude oil right at the production site, which would allow them to increase the value of their product and reduce transportation expenses. This provides opportunities for U.S. manufactures of equipment for mini refineries. Companies providing turn-key solutions have the best prospects.

Opportunities

As of today, Russia has about 30 major and 80 mini oil refineries with a total processing capacity of 5.6 million b/d. In 2008 (pre-crisis year), the Russian refining industry produced 36 million tons of gasoline, 69 million tons of diesel fuel, and 64 million tons of fuel oil.

Most of the Russian oil refineries were built in the two postwar decades: 16 plants, more than half of those currently active, were commissioned between 1945 and1965. Only two refineries, with the total capacity of about 70,000 b/d, were launched in Russia after the collapse of the Soviet Union. Thus, overall, plants built during the Soviet time are currently recycling about 98% of oil, and until recently, only a few had gone through significant technological upgrade. It is not surprising, therefore, that experts unanimously admit a high level of depreciation (60-75%) and use of old technologies in the Russian refining industry. Despite certain positive changes that have taken place recently, the quality of the product leaves much to be desired and the depth of oil refining is still extremely low: The average depth of oil processing in Russia does not exceed 72%. In addition, the hydroskimming capacity of the Russian refining industry exceeds its capacity to produce refined petroleum products, which is explained by the fact that the Soviet oil refining industry was focused on the production of diesel fuel and fuel oil, while demand for gasoline was relatively low. Today, companies produce more low quality petroleum half-stuff than they can process to the finished product level, and therefore, often have to export the semi-finished product at a discounted price.

The period of economic reforms in the 90s did not bring any positive changes to the Russian oil refining and petrochemical industries. In fact, due to the sharp decrease in domestic oil consumption, these years witnessed a significant decline in the actual volume of processed materials. In 2000, Russian refineries processed only 168.7 million tons of crude material, thus making no use of almost half of their total capacity (296 million tons per year).

"Contemporary history" of the Russian refining industry, as well as the prospects for its future, are to a big extent conditioned by the vertically integrated character of the sector: About 90% of oil refining capacities are controlled by ten major vertically integrated oil and gas companies.

According to varying assessments, technical upgrades in the industry require $30 to $50 billion. Most of this burden falls on the oil majors. With the pay-back period for investments in technological upgrades of refining facilities being 5 to7 years, and crude oil production and transport paying back much quicker, companies used to take on refining projects based on what remained in their budgets. However, recent efforts of the Russian government made Russian oil majors change those policies and start allocating substantial resources to oil refining. The result of this policy change is broad-scale reconstruction of existing Russian refineries and construction of new ones, which creates opportunities for U.S. technologies and equipment suppliers.

U.S. engineering services and equipment suppliers enjoy a relatively sound position in the Russian import market, and can look forward to opportunities to increase their share further if new projects become sustainable, and if their market development efforts are commensurate with the market's potential.

References & Key Contacts

Information on Russian and Central Asian refinery projects: http://abarrelfull.wikidot.com/russian-and-central-asia-refinery-projects

Rosneft refineries: http://www.rosneft.com/Downstream/refining

Russian Ministry of Energy Tel: 7 (495) 631 9858 minenergo@minenergo.gov.ru http://www.minenergo.gov.ru

Russian Association of Oil and Gas Equipment Producers Tel: 7 (495) 514 5856 info@n-g-k.ru http://www.eng.derrick.ru

Commercial Service Contact Gulnara Kenzhebulatova, Commercial Specialist Tel: 7 (495) 728 5405 Gulnara.Kenzhebulatova@trade.gov

SAFETY & SECURITY EQUIPMENT

Unit: USD thousands

	2009	2010	2011 (estimate)	2012 (estimate)
Total Market	5,650,000	6,180,000	7,008,000	8,059,000
Services	4,000,000	4,200,000	4,830,000	5,554,000
Equipment	1,650,000	1,980,000	2,178,000	2,505,000
Local Production	330,000	600,000	660,000	759,000
Exports	250,000	400,000	440,000	506,000
Imports	1,570,000	1,780,000	1,958,000	2,252,000
Imports from the U.S.	80,000	90,000	100,000	115,000

The Russian market for safety and security has the potential for steady development because of the country's vast infrastructure, large area, and number of potential security threats.

Before the financial crisis in 2008, the Russian market for safety and security systems had been developing rapidly, offering strong potential for U.S. companies. One of the reasons was the construction boom which correlates with safety and security products purchases. Beginning in mid 2009, the safety and security market entered the stage of revival.

Regarding regional segments, 65% of the market is concentrated in Moscow and St. Petersburg, 17% in the Urals Federal District, 7% in the Siberian Federal District, and 6% in the Northwest Federal District. The rest of the market is divided among the Volga, Far East and Southern Regions. This order may change over the next two years as the 2014 Olympic Games will require substantial investment in safety and security infrastructure in the Sochi region. However, key management decisions on that project are made in Moscow. Thus, the southern regions may take an insignificant market share from Moscow and St. Petersburg.

The safety and security equipment market is divided into four main product segments:

CCTV and Video Surveillance
Access Systems
Fire Safety Systems
Perimeter Security and Control Systems

2010 Safety and Security Equipment Market (Sales/Share)

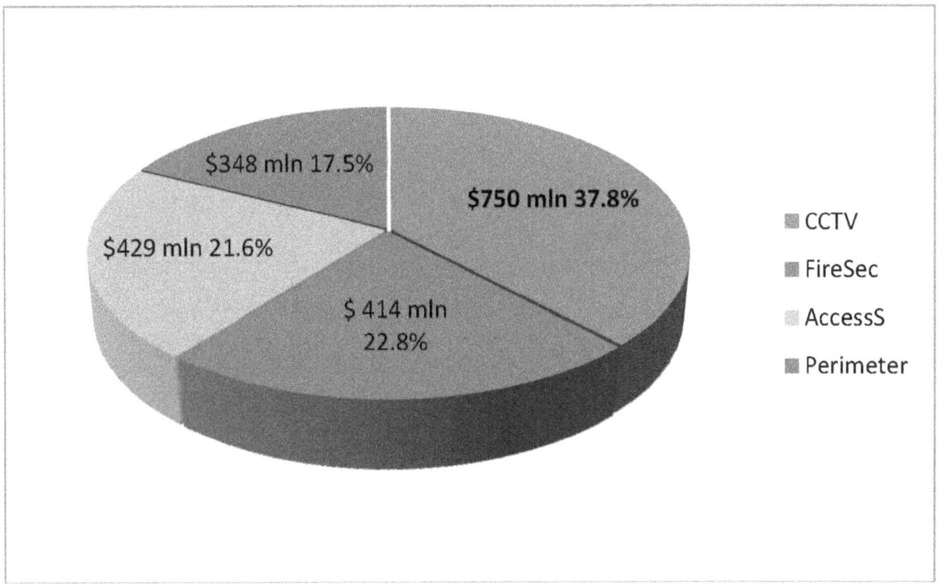

In 2010, the Russian CCTV and access systems segments totaled just over $1.2 billion, or 60% of the equipment market. It is considered the most developed and competitive segment. The size of the security and fire alarm segment was approximately $414 million (21.6% of the equipment market), historically increasing 12% to 15% annually. This segment grew substantially in 2010 because of the heavy fires that occurred in the summer throughout the country. Moreover the government is working on a fire security development program, with the Ministry of Emergency Situations in charge of the key points of the development agenda.

Major Consumers of Safety and Security Products and Services in 2010

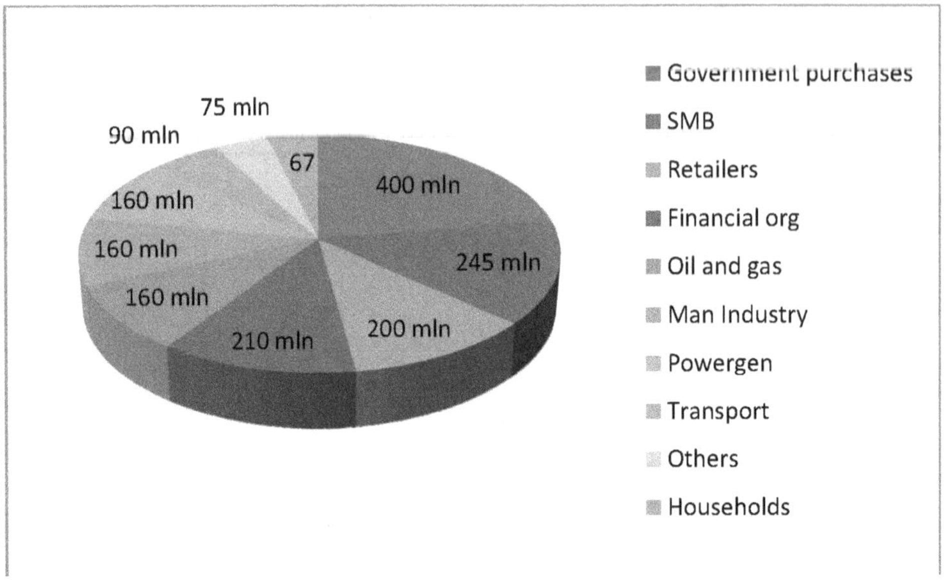

Depending on the segment, the share of imported products ranges from 50% to 95%. Experts estimate that up to 80% of access control, about 50% of intruder and fire alarms, and more than 95% of CCTV systems are imported. Even locally manufactured equipment contains 60% to 95% imported components. Hi-tech solutions come from China, Taiwan, and Korea and are popular in Russian regions outside of Moscow and St. Petersburg. Premium systems are imported from the United States, Europe (Great Britain, Germany, France, Italy, and Poland), Japan, and Israel, though the majority of the components even in these systems originate from China.

Government is the main end-user of products and services in this industry, with over $400 million in 2010. Its share is constantly increasing as the government remains concerned about terrorist activities and possible calamities related to the nation's infrastructure and major construction activities.

While Russian government procurement is substantial, private entities, mainly in real estate, banking, retail, and oil and gas, are also important buyers and end users of a wide variety of security equipment. Currently, there are over 300 distribution companies working in the Russian security market. Sixty-five percent of these companies are located in the Moscow and St. Petersburg regions.

Finding a local partner knowledgeable in the industry and experienced in procurement tenders would be the shortest path to successfully entering the Russian market. All Government purchases are made through http://www.zakupki.gov.ru , a large web-based resource consolidating all procurement enquiries from state organizations and agencies. It operates only in Russian. It is essential to cooperate with a Russian company or to open a representative office inside the country to handle operations related to government tenders. Moreover, companies working in this business need steady and long-term relations with law enforcement and emergency agencies, which are the main consumers of the safety and security products.

Sub-Sector Best Prospects

Industry specialists note that one recent trend is the convergence of information and safety and security technologies, which creates more opportunities for high quality U.S. technology exports. The IP-based CCTV segment is expected to maintain its growth in the future as it is an essential part of any security system. Color CCTV cameras have almost replaced monochrome units.

A new trend is comprehensive fire security alarms. The summer 2010 peat fires in Russia that injured hundreds of people forced the government to implement major changes in the Fire Service, which is a part of the Emergency Ministry. Much attention is being paid at the moment to fire security in public places and forests.

The Russian Government continues to show concern for possible terrorist attacks. Companies selling metal detectors expect an increase in sales, as luggage and individual inspection may become mandatory at rail stations and other transportation related areas.

One of the most important opportunities is the 2014 Olympic Games in Sochi. The total budget for the Games is about $13 billion. The cost of safety and security equipment is estimated at 17% of the construction cost, thus creating a $2 billion market for safety and security products. Additionally, U.S. companies may be presented with opportunities related to the 2018 FIFA World Cup.

The best prospects for sales of U.S. manufactured hardware in 2010-11 are:

IP-based solutions in various equipment segments (surveillance, detection, day/night surveillance and infrared systems) especially high end systems

Access control systems

Fire/intruder alarm systems, especially for public places

Integrated control systems

Biometric equipment, identifiers and readers

Antiterrorist equipment, especially bomb-detection equipment

Anti-theft systems, radar detection, recording equipment (wireless)

Experts consider that growth for these groups of products could reach 10-15% in 2011. Companies should be aware of possible U.S. export control regulations related to the export of these types of technologies and equipment.

Opportunities

The strength of the safety and security systems market is in constant innovation and price competitiveness. New concepts and products may create market entry opportunities.

Participation in industry events is very important in this Russian market and it also facilitates successful market entry. There are several key events in the Russian safety and security industry. Key companies in the sector participate in the Moscow International Exhibition for Protection, Security & Fire Safety (MIPS), a show that has received government support as well as Interpolitex.

Interpolitex is a specialized trade show dedicated only to emergency and law enforcement; it is supported by the Ministry of the Interior. Companies exhibiting at this trade fair work closely with this Ministry and its law enforcement agencies.

Organizations

Russian Security Industry Association http://www.rasi.ru/index_eng.php

VNIIPO; All-Russian Scientific-Research Institute for Fire Prevention (Fire security equipment certification body) http://www.vniipo.ru

Publications

Safety Systems Magazine published by Groteck Company http://www.groteck.net

Sec.ru http://www.sec.ru

Commercial Service Contact Timur Uddin, Commercial Specialist Tel: 7 (495) 728-5526 Timur.Uddin@trade.gov

TRAVEL & TOURISM TO U.S.

Source: Q1 Russian Tourism Report, BMI 2011; Office of Travel & Tourism, U.S. Dept of Commerce; CS Russia informal estimates

	2009	2010	2011 (estimate)	2012 (estimate)

Russians Traveling Abroad	20,157,000	21,437,000	22,846,000	24,300,000
Russians Traveling to U.S.	143,000	172,000	205,000	247,000

With a population of over 140 million, Russia is the ninth largest outbound market in the world. Over 21 million Russians traveled abroad in 2010. As the growing Russian middle class discovers new routes that cater to their tastes and budget, U.S. destinations are becoming more popular among Russian tourists. New direct passenger flights to the United States, simplified U.S. visa procedures and the depreciation of the

U.S. dollar against the Euro have helped make travel to the United States more attractive and affordable for Russian travelers. While the financial crisis of 2009 interrupted the rapid growth of the Russian T&T market, 2010 showed continuation of the positive dynamics, and experts' longer-term forecasts are extremely optimistic.

Sub-Sector Best Prospects

Based on the results of the survey of Russian tour operators conducted by CS Moscow, the most promising destinations in the United States include:

Cities: New York City, Miami, Las Vegas

National Parks

Ski / Winter Resorts

Leisure / Entertainment Complexes

New York City has been and will likely remain the most popular city destination for Russian tourists in the near future. Russians will often combine their business travel to NYC with a pleasure trip. Their family, historical and cultural ties to NYC put it on the top of the list for brand awareness, followed by Miami and other locations in Florida famous for their comfort and opportunities for various forms of leisure. As more Russian tourists reach the U.S. West Coast, California resorts and attractions are becoming increasingly popular in this respect as well. Las Vegas is another destination that historically was considered by many Russians the gambling and entertainment capital of the world and has gained even bigger popularity after July 1, 2009, when gambling was officially banned in Russia. Interest in national parks is growing as Russian tourists hear more about what they have to offer. Ski and winter sports resorts have become more popular in recent years as they provide a unique travel experience in terms of variety, beauty and quality of service. Because of the current U.S. dollar/Euro exchange rate, these resorts have become more economical than European destinations.

Opportunities

Increased prices for domestic travel destinations and the development of outbound travel services triggered Russians' growing interest in travel to destinations outside Russia. Turkey, China and Egypt have held the top places in the number of Russian tourists for the past several years. These countries, along with Finland, Italy, Spain, Greece, Bulgaria and Thailand still constitute the core of mass tourism destinations for Russian travelers. However, recent outbound traffic statistics indicate that, in addition to traditional warm and seaside destinations, more Russians are choosing countries where they may supplement time on the beach with other activities, such as cultural and sporting events, shopping and recreation. Moreover, Russians who have traveled to Asia and Europe in the past are willing to explore destinations other than those they have already visited. While the activity may be similar, the different destination is appealing. For example, skiers who have visited the Alps for their proximity look to Colorado, Utah and Vermont for their next trip.

The popularity of the United States as a tourist destination has grown steadily since 2003, after a downward trend following the events of September 11, 2001. Russian tourist numbers accelerated dramatically over the last few years. According to international arrival data from the Office of Travel and Tourism at the U.S. Department of Commerce, the number of Russians traveling to the United States totaled 115,000 in 2007, up 21% from 2006. In 2008, it reached 143,000, a record annual increase of 25%. Even during the crisis year 2009, the number remained relatively stable. It resumed its progressive change in 2010, showing an annual increase of 20% and reaching 172,000 travelers.

An important factor accounting for the steady growth in the number of Russian travelers to the United States is the significant improvement in the visa application process that has taken place in recent years. The U.S. Embassy has made great progress in streamlining the process in the face of a rapidly growing number of applications and has made visa information available online in Russian. Applicants are now able to send their application fee and supporting documents to the Embassy via a courier service with offices across Russia and have the opportunity to secure a two-year, multiple entry visa. For those wishing to renew a visa, the requirement to appear for an interview is waived if they apply within six months following their previous visa expiration date. The availability of visa information online has made it possible to counter the market's impression that

U.S. visas are expensive, difficult to obtain and take a long time to process. Russian tour operators are also educating their travelers regarding these improvements. Visit USA Russia, a young yet very active organization registered in Moscow in April 2010, is contributing to this effort by organizing meetings of Russian travel industry professionals with U.S. Consular officers working in the U.S. Embassy in Moscow and U.S. Consulates throughout the country.

Another significant improvement is the fact that more airlines, both U.S. and international, have launched non-stop service connecting Moscow with U.S. destinations. Delta Airlines, United Airlines, Aeroflot Russian Airlines, Transaero and Singapore Airlines all offer direct flights to U.S. cities. Aeroflot flies to New York, Washington DC and Los Angeles; Delta flies to New York and Atlanta; United to Washington, DC; Transaero has recently launched flights to New York and Miami, and Singapore Airlines flies to Houston. The increase in the number of direct flights between Moscow and U.S. cities is a reflection of the growing market demand for this kind of service. As the market becomes more educated about U.S. destinations, visa processing, flight availability and purchase value, the Russian market is looking increasingly to the United States for tourist destinations.

Within several months of its existence, Visit USA Russia has attracted 48 companies interested in further development of Russian outbound travel to the United States. This rapidly growing organization has already conducted a number of broad-scale, highly successful projects aimed at promoting U.S. destinations in Russia, and has an even more ambitious agenda for 2011.

Web Resources

Major Russian Cities http://www.visit-usa.ru/en/node/379

Moscow Ski Salon October 29-31, 2011 *Moscow* http://skiexpo.ru/msalon/eng/

Margarita Babayan, Chair Tel: 7 (495) 935-7925/36 Cell: 7 (906) 756-1883 chair@visit-usa.ru http://www.visit-usa.ru/en

Transaero 47 B. Polyanka Street, Bld. 1 Moscow Tel: 7 (495) 937-8477 http://transaero.ru/en
Aeroflot Russian Airlines 37 Leningradsky Prospect, bldg. 9 Moscow Tel: 7 (495) 223-5555 http://www.aeroflot.ru/cms/en
American Airlines 20 Sadovaya-Kudrinskya str., Office 206 Moscow Tel: 7 (495) 234-4074; 234-4075 http://www.aa.com
United Airlines 40/2 Prechistenka Street, Block 1, Entrance 3, Office 32 Moscow Tel: 7 (495) 980-0882 http://www.united.com/
Delta Airlines 11 Gogolevsky Blvd., 2nd floor Moscow Tel: 7 (495) 937-9090 http://www.delta.com
Singapore Airlines Hotel Renaissance, 18/1, Olympisky Prospect Moscow Tel: 7 (495) 937-5920 http://www.singaporeair.com
U.S. Travel Association 1100 New York Avenue, NW Suite 450 Washington, DC 20005-3934 http://www.tia.org

International Trade Administration Office of Travel & Tourism Industries U.S. Department of Commerce http://tinet.ita.doc.gov

U.S. Department of Homeland Security, US-Visit Program 1616 N. Fort Myer Drive Arlington, VA 22209 Tel: (202) 298-5200 http://www.dhs.gov/usvisit

B-FOR International Bjorn Bieneck, President & CEO 805 Princess Anne Street, Suite 1 Fredericksburg, VA 22401 Tel: (540) 373-9935 http://www.b-for.com

Russian Travel Industry Union Sergey Shpilko, President 11, Stoleshnikov per., office 426 Moscow, 107031 Russia Tel: 7 (495) 692-2464 E-mail: rata@rata.ru http://www.rustourunion.ru/

Commercial Service Contact Gulnara Kenzhebulatova, Commercial Specialist Tel: 7 (495) 728-5405 Gulnara.Kenzhebulatova@trade.gov

AGRICULTURAL SECTOR

Russia's agricultural imports rebounded in 2010 and reached approximately $31.7 billion. This level signals a remarkable recovery, nearly as high as the record of 2008. However the situation for U.S. exports is not quite as optimistic. Based on official data,

U.S. exports to Russia continued to decline at $1.3 billion in 2010, down from $1.7 billion in 2009. While U.S. exports of beef, fresh fruits, fish, nuts and dairy continued to expand, market access barriers severely restricted opportunities for pork and poultry – which in the past decade have been the United States' two largest agricultural exports to Russia.

Year-on-year and average annual growth in Russian agricultural imports can be seen in the following table:

	2006	2007	2008	2009	2010
Agricultural Imports (billion dollars1)	19.7	24.9	31.9	26.6	31.7
Growth Year-on-Year (percent)	24.6	26.8	28.16	-16.7	19.1

* UDG: WTO 2010; Source: Global Trade Atlas

2010 began with the introduction of the Customs Union between Russia, Kazakhstan, and Belarus. Few changes were made to agricultural tariffs and the average continues to be approximately 18% ad valorem. Tariff rate quotas for beef, poultry and pork remain under the Customs Union although the 2010 volumes for poultry and pork were slashed from the previously negotiated levels. Access beyond 2011 is uncertain and will be subject to WTO negotiations. Significant changes for imports are resulting from the evolving harmonization of sanitary, veterinary and phytosanitary regulations. While discussions are ongoing within the context of Russia's WTO accession to eliminate trade barriers and ensure Russia's requirements are consistent with internationally accepted practices, the transition from Russian requirements to Custom Union requirements is continually creating new challenges for U.S. exporters.

Russia's retail sector had been growing at a pace of 20% to 30% annually until 2009 when it posted a 5.5% decline. Projected sales for 2010 to 2011 are expected to stabilize or grow slightly. According to data from the Federal State Statistics Service (Rosstat), the value of the food and beverage market in Russia was $222 billion in 2009 and contributed to 48.6% of retail sales, up from 45% in 2008. In 2009, the value of food sales decreased 2.5%.

Because retailers demand consistent quality and adherence to contract specifications and penalize suppliers for failure to meet requirements, foreign suppliers continue to be competitive in the Russian market as they are more accustomed than Russian agricultural producers to meeting such strict specifications.

The structural evolution of the Russian retail market continues to be led by large retailers with annual turnover exceeding $1 billion. Discounters have outpaced hypermarkets and supermarkets in sales and expansion. For example, the X5 Retail Group plans to open 200-250 discounters in 2010 and only 15 supermarkets and 7-10 hypermarkets. Magnit plans to open 450-550 discount stores and 25-30 hypermarkets, and Dixie plans to spend about $100 million to open low-cost stores. The expansion has been focused mainly on developing modern retail formats in large urban areas such as Moscow and the surrounding areas. Nationwide, retail chains occupy about 30 percent of the food retail market, but with higher concentrations in major urban centers (about 50% in Moscow and 80% in St. Petersburg); however, some retailers have made considerable efforts to expand into Russia's regions.

Open-air markets and older Soviet-style stores, including wet markets, are declining in popularity and losing market share to modern retail formats such as hypermarkets, supermarkets, and discounters. There were 155 fewer open-air markets in Russia in 2009, a decrease of 4% from 2008.

Currently the Russian retail market is highly fragmented with the 10 largest retailers (by revenue) controlling only 14% of the market, versus 80% for the 10 largest retailers in the U.S. Western-style "modern" retail chains currently account for 50% of food sales in Moscow and 80% in St. Petersburg. Russian retail giants such as the X5 Retail Group, Magnit, Seventh Continent, Dixie and the Kopeika chains are still among the top Russian retail players.

Russia's food processing sector showed some improvement in 2010 after the slowdown in 2008-2009. Food processing sectors that are showing strength include: meat products (including pork, poultry, sausages and semi-finished meat), dairy products, confectionary, dry baby food and dietary products with cereal. Food ingredients are imported, mainly from Denmark, Belgium, France, Germany, Austria, Great Britain, and the United States. Many Russian manufacturers are investing in modernization and expansion in order to strengthen their position in the market. The Russian food industry continues its dependence on imports and, thus, opportunities to supply the market with

U.S. products are plentiful.

According to Rosstat, inflation in 2010 increased to 9.1% from 8.8% in 2009. The 2010 drought led to a drastic decline in crop production and resulted in high inflation (13.7%) for food. Prices of bread and pasta were curbed in many provinces by administrative measures, and increased only by 7.6% and 4.7%, respectively. Prices of cereals and groats increased by 58.8%, mostly due a 200% increase in the price of buckwheat, one of Russia's staple food cereals. Inflation of fish and seafood prices was only 4.8% due to increased fish harvests and improved marketing policy. Inflation of meat and poultry prices was below the overall inflation rate, only 5.3% due to drought-related increase in slaughter. In the meantime, increased in the prices of eggs, milk, staple dairy products, sugar, creamy butter and vegetable oil surpassed the overall inflation rate and ranged from 13.2% (eggs) to 27.6% (vegetable oil). The prices of vegetables and fruits increased by 45.6%.

Russia continues to pursue the targets set out in the official Food Security Doctrine which sets the minimum self-sufficiency targets: 85% meat, 90% milk, 80% sugar and vegetable oil, and 95% in potato and grains. In 2010, we saw heightened restrictions on dairy, pork and poultry as both domestic programs and foreign trade policy may shift to favor domestic production in order to help secure some of these targets. For 2011, this could result in more challenges for meat, poultry and dairy products, but at the same time create new opportunities for high protein feeds and animal genetics.

Sub-Sector Best Prospects

Frozen Beef

In December 2009, Russia extended the tariff rate quotas (TRQ) for frozen beef (HS0202) from 2010 through 2012. For 2010, Russia increased the total in-quota quantity for frozen beef from 450,000 MT to 530,000 MT, and the United States' share from 18,500 MT to 21,700 MT. Russia left in-quota tariffs unchanged at 15% but not less than €0.20/kg while increasing the over-quota tariff to 50% but not less than €1.00/kg. Simultaneously, Russia restricted quota-exempt "high-quality" beef receiving the in-quota rate, as its definition of high quality beef was changed from €3/kg to €8/kg. Beef and beef by-products may only be shipped from approved plants that have undergone special inspections to ensure conformity with Russian inspection criteria. Through November 2010, U.S. exports of frozen beef to Russia had reached 23,000 MT (representing a record $91.6 million in export value).

In December 2010, Russia amended the 2011 TRQs by increasing the U.S. share of frozen beef TRQ from 21,700 to 41,700 MT. Russia offset this amount through a TRQ reduction to "other countries".

Animal Genetics

The Russian government has adopted several development plans to stimulate development of the dairy, poultry, pork, and beef sectors. As the access for meat continues to be limited through reduced quotas and SPS measures, the demand and opportunity for higher quality animal genetics will grow.

Russian government subsidies will continue to facilitate the annual import of 40-50,000 head of cattle from around the world, and the United States is well-positioned to be a top supplier into the future, especially for producers seeking the best genetics available. The imported bovine semen market continues to grow, as producers seek to utilize sexed semen technology. In 2010, imports of bovine semen will reach close to $3 million. While statistics are unavailable, imports of bovine embryos have been slower to develop but should increase in tandem with awareness and education. The market is currently estimated at $500,000, with large potential for growth in 2011. Historical demand has primarily targeted dairy cattle, specifically registered Holsteins, but interest in beef genetics continues to grow rapidly, especially for Angus, but includes others such as Hereford.

Hatching eggs and chicks are important for the expanding Russian poultry and egg sector, and as a result, most import tariffs have been made duty-free.

Swine genetics remain an area of opportunity; however, transit restrictions through the European Union have prevented U.S. trade with Russia. The import market for breeding swine is roughly $25 million.

Edible Tree Nuts

After a drop in imports in 2009 due to the economic crisis, nut imports are recovering. In 2010, Russia imported 75,549 MT of tree nuts (up 8% from 2009). In value terms, nuts imports increased by 14% and reached $334.5 million.

In 2010, the U.S. exported 14,572 MT of tree nuts to Russia and became the second largest supplier of tree nuts following Ukraine. U.S. market share dropped from 23% in 2009 to 19% in 2010 due to the drastic decrease in pistachio sales to Russia. The United States is traditionally the main almond supplier to Russia and captures 91% of the market. In 2010, Russia imported 10% more California almonds, 12,764 MT, due mainly to the tenfold increase in shelled almond sales (1,242 MT in 2010 versus 128 MT in 2009). The supply of American pistachios dropped from 3,821 MT in 2009 to 1,597 in 2010 due to competition from low-priced Iranian product.

The majority of imported nuts are packaged in Russia into consumer-ready packs or used in the confectionary, baking and dairy industries.

Fish and Seafood

For 2010, total fish and seafood exports from the U.S. hit a record $51.6 million, an 88% increase over 2009. Exports of frozen roe and livers in 2010 demonstrated remarkable growth and estimated at $21.5 million, an almost 500% increase over 2009. The rapid increase is attributed to poor domestic catch of salmon and strong demand for salmon roe and salmon in general. The largest increases were in live crustaceans and mollusks, with import share that increased from $1.4 million in 2009 to over 4.4 million in 2010. According to Rosstat, retail prices for fish and seafood in Russia increased 4.8% in 2010. The outlook for 2011 suggests higher demand for fish and an increase in per capita consumption, both in lower-priced segments such as herring, hake, and perch, compared with more expensive fish and processed products. Higher imports of chilled fish and ready-to-eat products are due to changes in eating habits, increased consumer demand, and economic recovery. Current annual per capita fish and seafood consumption is estimated at 15 kilograms.

Fish consumption patterns will continue to depend heavily on household income, prices, and preferences within the population. Among consumption preferences of the Russian population are herring, pollock, mackerel, salmon and trout. Frozen fish is also traditionally popular in Russia.

Fresh Fruit (Apples, Pears, Grapes, Citrus)

Russia remains the third largest importer of fruit in the world in value terms and the number one market for pears. According to the Russian Ministry of Economic Development, per capita fruit consumption rose in Russia to 52.7 kilograms per year in 2009. Russians mainly buy apples, bananas, pears, and citrus. Prospects for U.S. fresh fruit exports to Russia are even better for 2011 due to lower crops expected in Europe due to poor weather.

While Russia is expected to continue investing in domestic production of apples, the market remains highly dependent on imports. Traditionally, Italy and France were the main exporters of apples to Russia. But Poland, China, Azerbaijan and Moldova have become increasingly competitive and, indeed, have overtaken Italy and France as the main suppliers of apples. U.S. apple exports increased by 3.4% in 2010 to $7.15 million, making the United States the 13th largest supplier.

In the pear market, Belgium, Argentina, the Netherlands, Spain and China hold the top positions. U.S. pear exports made gains in 2010 exporting $9.6 million and becoming the seventh largest supplier to Russia.

In 2010, Russia's imports of U.S. grapes increased 16% to $7 million. The main competitor to the U.S. in the premium segment is Italy.

The United States is the eleventh largest supplier of oranges, after Egypt, South Africa and Turkey, among others. Sales were up 25% in 2010 to $1.37m. American oranges enjoy particularly good sales in the Russian Far East. Russia's largest food retail chain promoted fresh U.S. blueberries and strawberries in Moscow in the fall of 2010, and Russian importers are interested in expanding sales of American berries in the coming season.

Wine and Spirits

Russian wine imports reached $797.7 million in 2010, up 30% from 2009 but still below the $914.1 million imported in 2008. In 2010, U.S. wine sales decreased 8% to $6.85m or less than one percent of the Russian wine market. The major competitors are EU countries, especially France, Italy and Spain. These countries rebounded in 2010 with sales increasing from 37% to 79% in 2010. Russian imports of hard liquor were $933.7 million in 2010, up 34% from 2009. U.S. (including Puerto Rico) spirits exports to Russia were $47.82 million (5% of the Russian market) in 2010, with a 10% increase for American spirits and a dramatic 85% increase for Puerto Rican alcohol. American whiskies have started to make inroads in Russia in competition with the market-dominant Scotch whiskies and European brandies, Armenian cognac, and Ukrainian vodkas.

Oilseeds and Feedstuff

Since 2008, the government has aggressively supported the development of poultry, pig and dairy farming through subsidized interest rate loans for private investors. The influx of funds has resulted in the adoption of new production technology, intensive feeding methods and increased demand for both protein feeds and formula feeds ingredients. The shortages of feed supplies in 2011 will be even more severe due to the drought and fires in the Central, Volga, and Ural districts in 2010. Grain production in 2010 dropped

by more than 30 percent from last year to 60 million metric tons (MMT), and will be the lowest since 1999. The shortage of feed grain may reach 2.5-3.0 MMT by April-May 2011.

Web Resources

Organizations

U.S.exporters should consult reports from USDA's office in Moscow, which are posted on the website of the Foreign Agricultural Service under the "Attaché Reports" heading or go to http://gain.fas.usda.gov/Pages/Default.aspx. Of particular interest should be the annual *Exporter Guide* as well as periodic reporting on changes in tariffs, market opportunities, and Russian commodity trends. Exporters should consider exhibiting their products in the U.S. pavilions at the World Food trade show (September 2011) or the Golden Autumn trade show (October 2011). For further information on these shows, please contact the Moscow Agricultural Trade Office at atomoscow@fas.usda.gov .

U.S.Embassy

Scott Reynolds, Minister-Counselor for Agricultural Affairs 8, Bolshoy Devyatinskiy Pereulok, Moscow 121099 Tel: 7 (495) 728-5222, Fax: 7 (495) 728-5133 agmoscow@fas.usda.gov , atomoscow@fas.usda.gov

Washington-based U.S. Government contacts for Russia

U.S. Department of Agriculture, Foreign Agricultural Service Office of Country and Regional Affairs, Europe Division Kristina Horgan, Country Desk Officer Kristina.Horgan@fas.usda.gov

1400 Independence Avenue, S.W. Washington, DC 20250-1000 Tel: (202) 720-1330
Foreign Agricultural Service, USDA http://www.fas.usda.gov
Agricultural Attaché Reports http://www.fas.usda.gov/scriptsw/AttacheRep/default.asp
USDA office at the American Embassy, Moscow, Russia http://www.eng.usda.ru
Ministry of Agriculture http://www.mcx.ru
Ministry of Economic Development http://www.economy.gov.ru

TRADE REGULATIONS, CUSTOMS AND STANDARDS

IMPORT TARIFFS

Russia continues to maintain a number of barriers with respect to imports, including tariffs and tariff-rate quotas, discriminatory and prohibitive charges and fees, and discriminatory licensing, registration and certification regimes. This situation has become more complicated due to the entry into force on January 1, 2010, of the Customs Union (CU) among Russia, Belarus and Kazakhstan. All issues such as tariffs, tariff rate quotas and licensing and certification are being harmonized, although implementation so far has been uneven. For more detailed information concerning tariffs, please refer to the "Customs Regulations and Contact Information" section below. The following is a selection of tariff ranges for popular U.S. goods entering Russia.

Commodity Rate (%)

HS 02: Meat and edible meat products

(within quota, but not less than .20-.25 Euro/kilo) 15 (beyond quota, but not less than 1-1.5 Euro/kilo) 50-75 HS 0207 (within quota, but not less than .2 Euro/kilo) 25 (beyond quota, but not less than .7 Euro/kilo) 80 HS 24: Tobacco and manufactured tobacco/Unmanufactured tobacco 5-20

-Cigars and Cigarettes but not less than 3 Euro/1000 pcs 30 HS 28: Inorganic Chemicals 5-20 HS 38: Miscellaneous chemical products 5-15 HS 39: Plastics and Articles thereof 5-10

-Finished products 10-20 HS 73: Articles of iron and steel 5-20 HS 84: Nuclear reactors, boilers, machinery 0-20 HS 85: Electric Machinery 0-20 HS 87: Vehicles except railway and tramway 0-35

HS: 8708 Auto parts 0-10 HS 90: Optic, Photo, Medical and Surgical Instruments and devices 0-20 -Medical equipment 0-15

Current information on the harmonized tariffs of the CU can be found in Russian at: http://www.tsouz.ru/

As part of the negotiations for the CU, Russia changed many of its tariffs and tariff lines. While some of these changes remain in accordance with the international obligations of the Russian government to comply with HS codes and Russia's intention to enter the WTO, many do not. The new CU tariff schedule changed rates for over 100 categories of commodities, lowering the tariff ceiling for some categories, but raising them or making permanent previous temporary tariff increases for many others. Notable changes included lowering of import tariffs for pearls, diamonds and other precious stones from 20% to 10-15% and keeping the high "temporary" tariffs on agricultural equipment and off-highway trucks. Certain commodities continue to be regulated through seasonal duties and quotas.

In addition to tariffs, there are two other charges applied to imports: the ubiquitous Value Added Tax (VAT) and selective excise taxes. The universal 18% VAT rate effective January 1, 2004 (with the exception of foodstuffs, pharmaceuticals and medical supplies, for which VAT is 10%) is applied to the import price, tariff, and excise tax combined. There are some exemptions from VAT. For example, resolution No.19 of January 17, 2001, provides a list of vitally essential medical equipment to which no VAT is applied. The excise tax applies to a number of luxury goods, alcohol and cigarettes, and varies from 20% to 570%.

From December 2008 through February 2009, the Russian government announced a series of significant duty increases on cars, harvesters, certain steel products (including pipes, tube and rebar), and certain agricultural products (including butter, milk and soy meal). These duty increases, many of which the government renewed after their initial nine-month period, have now been included in the harmonized CU tariff schedule and will continue to be an obstacle to U.S. exports to Russia.

In 2010, the CU introduced several amendments to its import tariffs. In particular, the CU increased tariffs on polycarbonates, dairy items, tropical oils, plastic items, used and recapped tires, wine material, agricultural machines and some self-propelled wheeled machines, while decreasing tariffs on paper and paperboard, inputs for production of solar modules, wood sheets for veneering, wolfram and cement waste and scrap, wine material in bulk, equipment for ports and leased aircraft.

High import duties on finished vehicles (as much as 30% for new cars and at a prohibitive level for used cars older than five years) have forced companies to set up local assembly plants to get past the tariffs. A Russian regulation on vehicle assembly (known as Decree 166) provides tariff exemptions to foreign automakers that assemble locally, but stipulates that manufacturers must increase the locally sourced content of vehicles to 30% of parts within an agreed six- to seven-year period. As of February 2011, the assembly regulation is being amended to require a local content target of up to 60% of foreign-branded vehicles in order to qualify for tariff exemptions. The duty rates for harvesters were temporarily increased in 2008, by at least 200%, and made permanent in the CU tariff schedule. The duty increases, combined with a restriction on Russian government subsidies for financing of imported agricultural equipment, contributed to a nearly complete cessation of imports into Russia for the major U.S. and EU producers of agriculture equipment. Foreign producers have re-gained some market share, but the restrictions on access to the subsidies continue to limit market potential.

While it initially appeared that the Russian government imposed these measures mainly to protect domestic producers from competing imports during the global economic crisis, their new permanence in the CU tariff schedule indicates that Russia's goal is to focus on developing local industry over foreign producers.

In addition to duty increases, trade investigations conducted by the Russian Ministry of Industry and Trade (MIT) have resulted in additional duties on such products as certain steel products, large diameter pipes, mechanical fasteners, and cutlery and steel pipes. However, all of Russia's current safeguard and antidumping measures are being reviewed by the MIT in view of the CU Agreement of November 19, 2010, on the Application of Safeguard, Antidumping and Countervailing Measures during a Transition Period.

TRADE BARRIERS

In general, U.S. companies face a number of tariff and non-tariff trade barriers when exporting to Russia. A complaint frequently voiced by U.S. companies is Russia's complex system of standardization. As explained in detail in the "Standards" section below, Russia's regime remains extremely complex due to its lack of clarity and transparency, and overall redundancy. While the system has improved somewhat, U.S. companies are encouraged to obtain appropriate legal advice or assistance from experienced distributors or consultants, as well as the U.S. Commercial Service.

Discrimination against foreign providers of non-financial services is, in most cases, not the result of federal law, but stems from abuse of power, sub-national regulations and practices that may violate Russian law. For example, a few foreign service providers have noted that they are forced to pay a range of fees to obtain licenses from local authorities, fees that domestic companies allegedly bypass via bribes.

The 1996 federal law "On Banks and Banking Activity" permits foreign banks to establish subsidiaries in Russia. However, Russia does not allow foreign banks to establish branches in Russia. The 1990 federal law on banking activities, last amended in 2006, specifically states that any quota or limitation on the size of foreign charter capital in the banking sector would require a new law to be put forward by the government of Russia and agreed to by the Central Bank of Russia. In November 2006, Russia and the U.S. signed their WTO Bilateral Agreement, a major step in Russia's accession to the WTO. As part of this Agreement, Russia pledged to allow foreign ownership to account for as much as 70% of the country's total banking sector equity. Implementation of this provision will likely take place only after Russia's accession.

The Central Bank requires newly established banks, whether domestic or foreign subsidiaries, to have a minimum of 180 million rubles ($6 million) in capital. Already existing banks are required to have a minimum capital of 90 million rubles ($3 million). The government of Russia has tentatively approved a plan that has not yet become law for these minimum capital levels to increase in 2012 to 300 million rubles ($10 million) and 180 million rubles ($6 million), respectively. At least 75% of the bank's employees and 50% of the bank's management board must be of Russian nationality if the chairman is not a Russian citizen. Heads of foreign banks' Russian offices are required to be proficient in the Russian language.

In the insurance sector, foreign insurance firms are subject to a 49% equity restriction. Foreign firms that were active in Russia when this requirement came into effect, however, were grandfathered and are not subject to the foreign equity limit. Russia also has more generous operating provisions for insurance companies from the European Union, and has been permitting multinational companies to benefit from this more generous treatment provided they conduct their Russian investments via their EU-based offices. Once Russia becomes a WTO member and the United States grants permanent normal trade relations status,

U.S. insurance companies will be allowed to operate through subsidiaries, including 100% foreign-owned non-life insurance companies, and will be able to open direct branches at the end of a nine-year transition period. However, as in the banking sector, Russia maintains the discretion to limit foreign sourced charter capital in the insurance sector and if the ratio of foreign-sourced to total charter capital in the insurance sector ever exceeds the 50% cap, Russia's regulators will have the discretion to take certain actions specified in Russia's WTO commitments.

Until Russia's accession, EU firms will continue to enjoy an advantage over their counterparts from the United States and elsewhere, since they can offer life and mandatory forms of insurance in Russia directly, without the requirement to work through a majority Russian-owned partner. Russian law currently requires that chief executives and chief accountants of foreign insurers operating in Russia be Russian citizens.

In 2010 the law "On Private Detective and Security Activities" entered into force. The law states that no security company can be owned by a non-Russian entity, including a Russian subsidiary owned by a foreign entity, and includes restrictions on the use of foreign capital in the operation of such firms.

The Russian telecommunications sector is governed by the Law on Communications, dated July 2003 and the law on "Information, Information Technologies and Information Protection," dated July 2006. The latter law's impact on competitive alternative telecommunications operators, many of which enjoy large foreign investment, has been substantial, since these companies now fall under tight government regulation. In particular, regulations on interconnection -- the process by which alternative operators connect their networks to the Russian public telephone network -- place interconnection contracts and fees under the regulatory authority of the Ministry for Communications and Mass Media. Alternative operators fear that these fees will be raised to subsidize network upgrades of government-owned and ministry-controlled local and long distance operators.

The Land Code that was passed in 2001 allows equal treatment of domestic and foreign entities to buy land and buildings, although purchase of agricultural land by foreigners is still prohibited. Foreign entities are restricted from buying land close to federal borders and in areas that the President determines critical to national security. On January 12, 2011, Russia published a presidential decree listing 380 areas around the country, primarily along its borders, in which the sale of land to foreigners or foreign companies is forbidden. A ban on the ownership of real estate by foreigners has been in force in Russia's border areas since 2001, but the geographic scope of the ban had not been definitively established.

The government enacted the Strategic Sectors Law (SSL) in May 2008. The SSL introduced a list of 42 "strategic" sectors in which purchases of "controlling interests" by foreign investors must be pre-approved by the Russian government. The list of restricted sectors includes: enterprises in the nuclear industry or involved in handling radioactive materials; enterprises involved in work on infectious diseases; arms, munitions, and military equipment production, maintenance, or repair; the aviation and space industries; certain data-transmission (radio, television, telecommunications) infrastructure; production and distribution of encryption technologies and equipment; production and sales of goods and providing services under conditions of a "natural monopoly" (e.g., activities such as operating certain gas networks); newspapers with a circulation of more than one million; and natural resource extraction. Many observers, while welcoming more clarity on the rules of the game, have criticized the SSL for being overly broad in the number of sectors it covers, and have raised concerns regarding the transparency of the approval process.

Under the procedures created by the SSL, the Federal Antimonopoly Service conducts initial vetting of proposed foreign investments, and in some cases the Federal Security Service (FSB) conducts additional verification to determine whether the transaction would result in a foreign company gaining control over a strategic business. Once vetting is completed, the Government Commission on Foreign Investment, chaired by the Prime Minister, is charged under the SSL with reviewing proposed transactions and either approving or denying them, or deferring them for additional review. The Commission met eight times through the end of 2010 and declined very few proposed transactions. Many of the applications came from Russian-owned companies based offshore.

In conjunction with the SSL, amendments to the sub-soil legislation were also passed requiring governmental approval for foreign investment in excess of 10% in companies operating a "strategic" deposit, which includes major oil, gas, and other mineral deposits. While foreign oil and gas companies were concerned about the potential application of these provisions, so far implementation has not impeded any investments.

The Russian government may be reconsidering its policy of not entering into any further Production Sharing Agreements (PSAs), designed for energy projects that require high capital expenditures and a long period before profits or significant tax revenues are generated. In a December 2010 speech at the Duma, Energy Minister Shmatko raised the possibility of reintroducing PSA-type agreements, but did not give details or a timeline. The two remaining major PSAs are ExxonMobil-led Sakhalin I and Total-led Kharyaga.

After declining marginally in 2008 for the first time since 2000, oil production rebounded slightly in 2009, and increased by 2.2% in 2010, surpassing 10 million barrels per day. Limited tax breaks for oil production and new output from several major fields, primarily from state-owned Rosneft's giant Vankor field, have helped recent production increases. However, many analysts and oil sector executives continue to predict oil production stagnation and decline without further fundamental reforms to the sector's onerous tax structure. Oil taxes are levied on revenues, instead of on profits, hindering needed large investments in new fields.

Russia's power generation sector is in urgent need of modernization and extension of generation capacity. Further delay in expanding electricity output could result in a drag on industrial growth. Russia's Ministry of Energy estimates that the country must invest $80 billion in the next 10 years to refurbish or replace aging generation assets, and that Russia must build 80 gigawatts of thermal power generation capacity in the next 20 years. According to the Ministry, the average energy efficiency of gas-fired power stations in Russia is only 38%; its goal is to raise that efficiency to 53% by 2030.

In aviation, many of the Russian-flagged carriers have aging fleets and use outmoded avionics and engines. Several are seriously considering significant purchases or wet-leases of foreign aircraft in an attempt to be more competitive with Western airlines.

When purchases do occur however, the effect of tariffs, VAT, and customs handling fees on aircraft is equivalent to a 40% tax, making it virtually impossible for Russian airlines to afford to purchase foreign planes. That said, under the latest Customs Union decision related to aircraft tariffs, passed last fall, exemptions were created to facilitate key purchases for leading airlines. Regulations and tariff levels in this area remain subject to change and potential market entrants should check on current conditions.

New regulations have also been introduced for certain cargo aircraft. Previously, cargo aircraft were subject to general regulations and were not classified into separate categories. Under the new regulations, the customs duty rate applicable to cargo aircraft having a maximum take-off weight in excess of 370,000 kg depends on whether such aircraft have an installed cargo ramp. If a cargo aircraft has a maximum take-off weight in excess of 370,000 kg and an installed cargo ramp, it is subject to 20% customs duty. If such aircraft has no cargo ramp, it is subject to a 0% customs duty.

In January 2011, the Russian government extended the 2010 export tariff on timber into 2011, thus implementing part of Russia's December 2010 commitment with the EU that Russia would not change export duties on timber from the current level of 25% until Russia's WTO accession. Russia has reportedly agreed to lower its export duties on timber to 5%-15%, depending on the type of timber, following Russia's WTO accession. Previously, the Russian authorities had planned to introduce a prohibitive 80% export tariff (but no less than 50 euros per cubic meter), starting in January 1, 2009, and then delayed the increase to January 1, 2011.

The "The Russian Coordinating Center of the National Internet Domain" (the Coordination Center) issued a regulation, "Provisions on Priority Registration of Domain Names in the РФ (RF) Domain" that stipulates that domain names must either reproduce or match word designations contained in trademarks. Trademark owners with a ".RU" (Russia) domain name can keep the ".RU," but now have the option of obtaining a ".РФ" (RF). .РФ domain names may be registered for a fee of approximately $20 for a one-year period, with the possibility of subsequent renewal of the domain name's registration annually. During the priority registration phase more than 18,000 domain names were registered for government entities and trademark holders. Despite the early registration for trademark holders, there is still a potential issue with cyber-squatting. The Coordination Center did not specify that domain names that are derived from the trademark holders would be protected.

On November 11, 2010, the second stage of the registration for Cyrillic domain names began. Now any individual or legal person registered in the Russian Federation may obtain a domain name through the registration process. Priority registration for the Cyrillic domain name zone began November 2009 for government entities and trademark holders. Only Russian citizens and businesses registered in the country are able to buy domains. The Coordination Center for the National Internet Domain registered 184,352 addresses for the general public on the first day of open registration. The .РФ domain has over 500,000 registered addresses.

A law on electronic digital signatures went into effect on January 14, 2002. This law does not follow the Model Law on Electronic Signatures of the U.N. Commission on International Trade Law, but rather defines electronic signatures narrowly, making public-key technology the sole acceptable digital signature technology. It also requires that hardware and software used in digital signature authentication programs be certified in Russia. This requirement gives the Russian government the right to insist on the de-compilation of electronic signature programs.

These requirements, in addition to the licensing requirements related to goods with encryption technology, present serious obstacles to trade in goods that Russia requires for further development of electronic commerce. Currently, any IT product requires a notification from the Russia's Federal Security Service (FSB), which a company should be able to obtain in 10 days. If the product contains low levels of cryptography, the FSB can grant authorization to import. If the product contains higher levels of cryptography, the FSB informs the importer of the need to apply for an import license from the Ministry of Industry and Trade. This permission and licensing process can take six months or longer to complete. Leading U.S. IT companies contend that the current system impedes imports, delays the creation of an innovation and knowledge-based economy in Russia, and hampers the further development of their R&D centers in Russia.

Both Russian and foreign businesses frequently complain about so-called "raiding" ("reiderstvo"), a practice which refers to the criminal takeover of a business through corruptly obtained legal documents. Raids are often carried out by professional raiders, sometimes working in tandem with corrupt officials and former employees or business partners of the victim company. Raids can be difficult to protect against as they rely on legal documents and frequently result in the victim being tied up in litigation for extended periods of time while the assets are transferred through a series of shell companies to an ostensible good faith purchaser. To minimize the risk of such attacks, investors are urged to vet local partners, review all business documents and make sure that documents are properly secured.

As many details regarding the operation and implementation of the Customs Union are still being worked out, there is much confusion in many areas such as import licenses, customs procedures and IPR enforcement. As part of the CU preparations, the GOR is planning to standardize Russia's technical regulations with European ones. These proposed regulations will increase restrictions on trade practices and are likely to have a large impact on U.S. exports to Russia.

IMPORT REQUIREMENTS AND DOCUMENTATION

The CU harmonized tariffs entered into effect on 1 January 2010, and the unified Customs Code took effect on July 1, 2010. These two documents now regulate trade in the integrated customs zone. The CU continues to implement the new regulations governing its structure and tariffs, as well as determining revenue sharing, and organizing logistical procedures for shipments. As a result, U.S. exporters have been facing additional delays, valuation questions, and other issues.

Customs clearance as a general rule should be performed in the jurisdiction of the respective participants in foreign economic operations. Starting January 1, 2010, goods transiting to Russia and/or Kazakhstan from foreign suppliers through Belarus are customs cleared at the CU's external frontier in Belarus. It is also planned that, starting July 1, 2011, goods imported through Kazakhstan should be customs cleared on the Kazakhstan border.

Importers are required to complete a Russian customs freight declaration for every item imported. A declaration must be supported by the following documents: contracts, commercial documents such as commercial invoices and packing lists, transport documents, import licenses (if applicable), certificates of conformity and/or safety (see "Product Standards" below) certificates of origin (if applicable), sanitary certificate (if applicable), import permission and licenses for products containing encryption technology, and documents confirming legitimacy of declarants/brokers/importers.

As for all exports, U.S. exporting firms are required to complete a Shipper's Export Declaration (SED), but this document does not need to be presented to Russian Customs, although they may ask for it. Exporters must present the appropriate export license (see next section), if one had to be obtained, at customs. Customs officials may seek other documentation to substantiate the declared value of any shipment.

In addition, currency control regulations require issuance of a "transaction passport" for both exports and imports to ensure that hard currency earnings are repatriated to Russia. The regulations also ensure that transfers of hard currency payments for imports are for goods actually received and properly valued.

U.S. EXPORT CONTROLS

The U.S. Department of Commerce's Bureau of Industry and Security (BIS) is responsible for implementing and enforcing the Export Administration Regulations (EAR), which regulate the export and re-export of some commercial items, including "production" and "development" technology. The items that BIS regulates are often referred to as "dual use" since they have both commercial and military applications. Please note that even commercial items without an obvious military application may be subject to the EAR and may even require an export license. Items with an Export Control Classification Number (ECCN) that are regulated for Chemical and Biological Weapons (CB), National Security (NS), Missile Technology (MT), Regional Stability (RS) or Crime Control (Column 1 or 2) purposes may require a license from BIS for export to Russia.

Further information on export controls is available at: http://www.bis.doc.gov/licensing/exportingbasics.htm

BIS has developed a list of "red flags," or warning signs, intended to discover possible violations of the EAR. These are posted at: http://www.bis.doc.gov/enforcement/redflags.htm

Also, BIS has "Know Your Customer" guidance at: http://www.bis.doc.gov/Enforcement/knowcust.htm

If there is reason to believe a violation is taking place or has occurred, report it to the Department of Commerce by calling the 24-hour hotline at 1(800) 424-2980, or via the confidential lead page at: https://www.bis.doc.gov/forms/eeleadsntips.html

The EAR does not control all goods, services, and technologies. Other U.S. government agencies regulate more specialized exports. For example, the U.S. Department of State has authority over defense articles and services. A list of other agencies involved in export control can be found on the BIS web site or in Supplement No. 3 to Part 730 of the EAR, which is available on the Government Printing Office Web site at: http://www.access.gpo.gov/bis/ear/ear_data.html .

BIS provides a variety of training sessions to U.S. exporters throughout the year. These sessions range from one to two day seminars and focus on the basics of exporting as well as more advanced topics. A list of upcoming seminars can be found at: https://www.bis.doc.gov/seminarsandtraining/index.htm

For further details about the Bureau of Industry and Security and its programs, please visit the BIS website at: http://www.bis.doc.gov

TEMPORARY ENTRY

Temporary entry of goods is allowed with full or partial relief from customs duties and import VAT for a period of up to two years. Russian Customs issues authorization for temporary entry of goods based on a written application submitted by an importer. The list of goods for temporary entry with full relief from customs duties and taxes as well as terms of such relief is regulated by the Customs Union.

Full conditional relief from customs duties is allowed when it does not affect the Russian economy, such as the temporary import of:

Containers, pallets, and other types of containers and packages for repeated use;

Goods for the purposes of the development of international relations in the scientific, cultural, sports, cinematography and tourism fields;

Products for international assistance;

Commercial samples, not for sale, used at trade shows and exhibitions.

All goods falling outside of this list are subject to partial relief only, as established by the Customs Code. The Customs Code provides for temporary import with a partial exemption from customs duties for 34 months when goods are classified as main production assets on the condition that such goods are not owned by the Russian entities using them in the territory of the Russian Federation. When partial relief from customs duties is applied, 3% of the amount of customs duties and taxes should be paid on a monthly basis for the period when goods are located in the customs territory of the Russian Federation. In practice, however, many U.S. companies bringing in commercial samples have had problems with Russian Customs. Sometimes officials demand that the importer pay a bond to cover any applicable import duties if the goods are sold in Russia. Russian Customs accepts the use of ATA Carnets, which are widely and effectively used.

For further information, please refer to the Customs Union Website: www.tsouz.ru or Russian Federal Customs Service Website: http://www.customs.ru/en , or http://www.tks.ru .

Labeling and Marking Requirements Labels on food items must feature the following information in the Russian language:

Type and name of the product;

Legal address of the producer (may be given in Latin letters);

Weight/volume of the product (if item is preserved in liquid, weight without liquid mass);

Food contents (name of basic ingredients/additives listed by weight in decreasing order);

Nutritional value (calories, vitamins if their content is significant or if product is intended for children, for medical, or for dietary use);

Conditions of storage;

Expiration date (or production date and period of storage);

Directions for preparation of semi-finished goods or children's foodstuffs;

Warning information with regard to any restrictions and side effects;

Terms and conditions of use.

Labels on nonfood items must include:

Name of the product;

Country of origin and name of manufacturer (may be given in Latin letters);

Usage instructions;

Main characteristics, rules and conditions for effective and safe use of product;

Any other information determined by the state regulation body.

It is advisable to place the Rostest mark on the label for products that have appropriate Rostest and sanitary- epidemiological certificates. This rule is applicable to both food and nonfood items.

Prohibited and Restricted Imports

The import and export of goods in Russia is carried out in accordance with the Federal Law on "Government Regulation of International Trade Activities" of 2003, which stipulates the application of quotas, licenses and other temporary restrictions on such operations.

Import licenses are issued by the Russian Ministry of Industry and Trade or its regional branches, and controlled by the Federal Customs Service. Licenses for sporting weapons and self-defense articles are issued by the Interior Ministry. Licenses are required for many other items as well including:

Alloys
Carpets
Color televisions (14, 21, and 25-inch)
Combat and sporting weapons
Ethyl alcohol
Explosives
Medicine, also used for veterinary purposes
Military and ciphering equipment
Precious metals
Radioactive materials and waste
Self-defense articles
Stones
Strong poisons and narcotics
Tobacco products
Vodka and many other types of alcoholic beverages
Poultry meat
Cattle meat, chilled and frozen
Pork
Technical means purposed for receiving non-disclosed information
O-zone damaging substances
Chemicals used for plant's protection
Sturgeon fish species, including caviar
Crayfish
Wild animals, wild plants, ivory, and corals
Valuable wood species
Cultural valuables

To learn whether an import license is needed for a particular product, contact the Russian Ministry of Industry and Trade licensing department (www.minpromtorg.gov.ru).

Customs Regulations and Contact Information

As a member of the World Customs Organization, the Convention of Temporary Imports and the International Convention on Harmonized Commodity Description and Coding System, Russia is obligated to adhere to internationally accepted customs regulations and practices. In January 2004, Russia implemented a new Customs Code as part of its WTO accession efforts. The new code reduced the time for customs clearance from ten to three days. It also offered advance declaration of cargo before arrival at customs. Other important changes introduced by the Code included:

Restricting the Russian Federation State Customs Committee from issuing contradictory additional regulatory acts;

Making possible the settlement of disputes with customs authorities directly in a court of law;

Establishing a definitive and comprehensive list of documents that must be submitted for customs clearance;

Prohibiting customs authorities from refusing to accept a declaration containing inaccuracies, if the inaccurate information has no impact on the defrayal of customs payments, or does not place restrictions in foreign trade;

Allowing clearance of goods through any customs office;

Providing urgent customs clearance for perishable goods, express cargoes, or time-sensitive materials for the mass media.

In 2010, Russia's existing Customs Code was replaced by the unified Customs Code of the Customs Union and the Law on Customs Regulation, which took effect as of July 1 and December 2010, respectively. The

Law on Customs Regulation, in particular, contains the "ex-officio amendment," a key part of Russia's commitments under the 2006 U.S.-Russia Bilateral Agreement on IPR.

Recently, the priorities for customs modernization included improvement in regulations, implementation of IT systems and enhanced dialogue with market participants. There is also a clearer understanding of the continued need for customs to take effective action against significant levels of grey market practices and to implement effective control coordinated on a global scale. However, many examples of arbitrary practices by local customs officials still exist and are encouraged by ambiguities in customs legislation. Small and medium-sized enterprises remain most vulnerable to these arbitrary practices.

CUSTOMS VALUATION

The customs value is generally considered to be the CIF (cost-insurance-freight) price of the imported goods. A customs-processing fee is also levied. If customs officials do not agree with the customs value of goods declared they are authorized to request additional documents that support the declared customs value. It is often normal practice for customs officials to request the Shippers Export Declaration (SED), which they consider to be proof of the customs value. However, presenting SED is not mandatory and the importer can present other available documents, including an official company letter that attests to the shipment's correct value. Since 2008, Russian Customs has been particularly zealous in its efforts to determine the highest possible value for imported goods. In fact, it has recently highlighted its role in "revenue generation," whose income comprises about 50% of Russia's state budget.

For further information, please refer to the Russian Federal Customs Service Website: http://www.customs.ru/en

STANDARDS

Despite positive changes in the last several years, the standards regime in Russia still lacks transparency. Russia continues to rely on product testing as a key element of the product approval process. Other types of product safety assurance, such as plant auditing, quality systems, and post market vigilance, are underdeveloped. Russia continues to adhere to redundant practices of further testing of internationally accepted certified products, which can delay entry of a variety of products into the country.

In addition, the former federal authority on standardization, Gosstandart, has been restructured twice as part of a larger government reorganization begun in May 2004, which led to some uncertainty as to exactly who in the agency did what, further adding to delays in discharging its functions. The current government authority for standardization, metrology and certification matters is the Federal Agency for Technical Regulations and Metrology (whose abbreviated name is Rosstandart) an agency of the Ministry of Industry and Trade. Until June 2010, the abbreviated name was Rostekhregulirovanie, but it was then changed to Rosstandart because it is very close to the former abbreviation Gosstandart that was widely used in Soviet times. Affiliated with this new agency are 485 technical committees, comprised of research institutes, which develop standards.

Standards Organizations

The following are the key government standards organizations in Russia.
Federal Agency for Technical Regulations and Metrology (Rosstandart)
9, Leninsky Prospect Moscow, 119991 Tel: 7 (499) 236-03-00 Fax: 7 (499) 236-62-31 E-mail: stand@gost.ru http:// www.gost.ru /

Federal Service for Control over Healthcare and Social Development (Roszdravnadzor) issues special regulatory approval documents for pharmaceutical products and medical devices) Slavyanskaya sq. 4, building 1 Moscow, 109074 Tel.: 7 (495) 698-45-38 E-mail: info@rosdravnadzor.ru http://www.roszdravnadzor.ru

Federal Service for Supervision of Consumers Protection and Welfare (Rospotrebnadzor) Vadkovskiy pereulok, house 18, stroenie 5 and 7 Moscow, 127994 Tel.: 7 (499) 973-26-90 E-mail: depart@gsen.ru http://www.rospotrebnadzor.ru/

Federal Service for Ecological, Technological and Nuclear Surveillance (Rostechnadzor) ul. Luykyanova, house 4, korpus 8 Moscow, 105066 Tel.: 7 (495) 411-60-20 Fax: 7 (495) 411-60-52 E-mail: rostehnadzor@gosnadzor.ru http://www.gosnadzor.ru/

Federal Agency of Svyaz (Rossvyaz) Ministry of Communications and Mass Media 7 Tverskaya Street Moscow, 125375 Mr. Vitaliy Kreindelin Head of Conformity Department Tel: 7(495) 771-85-59 Fax: 7(495) 771-87-10 E-mail: office@minsvyaz.ru http://www.rossvyaz.ru

VNIIS (Research Institute for Certification) 3/10, Elektrichesky Pereulok, Building 1 Moscow,123557 Phone: 7 (499) 253-70-06 Fax: 7 (499) 253-33-60 E-mail: vniis@vniis.ru http://www.vniis.ru

NIST Notify U.S. Service

Member countries of the World Trade Organization (WTO) are required under the Agreement on Technical Barriers to Trade (TBT Agreement) to report to the WTO all proposed technical regulations that could affect trade with other Member countries. Notify U.S. is a free, web-based e-mail subscription service that offers an opportunity to review and comment on proposed foreign technical regulations that can affect your access to international markets. Register online at Internet URL: http://www.nist.gov/notifyus/

Conformity Assessment

In recent years there has been a substantial movement toward the adoption of common international language on product standards and certification procedures, and some improvements have been made. In 1998, the Russian government established a public information service for regulations covered by the Technical Barriers to Trade (TBT) Agreement in the WTO; however, technical difficulties have plagued this service and it has not been an easily accessible or reliable source of information. On July 31, 1998, amendments to Federal Law No. 5151-1 "On Certification of Products and Services" (enacted on June 10, 1993) went into effect, which generally meet requirements of the TBT Agreement. The law allows a manufacturer to submit a declaration of conformity in the certification procedure for a limited number of products. The government has established a list of 200 products eligible for this procedure, which periodically changes.

Federal Law No. 184-FZ "On Technical Regulations" of December 27, 2002, was intended to change the existing cumbersome standardization and certification systems and harmonize Russian legislation with international standards by transitioning from a mandatory certification system to a modern system based on self-declaration. To that end, the government approved three consecutive programs aimed at developing 400 technical regulations that should be used instead of the old GOST standards. Only 24 technical regulations were developed, however, which are in operation today. One of the reasons cited for the delay of this reform is the complicated system of approval. Also, a number of government bodies resisted the creation of these technical regulations because they wanted to return to the old system where they controlled these regulations. One of the main supporters of the old system was Rosstandart, formerly Gosstandart.

To move this reform process along, in December 2009 amendments to Federal Law No. 184-FZ were approved. According to these amendments, a special government body would use a much simpler process of approving technical regulations. Many experts assumed that Rosstandart would become that government body, but on January 20, 2010, President Medvedev announced that the functions in this area will be divided between the Ministry of Industry and Trade and Rosstandart, which is, in fact, under the Ministry's jurisdiction. Currently the program of development of 70 technical regulations (of which 47 are in conjunction with the CU) is being executed. In addition the priority of the CU over national technical regulations is being discussed.

Product Certification

As the result of the establishment of the Custom's Union among Russia, Kazahstan and Belarus, the system of certification has changed. Now there are two sets of documents dedicated to Technical Regulations and Sanitary Regulations.

Technical Regulations (Certificate of Conformity/Declaration of Conformity)

As of July 1, 2010, new rules for conformity assessment, established in the CU, came into effect. As the result, manufactures can obtain certificates of conformity and declaration of conformity according to these new rules, and unified letterhead for all three countries is used. The full set of the documents, including the unified list of accredited bodies and laboratories that governs this process, is published on the CU website (www.tsouz.ru). A "Unified list of products" was also established and according to this list, those products included need to have certificates of conformity/declarations of conformity. If a product is not included, then it should go through the conformity process according to the national standards of Russia, Kazahstan, or Belarus. Until January 1, 2012, manufactures may choose to obtain these documents according to the national standards of Russia, Belarus or Kazahstan or according to the Unified standards of the CU. In the manufacturer chooses the first option, its products can only be sold in the territory of the country where the documents were obtained. After January 1, 2012, certificates of conformity/declaration of conformity can only be obtained according to the Unified standards of the CU.

Sanitary Regulation (Certificate of State Registration)

State registration is one of the forms of conformity assessment, so it can be concluded that the Certificate of State Registration is the same document of conformity, as the conformity certificate and declaration of conformity. On July 1, 2010, the sanitary certificate was abolished due to the fact that no such provisions exist in the CU document. Products which need a Certificate of State Registration are listed in part II of the "Unified list" that was approved by the CU Commission on May 28, 2010, No. 299 (last edition No. 456 dated November, 11, 2010). Starting January 1, 2011, only Certificates of State Registration, according to the CU principles are being issued.

A number of other mandatory and voluntary certification systems also exist, which are partly managed by other ministries or agencies. Below are the most widely used certificates:

Fire Safety Certificate: The Federal Law No. 123-FZ "Technical Regulations of Requirement for Fire Safety," which came into effect on May 1, 2009, now governs this process. Products requiring this certificate are listed in Government Decree No. 241 dated March 3, 2009.

Certificate of Conformity/Declaration of Conformity for Systems of Communications

(system of certification in the area of communication) confirms that the equipment conforms to technical requirements. It is issued by accredited bodies and laboratories of Rossvyaz, with an updated list published on its website. Rossvyaz obtained this function due to Government Decree No. 320 dated June 30, 2004. The list of communication devices which require a certificate of conformity can be found in Government Decree No. 532 dated June 25, 2005.

License (permission) from Rostekhnadzor allows the manufacture, installation and use of industrial machinery and equipment for the petrochemical, metallurgical and other industrial facilities in Russia. The process and list of products requiring this certificate are listed in Rostekhnadzor's Order No. 112 dated February 29, 2008.

Approval for Encrypted Products is issued by the Federal Security Service (FSB), while an import license is issued by the Ministry of Industry and Trade.

Russia participates in the following international certification systems:

System of the International Electrotechnical Commission (IEC) for tests of electrical, electronic and related equipment on conformity to safety standards (http://www.iec.ch; http://www.iecq.org)

System of certification of passenger cars, trucks, buses and other transport vehicles (http://www.unece.org)

System of certification of handguns and ammunition (http://www.com-i-p.com) OIML Certificate System of Measuring Instruments (http://www.oimi.org)

Russia's complicated, cumbersome and often changing system of certification as well as cultural and language barriers are a challenge for foreign companies attempting to certify products without appropriate legal advice or assistance from experienced distributors or consultants. In order to minimize time and expenses, it is recommended that U.S. companies work with reliable partners and consulting companies on registration and certification issues. For additional information regarding certification, please contact the

U.S. Commercial Service.

Certification Service Providers (this list is not exhaustive and is not to be construed as an endorsement of the companies listed below).

Russia

Rostest Moscow (various products)

Russian Center for Tests and Certification 31 Nakhimovsky Prospect, Moscow, 117418 Phone: 7 (495) 544-00-00 E-mail: info@rostest.ru http://www.rostest.ru /

Consult Business Group (Medinform Ltd., Pharminform Ltd.) (pharmaceutical products including biological active supplements, medical equipment and cosmetics)

Butyrksaya ul, 77, Business Center “Diagonal House”, 8 floor Moscow, 127015 Tel.: 7 (495) 797-49-63 E-mail: info@c-b-g.ru http://www.c-b-g.ru/about

Eurotest

4 Krutitskiy pereulok, house 14 Moscow, 109044 Tel. 7 (495) 660-52-28 E-mail: eurotest@eurotest.ru http://www.eurotest.ru

United States

Velosi Group (Oil & gas, petrochemical and refining industries) http://www.velosi.com

Nemko http://www.nemko.com

Russian Standard, Russian Certification Center (almost all areas, except aviation equipment and aviation instruments, military products, telecommunication equipment) http://www.rosstandard.com

TUV America Inc. http://tvuamerica.com

TUV Rheinland http://www.tuv.com

Underwriters Laboratories (UL) http://www.ul.com

Accreditation

Presently in Russia, various federal executive authorities carry out accreditation in accordance with the relevant legislation. There are 16 government agencies that were in charge of accrediatitation, including Rosstandart, Rostechnadzor, Rospotrebnadzor, Rossvyaz. Bureaucratic incongruities, overlapping fields of activity and the application of different procedures and criteria in the accreditation process are common occurrences. Often, the accreditation and certification activities of several federal executive authorities overlap.

Certification authorities and test laboratories, both Russian and foreign, are accredited in accordance with the following documents: GOST-R ISO/IEC 65-2000, GOST-R ISO/IEC 17021-2008, GOST-R ISO/IEC 17025-2006, GOST-R 51000.4-2008, GOST-R 51000.62008.

Currently, each individual Ministry, Rosstandart and the Research Institute for Certification (VNIIS) can accredit laboratories in their relevant industry sectors. Rosstandart runs the state registry of all accredited organizations.

Government Decree No. 163 “About Accreditation of Organizations that Assess Compliance with Technical Regulations” dated February 24, 2009, is published on Rosstandart’s website. In addition, Rosstandart prepared comments on this decree that are also published on its website.

In the near future a new "approval" agency – Federal Accreditation Agency will be established. Now the main goal of this agency is to put the whole certification system in order. President Medvedev signed Presidential Decree No 86 on January 24, 2011, "On Unified National System of Accreditation". This Agency will report to the Ministry of Economic Development and will be responsible for the establishment of the Unified National System of Accreditation. But most importantly, it will control all legal entities and entrepreneurs, who are accredited as testing laboratories, and issue certificates to organizations. It is expected that a number of new private companies and entrepreneurs will enter this market and, as a result of competition, prices in this sector will decrease, which will in turn drive down the consumer prices. It is expected that the certificates will be recognized by other countries, so companies will not have to go through both a national and international certification process.

The Federal Accreditation Agency should receive all its functions and be fully operational by January 1, 2012.

Publication of Technical Regulations

Proposed technical regulations are published (in Russian) on the Rosstandart website (http://www.gost.ru) for two months. Any Russian or foreign entity may comment in Russian to the contact listed on the website. Draft and final documents are published in the monthly "Vestnik of Technicheskogo Regulirovania" ("Journal of Technical Regulations"). This journal is an official publication of Rosstandart for its official documents, instructions, rules, and decrees. "Vestnik of Technicheskogo Regulirovania" is the country's effort to ensure transparency in the development of national standards required for WTO compliance. WTO membership presumes that all changes in the standardization system will be transparent, thereby avoiding hidden obstacles (non-tariff barriers) in trading relations with WTO partners.

Another publication that can be found on Rosstandart's website is "Mir Standartov" ("World of Standards").

Labeling and Marking

Please see the "Labeling and Marking" section above.

Contacts
U.S. Commercial Service - Moscow
8 Bolshoy Deviatinsky pereulok Moscow 121099, Russia Tel: 7 (495) 728-5580 Fax: 7 (495) 728-5585 E-mail: Moscow.Office.Box@mail.doc.gov

TRADE AGREEMENTS

Russia currently participates in a free trade agreement with the Commonwealth of Independent States and the Customs Union with Belarus and Kazakhstan. Russia also has an association agreement with the European Union and has historically received NTR and GSP status from the United States.

Web Resources

Bureau of Industry & Security, U.S. Department of Commerce

Main site: www.bis.doc.gov Export Controls: www.bis.doc.gov/licensing/exportingbasics.htm Possible Violations: www.bis.doc.gov/enforcement/redflags.htm Forms: https://www.bis.doc.gov/forms/eeleadsntips.html

Russian Federal Customs Service: www.customs.ru/en

Russian Ministry for Economic Development: http://www.economy.gov.ru

Russian Ministry of Industry and Trade: http://www.minprom.gov.ru/eng

TRADE AND PROJECT FINANCING

METHODS OF PAYMENT

Payment methods and terms vary depending upon the U.S. company's business model and relationship with its Russian trading partner. For new-to-market companies, requesting advance payment for goods and services from a Russian customer may be a prudent course to follow until both parties establish a positive record of payment. Once a U.S. firm has established a strong relationship with a Russian trading partner, it may consider extending short- and eventually longer term credit as a way to bolster sales volume. This should be done with caution and only after careful evaluation and establishment of successful payments.

For some large transactions, advance payment from a Russian buyer may be impractical. In such cases, financing may be provided by a bank, export credit agency or venture fund. Exporters' risk can be minimized with a bank or insurance guarantee from a Russian bank that would be acceptable to a U.S. bank. In leasing deals, exporters should insist on an upfront payment of three to fourth months upon delivery as a way to mitigate some of the risk.

Leasing has become increasingly attractive to both lessees and lessors because of its economic effectiveness, flexibility and accessibility in comparison to bank finance. Most large Russian banks have leasing programs that they can offer their clients in such cases, and there is a growing list of foreign leasing companies operating in Russia that can offer Russian clients leasing terms for imported equipment. Aviation, energy, mining, construction, transportation, pharmaceutical, forestry and fishing industries equipment which may be too expensive for Russian customers to purchase, are often leased.

HOW DOES THE BANKING SYSTEM OPERATE

Despite improvement over the last several years, the Russian banking system is still evolving in terms of being able to meet the capital and credit needs of a rapidly growing and dynamic market economy. However, while the banking services available from Russian banks is still limited compared to what is available in the U.S., a company doing business in Russia can access an expanding range of basic services offered by a larger commercial bank.

The Russian banking sector is highly segmented, with the top five banks controlling 48% of assets. There are over 1000 banks in Russia; 80 are 100% foreign-owned. The number of small banks is gradually decreasing due to insolvency and consolidation. The top two banks, Sberbank (controlled by the Central Bank) and VTB (controlled by the government), together own about one-third of the banking sector assets in Russia. The Russian government has approved a list of 11 state-controlled companies whose stakes are to be privatized in 2011-2013, which includes Sberbank and VTB. This mass privatization began with the sale of a 10% stake in VTB for $3.3 billion in February 2011.

FOREIGN-EXCHANGE CONTROLS

Currency control legislation has been liberalized considerably in the last few years. For payments related to the import of goods, there are no significant restrictions. However, the bank of the Russian importer is obliged to ensure compliance of payments with the currency regulations. Therefore, the Russian importer and its bank set up a "transaction passport" for each contract. The foreign exporter is not directly involved, but may be affected due to the need for the Russian importer to obtain documents and information from the exporter.

U.S. BANKS AND LOCAL CORRESPONDENT BANKS

Most foreign businesses prefer to deal with foreign-owned banks, as they are more stable, more experienced and generally offer higher levels of service. Until recently, these banks concentrated their activity in highly profitable financial markets and were not interested in commercial banking. However, demand led them to diversify their services to include foreign trade transactions and commercial banking. Many foreign banks now provide regular commercial services, including accounts, transfers, currency exchange, credit, documentary operations, letters of credit and trade financing. Some of these banks will establish individual accounts for non-residents and employees of their institutional clientele.

Unfortunately, the lack of nationwide branches makes these services largely unavailable to customers operating outside the major metropolitan centers of Moscow and St. Petersburg. U.S. banks have increased their share of the Russian banking market. Citibank has been present in the Russian market for many years, but has recently increased its presence via aggressive expansion into retail banking. GE Money Bank has also made inroads in the sector.

State-Owned Banks

Two state-controlled banks, Sberbank and Vneshtorgbank (VTB), continue to dominate the corporate and retail banking sectors in Russia. The state also controls a number of smaller banks. The Russian government has repeatedly urged Russia's state-controlled banks to modernize in order to play a more active role in the economy. These public criticisms aside, state banks have been the primary beneficiaries of the government's efforts to supply short- and long-term liquidity to the economy to mitigate the economic crisis.

Russian Private Commercial Banks

Other viable Russian banks include emerging service-oriented banks and large banks owned by financial-industrial groups. They are competitive and likely to remain customer oriented and to find creative solutions to Russia's business complexities. A potential weakness is their limited capacity to provide services comparable to those of large international banks. Furthermore, they lack nationwide coverage.

Russia's 10 largest commercial banks are:

Sberbank
VTB
Gazprombank
Rosselkhozbank
Bank of Moscow
Alfa-Bank
UniCredit Bank
ZAO Raiffeisen Bank
VTB24
Rosbank

EXPORT FINANCING

The Export-Import Bank of the United States (Ex-Im Bank) is the official export credit agency of the Unites States. Ex-Im Bank's mission is to assist in financing the export of

U.S. goods and services to international markets.

Ex-Im Bank offers guarantees and direct loans to finance the construction and operation of projects through structured finance transactions, including limited recourse project finance in which project cash flows are used for repayment of the financing.

Since Ex-Im Bank began lending to support U.S. exports in Russia, total authorizations have been US $5.0 billion (total exposure in Russia as of FY'10 is $439 million). Today, Ex-Im Bank's outstanding portfolio in Russia includes transactions in such sectors as oil & gas, agriculture, transportation, and financial services. In fiscal year 2010 (from October 2009 to September 2010), Ex-Im Bank authorized approximately $96 million worth of exports to Russia, up 35% over the same period last year.

As of fiscal year 2010, the Bank reported a second consecutive record-breaking year of $24.5 billion in export financing, up 70% from FY 2008. These transactions supported $34.4 billion worth of American exports and an estimated 227,000 American jobs.

For additional information on the U.S. Ex-Im Bank's financing options and its projects in Russia, please contact the Bank directly.

Brian Sant Angelo Global Business Development Export-Import Bank of the United States Phone: (202) 565-3484 Fax: (202) 565-3677 The European Bank for Reconstruction and Development (EBRD), whose largest shareholder is the US Government, offers a full range of financial services to US investors in Russia. Using its AAA credit rating, the EBRD can provide debt, equity, quasi-equity, syndications, and trade finance in both local and foreign currency at competitive commercial rates and with longer tenors than is usually supplied by commercial lenders. The EBRD's lending priorities are for private sector-led investment, but sovereign lending is also a feature of the bank, particularly for water, transport and energy needs at the municipal level. For sovereign loans, the EBRD requires open, competitive tenders that can offer an opportunity to supply US goods and services."

Web Resources Export-Import Bank of the United States: http://www.exim.gov Oveseas Private Investment Corporation: http://www.opic.gov

U.S.Trade and Development Agency: http://www.tda.gov SBA's Office of International Trade: http://www.sba.gov/oit USDA Commodity Credit Corporation: http://www.fsa.usda.gov/ccc/default.htm

U.S.Agency for International Development: http://www.usaid.gov European Bank for Reconstruction and Development:

http://www.ebrd.com/pages/country/russia.shtml

BUSINESS TRAVEL

BUSINESS CUSTOMS

The Russian market is extremely competitive. Salesmanship is a key factor and U.S. firms should be prepared to describe the competitive advantages and factors that distinguish them in the marketplace.

Establishing a personal relationship with business partners is a critical factor in the successful negotiation of major projects, government procurement or in developing long-term business relationships. Scheduling meetings with potential Russian business partners can be challenging. It may take weeks to get a response to an email, fax or a telephone request for a meeting. Once contact has been established, patience may still be required to confirm a date and time to meet. U.S. business visitors to Moscow or St. Petersburg are advised to factor traffic into scheduling.

Russian language ability is a must and an interpreter should be hired if necessary. An increasing number of Russian businesspeople speak a courtesy level of English; however, many prefer to conduct business discussions in Russian. The U.S. Commercial Service can arrange for the services of qualified interpreters.

Business cards are important and are exchanged freely. Cards should have regular contact information and an email address and website if available. Most foreign businesspeople in Russia carry bilingual English/Russian business cards (one side English, the other Russian).

Promotional materials in Russian are an important tool for creating interest in a company's products in the Russian market. It is very important that the translation be accurate and of high quality. Many companies interested in the Russian market have used on-line translation services for translation of their promotional material, only to learn that the translation was inferior and did not serve the intended purpose. For the best results, it is highly recommended that professional translation services be used. The Commercial Service can recommend fully qualified translators upon request.

TRAVEL ADVISORY

Travel Warnings are issued when the State Department recommends that Americans avoid a certain country, and issues travel advisories when warranted by local conditions. If you are traveling to Russia, please check travel.state.gov before your departure for updated information, and be sure to register your travel through the State Department at https://travelregistration.state.gov/ibrs/ui/.

At this writing, the Department of State's Consular Information Sheet for Russia contains the following information on Safety and Security for U.S. citizens in the Russian Federation:

"Given continued civil and political unrest throughout much of the Caucasus region, the Department of State continues to warn U.S. citizens against travel to Chechnya and all areas that border it: North Ossetia, Ingushetia, Dagestan, Stavropol, Karachayevo-Cherkessiya, and Kabardino-Balkariya. The U.S. government's ability to assist Americans who travel to the northern Caucasus is extremely limited. Throughout the region, local criminal gangs have kidnapped foreigners, including Americans, for ransom. U.S. citizens have disappeared in Chechnya and remain missing. Close contacts with the local population do not guarantee safety. There have been several kidnappings of foreigners and Russians working for media and non-governmental organizations in the region. Because of ongoing security concerns, U.S. government travel to the area is very limited. American citizens residing in these areas should depart immediately as the safety of Americans and other foreigners cannot be effectively guaranteed.

Occasional acts of terrorism, including bombings and hostage taking, have occurred in Russia over the last several years. Bombings have occurred at Russian government buildings, hotels, tourist sites, markets, entertainment venues, schools, residential complexes, and on public transportation including an airport, subways, buses, trains, and scheduled commercial flights.

There is no current indication that American institutions or citizens are targets, but there is a general risk of American citizens being victims of indiscriminate terrorist attacks. American citizens in Russia should be aware of their personal surroundings and follow good security practices. Americans are urged to remain vigilant and exercise good judgment and discretion when using any form of public transportation. When traveling, Americans may wish to provide a friend, family member, or coworker a copy of their itinerary. Americans should avoid large crowds and public gatherings that lack enhanced security measures. Travelers should also exercise a high degree of caution and remain alert when patronizing restaurants, casinos, nightclubs, bars, theaters, etc., especially during peak hours of business.

American citizens living in Russia or traveling there for even a few days are strongly urged to register with the U.S. Embassy or nearest Consulate General. Registration will allow the embassy to provide direct information on the security situation as necessary. Registration can be done on-line (https://travelregistration.state.gov/ibrs/ui/) and can be done in advance of travel.

For the latest security information, Americans traveling abroad should regularly monitor the Department of State, Bureau of Consular Affairs' website at http://travel.state.gov, where the current Travel Warnings and Travel Alerts, as well as the Worldwide Caution, can be found.

Up-to-date information on safety and security can also be obtained by calling 1-888-4074747 toll free in the U.S. and Canada, or for callers outside the United States and Canada, a regular toll-line at 1-202-501-4444. These numbers are available from 8:00 a.m. to 8:00 p.m. Eastern Time, Monday through Friday (except U.S. federal holidays).

The Department of State urges American citizens to take responsibility for their own personal security while traveling overseas. For general information about appropriate measures travelers can take to protect themselves in an overseas environment, see the Department of State's pamphlet A Safe Trip Abroad." This information is updated regularly. Always check http://travel.state.gov prior to travel.

TRAVEL TIPS

Hotels: While world-class tourist and business facilities exist in Moscow and St. Petersburg, they are under-developed in much of Russia, and many goods and services taken for granted in other countries are not yet available. Moscow, St. Petersburg, Novgorod, Nizhniy Novgorod, Nizhnevartovsk, Perm, Samara, Yekaterinburg, Perm, Sochi, Yuzhno Sakhalinsk and Vladivostok, among other cities, have Western-style hotels, though often priced at a premium compared with other major cities of the world. Outside major cities, traditional Russian hotels offer modest accommodations at modest rates. Some regional hotels raise rates for foreign guests. It is possible to find well-appointed hotels in some small towns; it is equally possible to be temporarily without water or electricity when visiting some regions of Russia.

Clothing: Russian businessmen and women predominately wear business suits. For women, dresses, skirts or pants are acceptable. Winters can be extremely cold in Russia with occasional temperatures in the minus-20 Fahrenheit range in northern and Siberian cities; Moscow and St. Petersburg can be quite cold as well, with temperatures in the teens F. not uncommon. Winter clothes may be needed as early as October or as late as April. During the winter months people dress for warmth. Travelers are advised to bring boots or other protective footwear, as streets and sidewalks in winter are frequently slushy or icy. Summers, while brief, can be surprisingly hot, and air conditioning is still rare outside big-city hotels and offices.

Food: A meal in a hotel or top restaurant in Moscow and St. Petersburg can be very expensive by U.S. standards. Nevertheless, in these cities there is an increasing variety of less expensive restaurants, including pizza, and fast food establishments. Russian food can be bland to American tastes, while many visitors find Caucasian, Georgian and Uzbek cuisines to be interesting contrasts. Regardless of the city or hotel, bottled water served with no ice is recommended.

Money: Russia is a predominately cash economy with the Russian ruble as the only legal tender for local transactions. It is illegal to pay for goods and services in U.S. dollars or other foreign currency. Old, worn, or marked bills are often not accepted at banks and exchanges. In Moscow and St. Petersburg, currency exchange offices are available in most shopping areas and provide reliable service. Credit cards are now accepted at many modern businesses in Moscow and St. Petersburg, and at some hotels and restaurants in larger regional cities, but frequently only in major stores. Traveler checks are not widely accepted in Russia. Travelers to regional cities or towns are advised to carry enough cash to cover foreseeable expenses. Major hotels and the American Express offices in Moscow and St. Petersburg may be able to suggest locations for cashing traveler's checks or obtaining cash advances on credit cards. Rubles (and dollars, if needed) may be obtained from bank ATMs that are connected to the PLUS and CIRRUS systems using U.S. debit/credit cards. It is not recommended to use credit/debit cards for small purchases or in standalone ATMs (those not physically located at a bank). ATMs are common in the larger cities, although there have been some instances of theft from card numbers used in these systems. Western Union has many agents in Moscow, and other cities in Russia, which disburse money wired from the United States.

Mail Services: The following companies, with offices in Moscow, offer priority mail services between the United States and Russia:

DHL
Federal Express
Pony Express
TNT
UPS

PERSONAL SECURITY

Incidents of unprovoked, violent harassment against racial and ethnic minorities regularly occur throughout the Russian Federation. The U.S. Embassy and Consulates General continue to receive reports of American citizens, often members of minority groups, having been victimized in violent attacks by "skinheads" or other extremists. Travelers are urged to exercise caution in areas frequented by such individuals and wherever large crowds have gathered. Americans most at risk are those of African, South Asian or East Asian descent, or those who, because of their complexion, are perceived to be from the Caucasus region or the Middle East. These Americans are also at risk of harassment by police authorities.

Visitors to Russia need to be alert to their surroundings. In large cities, they need to take the same precautions against assault, robbery, or pickpockets that they would take in any large U.S. city:

keep billfolds in inner front pockets,

carry purses tucked securely under arms,

wear the shoulder strap of cameras or bags across the chest,

walk away from the curb and carry purses and other bags away from the street.

The most vulnerable areas include underground walkways and the subway, overnight trains, train stations, airports, markets, tourist attractions, and restaurants.

Groups of children and adolescents have been aggressive in some cities, swarming victims, or assaulting and knocking them down. They frequently target persons who are perceived as vulnerable, especially elderly tourists or persons traveling alone. Some victims report that the attackers use knives. Persons carrying valuables in backpacks, in back pockets of pants and in coat pockets are especially vulnerable to pickpockets. Recently, groups of older teen males have also swarmed Metro passengers and forcibly stolen personal belongings.

Foreigners who have been drinking alcohol are especially vulnerable to assault and robbery in or around nightclubs or bars, or on their way home. Some travelers have been drugged at bars, while others have taken strangers back to their lodgings, where they were drugged, robbed and/or assaulted. The Russian media report that the drug GHB is reportedly gaining popularity in local nightclubs, under the names butyrate or oxybutyrate. This drug can also cause amnesia, loss of consciousness, extreme intoxication when mixed with alcohol, and death. The drug, typically a capful of liquid mixed with a beverage, gained notoriety in the United States after incidents of date rape and death.

In many cases, stolen credit cards are used immediately. Victims of credit card or ATM card theft should report the theft to the credit card company or issuing bank immediately. Travelers are advised to be vigilant in bus and train stations and on public transport. Travelers have generally found it safer to travel in groups organized by reputable tour agencies. Visitors are strongly discouraged from using unmarked, "gypsy" taxis. Passengers have been victims of robbery, kidnapping, extortion and theft. Criminals using these taxis to rob passengers often wait outside bars or restaurants to find passengers who have been drinking and therefore more susceptible to robbery. Robberies may also occur in taxis shared with strangers. Although there are few registered taxi services in Russia, travelers should always use authorized services when arriving at major airports.

A common street scam in Russia is the "turkey drop" in which an individual "accidentally" drops money on the ground in front of an intended victim, while an accomplice either waits for the money to be picked up, or picks up the money him/herself and offers to split it with the pedestrian. The individual who dropped the currency then returns, aggressively accusing both of stealing the money. This confrontation generally results in the pedestrian's money being stolen. Avoidance is the best defense. Do not get trapped into picking up the money, and walk quickly away from the scene.

To avoid highway crime, travelers should try not to drive at night, especially when alone, or sleep in vehicles along the road. Travelers should, under no circumstances, pick up hitchhikers; they not only pose a threat to physical safety, but also put the driver in danger of being arrested for unwittingly transporting narcotics.

Extortion and corruption are common in the business environment. Threats of violence and acts of violence are commonly resorted to in business disputes. Organized criminal groups and sometimes local police target foreign businesses in many cities and have been known to demand protection money. Many Western firms hire security services that have improved their overall security, although this is no guarantee. Small businesses are particularly vulnerable. American citizens are encouraged to report all extortion attempts to the Russian authorities and to inform consular officials at the U.S. Embassy or nearest Consulate General.

Travelers should be aware that certain activities that would be normal business activities in the United States and other countries are either illegal under the Russian legal code or are considered suspect by the Federal Security Service (FSB). U.S. citizens should be particularly aware of potential risks involved in any commercial activity with the Russian military-industrial complex, including research institutes, design bureaus, production facilities or other high technology, government-related institutions. Any misunderstanding or dispute in such transactions can attract the involvement of the security services and lead to investigation or prosecution for espionage. Rules governing the treatment of information remain poorly defined.

It is not uncommon for foreigners in general to become victims of harassment, mistreatment and extortion by law enforcement and other officials. Police do not need to show probable cause in order to stop, question or detain individuals. If stopped, travelers should try to obtain, if safe to do so, the officer's name, badge number, and patrol car number, and note where the stop happened, as this information assists local officials in identifying the perpetrators in cases where the incident is not for legitimate purposes. Authorities are concerned about these incidents and have cooperated in investigating such cases. Travelers should report crimes to the U.S. Embassy or the nearest Consulate General.

Consular Services: All Americans who travel to Russia are encouraged to register at the U.S. Embassy or at one of the U.S. Consulates, listed below. In addition to providing updated travel and security information, registration facilitates replacement of a lost or stolen passport as well as contact in case of emergency.

U.S. EMBASSY - MOSCOW

Ambassador - 8 Bolshoy Deviatinsky Pereulok, Moscow 121099 American Citizen Services, Consular Section 21 Novinskiy Blvd, Moscow 123242 Tel: 7 (495) 728-5577, Fax: 7 (495) 728-5084 After-hours (emergencies): Tel: 7 (495) 728-5025/728-5000

U.S. Consulate General - St. Petersburg

Consul General Sheila S. Gwaltney 15 Furshtadkskaya Street, St.Petersburg 191028 Tel: 7 (812) 331-2600, Fax: 7 (812) 331-2852 After-hours emergencies: Tel: 7 (812) 271-6455 or 939-5794

U.S. Consulate General - Vladivostok

Consul General Sylvia Curran 32 Pushkinskaya Street, Vladivostok 690001 Tel: 7 (4232) 300-070, Fax: 7 (4232) 499-371/2

(4232) 300-091 (visa section) After-hours emergencies: Tel: 7 (4232) 710-067

U.S. Consulate General – Yekaterinburg

Consul General Mike Reinert 15 Gogol Street, 4th Floor, Yekaterinburg 620151 Tel: 7 (343) 379-3001/379-4619/91, Fax: 7 (343) 379-4515

VISA REQUIREMENTS

The Russian government requires visas and residence permits for businessmen and investors. Work and residence permits must be renewed periodically -- a cumbersome process. Russia's visa system for residence and work permits is very complicated, and potential investors would be well-advised to consult the State Department and U.S. Embassy websites for the latest information on Russian visas: http://moscow.usembassy.gov/russian-visas.html and http://travel.state.gov/travel/cis_pa_tw/cis/cis_1006.html . In some sectors, requirements that a certain percentage of staff be Russian citizens may have a negative impact on foreign investors.

ENTRY/EXIT REQUIREMENTS: The Russian government maintains a restrictive and complicated visa regime for foreigners who visit, transit, or reside in the Russian Federation. A U.S. citizen who does not comply with Russian visa laws can be subject to arrest, fines, and/or deportation. Russian authorities will not allow a U.S. citizen traveler with an expired visa to depart the country, effectively stranding the person for up to 20 days, until local authorities grant an exit visa.

The Government of Russia does not consistently recognize the standing of the U.S. diplomatic mission to intervene in visa matters, including situations in which an American is stranded because of an expired visa. U.S. citizens should also be aware that Russian immigration and visa laws change regularly, and the implementation of new regulations has not always been transparent or predictable; it is recommended that Americans consult with the U.S. Embassy and, possibly, an immigration specialist for assistance in more complex residency and work-related issues.

The Russian visa system includes a number of provisions that may be unfamiliar to Americans, including:

Sponsorship
Entry Visas
Limitations on Length of Stay
Exit Visas
Migration Cards
Visa Registration
Transit Visas
Work Visas
Restricted Areas

Dual citizens who also carry Russian passports face additional complicated regulations.

Sponsorship: Under Russian law, every foreign traveler must have a Russian-based sponsor, which could be a hotel, tour company, relative, employer, university, etc. Even if a visa was obtained through a travel agency in the United States, there is always a Russian legal entity whose name is indicated on the visa and who is considered to be the legal sponsor. Russian law requires that the sponsor must apply on the traveler's behalf for replacement, extension, or changes to a Russian visa. U.S. citizens are strongly advised to ensure that the sponsor listed on their visa is a known, legal entity, and that the traveler holds contact information for the visa sponsor prior to arrival in Russia, as the sponsor's assistance will be essential to resolve any visa problems or assist in cases of emergency.

Entry Visas: To enter Russia for any purpose, a U.S. citizen must possess a valid U.S. passport and a visa issued by a Russian Embassy or Consulate. It is impossible to obtain an entry visa upon arrival, so travelers must apply for their visas well in advance.

U.S.citizens who apply for Russian visas in third countries (e.g., countries bordering the Russian Federation) where they do not have residence, may face considerable delays in visa processing. Travelers who arrive in Russia without an entry visa will not be permitted to enter the country, and face immediate return to the point of embarkation at their own expense.

Russian tourist visas are often granted only for the specific dates mentioned in the invitation letter provided by the sponsor. U.S. citizens sometimes receive visas valid for periods as short as 24 hours. Even if the visa is misdated through error of a Russian Embassy or Consulate, the traveler will still not be allowed into Russia before the visa start date or be allowed to leave after the visa expiration date. Any mistakes in visa dates must be corrected before the traveler enters Russia. It is helpful to have someone who reads Russian check the visa before departing the United States. Travelers should ensure that their visas reflect intended activities in Russia (e.g., tourism, study, business, etc.). Travelers are advised to request visas for a period of five days before and after the anticipated stay, if possible, in order to manage unanticipated changes of travel plans.

U.S.citizens who are denied visas may seek a clarification from the Ministry of Foreign Affairs, 32/34 Smolenskaya-Sennaya Pl., Moscow, Russia, 119200, e-mail ministry@mid.ru .

Limitations on Length of Stay: Unless a visa specifically authorizes employment or study, a foreigner may stay in Russia only 90 days in any 180-day period. This applies to business, tourist, humanitarian and cultural visas, among other categories.

Exit Visas: A valid visa is necessary to depart Russia. Travelers who overstay their visa's validity, even for one day, will be prevented from leaving until their visa is extended (usually at the airport). If a visa has expired more than three days prior to departure, Russian authorities may take up to 20 calendar days to authorize an exit visa, during which time the traveler will be stranded in Russia at his or her own expense. The ability of the Embassy or Consulates General to intervene in these situations is limited.

Russian law prohibits licensed lodging establishments in Russia from housing foreign travelers with expired visas. There are few adequate public shelters or safe havens in Russia, and neither the U.S. Embassy nor the Consulates General have means to accommodate such stranded travelers.

Visitors who lose their U.S. passports and Russian visas to accident or theft must immediately replace their passports at the U.S. Embassy or one of the Consulates General. The traveler must then enlist the visa sponsor to obtain a new visa in order to depart the country. It is helpful to make a photocopy of your visa in the event of loss, but a copy is not sufficient to permit departure.

Visas for students and English teachers sometimes allow only one entry. In these cases, the sponsoring school is responsible for registering the visa and migration card and obtaining an exit visa. Obtaining an exit visa can take up to twenty days so students and teachers need to plan accordingly. Please see the section below regarding Teaching in Russia.

Migration Cards: All foreigners entering Russia must fill out a two-part migration card upon arrival. The traveler deposits one part of the card with immigration authorities at the port of entry, and keeps the other part for the duration of his or her stay. Upon departure, the traveler must submit his or her card to immigration authorities. Foreign visitors to Russia are normally required to present their migration cards in order to register at hotels.

Migration cards, in theory, are available at all ports of entry from Russian immigration officials (Border Guards). The cards are generally distributed to passengers on incoming flights and left in literature racks at arrival points. Officials at borders and airports usually do not point out these cards to travelers; it is up to the individual travelers to find them and fill them out.

Replacing a lost or stolen migration card is extremely difficult. While authorities will not prevent foreigners from leaving the country if they cannot present their migration cards, travelers could experience problems when trying to re-enter Russia at a future date.

Although Russia and Belarus use the same migration card, travelers should be aware that each country maintains its own visa regime. U.S. citizens wishing to travel to both nations must apply for two separate visas. A traveler entering Russia directly from Belarus is not required to obtain a new migration card, but at his or her option may do so if blank ones are available at the time of entry.

Visa Registration: Travelers must register their visa and migration card through their sponsor, in any location in Russian at which they spend more than three days. If a traveler chooses not to register a stay of less than three days, he or she is advised to keep copies of tickets, hotel bills, or itineraries in order to prove compliance with the law.

U.S. citizens should be aware that Russian police officers have the authority to stop people and request their identity and travel documents at any time, and without cause. Due to the possibility of random document checks by police, travelers should carry their original passports, migration cards, and visas with them at all times.

Transit Visas: Travelers intending to transit through Russia en route to a third country must have a Russian transit visa. Even travelers who are simply changing planes in Moscow or another international airport in Russia for an onward destination will be asked to present a transit visa issued by a Russian Embassy or Consulate. Russian authorities may refuse to allow a U.S. citizen who does not have a transit visa to continue with his or her travel, obliging the person to immediately return to the point of embarkation at the traveler's own expense.

Work Visas: There are quotas on invitations to foreigners to enter Russia in order to work. These quotas are established by territorial agencies in the regions and are approved annually by the Russian Government. According to the law, quotas take into account the demographic situation in the relevant region of Russia and its ability to accommodate foreign nationals. This is theoretically based on the principle that priority should be given to the use of domestic labor. The prospective employer must initiate the application process for this type of visa at Pasportny Stol/PVU. Prospective employers who hire foreigners must also receive permission from the local branch of the Ministry of Interior's Federal Migration Service. The Federal Migration Service then issues the foreigner a document confirming his legal employment. Please note that Russian authorities may require tests for drugs and infectious diseases for holders of work visas.

There are a few categories of foreigners who can be employed without such a permit: those who have a Russian residency permit or permanent registration with police; church employees; technical experts who come for a short period to assemble imported equipment; and those who come for educational activities

Restricted Areas: U.S. citizens should be aware that there are several closed cities and regions in Russia. Travelers who attempt to enter these areas without prior authorization are subject to arrest, fines, and/or deportation. A traveler must list on the visa application all areas to be visited and subsequently register with authorities upon arrival at each destination. Travelers should check with their sponsor, hotel, or the nearest office of the Russian Federal Migration Service before traveling to unfamiliar cities and towns.

American Citizens Also Holding Russian Passports: Dual U.S./Russian nationals who enter Russia on Russian passports face several possible difficulties. Russian authorities will not permit departure from Russia if the person's Russian passport has expired or has been lost, whether or not the traveler also has a valid U.S. passport. In these cases the traveler will be required to obtain a new Russian passport, a process that can take several. In order to apply for a Russian visa in a U.S. passport, however, Russian consular officials require a person to renounce his or her Russian citizenship.

Russian external passports extended by Russian Consulates or Embassies overseas are not considered valid for departure from Russia no matter how long the extension. Bearers of such passports will have to apply for a new passport inside the country. Males of conscript age (18 - 27 years old) who are deemed to be Russian citizens may experience problems if they have not satisfied their military service requirement.

For further Information, please see the Department of State's webpage on dual nationality .

U.S. Companies that require travel of foreign businesspersons to the United States should be advised that security options are handled via an interagency process. Visa applicants should go to the following links.

State Department Visa Website: http://travel.state.gov/visa/index.html

United States Visas.gov: http://www.unitedstatesvisas.gov

U.S. Embassy Moscow website: http://moscow.usembassy.gov/visas.html

For visitors to Russia, it is mandatory to carry your passport and visa with you at all times. Random document checks by police on foreigners are frequent. Failure to present proper documentation can lead to detention and/or fines.

Below is contact information for the Russian Embassy and Consulates in the U.S.

Russian Embassy and Consulate in Washington, D.C. Tel: (202) 939-8902/07/13/18 Fax: (202) 483-7579

Russian Consulate in New York City Tel: (212) 348-0926/55 Fax: (212) 831-9162

Russian Consulate in San Francisco Tel: (415) 928-6878, 202-9800/01 (415) 929-0862 (visas) Fax: (415) 929-0306

Russian Consulate in Seattle Tel: (216) 728-1910 Fax: (216) 728-1871

Russian Consulate in Houston Tel: (713) 337-3300 Fax: (713) 337-3305

U.S. Companies that require travel of foreign businesspersons to the United States should be advised that security evaluations are handled via an interagency process. Visa applicants should go to the following links.

State Department Visa Website: http://travel.state.gov/visa/

TELECOMMUNICATIONS

Internet Accessibility: The level of penetration and Internet awareness continues to increase in Russia. Recent figures show that about 43.6% of the Russian population uses the Internet on a regular basis and this figure is expected to grow to 52% by the end of 2011. The largest players in Russian language e-mail services and search engines are Mail.ru, Rambler and Yandex. Internet is widely available in the major cities.

Wi-Fi is increasingly available in Russia. Currently, there are about 3,500 hot spots active in Russia that are primarily located in Moscow, St. Petersburg and other large cities. Launching WIMAX services combined with Wi-Fi will be the driver for further proliferation of wireless Internet access.

Mobile Technology: Mobile services are provided in the GSM, CDMA-450, AMPS and DAMPS standards. GSM dominates the market, with 3G gaining some share. The major cellular operators in the market are Mobile TeleSystems (MTS), Vimpelcom and Megafon.

Long distance telephone calls can usually be made from any place in the city using IP phone cards or SKYPE, if you have an available Internet connection. Check with your provider to make sure coverage is available. With a pre-paid, locally purchased phone card, you can also make calls from phone kiosks located near metro and train stations, tourist attractions and in downtown areas.

A rudimentary knowledge of Russian is extremely helpful for those placing a call through local telephone and telegraph offices. Moscow is eight hours ahead of Washington,

D.C. To reach Moscow by phone from the United States you need to access an international line, and then dial Russia Country Code "7," Moscow City Code "495" followed by the phone number. Some new numbers use "499" for Moscow, and calling cell phones in Russia often require a different dialing string.

TRANSPORTATION

The U.S. Federal Aviation Administration (FAA) has assessed the Russia government as being in compliance with the ICAO international aviation safety standards for oversight of Russia air carriers operations. See http://www.faa.gov/about/initiatives/iasa/ for more information.

Travelers should be aware some local airlines do not have advance reservation systems but sell tickets for cash at the airport. Flights often are canceled if more than 30% of the seats remain unsold. Travelers should have their passport with them at all times. Air travel within western Russia is occasionally erratic but generally stays on schedule; the quality of service continues to improve. Flights within the Russian Far East are often delayed or cancelled in winter months due to snow or fog. International Russian carriers such as Aeroflot and Transaero usually use western equipment and meet higher standards than domestic carriers.

Moscow has three major airports (Sheremetyevo, Domodedovo and Vnukovo); a fourth airport, Bykovo, deals primarily with cargo and emergency flights. International flights generally enter Moscow through Sheremetyevo and Domodedovo. Most international flights arrive in Sheremetyevo-2 (renamed SVO-F in December 2009) while Sheremetyevo-1 (renamed SVO-B in March 2010) handles most domestic traffic. With the opening of terminal C (SVO-C) in March 2007 and the opening of terminal D (SVOD) in November 2009, some international and domestic travel has been diverted to these facilities. Terminal E (SVO-E) was completed in April 2010 and also receives international flights. In July 2010, terminals F, D, and E were connected to allow for more convenient passenger movements throughout the terminals.

Travelers may continue to other Russian cities from Sheremeyevo, Vnukovo or Domodedovo airports. However, travel time between airports or to the city center can take as much as three hours, and ample time must be allowed for passport control, customs clearance and baggage retrieval. St. Petersburg's airport has two terminals: Pulkovo-1 (domestic flights) and Pulkovo-2 (international flights).

Train travel in Russia is generally reliable and convenient as stations are located in the city center. From St. Petersburg to Moscow, travelers often ride overnight trains, although unaccompanied passengers are reminded to keep an eye on their valuables and lock their doors at night (if in a sleeping compartment), as some incidents of pick-pocketing have been reported. Inclement weather, erratic maintenance and a culture of aggressive driving make road conditions throughout Russia highly variable. Drivers and pedestrians should exercise extreme caution to avoid accidents. Traffic police sometimes stop motorists to levy cash "fines," and criminals occasionally prey on travelers, especially in isolated areas.

In Moscow and St. Petersburg, the metro (subway) can be an efficient and inexpensive means of transportation. However, for non-Russian speakers, it can be difficult unless prepared in advance. Be sure to carry a metro map with you and learning Cyrillic alphabet is helpful. Marked taxis are increasingly present in Moscow and St. Petersburg. Short-term business travelers may wish to consider renting a car and driver for extensive excursions, or hire taxis through their hotels for shorter jaunts. Car rentals are another option that has opened up in the last couple of years, although driving in Russia can be difficult for the uninitiated.

LANGUAGE

Though many better-educated Russians in major cities speak English, you should be prepared to conduct business in Russian. Many first-time visitors are surprised by how difficult it can be to find anyone who speaks English. U.S. businesses should hire a reputable interpreter when conducting important negotiations. Not having product literature in Russian will put your company at a disadvantage relative to your European and Asian competitors, not to mention local firms.

HEALTH

As in many countries of the world, travelers should drink only boiled or bottled water, with the possible exception of Moscow. Medical care is usually below western standards, with occasional shortages of basic medical supplies. In Moscow and St. Petersburg, there are now a number of Western managed medical and dental clinics that provide adequate ambulatory care. Such facilities usually require cash payment at Western rates upon admission. The U.S. Embassy and Consulates maintain lists of such facilities and of English speaking doctors (http://moscow.usembassy.gov/medical.html). For serious medical conditions, it may be necessary to travel to western Europe or return to the U.S., and this can be very expensive if undertaken under emergency conditions. The cost of a medical evacuation (in an air ambulance) from some Russian regions exceeds $100,000. The Embassy strongly urges all travelers who visit Russia to purchase traveler's medical insurance, which includes coverage for a medical evacuation. Elderly travelers and those with preexisting health problems may be at particular risk. Further information on health matters can be obtained from the Centers for Disease Control and Prevention's international traveler's hotline at 1-877-394-8747, or via the CDC home page at http://www.cdc.gov .

LOCAL TIME, BUSINESS HOURS, AND HOLIDAYS

There are 9 time zones across Russia. Moscow is eight hours ahead of Eastern Standard/Daylight Time. Russian changes relative to daylight savings time are made on the last Sundays of March and October, at 2 am. In February 2011, President Medvedev announced the abolition of daylight saving time starting autumn 2011. Most companies and offices maintain business hours of 9:00 a.m. - 6:00 p.m. Many shopping centers and supermarkets are open from 10:00 a.m. - 8:00 p.m. Increasingly, major supermarket chains are open 24 hours, 7 days per week.

Russian Holidays: The holidays listed on the U.S. Embassy's website are not an exclusive list. Occasionally days off will be declared by the government to create a long weekend, particularly at Christmas (when holidays fall on weekends, Russian authorities generally announce during the week prior to the holiday whether it will be celebrated on the previous Friday or the following Monday). Travelers should be aware that little business is done from mid-December through mid-January. The country essentially shuts down for business from New Years to Russian Orthodox Christmas (January 7). Government offices, most businesses and even much of the press close during this period. The period from May 1 through May 9 is similar.

U.S. Embassy Official Holidays for 2011: http://moscow.usembassy.gov/holidays.html

TEMPORARY ENTRY OF MATERIALS AND PERSONAL BELONGINGS

Russian customs procedures include entry and exit declaration forms. Foreigners are allowed to export up to $3,000 without providing a customs declaration or proof of how the money was obtained. Foreigners may also export up to $10,000 by simply filling out a customs declaration upon exit. More than $10,000 can be exported upon proof that it was imported into Russia legally (a stamped customs declaration or proof of a legal bank or wire transfer must be presented to export currency). Failure to follow these procedures can and does result in delays, detentions, confiscation of the currency, and even imprisonment. Lost or stolen customs forms should be reported to the Russian police, and a police report (spravka) should be obtained to present to customs officials upon departure. Often, however, the traveler will find that the lost customs declaration cannot be replaced.

Generally speaking, you should obtain a receipt for all items of value – including caviar – purchased in Russia. Furthermore, old artifacts and antiques must have a certificate indicating that they have no historical value. For further information, call Russian Customs at 7 (495) 265-6628 or 208-2808. Additional information can also be found at www.customs.ru .

Export duties may be imposed on any items that are determined by customs officials at the point of departure to be of commercial use. Items which may appear to have historical or cultural value -- icons, rugs, art, antiques, etc. -- may be taken out of Russia only with prior written approval of the Ministry of Culture and payment of a 100% duty. Occasionally, dealers of quality items may be able to arrange this approval at considerably less cost. Certain items, such as caviar, medications, jewelry, precious/semi-precious stones or metals, and fuel may be exported duty-free in limited amounts only.

Computers, electronic notebooks and related hardware must be presented to customs officials at the airport for scanning at least two hours prior to departure. The Embassy understands that customs officials may require "information storage devices" to be submitted 24 hours before departure. The law is often neglected but can be enforced on a-case-by-case basis. Failure to follow the customs regulations may result in penalties ranging from confiscation of the property in question and/or imposition of fines or arrest.

To prevent possible difficulties in taking currency and valuables back out of Russia, travelers are highly advised to ensure that their passenger declaration form is completed and is stamped by customs officials at the point of entry. This customs declaration should be kept and made available when exiting Russia.

Web Resources

U.S.Department of State Website: http://www.travel.state.gov Centers for Disease Control and Prevention: http://www.cdc.gov

U.S.Embassy Moscow Website: http://moscow.usembassy.gov

U.S.Federal Aviation Administration (FAA) http://www.faa.gov/about/initiatives/iasa

IMPORTANT CONTACTS

RUSSIAN GOVERNMENT OFFICES

Ministry of Economic Development Ms. Elvira Nabiullina, Minister 1/3, 1st Tverskaya-Yamskaya Street, Moscow 125993 Tel: 7 (495) 694-0353; 950-9263 (The Americas Dept.), Fax: 7 (499) 251-6965 http://www.economy.gov.ru

Ministry of Finance 9 Ilyinka Street, Entrance 1, Moscow 103097 Tel: 7 (495) 987-9101/-9130/-9140/-9868; Fax: 7(495) 625-0889 http://www.minfin.ru

Ministry of Industry and Trade Mr. Viktor Khristenko, Minister 7 Kitaigorodskiy Proyezd, Moscow 109074 Tel: 7 (495) 710-4888; Fax: 7 (495) 710-5150 (International Dept.) http://www.minprom.gov.ru

Ministry of Energy

Mr. Sergey Shmatko, Minister 42 Shchepkina Street, GSP-6, Moscow 107996 Tel: 7 (495) 631-98-58; Fax: 7 (495) 631-8364 http://minenergo.com

Ministry of Information and Mass Communications

Mr. Igor Shegolev, Minister 7 Tverskaya Street, Moscow 125375 Tel: 7 (495) 771-8100; Fax: 7 (495) 771-8710 http://english.minsvyaz.ru/enter.shtml

Ministry of Transportation

Mr. Igor Levitin, Minister 1/1 Rozhdestevenka Street, Moscow 109012 Tel: 7 (495) 626-1000, Fax: 7 (495) 626-9128, 626-9038 http://www.mintrans.ru

Ministry of Health and Social Development

Ms. Tatyana Golikova, Minister 3 Rakhmanovsky Per., GSP-4, Moscow 127994 Tel.: 7 (495) 628-4453, Fax: 7 (495) 627-2944 http://www.minzdravsoc.ru

Ministry of Agriculture

Ms. Yelena Skrynnik 1/11 Orlikov Pereulok, Moscow 107139 Tel: 7 (495) 607-8000; Fax: 7 (495) 607-8362 http://www.mcx.ru

Ministry of the Interior Mr. Rashid Nurgaliyev Economic Security Department 16, Zhitnaya St., Moscow 119049 Tel: 7 (495) 667 2221 http://eng.mvdrf.ru

Ministry of Regional Development Mr. Viktor Basargin Sadovaya-Samotechnaya St., 10/23, bldg. 1, Moscow 127994 Tel: (495) 980-25-47; Fax: (495) 699-38-41 http://www.minregion.ru

Federal Customs Service

Mr. Andrey Belyaninov 11/5, Novozavodskaya St., 121087 Moscow Tel: 7 (495) 449 7252 http://www.customs.ru/en

Federal State Statistics Service (Goskomstat)

Mr. Alexander Surinov 39 Myasnitskaya St., Moscow 107450 Tel: 7 (495) 607 4902; Fax: 7 (495) 607 4087 http://www.gks.ru/wps/wcm/connect/rosstat/rosstatsite.eng/

Russian Agency for Patents and Trademarks (Rospatent)

Dr. Boris Simonov, Director General 30-1 Berezhkovskaya Nab., G-59, GSP-5, Moscow 123995 Tel. 7 (495) 240-6138, 240-6015; Fax: 7 (495) 243-3337 http://www.fips.ru/rospatent/index.htm

Central Bank of Russia

Mr. Sergey Ignatyev, Chairman Sergey Tatarinov, Head of External and Public Relations 12 Neglinnaya Street, Moscow 107016 Tel: 7 (495) 771-9100; Fax: 7(495) 621-6465 http://www.cbr.ru /

SELECTED REGIONAL GOVERNMENTS

Moscow City Administration

Sergey Sobyanin, Mayor of the City of Moscow 13 Tverskaya Street, Moscow 125032 Tel/Fax: 7 (495) 692-1637 http://www.mos.ru

St. Petersburg City Administration

Governor of St. Petersburg Aleksander Prokhorenko, Chairman Committee for External Relations Smolny, St. Petersburg 191060 Tel: 7 (812) 576-7113; Fax: 7(812) 576-7633 http://www.kvs.spb.ru/?lang=eng http://eng.gov.spb.ru

Vladivostok City Administration

Igor Pushkaryov, Mayor of Vladivostok Okeanskiy prospect, Vladivostok 690950 Tel: 7 (4232) 614-223 http://www.vlc.ru

Chukotsky Autonomous Okrug Government

Roman Kopin, Governor 20 Bering Street, Anadyr 689000 Tel: 7 (42722) 290 86, Fax: 7 (42722) 290 87 http://www.chukotka.org/en/main

Kamchatka Oblast Territorial Administration

Aleksey Kuzmitskiy, Governor 1 Lenin Square, Petropavlovsk Kamchatsky 683040 Tel: 7 (4152) 412 096; Fax: 7 (4152) 423 503 http://www.kamchatka.gov.ru/en/

Natalia Labkovskaya, Director Department of Foreign Economic Relations and Protocol Tel/Fax: 7 (4152) 42 53 06 E-mail: orgotdel@kamchatka.gov.ru http://www.kamchatka.gov.ru

Khabarovsk Territorial Government

Aleksandr Levintal, Vice-Chairman, Minister Ministry of Economic Development & Foreign Relations 19 Muravjeva-Amurskogo Street, Khabarovsk 680002 Tel: 7 (4212) 329 739; Fax: 7 (4212) 324-153 E-mail: econ@adm.khv.ru http://gov.khabkrai.ru/

Leningrad Oblast

Vladimir Kolesnikov, Chairman

Committee for International and Regional Relations 67 Suvorovsky Prospect, St. Petersburg 193311 Tel: 7 (812) 274-4742; Fax: 7 (812) 274-5986 E-mail: kvs@lenreg.ru http://www.lenobl.ru/

Primorskiy Territorial Administration

Yevgeniy Markin, Director Department of International Relations and Tourism 22 Svetlanskaya Street, Vladivostok 690110 Tel: 7 (4232) 208 340; Fax: 7 (4232) 209 259 E-mail: intnlcmt@primorsky.ru http://www.primorsky.ru

Sakhalin Regional Administration

Vadim Rokotov, Chairman Committee for International, Foreign Economic and Regional Relations 32 Kommunisticheskiy Prospect, Yuzhno-Sakhalinsk 693000 Tel: 7 (4242) 727 494; Fax: 7 (4242) 727 493 E-mail: kom_mvms@adm.sakhalin.ru http://www.adm.sakhalin.ru/

Sverdlovsk Oblast Administration

Ministry for International and Foreign Economic Relations Alexander Kharlov, Minister 1 Oktyabrskaya Ploshchad, Yekaterinburg 620031 Tel: 7 (343) 217-86-72/73; Fax: 7 (343) 217-89-07/11 http://www.midural.ru/

Tatarstan Republic Administration

Interantiona Foreign Economic Relations Department Eskander Muflikhanov, 1 Ploschad Svobody, Kazan Tel: 7 (843) 264-7723 http://prav.tatar.ru/eng/

Yekaterinburg City Administration

Svetlana Garipova, Chairman Foreign Relations Department 24a Lenina Prospect, Yekaterinburg 620014 Tel: 7 (343) 377-55-67, 51-43-83; Fax: 7 (3432) 51-90-05 Email: garipova@adm-ekburg.ru http://www.ekburg.ru/english_version/

AMERICAN CHAMBER OF COMMERCE IN RUSSIA

American Chamber of Commerce in Russia Andrew Somers, President Tatiana Raguzina, Sr. VP for Policy and Membership

7 Dolgorukovskaya Street, Moscow 127006 Tel: 7 (495) 961-2141; Fax: 7 (495) 961-2142 E-mail: amcham@amcham.ru http://www.amcham.ru

American Chamber of Commerce in St. Petersburg

Ms. Maria Chernobrovkina, Executive Director "Na Novo-Isaakievskoy" Business Center Ulitsa Yakubovicha 24, left wing, 3rd floor St. Petersburg 190000 Tel: 7 (812) 448 1646; Fax: 7 (812) 448 1645 E-mail: all@spb.amcham.ru http://www.amcham.ru/spb/

RUSSIA-FOCUSED CHAMBERS OF COMMERCE AND INDUSTRY AND TRADE ASSOCIATIONS IN THE UNITED STATES

U.S.-Russia Business Council

Edward Verona, President and CEO 1110 Vermont Avenue, NW, Suite 350, Washington, DC 20005 Tel: (202) 739-9180, Fax: (202) 659-5920 http://www.usrbc.org

Lotte Plaza Business Center Novinskiy boulevard 8, office 907 Moscow 121099 Tel: 7 (495) 228 58 96; Fax: 7 (495) 228 58 97 http://www.usrbc.org

American-Russian Chamber of Commerce and Industry

Helen Teplitskaya, President Aon Center, 200 E Randolph St., Suite 2200 Chicago, IL 60601 Tel: (312) 494-6562; Fax: (312) 494-9840 E-mail: info@arcci.org http://www.arcci.org/

Foundation for Russian-American Economic Cooperation

Carol Vipperman, President 2601 Fourth Avenue, Suite 600, Seattle, WA 98121 Tel: (206) 443-1935; Fax: (206) 443-0954 E-mail: fraec@fraec.org http://www.fraec.org

Mid-Atlantic Russia Business Council

Val Kogan, President and CEO 1760 Market Street, Suite 1100, Philadelphia, PA 19103 Tel: (215) 708-2628; Fax: (215) 963-9104 E-mail: info@ma-rbc.org http://www.ma-rbc.org

Russian-American Chamber of Commerce

Sergio Millian, President 1552 Pennsylvania St. Denver, CO 80203 Tel/Fax: (303) 831-9181 E-mail: sergio@russianamericanchamber.com http://www.russianamericanchamber.com

RUSSIAN CHAMBERS OF COMMERCE AND INDUSTRY AND TRADE ASSOCIATIONS

Council for Trade and Economic Cooperation (Russia-USA)

Boris Alekseyev, President 3 Naberezhnaya Tarasa Shevchenko, Moscow 121248 Tel: 7 (495) 243-5514, -5494; Fax: 7 (495) 243-4156 E-mail: info@ctec.ru http://www.ctec.ru/eng

Veronika Krasheninnikova, Ph.D., President 445 Park Avenue, 10th Floor New York, NY 10022 Tel: (212) 829 5724; Fax: (917) 322 2105 Email: info-usa@ctec.ru

Moscow Chamber of Commerce and Industry

Leonid Govorov, President 38/1, Sharikopodshipnikovskaya Street Moscow, 115088 Russia Tel.: 7 (499) 132-0733 Fax: 7 (499) 132-764 E-mail: mtpp@mtpp.org http://www.mostpp.ru/eng

Chamber of Commerce and Industry of the Russian Federation

Yevgeniy Primakov, President 6 Ilyinka Street, Moscow 109012 Tel: 7 (495) 620-0009 Fax: 7 (495) 620-0360 E-mail: tpprf@tpprf.ru http://www.tpprf.ru/

Russian Union of Industrialists and Entrepreneurs (RSPP)

Alexander Shokhin, President 10/4 Staraya Ploshad, Moscow 103070 Tel: 7 (495) 748-41-11 Fax: 7 (495) 606-11-29 E-mail: rspp@rspp.ru http://www.rspp.ru

St. Petersburg Chamber of Commerce and Industry Vladimir Katenev, President Ms. Tatyana M. Radion, Director of External Relations Department

46-48 Chaikovskogo Street, St. Petersburg 191123 Tel: 7 (812) 273-5908; Fax: 7 (812) 272-8612 E-Mail: spbcci@spbcci.ru http://www.spbcci.ru/english

Russian-American Business Council (RABC)

Ednan T. Agayev, Vice President 17 Kotelnicheskaya Nab. Office 324, Moscow 115184 Tel: 7 (495) 970-13-89 Fax: 7 (495) 970-13-88 E-mail: rabc@rabc.ru http://www.rabc.ru

U.S. COMMERCIAL SERVICE CONTACTS IN RUSSIA

CS Russia has offices in Moscow, St. Petersburg, and Vladivostok. For a complete list of services, upcoming events and industry specific contacts, please visit: http://www.buyusa.gov/russia/en

Moscow

U.S. Embassy, U.S. Commercial Service 8, Bolshoy Deviatinsky Pereulok Moscow 121099, Russia Phone: 7 (495) 728-5580, Fax: 7 (495) 728-5585 Email: Moscow.Office.Box@mail.doc.gov

St. Petersburg

U.S. Consulate General, U.S. Commercial Service 15 Ulitsa Furshtatskaya St. Petersburg 191028 Tel: 7 (812) 326-2560, Fax: 7 (812)326-2561 Email: StPetersburg.Office.Box@mail.doc.gov

Vladivostok

U.S.Consulate General, U.S. Commercial Service 32 Pushkinskaya Street, Vladivostok, 690001 Phone: 7 (4232) 499-381, Fax: 7 (4232) 30-00-92 Email: Vladivostok.Office.Box@mail.doc.gov Vladivostok.Office.Box@mail.doc.gov

U.S.EMBASSY AND CONSULATE CONTACTS

U.S.Embassy

8 Bolshoy Deviatinsky Pereulok Moscow 121099, Russia Tel: 7 (495) 728-5000; Fax: 7 (495) 728-5159 After-hours (emergencies): Tel: 7 (495) 728-5025 http://moscow.usembassy.gov

U.S. Consulate-General - St. Petersburg

15 Ulitsa Furshtatskaya, St. Petersburg Tel: 7 (812) 331-2600; Fax: (812) 331-2852 After-hours emergencies: Tel: 7 (812) 331-2600 http://stpetersburg.usconsulate.gov/

U.S. Consulate General - Vladivostok

32 Pushkinskaya Street, Vladivostok 690001 Tel: 7 (4232) 300-070, Fax: 7 (4232) 499-372 http://vladivostok.usconsulate.gov/

U.S. Consulate-General – Yekaterinburg

15 Gogolya Street, 4th Floor, Yekaterinburg Tel: (343) 379-30-01, 379-46-19, 379-46-91, 379-45-51 Fax: (343) 379-45-15 http://yekaterinburg.usconsulate.gov/

Market Research

To view market research reports produced by the U.S. Commercial Service please go to the following website: http://www.export.gov/mrktresearch/index.asp and click on Country and Industry Market Reports.

Please note that these reports are only available to U.S. citizens and U.S. companies. Registration to the site is required, and is free.

Trade Events Please click on the link below for information on upcoming trade events.

http://www.export.gov/tradeevents/index.asp

LOCAL GOVERNMENT CONTACTS

ADYGEY REPUBLIC

Address: Ul. Zhukovskogo 22, Maykop 352800
Tel.: (87722) 219-00, 719-00, 219-01
Fax: (87722) 259-58
Representation in Moscow
Yuri Mossovich Naatyzh
Address: Stary Tolmachovsky Per. 6, 115184
Tel.: (095) 230-0748
Fax: (095) 230-3401
Adygey Republic Chamber of Commerce and Industry
Yuri Shumafovich Autlev, First Deputy Minister on Economic Development and Trade
E-mail: maykop@rfcci.rospac.msk.su
Address: Ul. Pionerskaya 199, Maykop 385000
Tel.: (87722) 251-10
Fax: (87722) 226-12

ALTAI KRAI

Address: Prospect Lenina 59, Barnaul 656035
Tel.: (3852) 36-32-05
Fax: (3852) 36-38-63
Representation in Moscow
Timur Surenovich Bablumyan
Address: Per. Bolshoy Tolmachovsky 5, Bldg. 9, 109017
Tel.: (095) 951-0157
Fax: (095) 953-0184
Altai Krai Chamber of Commerce and Industry
Nikita Lvovich Yevtushenko, President
E-mail: altai@rfcci.rospac.msk.su
Address: Ul. Proletarskaya 65, Barnaul 656056
Tel.: (3852) 26-20-50, 26-23-61, 26-23-67
Fax: (3852) 26-23-67

ALTAI REPUBLIC

Address: Ul. Chaptynova 24, Gorno-Altaysk 649000
Tel.: (38822) 2-27-61
Fax: (38822) 9-51-21
Representation in Moscow
i. o. Vadim Aleksandrovich Mikhailov
Address: Ul. Malaya Dmitrovka 3
Tel.: (095) 299-5087, 299-4194
Fax: (095) 299-8197
Chamber of Commerce and Industry of Altai Republic
Svetlana Anatolievna Saduakasova, Chairwoman
E-mail: tppra@mail.gorny.ru
Address: Ul. Ulagasheva 13, P.O. Box 208, Gorno-Altaisk 649000, Altai Republic
Tel./Fax: (38822) 3-12-34

AMUR OBLAST

Address: Ul. Lenina 135, Blagoveschensk 675023
Tel.: (4162) 42-42-03, 44-03-22
Fax: (4162) 44-62-01
Representation in Moscow
Sergey Aleksandrovich Lavrikov
Address: Ul. Malaya Dmitrovka 3, room 506, 103728
Tel: (095) 299-3863, 299-4163, 299-4608
Fax: (095) 299-4202
Amur Oblast Chamber of Commerce and Industry
Sergey Nikolayevich Litvinenko, President
E-mail: amur@rfcci.rospac.msk.su
Address: Ul. Gorkogo 240/3, Blagoveschensk 675011
Tel./Fax: (4162) 42-05-76

ARKHANGELSK OBLAST

Address: Troitsky Prospect 49, Arkhangelsk 163061
Tel.: (8182) 65-30-41
Fax: (8182) 64-65-11
Svetlana Pavlovna Gorlanova, Chairman of Committee of International Relations
Tel.: (8182) 64-67-50
Fax: (8182) 21-12-03
Representation in Moscow
Viktor Vladimirovich Mitin
Address: Ul. Malaya Dmitrovka 3, office 217, 103728
Tel.: (095) 299-4412, 299-6862
Fax: (095) 299-7858
Arkhangelsk Oblast Chamber of Commerce and Industry
Gumyar Khafizovich Nurgaliyev, President
E-mail: arkhangelsk@rfcci.rospac.msk.su
Address: Troitsky Prospect 52, office 926, Arkhangelsk 163061
Tel.: (8182) 64-05-98, 64-01-73
Fax: (8182) 64-01-58, 65-50-26

Astrakhan Oblast
Address: Ul. Sovetskaya 15, Astrakhan 414008
Tel.: (8512) 22-85-19, 22-17-67, 22-29-93
Fax: (8512) 22-95-14
i. o. Natalya Aleksandrovna Korchagina, Deputy Head of Administration for International Relations

Address: Ul. Trusova 45, Astrakhan 414000
Tel.: (8512) 22-65-07
Fax: (8512) 22-17-09
Representation in Moscow
Anatoly Andreyevich Volodin
Address: Prospect Mira 3
Tel.: (095) 251-0719
Fax: (095) 251-0696
Astrakhan Oblast Chamber of Commerce and Industry
Aleksey Dmitriyevich Kantemirov, President
E-mail:astrahan@rfcci.rospac.msk.su
Address: Ul. Zhelyabova 50, Astrakhan 414040
Tel.: (8512) 24-77-15, 24-59-15, 25-58-44
Fax: (8512) 24-71-52

BASHKORTOSTAN REPUBLIC

Tel.: (3472) 50-27-24, 52-96-55
Fax: (3472) 50-02-81
Boris Grigoryevich Kolbin, Minister of Foreign Relations
Tel: (3472) 79-96-21
Fax: (3472) 79-96-25
Representation in Moscow
Albert Maratovich Kharisov
Address: Ul. Dobroslobodskaya 6, Bldg. 2
Tel.: (095) 933-9000
Fax: (095) 933-9043
Bashkortostan Republic Chamber of Commerce and Industry
Zinnat Kharrasovich Khayrullin, Chairman
E-mail: tpp6@rfcci.rospac.msk.su
Address: Ul. Vorovskogo 22, Ufa 450057
Tel.: (3472) 23-23-80
Fax: (3472) 51-70-79

Belgorod Oblast
Yevgeny Stepanovich Savchenko, Head of the Administration
Address: Pl. Revolutsii 4, Belgorod 308005
Tel.: (0722) 22-42-47, 22-45-77, 22-54-56
Fax: (0722) 22-33-43, 33-67-05
Representation in Moscow
Aleksander Grigoryevich Matsepuro
Address: Zagorodnoye Shosse 5, Bldg. 21, 117152
Tel.: (095) 952-0203, 952-3063, 952-5930
Fax: (095) 952-2836
Belgorod Oblast Chamber of Commerce and Industry
Valeriy Stepanovich Skrug, President
E-mail: belgorod@rfcci.rospac.msk.su
Address: Ul. Litvinova 110, 308600
Tel.: (0722) 26-89-50, 31-14-54
Fax: (0722) 31-14-51

BRYANSK OBLAST

Address: Prospect Lenina 33, Bryansk 241002
Tel.: (0832) 46-26-11
Fax: (0832) 41-38-95
Representation in Moscow
Nikolay Alekseyevich Moskin
Address: Ul. Novy Arbat 19, Rooms 1901, 1902, 1904, 127025
Tel./Fax: (095) 203-5052
Bryansk Oblast Chamber of Commerce and Industry
Tatyana Fedorovna Suvorova, President
E-mail: brjansk@rfcci.rospac.msk.su
Address: Ul. Komsomolskaya 11, Bryansk 241035
Tel.: (0832) 56-68-06, 56-76-63
Fax: (0832) 56-44-24

BURYAT REPUBLIC

Address: Ul. Sukhe-Batora 9, Ulan-Ude 670001
Tel.: (3012) 21-46-52, 21-44-29
Fax: (3012) 21-25-55
Representation in Moscow
Bair Gvibalovich Balzhirov
Address: Ul. Myasnitskaya 43, Bldg. 2, 107178
Tel.: (095) 925-9500
Fax: (095) 923-6046
Buryat Republic Chamber of Commerce and Industry
Gennady Monkhorovich Berbidayev, President
E-mail: tpprb@buryatia.ru
Address: Ul. Sakhyanovoy 5, P.O. Box 4284, Ulan-Ude 670047
Tel./Fax: (3012) 37-34-34

BURYAT-AGINSKY AUTONOMOUS DISTRICT

Address: Ul. Bazara Rinchino 92, Aginskoye, Chita Oblast 674460
Tel.: (30239) 341-52
Fax: (30239) 349-59
Representation in Moscow
Ochir Damdinovich Damdinov
Address: Ul. Novy Arbat 19, Room 1733, 127025
Tel.: (095) 203-9509
Fax: (095) 203-8014

BURYAT UST-ORDYNSKY AUTONOMOUS AREA

Address: Ul. Lenina 18, Ust-Ordynsky, Irkutsk Oblast 669001
Tel.: (39541) 2-12-62
Fax: (39541) 2-25-93
Representation in Moscow
Oleg Borisovich Batorov

Address: Ul. Novy Arbat 19, Room 1730, 127025
Tel.: (095) 203-5256
Fax: (095) 203-6404

CHELYABINSK OBLAST

Address: Ul. Tsvillinga 27, Chelyabinsk 454089
Tel: (3512) 33-92-41
Fax: (3512) 36-25-90
Representation in Moscow
Valery Aleksandrovich Shubin
Address: Dmitrovsky Proezd 4A, 125422
Tel: (095) 210-8857, 210-8859
Fax: (095) 977-0835
South-Ural Chamber of Commerce and Industry
Fedor Lukitch Degtyarev, President
E-mail: cheliabinsk@rfcci.rospac.msk.su, suci@ural.chel.su
Address: Ul. Vasenko 63, Chelyabinsk 454000
Tel: (3512) 66-18-16
Fax: (3512) 66-52-23

CHITA OBLAST

Address: Ul. Tchaikovskogo 8, Chita 672021
Tel: (3022) 23-34-93, 23-21-84
Fax: (3022) 26-33-19
Representation in Moscow
Viktor Mikhailovich Stolyarov
Address: Ul. Novy Arbat 19, Room 2003, 2007, 2009, 2011
Tel: (095) 203-33-28
Fax: (095) 203-4539
Chita Oblast Chamber of Commerce and Industry
Vladimir Anatolyevich Maltsev, Chairman
E-mail: tpp@mail.chita.ru
Address: Ul. Lenina 27, P.O. Box 495, Chita 672010
Tel: (3022) 32-29-28, 26-57-54
Fax: (3022) 32-29-28

CHUKOTKA AUTONOMOUS DISTRICT

Address: Ul. Beringa 20, Anadyr 689000
Tel: (42722) 2-42-62
Fax: (42722) 2-27-25
Representation in Moscow
Aleksander Viktorovich Moskalenko
Address: Kursovoy Per. 4, 119034
Tel: (095) 502-9730
Fax: (095) 937-6580

CHUVASH REPUBLIC

Address: Pl. Respubliki 1, Dom Parlamenta, Cheboksary 428004
Tel: (8352) 62-46-87, 62-01-71
Fax: 973-2238 (satellite), (8352) 62-17-99
International Relations Department
Vladimir Ilyich Spiridonov, Chairman
E-mail: torg5@chuvashia.net.ru
Tel.: (8352) 62-06-49, 62-46-91
Fax: (8352) 62-13-37
Representation in Moscow
Anatoly Ivanovich Grigoryev
Address: Ul. Bolshaya Ordynka 46/1, 109017
Tel: (095) 953-9849, 953-1627, 953-2159
Fax: (095) 953-2159
Chuvash Republic Chamber of Commerce and Industry
Igor Vladimirovich Kustarin, President
E-mail: tppchr@vti.co.ru
Address: Prospect Yakovleva 4/2, Cheboksary 428029
Tel: (8352) 20-43-80, 20-37-86, 20-02-94, 21-16-68
Fax: 937-0116 (satellite), (8352) 20-64-64

DAGESTAN REPUBLIC

Address: Pl. Lenina 1, Makhachkala 367012
Tel: (8722) 67-30-60, 67-30-59
Fax: (8722) 67-30-21
Representation in Moscow
Ramazan Shakhbanovich Mamedov
Address: Ul. Pokrovka 28
Tel: (095) 916-0673, 916-1536, 928-3375
Fax: (095) 928-4112
Dagestan Republic Chamber of Commerce and Industry
Said Gaziyevich Gaziyev, Chairman
E-mail:dagestan@rfcci.rospac.msk.su
Address: Pl. Lenina 2, Makhachkala 367012
Tel: (8722) 67-04-61, 67-04-62
Fax: (8722) 67-20-21

EVENKIYSKY AUTONOMOUS AREA

Address: Ul. Sovetskaya 2, Tura 648000
Tel: (095) 789-3126, 27
Fax: (3912) 63-63-56
Representation in Moscow
Yelena Konstantinovna Batygina
Address: Ulansky Per. 24, office 616, 103045
Tel: (095) 956-1910
Fax: (095) 207-7594

INGUSH REPUBLIC

Address: Administration of the President, Pl. Respubliki 2, Magas 386102

Tel: (87322) 255-11
Fax: (095) 334-2039
Representation in Moscow
Khamzat Magomedovich Beyakharoyev
Address: Ul. Vorontsovskaya 22, Bldg. 2
Tel: (095) 912-9275, 912-9309
Fax: (095) 912-9275

Irkutsk Oblast
Boris Aleksandrovich Govorin, Governor
Address: Ul. Lenina 1a, Irkutsk 664027
Tel.: (3952) 27-67-60
Fax: (3952) 24-33-40
Representation in Moscow
Ivan Vasilyevich Fedoseyev
Address: Durasovsky Per. 3, Bldg. 2, 109028
Tel: (095) 916-1708
Fax: (095) 915-70-58
East-Siberian Chamber of Commerce and Industry
Konstantin Semenovich Shavrin, President
E-mail:tpp23@rfcci.rospac.msk.su
Address: Ul. Sukhe-Batora 16, Irkutsk 664003
Tel: (3952) 33-50-60, 33-51-16, 34-27-47, 33-51-32
Fax: (3952) 33-50-66, 34-37-93

IVANOVO OBLAST

Address: Ul. Baturina 5, Ivanovo 153000
Tel.: (0932) 41-77-05
Fax: (0932) 41-92-31
Representation in Moscow
Address: Ul. Novy Arbat 19
Tel: (095) 203-4134, 203-4144, 203-4185
Fax: (095) 203-9345
Ivanovo Oblast Chamber of Commerce and Industry
Vladimir Sergeyevich Sokov, President
E-mail: ivanovo@rfcci.rospac.msk.su
Address: Ul. Baturina 8, Ivanovo 153002
Tel.: (0932) 32-73-48
Fax: (0932) 30-89-66

JEWISH AUTONOMOUS OBLAST

E-mail: birobidzhan@rfcci.rospac.msk.su
Address: Prospect 60-let USSR 18, Birobidzhan 679000
Tel.: (42622) 602-42
Fax: (42622) 407-25
Valery Solomonovich Gurevich, Deputy Head of Administration
E-mail: gurevich@on-line.jar.ru
Tel: (42622) 626-72, 636-63
Fax: (42622) 626-72
Jewish Autonomous Oblast Chamber of Commerce and Industry
Yevgeniya Nikolayevna Stolbova, Executive Director
Address: Ul. Shalom – Aleykheima 60a, Birobidzhan 679000
Tel: (42622) 6-85-80, 4-05-87
Fax: (42622) 4-05-87

KABARDIN-BALKAR REPUBLIC

Address: Prospect Lenina 27, Parliament house, Nalchik 360028
Tel: (86622) 40-21-42
Fax: (86622) 761-74
Representation in Moscow
Mukhamed Mayevich Shogenov
Address: Ul. Bol. Kommunisticheskaya 4, Bldg. 1, 109004
Tel: (095) 911-1852, 911-2834, 911-0697
Fax: (095) 912-4053
Kabardin-Balkar Republic Chamber of Commerce and Industry
Meri Khazrailovna Ashakhmetova, Chairman
E-mail: tppkbr@digsys.ru
Address: Prospect Shogentsukova 10, Nalchik 360000
Tel: (86622) 2-60-76, 2-69-81
Fax: (86622) 2-60-76

KALININGRAD OBLAST

Address: Ul. Dmitriya Donskogo 1, Kaliningrad 236007
Tel/Fax: (0112) 46-75-45
Representation in Moscow
Yevgeny Ivanovich Izotov
Address: Ul. Krasnaya Presnya 7, 123022
Tel/Fax: (095) 258-4401
Kaliningrad Oblast Chamber of Commerce and Industry
Igor Vyacheslavovich Tsarkov, President
E-mail: kaliningrad_cci@baltnet.ru
Address: Ul. Vatutina 20, Kaliningrad 236010
Tel: (0112) 21-87-15, 21-55-07
Fax: (0112) 21-87-15

KALMYKIA (KHALMG TANGCH) REPUBLIC

Address: Ploshchad Lenina, Dom Pravitelstva, Elista 358000
Tel: (84722) 613-88
Fax: (84722) 607-66
Representation in Moscow
Aleksey Maratovich Orlov
Address: Ul. Poklonnaya 12/2
Tel: (095) 249-8730, 249-8736
Fax: (095) 249-8741
Kalmykia Republic Chamber of Commerce and Industry
Nadezhda Pavlovna Ilyanova, Chairman

E-mail: kalmykia@rfcci.rospac.msk.su
Address: Ul. Gubarevicha 2, Elista 358001
Tel: (84722) 575-72, 524-05, 543-95
Fax: (84722) 575-72

KALUGA OBLAST

Address: Ploschad Stary Torg 2, Kaluga 248600
Tel: (0842) 56-23-57
Fax: (0842) 53-13-09
Nikolay Yevgenyevich Shubin, Director of the Department of Interregional Economic Relations
Tel: (0842) 57-56-90
Fax: (0842) 59-15-76
Representation in Moscow
Vladimir Vasilyevich Potemkin
Address: Ul. Tverskaya 9A, Bldg. 5A, 103032
Tel: (095) 203-1712, 229-9825
Fax: (095) 229-9805
Kaluga Oblast Chamber of Commerce and Industry
Aleksander Nikolayevich Malyshev, President
E-mail: kaluga@rfcci.rospac.msk.su
Address: Ploschad Stary Torg 9, Kaluga 248600
Tel: (0842) 57-01-17
Fax: (0842) 57-01-17, 56-47-98

KAMCHATKA OBLAST

Address: Ploschad Lenina 1, Petropavlovsk-Kamchatsky 683040
Tel: (4152) 11-20-96
Fax: (41522) 7-38-43
Representation in Moscow
Aleksandra Georgievna Balenko
Address: Denezhny Per. 12, k. 16, 119002
Tel: (095) 241-0313, 241-3929
Fax: (095) 241-3546
Kamchatka Oblast Chamber of Commerce and Industry
Alla Vasilyevna Parkhomchuk, President
E-mail: kamtpp@iks.ru
Address: Ul. Leninskaya 38, Suite 208, Petropavlovsk-Kamchatsky 683000
Tel: (4152) 12-35-10, 12-35-44
Fax: (4152) 12-35-10

KARACHAYEVO-CHERKESS REPUBLIC

Address: Ploschad Lenina, Dom Pravitelstva, Cherkessk 369000
Tel: (87822) 540-11
Fax: (87822) 529-80
Representation in Moscow
Oleg Viktorovich Mischerin
Address: Ul. Sadovnicheskaya 71, 115035
Tel: (095) 959-55-15, 951-2312
Fax: (095) 959-55-15
Karachayevo-Cherkess Republic Chamber of Commerce and Industry
Anatoly Magometovich Abitov, President
E-mail: cherkessk@rfcci.rospac.msk.su
Address: Ul. Kooperativnaya 6, Cherkessk 369000
Tel: (87822) 511-77, 516-37
Fax: (87822) 516-37

KARELIA REPUBLIC

Address: Prospect Lenina 19, Petrozavodsk 185028
Tel: (8142) 76-41-41, 76-24-42
Fax: (8142) 76-41-48
Representation in Moscow
Anatoly Arkadyevich Markov
Address: Arkhangelsky Per. 1, Room 555
Tel: (095) 207-8724
Fax: (095) 208-0318
Karelia Republic Chamber of Commerce and Industry
Aleksander Aleksandrovich Pankratov, President
E-mail: chamber@karelia.ru
Address: Ul. Engelsa 4, Petrozavodsk 185035
Tel./Fax: (8142) 78-30-40, 76-54-78

KEMEROVO OBLAST

Address: Sovetskiy Prospect 62, Kemerovo 650099
Tel.: (3842) 36-43-33, 36-34-09
Fax: (3842) 58-31-56
Representation in Moscow
Natalya Vasilyevna Khapiy
Address: Ul. Bolshaya Tatarskaya 5/14, Bldg. 9, Moscow 113184
Tel/Fax: (095) 953-5489

Kuzbass Chamber of Commerce and Industry
Tatiana Olegovna Alekseyeva, President
E-mail: ktpp@mail.kuzbass.net
Address: Prospect Sovetsky 63, Suite 407, Kemerovo 650099
Tel./Fax: (3842) 58-77-64

KHABAROVSK KRAI

Address: Ul. Karla Marksa 56, Khabarovsk 680000
Tel.: (4212) 32-51-21
Fax: (4212) 32-87-56
Representation in Moscow
Andrey Borisovich Chirkin
Address: Ul. Novy Arbat 19, Room 2029, 127025
Tel: (095) 203-8325, 203-53-47
Fax: (095) 203-8325
Far Eastern Chamber of Commerce and

Industry
Mikhail Vasilyevich Kruglikov, President
E-mail: tpp25@rfcci.rospac.msk.su
Address: Ul. Sheronova 113, Khabarovsk 680000
Tel.: (4212) 30-47-70
Fax: (4212) 23-54-58, 32-82-33

KHAKASS REPUBLIC

Address: Prospect Lenina 67, Abakan 662600
Tel.: (39022) 633-22, 660-86
Fax: (39022) 650-96
Representation in Moscow
Mikhail Mikhailovich Bergman
Address: Ul. Novy Arbat 19, Room 830, 127025
Tel: (095) 203-8341, 203-5732
Fax: (095) 203-8345
Khakass Republic Chamber of Commerce and Industry
Serzh Bakhshiyevich Adamyan, Chairman
E-mail: tpp34@rfcci.rospac.msk.su
Address: Ul. Sovetskaya 45a, Abakan 655019
Tel.: (39022) 665-86, 645-25
Fax: (39022) 672-73

KHANTY-MANSI AUTONOMOUS AREA

Address: Soviet House, Ul. Mira 5, Khanty-Mansiysk 628011
Tel.: (34671) 320-27, 320-95, 329-67
Fax: (34671) 334-60
Representation in Moscow
Vladimir Alekseyevich Khariton
Address: Starokonyushenny Per. 10/10, Bldg. 2, 109004
Tel.: (095) 291-1293
Fax: (095) 291-1762

E-mail:hanty@rfcci.rospac.msk.su
Address: Ul. Gagarina 128, Khanty-Mansiysk 628002
Tel.: (34671) 2-14-25
Fax: (34671) 2-14-26

KIROV OBLAST

Vladimir Nilovich Sergeyenkov, Governor
Address: Ul. Karla Libknekhta 69, Kirov 610019
Tel.: (8332) 62-95-64
Fax: (8332) 62-89-58
Representation in Moscow
Petr Ivanovich Dmitriev
Address: Kutuzovsky Prospect 12, floor 4, 121348
Tel: (095) 243-2351
Fax: (094) 243-2336
Vyatka Chamber of Commerce and Industry
Nikolay Mikhailovich Lipatnikov, President
E-mail: tpp48@rfcci.rospac.msk.su
Address: Ul. Gertsena 37, Kirov 610000
Tel.: (8332) 67-93-43, 67-37-00
Fax: (8332) 67-93-43

KOMI REPUBLIC

Address: Ul. Kommunisticheskaya 9, Syktyvkar 167010
Tel.: (8212) 28-51-05, 28-51-12
Fax: (8212) 21-43-84
Representation in Moscow
Stepan Vladimirovich Ignatov
Address: Volokolamskoe Shosse 62, 125367
Tel./Fax: (095) 490-10-80
Komi Republic Chamber of Commerce and Industry
Sarkiz Vilenovich Manasaryants, President
E-mail: palata@online.ru
Address: Ul. Internatsionalnaya 100, Syktyvkar 167610
Tel.: (8212) 44-19-43
Fax: (8212) 29-21-31

Address: Ul. 50-letiya Oktyabrya 33, Kudymkar 619000
Tel.: (34260) 4-59-03
Fax: (34260) 4-12-74, 4-21-28
Representation in Moscow
Tamara Aleksandrovna Systerova
Address: Ul. Novy Arbat 19, Rooms 1827, 1829, 127025
Tel: (095) 203-9408, 203-7917
Fax: (095) 203-7476
Komi-Permyak Area Chamber of Commerce and Industry
Andrey Arkadyevich Klimov, President
Address: Ul. 50-letiya Oktyabrya 30, Kudymkar 617240
Tel.: (3422) 34-02-98, 34-92-37
Fax: (3422) 34-27-47

KORYAK AUTONOMOUS AREA

Address: Ul. Porotova 22, Palana 688000
Tel.: (41543) 313-80, 313-83, 315-60
Fax: (41543) 313-70
Representation in Moscow
Vladimir Mikhailovich Shevelenko
Address: Ul. Bolshaya Dmitrovka 9, Bldg. 7, 125009
Tel: (095) 229-5421
Fax: (095) 229-9837

KOSTROMA OBLAST

Address: Ul. Dzerzhinskogo 15, Kostroma 156006
Tel.: (0942) 31-34-72

Tel/Fax: (0942) 31-33-95
Representation in Moscow
Vasiliy Mikhailovich Duma
Address: Ul. Novy Arbat 19, Rooms 1811, 1113, 127025
Tel: (095) 203-4244, 203-5714
Fax: (095) 203-4169
Kostroma Oblast Chamber of Commerce and Industry
Yury Alekseyevich Mikhailov, President
E-mail: kostorma@rfcci.rospac.msk.su
Address: Ul. Kalinovskaya 38, Kostroma 156013
Tel: (0942) 55-62-62, 31-34-84
Fax: (0942) 55-62-62

KRASNODAR KRAI

Address: Ul. Krasnaya 35, Krasnodar 350014
Tel: (8612) 62-45-38
Fax: (8612) 68-43-00
Representation in Moscow
Dmitry Leonidovich Mikheev
Address: 2 Kazachy Per. 6, 119180
Tel./Fax: (095) 238-2028
Krasnodar Krai Chamber of Commerce and Industry
Yury Nikolayevich Tkachenko, Chairman
E-mail: tppkk@tppkuban.ru
Address: Ul. Kommunarov 8, Krasnodar 350063
Tel: (8612) 68-22-13, 68-22-74
Fax: (8612) 68-22-13, 62-91-19

KRASNOYARSK KRAI

Address: Prospect Mira 110, Krasnoyarsk 660009
Tel: (3912) 49-31-11
Fax: (3912) 22-11-78
Representation in Moscow
Yevgeny Viktorovich Ivanov
Address: Ul. Gilyarovskogo 31, bldg.2, 107996
Tel: (095) 284-8579, 284-8656, 284-8685
Fax: (095) 284-8241
Central Siberian Chamber of Commerce and Industry
Valery Alekseyevich Kostin, Chairman
E-mail: cstp@rfcci.rospac.msk.su
Address: Ul. Kirova 26, Krasnoyarsk 660049
Tel.: (3912) 23-96-13
Fax: (3912) 23-96-83

KURGAN OBLAST

Address: Ul. Gogolya 56, Kurgan 640663
Tel.: (3522) 41-70-33
Fax: (3522) 41-71-32
Representation in Moscow
Sergey Nikolaevich Yagovitin
Address: Ul. Malaya Dmitrovka 3, Rooms 313, 314, 103795
Tel./Fax: (095) 200-3978
Kurgan Oblast Chamber of Commerce and Industry
Yevgeny Aleksandrovich Sochnev, President
E-mail: kcci@kurgan.isp.ru
Address: Ul. Dzerzhinskogo 1a, Kurgan 640007
Tel.: (3522) 42-69-99, 27-85-42
Fax: (3522) 42-69-99

KURSK OBLAST

Address: Soviet House, Krasnaya Ploschad, Kursk 305002
Tel.: (0712) 22-62-62, 56-65-73
Fax: (0712) 56-65-73
Representation in Moscow
Sergey Mikhailovich Klushin
Address: Ul. Novy Arbat 19, Rooms 1502, 1504, 1506, 127025
Tel.: (095) 203-4641, 203-7487
Fax: (095) 203-4641
Kursk Oblast Chamber of Commerce and Industry
Valentina Grigoryevna Ordynets, President
E-mail: kursk@rfcci.rospac.msk.su
Address: Ul. Kirova 7, Kursk 305000
Tel.: (0712) 56-24-69
Fax: (0712) 56-24-62, 56-24-69

LENINGRAD OBLAST

Address: Suvorovsky Prospect 67, St. Petersburg 193311
Tel: (812) 274-3563
Fax: (812) 315-8665
Sergey Yevgenyevich Naryshkin, Chairman of Committee for Foreign Economic Relations
Tel: (812) 2744742
Fax: (812) 2745986
Representation in Moscow
Aleksey Ivanovich Okulov
Address: Ul. Novy Arbat 15, Bldg. 1, 121019
Tel.: (095) 291-3355
Fax: (095) 291-4454
St. Petersburg and Leningrad Region Chamber of Commerce and Industry
Aleksander Vadimovich Chistoserdov, President
E-Mail: sptpp@rfcci.rospac.msk.su
Address: Ul. Tchaikovskogo 46-48, St. Petersburg 191123
Tel: (812) 273-4896, 272-1148, 272-8612, 279-0968
Fax: (812) 272-6406, 272-8612

LIPETSK OBLAST

Address: Sobornaya Ploschad 1, Lipetsk 398014
Tel: (0742) 24-25-65, 24-14-52
Fax: (0742) 72-24-26
Lipetsk Oblast Chamber of Commerce and Industry
Liliya Danilovna Pogodina, President
E-mail: lipetsk@rfcci.rospac.msk.su
Address: Ul. Skorokhodova 2, Lipetsk 398019
Tel: (0742) 45-60-04, 45-60-69, 45-60-83
Fax: (0742) 72-05-04

MAGADAN OBLAST

Address: Ploschad Gorkogo 6, Magadan 685000
Tel: (41322) 2-31-34
Fax: (41322) 9-71-61, 9-78-07
Representation in Moscow
Address: Ul. Novy Arbat 19, Room 2204, 127025
Tel: (095) 203-7828
Fax: (095) 203-5917
Magadan Oblast Chamber of Commerce and Industry
Galina Sergeyevna Chubarova, Chairman
E-mail: magadan@rfcci.rospac.msk.su
Address: Ul. Proletarskaya12, Suite 72, Magadan 685000
Tel: (41322) 2-81-61
Fax: (41322) 7-65-17

MARI-EL REPUBLIC

Address: Leninsky Prospect 29, Yoshkar-Ola 424001
Tel: (8362) 63-04-08, 64-15-25
Fax: (8362) 64-19-21
Representation in Moscow
Zhaudat Gabdulganievich Khanafiev
Address: Ul. Novy Arbat 21, Room 1827, 119019
Tel./Fax: (095) 291-4838
Mari-El Republic Chamber of Commerce and Industry
German Aleksandrovich Dementyev, President
E-mail: mari_el@rfcci.rospac.msk.su
Address: Ul. Panfilova 39, room 13, Yoshkar-Ola 424001
Tel: (8362) 63-01-61, 73-63-13
Fax: (8362) 63-04-26

REPUBLIC MORDOVIA

Address: Ul. Sovetskaya 35, Saransk 430002
Tel: (8342) 17-54-71, 32-78-01, 17-77-95
Fax: (8342) 17-45-26

Address: Ul. Obraztsova 29, Moscow 127018
Tel: (095) 219-4049, 219-4050
Fax: (095) 218-0142
Mordovia Republic Chamber of Commerce and Industry
Konstantin Pavlovich Pakshin, Director
E-mail: saransk@rfcci.rospac.msk.su
Address: Ul. Moskovskaya 14, Saransk 430000
Tel.: (8342) 17-21-75, 17-52-04
Fax: (8342) 32-73-80

MOSCOW

Address: Ul. Tverskaya 13, Moscow 103032
Tel.: (095) 292-7238, 229-4887
Fax: (095) 234-3295
Iosif Nikolayevich Ordzhonikidze, Vice Mayor on Foreign Relations Department
Tel.: (095) 229-6360
Fax: (095) 230-2856

Moscow Chamber of Commerce and Industry
Yury Ivanovich Kotov, President
E-mail: moscow@rfcci.rospac.msk.su
Address: Ul. Akademika Pilyugina 22, Moscow 117393
Tel.: (095) 132-7510, 132-7418, 132-0001
Fax: (095) 132-0029

MOSCOW OBLAST

E-mail: pcci@podolsk.ru
Address: Staraya Ploschad 6, Moscow 103070
Tel.: (095) 206-6278, 206-6862
Fax: (095) 928-98-12
Tigran Aleksandrovich Karakhanov, Minister of Foreign Economic Relations
Tel.: (095) 727-1352
Moscow Oblast Chamber of Commerce and Industry (Balashikhinskaya)
Anatoly Vladimirovich Shestakov, President
E-mail: btpp@bues.ru
Address: Ploschad Slavy 1, Balashikha 143900
Tel: (095) 529-10-00, 529-16-41
Fax: (095) 529-16-41
Moscow Oblast Chamber of Commerce and Industry (Vostochnaya Mezhrayonmnaya)
Leonid Mikhaylovich Belas, President
E-mail: vmtpp@dts.ru
Address: Ploschad Revolutsii 4, Suite 112, Pavlovsky Posad 142500
Tel: (243) 2-25-17

Moscow Oblast Chamber of Commerce and Industry (Dmitrovskaya Mezhrayonmnaya)
Valery Vasilyevich Gavrilov, President
E-mail: mail@dmtpp.ru
Address: Ul. Professionalnaya 1a, Dmitrov 141800
Tel./Fax: (095) 993-78-53
Moscow Oblast Chamber of Commerce and

Industry (Dubna)
Vladimir Nikolayevich Bobrov, President
E-mail: zemlya@uni-dubna.ru
Address: Ul. Sovetskaya 14, Dubna 141980
Tel.: (221) 2-33-29, 2-29-64, 2-22-77
Fax: (221) 2-33-29

Moscow Oblast Chamber of Commerce and Industry (Zheleznodorozhny)
Andrey Viktorovich Petrenko, President
E-mail: etpp@keynet.ru
Address: Ul. Mayakovskogo 12, Zheleznodorozhny 143980
Tel.: (095) 527-75-38
Fax: (095) 522-34-84

Moscow Oblast Chamber of Commerce and Industry (Zhukovskaya)
Sergey Viktorovich Kuzmin, President
Address: Ul. Gagarina 2, Suite 64, Zhukovsky 140160
Tel.: (095) 556-13-39
Fax: (095) 556-25-93

Moscow Oblast Chamber of Commerce and Industry (Korolev)
Aleksander Aleksandrovich Medakin, President
Address: Ul. Karla Marks 3, Suite 51, Korolev 141070
Tel.: (095) 516-03-61, 516-60-92
Fax: (095) 516-03-61

Moscow Oblast Chamber of Commerce and Industry (Krasnogorsk)
Sergey Gennadyevich Shmakov, President
Address: Ul. Komsomolskaya 31, Krasnogorsk 143400
Tel./Fax: (095) 562-23-13

Moscow Oblast Chamber of Commerce and Industry (Lobnya)
Andrey Nikolayevich Tishkov, President
Address: Ul. Kalinina 5, Lobnya 141730
Tel./Fax: (095) 577-17-38

Moscow Oblast Chamber of Commerce and Industry (Odintsovo)
Arkady Alekseyevich Kornatsky, President
E-mail: kaskad@odintsovo.comcor.ru
Address: Ul. Molodezhnaya 18, Suite 404, Odintsovo 143000
Tel./Fax: (095) 599-15-65

Moscow Oblast Chamber of Commerce and Industry (Podolsk)
Grigory Alekseyevich Komarenko, President
E-mail: pcci@podolsk.ru
Address: Ul. Rabochaya 2/40, Podolsk 142109
Tel./Fax: (095) 137-97-49, (275) 4-12-54, 4-10-15

Moscow Oblast Chamber of Commerce and Industry (Reutovo)
Aleksander Nikolayevich Khodyrev, President
E-mail: rcci@bues.ru
Address: Ul. Novaya 19, Reutov 143966
Tel.: (095) 791-70-83
Fax: (095) 791-70-79

Moscow Oblast Chamber of Commerce and Industry (Sergiyev Posad)
Vasily Dmitriyevich Goncharov, President
E-mail: tppsp@rambler.ru
Address: Prospect Krasnoy Armii 131, Sergiyev Posad 141300
Tel.: (095) 786-22-78, (254) 49-826
Fax: (254) 27-909

Moscow Oblast Chamber of Commerce and Industry (Serpukhov)
Vladimir Leonidovich Novikov, President
Address: Ul. Gorkogo 1a, Serpukhov 142203
Tel./Fax: (0967) 72-76-25

Moscow Oblast Chamber of Commerce and Industry (Fryazino)
Aleksey Sergeyevich Petrukhin, President
Address: Ul. Vokzalnaya 6a, Fryazino 141120
Tel.: (256) 7-23-00, 7-23-66

Moscow Oblast Chamber of Commerce and Industry (Khimki)
Anatoly Vladimirovich Yurov, Chairman
E-mail: htpp@comintern.ru
Address: Ul. Moskovskaya 16, Khimki 141400
Tel.: (095) 572-51-00
Fax: (095) 572-22-72

Moscow Oblast Chamber of Commerce and Industry (Schelkovo)
Leonid Andreyevich Tverdokhlebov, President
E-mail: scheltpp@shelkovo.comcor.ru
Address: Ploschad Lenina 2, Suite 306, Schelkovo 141100
Tel.: (256) 11-149
Fax: (256) 11-149

MURMANSK OBLAST

Address: Prospect Lenina 75, Murmansk 183006
Tel: (8152) 48-62-01, 47-65-40
Fax: (8152) 47-65-03,45-10-54, 45-64-38, 45-89-87
Vladimir Mikhailovich Yevseyev, Chairman
Department for Foreign Economic Affairs
Svetlana Stepanovna Lobanova, Deputy Chairman
Tel: (8152) 47-72-64, 45-34-49
Fax: (8152) 47-65-03
Representation in Moscow

Anatoly Ivanovich Petrenko
Address: Ul. Bolshaya Nikitskaya 12, 103851
Tel: (095) 229-6977, 229-0331
Fax: (095) 229-5351
Northern Chamber of Commerce and Industry
Anatoly Mikhailovich Glushkov, Chairman
E-mail: murmansk@rfcci.rospac.msk.su
Address: Per. Rusanova 10, Murmansk 183766
Tel: (8152) 47-29-99, 47-27-89, 47-34-59
Fax: (8152) 47-39-78

NENETS AUTONOMOUS AREA

Address: Ul. Smidovicha 20, Naryan-Mar 166000
Tel.: (81853) 4-21-13
Fax: (81853) 4-22-69
Representation in Moscow
Tatyana Alekseyevna Malysheva
Address: Ul. Novy Arbat 19, Room 1122 127025
Tel: (095) 203-9039
Fax: (095) 203-9174

NIZHEGOROD OBLAST

Address: Kremlin 1, Nizhny Novgorod 603082
Tel: (8312) 39-13-30, 39-10-12
Fax: (8312) 39-00-48
Representation in Moscow
Semen Arkadyevich Bagdasarov
Address: Ul. 1 Brestskaya 35
Tel./Fax: (095) 250-2709
Nizhny Novgorod Chamber of Commerce and Industry (Dzerzhinsky District)
Olga Anatolyevna Kudryavtseva, President
E-mail: dztpp@sinn.ru
Address: Ploschad Dzerzhinskogo 3, Dzerzhinsk 606000, Nizhegorodskaya Oblast
Tel: (8313) 25-20-33
Fax: (8313) 33-44-09
Nizhny Novgorod Chamber of Commerce and Industry
Gennady Maksimovich Khodyrev, President
E-mail: tpp@rda.nnov.ru
Address: Ploschad Oktyabrskaya 1, Nizhny Novgorod 603005
Tel: (8312) 19-42-10, 19-77-04, 19-62-35, 19-54-08
Fax: (8312) 19-40-09

NORTH OSSETIA REPUBLIC (ALANIA)

Address: Ploschad Svobody 1, Vladikavkaz 362038
Tel.: (8672) 53-35-16, 53-35-24
Fax: (8672) 74-92-48
Representation in Moscow
Vladimir Anatolyevich Belikov
Address: Durasovsky Per. 1/9
Tel: (095) 916-2147
Fax: (095) 916-2522
North Ossetia Republic Chamber of Commerce and Industry
Kazbek Khazbievich Tuganov, President
E-mail: tpprso-a@osetia.ru
Address: Ul. Avgustovskikh Sobytiy 10, Vladikavkaz 362002
Tel.: (8672) 53-15-84, 53-94-70
Fax: (8672) 54-21-61

NOVGOROD OBLAST

Address: Sofiyskaya Ploschad 1, Velikiy Novgorod 173005
Tel.: (8162) 27-47-79, 13-12-02
Fax: (8162) 13-13-30
Olga Vasilyevna Andrianova, Chairman
Foreign Affairs Committee
Address: Sofiyskaya Ploschad 1, Velikiy Novgorod 173005
Tel/Fax: (8162) 13-13-69
Representation in Moscow
Vladimir Nikolayevich Podoprigora
Address: Ul. Malaya Dmitrovka 3, Room 220, 123075
Tel: (095) 299-4004
Fax: (095) 200-4538
Novgorod Oblast Chamber of Commerce and Industry
Viktor Abramovich Bykov, President
E-mail: gced@ncci.novline.ru
Address: Ul. Germana 1A, Velikiy Novgorod 173002
Tel.: (8162) 13-69-00, 13-94-03, 27-97-47
Fax: (8162) 13-20-46, 13-94-03

NOVOSIBIRSK OBLAST

Address: Krasny Prospect 18, Novosibirsk 630011
Tel.: (3832) 23-08-62, 23-29-95
Fax: (3832) 23-57-00
Representation in Moscow
Vadim Borisovich Filatov
Address: Ul. Myasnitskaya 35, Room 522, 101000
Tel.: (095) 204-1300
Fax: (095) 204-1302
Western Siberia Chamber of Commerce and Industry
Boris Viktorovich Brusilovsky, Chairman
E-mail: org@sbcnet.ru
Address: Prospect Marx 1, Novosibirsk 630064
Tel.: (3832) 46-41-50, 46-54-01
Fax: (3832) 46-30-47, 46-41-50

OMSK OBLAST

Address: Ul. Krasny Put 1, Omsk 644002
Tel.: (3812) 24-14-15, 24-40-11
Fax: (3812) 24-23-72
Foreign Economic Relations Committee
Viktor Stepanovich Bazhenov, Chairman
E-mail: vescom@ecrel.omsk.su
Tel.: (3812) 232-765
Fax: (3812) 232-765
Representation in Moscow
Boris Stepanovich Tsyba
Address: Bol. Kozlovsky Per. 14/15
Tel: (095) 921-6554, 921-4316
Fax: (095) 921-2157
Omsk Oblast Chamber of Commerce and Industry
Tatyana Aleksandrovna Khoroshavina, Chairman
E- mail: omtpp@omsknet.ru
Address: Ul. Krasny Put 18, Omsk 644099
Tel.: (3812) 23-05-23, 23-45-80, 25-33-33
Fax: (3812) 23-52-48

ORENBURG OBLAST

Address: Dom Sovetov, Orenburg 460015
Tel.: (3532) 77-69-31, 78-60-10
Fax: (3532) 77-09-62
Representation in Moscow
Vyacheslav Semenovich Ryabov
Address: Ul. Novy Arbat 19, Room 2014, 127025
Tel: (095) 203-8532
Fax: (095) 203-5976
Orenburg Oblast Chamber of Commerce and Industry
Viktor Andreyevich Sytezhev, President
E-mail: orenburg@rfcci.rospac.msk.su
Address: Parkovy Prospect 6, Orenburg 46000
Tel.: (3532) 77-02-35
Fax: (3532) 77-73-29

OREL OBLAST

Address: Ploschad Lenina 1, Orel 302021
Tel.: (0862) 41-63-13, 47-53-00
Fax: (0862) 41-25-30
Representation in Moscow
Marina Georgievna Rogocheva
Address: Ul. Goncharnaya 12, Bldg. 3, 109240
Tel: (095) 915-8614, 915-8551
Fax: (095) 915-8614
Orel Oblast Chamber of Commerce and Industry
Svyatoslav Aleksandrovich Komarov, President
E-mail: palata@orel.ru
Address: Proletarskaya Gora 7, Orel 302028
Tel.: (0862) 29-46-67, 29-54-69, 43-30-46
Fax: (0862) 29-54-69

PENZA OBLAST

Address: Ul. Moskovskaya 75, Penza 440025
Tel.: (8412) 66-11-94
Fax: (8412) 55-04-11
Representation in Moscow
Pavel Khaskelyevich Zaydfudim
Address: Ul. Novy Arbat 19, Room 1914, 127025
Tel: (095) 203-1075
Fax: (095) 203-4893, 203-6245
Penza Oblast Chamber of Commerce and Industry
Arnold Konstantinovich Mordovsky, Chairman
E-mail: penza@rfcci.rospac.msk.su
Address: Ul. Moskovskaya 56, Suite 21, Penza 440601
Tel.: (8412) 52-42-29
Fax: (8412) 56-21-99

PERM OBLAST

Address: Ul. Kuybysheva 14, Perm 614006
Tel.: (3422) 58-70-75
Fax: (3422) 34-89-52
Representation in Moscow
Aleksander Alekseyevich Potekhin
Address: Ul. Malaya Dmitrovka 3, Room 206, 103795
Tel: (095) 299-48-36
Fax: (095) 209-08-97
Perm Oblast Chamber of Commerce and Industry
Zamarayev Viktor Anatolyevich, Chairman
E-mail: permtpp@rfcci.rospac.msk.su
Address: Ul. Sovetskaya 24-b, Perm 614000
Tel.: (3422) 12-28-11, 12-86-88
Fax: (3422) 12-41-12

PRIMORSKY KRAI

Address: Ul. Svetlanskaya 22, Vladivostok 690110
Tel.: (4232) 22-38-00
Fax: (4232) 22-17-69
Representation in Moscow
Aleksei Valeryevich Bespalov
Address: 1 Krasnogvardeysky Proezd 9, 123100
Tel./Fax: (095) 255-8213
Primorsky Krai Chamber of Commerce and Industry (Free Economic Zone Nakhodka)
Konstantin Vasilyevich Goncharov, Chairman
E-mail: tpp-rfe@nhk.infosys.ru
Address: Nakhodkinsky Prospect 10, Nakhodka-4 692900
Tel.: (4236) 64-59-14, 64-18-45

Fax: (4236) 64-59-14
Primorsky Krai Chamber of Commerce and Industry
Vladimir Borisovich Brezhnev, Chairman
E-mail: tpp-rfe@nhk.infosys.ru
Address: Okeansky Prospect 13a, Vladivostok 690600
Tel.: (4232) 26-96-30, 26-13-80
Fax: (4232) 22-72-26

PSKOV OBLAST

Address: Ul. Nekrasova 23, Pskov 180001
Tel.: (8112) 16-22-03, 16-48-18
Fax: (8112) 16-03-90
Representation in Moscow
Igor Petrovich Novoselov
Address: Ul. Nikolskaya 10/2, Bldg. 2B, Room 415, 109012
Tel/fax: (095) 928-0795
Pskov Oblast Chamber of Commerce and Industry
Vladimir Anatolyevich Zubov, President
E-mail: pskov@rfcci.rospac.msk.su, tpp@zavet.pskov.su
Address: Ul. Sovetskaya 15a, Pskov 180000
Tel.: (8112) 16-38-83
Fax: (8112) 16-00-52

ROSTOV OBLAST

Address: Ul. Sotsialisticheskaya 112, Rostov-na-Donu 344050
Tel.: (8632) 44-18-10
Fax: (8632) 44-15-59
Valery Leonidovich Yevteyev, Head, Department of International and Foreign Economic Relations
Tel.: (8632) 40-55-29
Fax: (8632) 40-17-01
Representation in Moscow
Viktor Petrovich Vodolatsky
Address: Ul. Novy Arbat 19, Rooms 1909, 1911, 102025
Tel: (095) 203-9471
Fax: (095) 203-8958
Rostov Oblast Chamber of Commerce and Industry
Nikolay Ivanovich Prisyazhnyuk, President
E-mail: tpp@rost.ru
Address: Ul. Pushkinskaya 176, Rostov-na-Donu 344022
Tel.: (8632) 64-45-47
Fax: (8632) 64-45-47, 92-39-94

RYAZAN OBLAST

Address: Ul. Lenina 30, Ryazan 390000
Tel.: (0912) 27-45-07, 27-21-25
Fax: (0912) 44-25-68
Representation in Moscow
Viktor Aleksandrovich Rodionov
Address: Ul. Novy Arbat 19, Room 2213, 127025
Tel: (095) 203-6234, 203-9438, 203-6178
Fax: (095) 203-6185
Ryazan Oblast Chamber of Commerce and Industry
Tatyana Vasilyevna Guseva, President
E-mail: ryazancci@rtpp.ryazan.su
Address: Ul. Gorkogo 17, Ryazan 390023
Tel.: (0912) 77-20-67, 28-99-03/67/68/73/74
Fax: (0912) 28-99-02, 28-99-65

SAKHA REPUBLIC (YAKUTIA)

Vyacheslav Anatolyevich Shtyrov, President
Address: Ul. Kirova 11, Dom Pravitelstva, Yakutsk 677022
Tel.: (4112) 43-50-50
Fax: (4112) 43-55-57
Representation in Moscow
Nikolay Nikolayevich Yermolayev
Address: Myasnitsky Proezd 3/26, 107087
Tel: (095) 925-5281, 923-1097
Fax: (095) 928-4221
Sakha Republic Chamber of Commerce and Industry
Sergey Gennadyevich Bakulin, Chairman
E-mail: palata91@mail.ru
Address: Ul. Lenina 22, Suite 214, Yakutsk 677000
Tel.: (4112) 26-64-96

SAKHALIN OBLAST

Address: Kommunistichesky Prospect 39, Yuzhno-Sakhalinsk 639011
Tel.: (4242) 72-19-02
Fax: (4242) 72-18-01
Representation in Moscow
Vladimir Ivanovich Shapoval
Address: Ul. Novy Arbat 19, Room 1132, 127025
Tel: (095) 203-5141, 203-7909
Fax: (095) 203-8456
Sakhalin Oblast Chamber of Commerce and Industry
Yury Evgenyevich Bimayev
E-mail: sah_cci@svtc.ru
Address: Ul. Kryukova 53, Suite 10, Yuzhno-Sakhalinsk 693000
Tel.: (4242) 72-38-17, 72-25-48
Fax: (4242) 72-25-48

SAMARA OBLAST

Address: Ul. Molodogvardeyskaya 210, Samara 443006
Tel.: (8462) 32-22-68

Fax: (8462) 32-13-40
Representation in Moscow
Gennady Vasilyevich Gendin
Address: Veskovsky Per. 2, 127030
Tel: (095) 973-3620, 973-3616, 973-2497, 973-0481
Fax: (095) 973-0554
Middle Volga Chamber of Commerce and Industry
Boris Vasilyevich Ardalin, Chairman
E-mail: samara@rfcci.rospac.msk.su
Address: Ul. Alekseya Tolstogo 6, Samara 443099
Tel.: (8462) 32-11-59
Fax: (8462) 70-48-96

SARATOV OBLAST

Address: Ul. Moskovskaya 72, Saratov 410042
Tel.: (8452) 27-37-30
Fax: (8452) 72-52-54
Boris Leonidovich Shinchuk, Minister of International and Economic Relations
Tel: (8452) 24-13-76
Fax: (8652) 24-27-63
Representation in Moscow
Irina Viktorovna Silakova
Address: Podkopayevsky Per. 7, Bldg.3, 109028
Tel/fax: (095) 917-0542, 917-0519
Saratov Chamber of Commerce and Industry
Vladimir Vladimirovich Davydov, President
E-mail: secretary@sgtpp.overta.ru
Address: Ul. Bol. Kazatchya 30, Saratov 410600
Tel.: (8452) 27-70-78

SMOLENSK OBLAST

Administration
Address: Soviet House, Smolensk 214008
Tel.: (0812) 23-67-39, 23-68-51
Fax: (0812) 23-68-51
Smolensk Oblast Chamber of Commerce and Industry
Oleg Vladimirovich Lukirich, President
E-mail: smolensk@rfcci.rospac.msk.su
Address: Ul. Karla Marx 12, Smolensk 214000
Tel.: (0812) 23-74-50, 23-74-32
Fax: (0812) 23-74-50

ST. PETERSBURG CITY

Address: Smolny, St. Petersburg 193060
Tel.: (812) 271-7413, 273-5924
Fax: (812) 276-1772
Aleksander Vadimovich Prokhorenko, Vice Governor, Chairman of Foreign Relations Committee
Tel.: (812) 276-1204
Fax: (812) 276-1633
Representation in Moscow
Vagif Narimanovich Guseynov
Address: Ul. Spiridonovka 20, Bldg. 1, 103001
Tel: (095) 290-4364, 290-1794
Fax: (095) 203-5060

STAVROPOL KRA

Address: Ploschad Lenina 1, Stavropol 355025
Tel.: (8652) 35-22-52
Fax: (8652) 35-06-60
Representation in Moscow
Anatoly Leonidovich Koliev
Address: Ul. Novy Arbat 19, Room 1713, 127025
Tel: (095) 203-5536
Fax: (095) 203-5539
Stavropol Krai Chamber of Commerce and Industry
Vladimir Georgievich Konstantinov, President
E-mail: stavropol@rfcci.rospac.msk.su
Address: Ul. Lenina 384, Stavropol 355034
Tel.: (8652) 94-53-34
Fax: (8652) 34-05-10

SVERDLOVSK OBLAST

Address: Ploschad Oktyabrskaya 1, Yekaterinburg 620031
Tel.: (3432) 70-54-73, 70-54-68
Fax: (3432) 70-54-72, 71-27-49
Representation in Moscow
Vladimir Serafimovich Melentyev
Address: Ul. Nezhinskaya 14, Korpus 5, 119517
Tel: (095) 441-1180
Fax: (095) 441-1182
Ural Chamber of Commerce and Industry
Yury Petrovich Matushkin, President
E-mail: tpp16@rfcci.rospac.msk.su
Address: Ul. Vostochnaya 6, Yekaterinburg 620027
Tel.: (3432) 53-04-49, 55-81-27, 53-58-60
Fax: (3432) 53-58-63

TAIMYR DOLGANO-NENETS AUTONOMOUS AREA

Address: Ul. Sovetskaya 35, Dudinka 647000, Krasnoyarsk Krai
Tel.: (39111) 2-53-74, 2-11-60
Fax: (39111) 5-82-07
Representation in Moscow
Vladimir Petrovich Mekhanik
Address: Voznesensky Per. 22, 103009
Tel.: (095) 797-8280
Fax: (095) 786-8356
Taimyr Area Chamber of Commerce and Industry
Petr Radislavovich Gershanovich, President
E-mail: taimyr@rfcci.rospac.msk.su

Address: Ul. Begicheva 4, Dudinka 647000
Tel./Fax: (39111) 2-55-09

TAMBOV OBLAST

Address: Ul. Sovetskaya 106, Tambov 392017
Tel.: (0752) 22-10-61
Fax: (0752) 22-25-18
Tambov Oblast Chamber of Commerce and Industry
Nikolay Fedorovich Kalinov, President
E-mail: cmi@tmb.su
Address: Ul. Internatsionalnaya 118, Tambov 392622
Tel.: (0752) 72-49-35, 71-58-91
Fax: (0752) 71-58-91

TATARSTAN REPUBLIC

Mintimer Sharipovich Shaimiyev, President
Address: Kremlin, Kazan 420014
Tel.: (8432) 92-02-30
Fax: (8432) 92-70-88
Representation in Moscow
Nazif Muzagidanovich Mirikhanov
Address: 3 Kotelnichesky Per. 13/15, Bldg. 1, 115172
Tel: 915-3399, 915-3742, 915-5802
Fax: 915-3487, 915-0610
Tatarstan Republic Chamber of Commerce and Industry
Shamil Rakhimovich Ageyev, General Director
E-mail: kazan@rfcci.rospac.msk.su
Address: Ul. Pushkina 18, Kazan 420503
Tel.: (8432) 64-62-07
Fax: (8432) 36-09-66

TOMSK OBLAST

Address: Ploschad Lenina 6, Tomsk-69 634032
Tel.: (3822) 510-813
Fax: (3822) 510-730
Vladimir Aleksandrovich Zhidkikh, First Vice Governor
E-mail: tomskadm@chat.ru
Tel.: (3822) 51-03-05
Fax: (3822) 51-00-64
Representation in Moscow
Aleksander Nikolayevich Cherevko
Address: Ul. Malaya Dmitrovka 3, 103006
Tel.: (095) 973-2538, 973-2539, 200-3980
Fax: (095) 299-3611, 973-2538
Tomsk Oblast Chamber of Commerce and Industry
Arkady Yakovlevich Eskin, President
E-mail: tpp@cnti.tomsk.ru
Address: Ul. Komsomolskaya 3, Tomsk 634050
Tel.: (3822) 51-00-88, 51-00-33
Fax: (3822) 51-00-54

TULA OBLAST

Address: Prospect Lenina 2, Tula 300600
Tel.: (0872) 27-84-36
Fax: (0872) 20-63-26
Representation in Moscow
Boris Afanasyevich Grigoryev
Address: Veskovsky Per. 2, 103030
Tel: (095) 978-2205, 978-1456
Fax: (095) 978-0643
Tula Oblast Chamber of Commerce and Industry
Yury Mikhailovich Agafonov, President
E-mail: tula@rfcci.rospac.msk.su
Address: Krasnoarmeysky Prospect 25, Suite 206, 408, Tula 300041
Tel.: (0872) 36-45-17
Fax: (0872) 36-02-16

TUVA REPUBLIC

Address: Chulduma 18, Dom Pravitelstva, Kyzyl 667000
Tel.: (39422) 3-69-12, 3-69-48
Fax: (39422) 1-13-54/46
Representation in Moscow
Orlan Oorzhakovich Cholbeney
Address: Ul. Donskaya 8, Bldg. 2, 117049
Tel.: (095) 236-4801
Fax: (095) 236-4553
Tuva Republic Chamber of Commerce and Industry
Tatiana Aleksandrovna Tyutrina, Chairman
E-mail: tpp@tuva.ru
Address: Ul. Tuvinskikh Dobrovoltsev 29, Kyzyl 667000
Tel.: (39422) 325-51
Fax: (39422) 367-22

TVER OBLAST

Address: Ul. Sovetskaya 44, Tver 170000
Tel.: (0822) 33-10-51
Fax: (0822) 42-55-08
Representation in Moscow
Anatoly Mikhailovich Dubodel
Address: Ul. Bolshaya Dmitrovka 26, Room 816, 103426
Tel./Fax: (095) 292-1485
Tver Oblast Chamber of Commerce and Industry
Andrey Alekseyevich Stroyev, Chairman
E-mail: tvertpp@rfcci.rospac.msk.su
Address: Vagzhanovsky Per. 9, Tver 170000
Tel.: (0822) 42-78-43, 42-61-19
Fax: (0822) 42-78-43

TYUMEN OBLAST

Address: Ul. Volodarskogo 45, Tyumen 625004
Tel.: (3452) 46-51-80, 46-77-20
Fax: (3452) 24-48-81, 46-55-42
Representation in Moscow
Vladimir Mikhailovich Goryunov
Address: Ul. Pyatnitskaya 47, Bldg.2 , 119017
Tel: (095) 953-0622
Fax: (095) 953-0324
Tyumen Oblast Chamber of Commerce and Industry
Nikolay Nikolayevich Karnaukhov, President
E-mail: tmntpp@sibtel.ru
Address: Ul. Respubliki 211a, Tyumen 625000
Tel.: (3452) 21-38-08, 21-08-09
Fax: (3452) 21-08-09

UDMURT REPUBLIC

Address: Ul. Pushkinskaya 214, Izhevsk 426007
Tel.: (3412) 49-70-10
Fax: (3412) 49-70-39
Viktor Arkadievich Vikulov, Minister of International Relations
E-mail: mir@interlink.udm.ru
Tel.: (3412) 25-91-20
Fax: (3412) 78-49-97
Representation in Moscow
Andrey Vladimirovich Sakovich
Address: Ul. Novy Arbat 19, Room 2024, 127025
Tel: (095) 203-5352
Fax: (095) 203-9147
Udmurt Republic Chamber of Commerce and Industry
Yevgeny Yuryevich Vylegzhanin, President
E-mail: izhtpp@rfcci.rospac.msk.su
Address: Ul. Galyansky Proselok 54a, Izhevsk 426063
Tel.: (3412) 75-03-08, 76-14-17, 75-13-19
Fax: (3412) 75-03-08

ULYANOVSK OBLAST

Address: Ploschad Lenina 1, Ulyanovsk 432700
Tel.: (8422) 41-29-43, 41-20-78
Fax: (8422) 32-52-44
Representation in Moscow
Aleksander Fedorovich Kotelevsky
Address: Denezhny Per. 12, floor 4, 119002
Tel: (095) 241-4374, 241-3142
Fax: (095) 241-3899
Ulyanovsk Oblast Chamber of Commerce and Industry
Yevgeny Stepanovich Balandin, President
E-mail: ultpp@mv.ru
Address: Ul. Engelsa 19, Ulyanovsk 432600
Tel.: (8422) 31-45-23, 31-83-44
Fax: (8422) 32-93-73

VLADIMIR OBLAST

Address: Oktyabrsky Prospect 21, Vladimir 600000
Tel.: (0922) 33-15-52
Fax: (0922) 35-34-45
Representation in Moscow
Andrey Veniaminovich Yarin
Tel.: (095) 911-1846, 299-6649
Vladimir Oblast Chamber of Commerce and Industry
Evgeny Borisovich Limonov, President
E-mail: root@cci.vladimir.ru
Address: Ul. Mira 29, Vladimir 600017
Tel.: (0922) 23-25-64, 23-69-54, 23-79-91
Fax: (0922) 23-69-54, 23-79-91

VOLGOGRAD OBLAST

Address: Prospect Lenina 9, Volgograd 400098
Tel.: (8442) 33-66-88, 33-52-03
Fax: (8442) 93-62-12
Representation in Moscow
Tatiana Yevgenyevna Trubitsyna
Address: Ul. Kastanayevskaya 13, Suite 1, 121098
Tel./ Fax: (095) 142-0973
Volgograd Oblast Chamber of Commerce and Industry
Aleksander Dmitrievich Belitsky, President
E-mail: volgograd@rfcci.rospac.msk.su
Address: Ul. 7 Gvardeyskaya 2, Volgograd 400005
Tel.: (8442) 34-67-34, 34-41-78, 93-61-35
Fax: (8442) 34-22-02

VOLOGDA OBLAST

Address: Ul. Gertsena 2, Vologda 160035
Tel.: (8172) 72-07-64, 72-23-80
Fax: (8172) 25-15-54
Leonid Genrikhovich Iogman, Head of Economic Department
E-mail: avo@vologda.ru
Tel.: (8172) 72-84-70
Fax: (8172) 72-27-19, 25-14-54
Representation in Moscow
Address: Starokonyushenny Per. 4, Bldg.5
Tel.: (095) 449-2655
Fax: (095) 449-2634
Vologda Oblast Chamber of Commerce and Industry
Galina Dmitriyevna Telegina, President
E-mail: grant@vologda.ru
Address: Ul. Lermontova 15, Vologda 160035
Tel.: (8172) 72-14-80, 72-49-00, 72-32-58
Fax: (8172) 72-32-58

VORONEZH OBLAST

Administration
Address: Ploschad Lenina 1, Voronezh 394015
Tel.: (0732) 55-27-37, 55-45-34
Fax: (0732) 55-38-78
Representation in Moscow
Aleksander Ivanovich Firsov
Address: Ul. 2 Tverskaya-Yamskaya 26, 125047
Tel./Fax: (095) 250-9855
Voronezh Oblast Chamber of Commerce and Industry
Vyacheslav Aleksandrovich Kondratyev, President
E-mail: voronezh@rfcci.rospac.msk.su
Address: Ul. Svobody 73, Voronezh 394006
Tel.: (0732) 52-21-17
Fax: (0732) 52-49-38, 77-24-87

YAMALO-NENETS AUTONOMOUS AREA

Address: Ul. Respubliki 72, Salekhard 629008
Tel.: (34922) 4-46-02, 4-00-66
Fax: (34922) 4-52-89, 4-79-99
Representation in Moscow
Nikolay Arkadyevich Borodulin
Address: Arkhangelsky Per. 15, Bldg. 3, 101000
Tel: (095) 924-6789, 923-2546
Fax: (095) 925-8338

YAROSLAVL OBLAST

Address: Sovetskaya Ploschad 1, Yaroslavl 150000
Tel.: (0852) 22-23-28
Fax: (0852) 32-84-14
Abrosimova Irina Viktorovna, Head of Department for Investments & Foreign Economic Activity
E-mail: abro@adm.yar.ru
Address: Sovetskaya Ploschad 3, Yaroslavl 150000
Tel.: (0852) 72-94-15
Fax: (0852) 32-78-35
Representation in Moscow
Vladimir Vasilyevich Redkin
Address: 123022 Moscow, Mansurovsky Per. 15, 119034
Tel: (095) 201-5965
Fax: (095) 201-2486
Yaroslavl Oblast Chamber of Commerce and Industry
Valery Aleksandrovich Lavrov, President
E-mail: tpp@adm.yar.ru
Address: Sovetskaya Ploschad 1/19, Yaroslavl 150000
Tel.: (0852) 32-88-85, 32-80-53
Fax: (0852) 32-88-85, 72-89-36

GOVERNMENT ORGANIZATIONS RESPONSIBLE FOR FOREIGN INVESTMENT

Ministry of the Economy of the Russian Federation (Minekonomiki of Russia)

Formulation and implementation of the State Policy for attracting foreign investment.
Coordination of the activities of the federal bodies regarding cooperation with foreign investors.
Establishment of free economic zones.
Arranging for and holding international tenders and bidding.
Arranging for Concession agreements and deals on production sharing.

Central Bank of the Russian Federation (Bank of Russia)
Administration of Exchange Control over Capital Transactions

Governing bank transactions with foreign capital.
Licensing of capital transactions in foreign currencies - including long-term credits.

Ministry of Finance of the Russian Federation
Department of Securities

Licensing the activities of financial and of the Russian Federation investment companies.
Governing the participation of foreign investment projects.

Ministry of Finance of the Russian Federation
Department of Tax Reforms

Drafting taxation laws and regulations.
Designing procedures for tax laws to be enforced.

State Property Committee (Goskomimushestvo of Russia - GKI)
Administration for Foreign Investment

Formulation of options for participation of foreign investors in privatization.
Administration of foreign investors participation in privatization.

Russian Fund for Federal Property (RFFP)

Arranging for and holding investment and monetary auctions in the privatization process of state property.
Control over the implementation of investment programs.

State Taxation Service of the Russian Federation (Gosnalogslujba of Russia)
Administration for Foreign Economic Relations and International Taxation

Explanation of the enforcement of tax laws.
Control over the implementation of tax laws.

State Customs Committee of the Russian Federation (SCC of Russia)

Arranging for the customs legalization of foreign economic transactions.
Customs regulation of foreign economic transactions.
Control over the use of customs incentives.

State Registration Chamber of the Ministry of Economy of Russia

Registration of ventures with foreign investments.
Accreditation of the missions of foreign companies.
Support in obtaining visas.

Foreign Investment Promotion Center (FIPC) of the Ministry of Economy of Russia

Informational and advisory services for foreign investors.
Dissemination of investment information - including information on investment projects in the Russian Federation.
Assistance to businessmen in their quest of investment opportunities and particular partners.
Coordination of the activities of the overseas investment offices.

Investment offices of the FIPC

Dissemination of investment information, including investment projects in the Russian Federation.
Promotion of investment projects in and offers of Russian enterprises.
Advisory services for potential investors.

Federal Center for Project Financing

Investment consulting.
drafting of business plans.

INTERNATIONAL AGREEMENTS - BILATERAL INVESTMENT PROTECTION TREATIES AND OTHER INVESTMENT LEGISLATION[3]

As of June 1997, there were 11 bilateral investment protection treaties (BITs) in the Russian Federation. Most of these treaties were concluded by the former Soviet Union but are recognized by Russia as the USSR's legal successor. Additional treaties are under negotiations

The BITs are reciprocal treaties between Russia and individual foreign states that provide legal guarantees to investors from treaty states in Russia as well as to Russian investors in treaty states. Such guarantees normally pertain to the transfer of funds related to foreign investment activities, expropriation and similar measures, losses as a result of armed conflict and civil disturbance as well as the legal succession of investment insurance agencies (subrogation). Under these treaties, foreign investors are assured of either:

1) "national treatment" - treatment no less favorable than the one accorded to Russian investors;
2) "most favored nation treatment" - treatment no less favorable than the one accorded to investors from any third country; and,
3) "full protection and security".

Furthermore, they provide international arbitration for the resolution of disputes arising under the treaties. Such recourse applies to disputes between the contracting states ("state-to-state disputes") and disputes between protected foreign investors and the host state ("investor disputes").

The treatment of "indirect" and "creeping" expropriations are some of the important differences between BITs - even though most of them have similar provisions. In several BITs, transfer guarantees are subject to qualifications.

Under the "umbrella clause", any obligation toward a protected investor that is not fulfilled is considered a violation of the BIT. In this way, investors can obtain treaty protection of their contractual rights against Russian agencies.

In theory, differences among the BITs should not work against the investor. Because of the most favored nation treatment (MFN) provisions, investors from any country that has concluded a BIT with Russia can invoke in their favor the guarantees under any treaty between Russia and any third country. Thus, German investors in Russia are entitled to all the guarantees provided in the BITs of Russia with Austria, Canada, China, etc. The MFN provisions link all the Russian investment related treaties into a

[3] For the complete texts of legislation, please contact Russian Info&Business Center, Inc. at (202) 546-2103

comprehensive network establishing the highest level of protection and investor freedoms envisaged under any one of these treaties.

MULTILATERAL CONVENTIONS

Russia is a member of several multilateral conventions which have the potential to affect the legal protection of investors on its territory. They include:

1 the 1988 **Multilateral Investment Guarantee Agency Convention** (the MIGA Convention) that facilitates the insurance against non-commercial risks in all signatory countries of investors from those countries;

2. the **Convention on the Recognition and Enforcement of Foreign Arbitrage Awards** signed in New York on June 10, 1958 (the New York Convention); and

3. the **Cooperation Agreement between Russia and the European Union.**

Other important conventions such as the one governing the settlement of investment disputes between states and nationals of other states - signed in Washington on March 18, 1965; the Convention on the International Center for the Settlements of Investment Disputes (ICSID Convention); and, the Energy Charter Treaty - signed in Lisbon on December 14, 1994 have not yet been ratified. The latter applies only to investments in the energy sector but lays out detailed standards for investment protection that reflect investment principles recognized internationally. Foreign investors may find this a useful reference in their negotiations with Russia.

RUSSIAN DOMESTIC LAWS

As of June 1997, most guarantees concerning foreign investment were embodied in the Foreign Investment Law. Foreign investors are assured of the following in Chapter 2 of this law:

1. Treatment no less favorable than that accorded to domestic investors (Article 6). Such national treatment, however, is subject to exceptions which may be established by domestic law, notably in the area of ownership or leasing of land and acquisition of rights to natural resources (Article 38) and in connection with privatization (Article 37).

2. Protection against nationalization, confiscation and illegal actions of state bodies and officials (Articles 7 and 8). Nationalization and confiscation measures require enacting legislation by Parliament - in case of confiscation by Parliament, the president or the government is responsible. Such procedures can be contested in Russian courts and must be accompanied by prompt, adequate and effective compensation. However, this guarantee does not explicitly extend to cases of so-called "indirect" and "creeping" expropriation, which are the main concern of investors. Russian authorities compute the amount of compensation after the official announcement of confiscation. However, the value of the affected property may already have been largely discounted in anticipation of the measure.

3. Transfer abroad of investment proceeds in foreign currency (Article 10). One has to keep in mind that 50 percent of the revenues from Russian exports must be converted into rubles at the official exchange rate.

4. Reinvestment or other use inside Russia of investment proceeds in local currency (Article 11). While the conversion of local currency proceeds is not guaranteed by the Foreign Investment Law, investors can buy hard currency for rubles through banks or currency exchanges; and

5. Recourse to Russian courts and, in some instances, arbitration proceedings for the settlement of investment disputes (Article 9). However, according to international treaties, foreign investors are entitled to international arbitration. Investors from countries that have a BIT with Russia have access to international arbitration while investors from other countries do not.

Although the investment protection guarantees of the Foreign Investment Law overlap with those found in the BITs of Russia, the latter are frequently more comprehensive, avoid technical loopholes and can be enforced through recourse to international arbitration and diplomatic protection. Article 5 of the Law is particularly important. It provides that international treaties apply directly to foreign investments in Russia and take precedence over domestic law in cases of conflict. However, the latter rule may be subject to question if a conflict arises between an international treaty's provision and the Constitution of Russia.

ECONOMIC STABILIZATION TOOLS

Russian legislation provides a number of stabilization mechanisms in order to limit the damage a foreign investor may suffer in a deteriorating investment climate. The **Foreign Investment Law** includes a provision that postpone for one year the enforcement of a law or any legal act that deteriorates the conditions of preexisting foreign investments. **Presidential Decree No. 1466 "On the Improvement of Work with Foreign Investment"**, adopted on September 27, 1993 provides that legal acts will not be applied to already existing wholly or partly foreign-owned enterprises for a period of three years if they introduce changes for the worse. The law provides that they will apply immediately if they improve the present conditions. **Presidential Decree No. 2285 "On Issues of Agreements on Production Sharing in the Mineral Resource Sector",** adopted on December 24, 1993, applies the "grandfather" clause to production-sharing agreements between foreign investors and Russian state bodies. The clause calls for the agreement to be modified in order to keep the foreign investors as a whole entity. Thus, the Russian side to the agreement is the one that solely shoulder all the losses.

While "grandfather" schemes may provide some comfort to foreign investors, they afford only limited protection. First, they do not encompass all the types of adverse legislative changes. Second, the one to three years "freezing periods" are frequently too short, especially when investment projects have considerable lead times before they yield returns. Third, and foremost, the grandfather clauses are themselves part of domestic Russian legislation. As with any other piece of legislation, they can, at any moment, be changed or repealed by the Russian legislature.

Under the Russian Constitution, considerable powers have devolved to the Federation's jurisdictions and even to its municipalities. Local legislation can affect federal legislation on the rights of foreign investors. To safeguard investors against this possibility, the two presidential decrees mentioned above have provisions that void sub-federal legislation impairing federal laws or decrees. The validity and scope of these provisions might, however, raise questions about their constitutionality.

DISPUTE RESOLUTION

As mentioned above, Russia is a member of the ICSID Convention - an important international convention for the resolution of disputes with foreign investors. This Convention was opened to signature on March 18, 1965 on behalf of member countries of the International Bank for Reconstruction and Development to provide facilities for the conciliation and arbitration of investment disputes between contracting states and nationals of other contracting states. There are clear indications that Russia might adhere to the Convention in the near future. According to Article 9 of the Foreign Investment Law, "investment disputes" are to be settled by the Supreme Court or by the Supreme Arbitration Court of the Russian Federation - if no other methods of settlement are stipulated by international agreements. Therefore, the Russian Foreign Investment Law leaves a door open for the international settlement of investment disputes.

Furthermore, Russia has subscribed to several bilateral treaties on investment protection - these usually incorporate provisions on the settlement of investment disputes. Foreign investors must keep in mind that the stipulation of international treaties prevail over Russian domestic legislation. As to "other disputes" where a treaties prevail over Russian foreign interest is involved, these would typically be decided by Russian Courts, unless the parties have agreed to have them settled by arbitration.

Disputes involving an enterprise with foreign interest are usually considered, under Russian law, as disputes having an international character. Therefore, upon agreement between the parties, such disputes can be submitted for arbitration in any country. The parties are free to choose either *ad hoc* or "institutional" arbitration, and under certain circumstances they have also the choice of the substantive law.

Several Russian bodies are members of the International Chamber of Commerce - though Russia is not a member of the ICC's International Court of Arbitration. Nevertheless, ICC arbitration is increasingly being adopted involving foreign investment in Russia.

Foreign investors are advised to pay particular attention when choosing the most appropriate provision for arbitration in their contractual relationships with Russian partners or Russian subjects, as well as in the relationships between their fully or partially owned Russian enterprise and other physical and legal persons.

Special courts have been set up in Russia to replace the previous body - State Arbitration or *Gosarbitrazh* - for the settlement of economic disputes. The jurisdiction of these courts (commonly referred to as arbitrage tribunals) should not generally apply to foreign investors and/or enterprises with foreign participation. Their jurisdiction would apply only if the disputing parties agree, or if stipulated by intergovernmental or international agreement. In certain areas - mainly administrative disputes - the competence of these tribunals is considered exclusive and mandatory.

INCENTIVES & PRIVILEGES FOR INVESTORS

Incentives are granted to producers and investors promoting the development of various regions or economic sectors. The system of incentives, however, is subject to frequent changes.

SPECIAL TAX INCENTIVES

The Foreign Investment Law (Article 28) provides that tax incentives may be granted to enterprises with foreign investments operating in priority areas and in certain regions. In practice, however, a two year tax break previously applicable to enterprises with foreign investment (three years in the Far East Region) was repealed. Special tax incentives currently available are extremely limited. At the present time, enterprises registered after January 1, 1994 are the beneficiaries - under those tax incentives - of a two year tax break (reduced to 25 percent and 50 percent of the base tax rate in years three and four, respectively) if they:

are involved in the material production activities, and;

have at least 30 percent paid in foreign equity participation - the sum must be equal to a minimum of $10 million.

Moreover, tax breaks are only available if the income from production activities during the first two years is greater than 70 percent of the enterprise's total income from all activities (90 percent during years three and four).

CUSTOMS INCENTIVES

Property imported into Russia by foreign investors as a contribution to the charter capital is exempt from customs duties upon importation (also see Chapter 5). Tariff incentives, such as return of earlier paid customs, lower tariff rates or total exemptions, apply to:

imported goods that will be contributed to the authorized capital;
certain products and exports;
property imported by foreign employees for their own needs.

With a special permission of the Russian Government, tariffs are reduced by 50 per- cent on certain goods imported as foreign investments if:

the foreign suppliers are, at the same time, the founders of enterprises producing similar goods on the Russian territory;
these enterprises use Russian raw materials and labor;
foreign companies invest into material production;
total investments into the enterprise are no less than US$ 100 million;
foreign contribution to the authorized capital of the enterprise is not less than US$ 10 million.

EXPORT AND IMPORT ACTIVITY

Foreign affiliates and enterprises with more than a 30 percent equity stake in Russian companies may export their products and import goods for their needs without any import or export license. Since 1994, export licenses have been required only for "strategic natural resources" products.

HARD CURRENCY RECEIPTS

Enterprises operating in Russia are obliged to exchange 50 percent of their hard-currency income into rubles on the domestic currency market. It is, however, possible to buy hard currency for import needs or for transfers abroad.

FINANCING FACILITIES

Presidential Decree No. 1928, "On Private Investments in the Russian Federation", adopted on September 17, 1994 authorizes the Russian Government to allocate 0.5 percent of its gross domestic product to finance highly efficient investment projects that have a commercial participation. The State contribution to such projects is usually 20 percent - it is no greater than 80 percent of the investment. The balance of funds in the project must be made up by private investors.

These are some of the possible forms that State participation can take in a project:

loan by the Russian Central Bank, denominated in foreign currency for a maximum of 24 months;
government purchases of equity in joint-stock companies that can be sold on the market once the project is profitable; and
special incentives for large investments when a foreign contribution exceeds 30 per- cent of share capital.

FREE ECONOMIC ZONES

Russia is eager to use free economic zones (FEZs) to encourage foreign investment. About 15 FEZs exist in Russia, the most advanced of which are in **Nachodka** - in the Far East - and **Yantar** - in Kaliningrad.

The conditions for investments in FEZs differ from zone to zone and are regulated by each zone's laws and regulations. Federal legislation regulates only the most important issues.

The incentives may be the following:

simplified registration of enterprises in the FEZs;
lower rates of taxation - they can, however, not be lower than 50 percent of the rate being applied on the Russian territory;
lower leasing rates for land and leasing terms up to 70 years;
lower tariffs on imports and exports, and expedient border procedures;
simplified procedures for the entry and exit of foreign citizens, including waiver of visa requirements.

All incentives are to be endorsed by the Russian Council of Ministers and approved by the Parliament.

Free Customs Zones and Bonded Warehouses are the two specific types of FEZs detailed in the Customs Code of the Russian Federation - adopted on June 18, 1993.

INVESTMENT PROMOTION

A system of foreign investment promotion has been established in the Russian Federation The Ministry of the Economy assumes the leading role in the promotion of foreign investment and is responsible for: drafting and implementing state policy aimed at attracting foreign investment; coordinating the activities of the federal and regional executive bodies regarding the cooperation with foreign investors; establishing free economic zones; arranging for and holding international tenders; arranging for concession agreements and production sharing deals; and, allocating loans provided by international financial organizations and foreign states. The Department for International Investment Cooperation has been established within the Ministry of the Economy for the purpose of dealing with the specific FDI promotion issues. This Department ensures the interaction with other executive bodies and deals practically with all major issues of state DFI policy.

The State Registration Chamber has been established within the Russian Ministry of the Economy. Registering ventures with foreign investments, keeping a State register of ventures, and accrediting the missions of foreign companies is authorized under the law.

Information and consultative services for foreign investors are rendered by the Foreign Investment Promotion Center (FIPC) - which is affiliated to the Ministry of the Economy.

The Federal Center for Project Financing makes pre-feasibility studies. It also makes expert analysis of international investment cooperation and the use of credits granted under the guarantees of the Russian government.

The Ministry of Finance, the State Property Committee (GKI), the Federal Property Fund, the State Tax Service, the State Customs Committee, and the Russian Central Bank also play an active role in foreign investment promotion.

ADVISORY COUNCIL ON FOREIGN INVESTMENT

In June 1994, the Advisory Council on Foreign Investment was created to promote foreign investment. It was created on the initiative of the Government of the Russian Federation and more than 20 representatives of major international corporations. The Advisory Group is chaired by Prime Minister .

Governmental Decree No. 1108 dated September 29, 1994 officially established the Advisory Group. According to the Decree the three working groups have been formed to draft proposals:

to upgrade Russia's attractiveness as an investment location, especially for foreign investors - this group is headed by the Minister of the Economy

to eliminate external barriers for Russian exporters - this group is headed Deputy Prime Minister and Minister of Foreign Economic Relations, and,

to improve tax legislation and incentive measures for foreign investments - this group is headed by the Minister of Finance

Proposals and recommendations were drafted by these groups and presented to the first meeting of the Advisory Council in November 1994. Many of the recommendations have been taken under consideration by the Government and proposed to the Duma. A special plan on implementing these recommendations has been developed by the different Russian ministries involved and by representatives of the work groups. The plan includes concrete measures which could improve banking and currency regulation, introduce changes in the tax law and clarify some articles concerning tax legislation.

FOREIGN INVESTMENT PROMOTION CENTER

The **Foreign Investment Promotion Center (FIPC)** was created in June 1997 as a standard framework for the long-term attraction of foreign capital. The FIPC, in accordance with Governmental Decree No. 657, adopted on June 30, 1997, is a government body subordinated to the Russian Ministry of the Economy.

The mission of the FIPC is to attract, facilitate and increase foreign investment into the Russian Federation.

The main objectives of the Centers are:

to effectively encourage foreign investment into the Russian economy;
to study investment projects and bring together potential partners;
to make it attractive for foreign investors to establish a presence in Russia;
to advocate laws and regulations to improve Russia's investment climate;
to offer pre- and post-investment services to foreign investors;
to give support and guidance to Russian regions and to their investment promotion agencies for local industries;

In accordance with its objectives the FIPC carries out the following services:

promulgates cooperation and ensures the assistance of Russian federal and regional executive government bodies to potential investors;
assists, advises and renders administrative support to foreign companies already present in Russia;
supplies information on new investment opportunities in Russia and its Regions and markets Russian investment projects abroad through FIPC's offices in Western Europe;
provides the foreign investor with all of the basic data he requires in order to structure his project and appraise it in advance;
informs foreign investors on the changes in the Russian foreign investment legislation and consults on the existing laws and regulations concerning foreign companies activities in Russia;
identifies Russian partners for foreign firms and business people looking for partnership in Russia and its different regions;
arranges contacts and prepares the itineraries for the prospective investors visiting business locations of Russian partners;
assists in the negotiation process between foreign investors and Russian partners and holds talks with potential investors on the required conditions to attract and use foreign investment credits in Russia.

In order to fulfill these objectives, the FIPCs decided to open overseas offices in Frankfurt, Paris, London and Milan during the next two years. The first two offices - Frankfurt and Paris - started their activities in the Fall of 1997.

The European Bank for Reconstruction assists the FIPC in its activities. The FIPC has elaborated its investment promotion methodology based on the practices which have been successfully developed by such prominent investment promotion institutions as the Industrial Development Agency of Ireland and the Foreign Investment Advisory Service and Multilateral investment Guarantee Agency - both divisions of the World Bank.

According to the existing foreign investment promotional techniques, the following forms of activity will be undertaken by FIPC through its Moscow led network of offices:
advertising,
direct mailing;
investment seminars;
investment missions;
participation in trade shows and exhibitions;
distribution of literature;
one-to-one direct mailing efforts;
preparation for the visits of prospective investors;
matching prospective investors with local partners;
acquiring permits and approvals from various governmental departments;
preparing project proposals;
conducting feasibility studies;
providing services to investors after the projects have become operational.

Russian Foreign Investment Promotion Center:
Smolensky Bulvar, 3/5, Moscow, Russia,.
Tel: 7 095 245 21 71 or 7 095 246 94 39, Fax: 7 095 246 94 39.

OTHER ORGANIZATIONS

Several "joint ventures" associations and clubs are currently in existence in Russia. Two of the most prominent ones - the Association of joint Ventures and the International Associations and Organizations - unite joint ventures and 100% foreign owned enterprises from all over the country. Similar organizations exist in Moscow and St. Petersburg. The aim of these organizations is to bring together managers with similar purposes and problems, to exchange information, to support business conferences, to help in the search of partners, to provide legal support, etc.

Recently, several State and privately-owned insurance companies have begun to operate with foreign investors covering non-commercial risks. One of them is the International Agency for Insurance of Non-Commercial Risks. This Agency is supported by the Russian Government.

Foreign investors can also apply to the Russian Finance Corporation - created in April 1993. It primarily works as an agent of the Russian Government and finances investment projects with centralized finance and credit resources. The Corporation has preferential treatment when it comes to finance and foreign trade operations.

Foreign firms can also get the support from the Russian Chamber of Commerce and Industry, the Ministry of Foreign Economic Relations, various Russian-foreign associations, and others - all of them well-known in the Russian Federation Foreign Economic Relations.

BASIC TITLES ON RUSSIA

title	ISBN
Russia 1000 Largest Industrial Companies Directory	1438740158
Russia 1000 Largest Industrial Companies Directory	1433041111
Russia 500 Largest Industrial Companies Directory	1438740166
Russia 500 Largest Industrial Companies Directory	143304112X
Russia A "Spy" Guide - Strategic Information and Developments	1433041138
Russia A Spy" Guide"	1438740174
Russia Advertising Directory	1438740182
Russia Advertising Directory	1433041146
Russia Air Force Handbook	1438740190
Russia Air Force Handbook	1433041154
Russia and CIS Countries Chambers of Commerce Directory	1438740204
Russia and CIS Countries Chambers of Commerce Directory	1433041162
Russia and NIS Mineral Industry Handbook - Strategic Information and Regulations Vol. 1	1438740212
Russia and NIS Mineral Industry Handbook - Strategic Information and Regulations Vol. 1	1433041170
Russia and NIS Mineral Industry Handbook - Strategic Information and Regulations Vol. 2	1438740220
Russia and NIS Mineral Industry Handbook - Strategic Information and Regulations Vol. 2	1433041189
Russia Army Weapon Systems Handbook	1433061899
Russia Army Weapon Systems Handbook	1433061899
Russia Army Weapon Systems Handbook	1433061899
Russia Army, National Security and Defense Policy Handbook	1438740239
Russia Army, National Security and Defense Policy Handbook	1433041197
Russia Automobile Industry Directory	1438740247
Russia Automobile Industry Directory	1433041200
Russia Aviation and Aerospace Industry Handbook Vol. 1	1438740255
Russia Aviation and Aerospace Industry Handbook Vol. 1	1433041219
Russia Aviation and Aerospace Industry Handbook Vol. 1	1433041219
Russia Aviation and Aerospace Industry Handbook Vol. 2	1438740263
Russia Aviation and Aerospace Industry Handbook Vol. 2	1433041227
Russia Banking & Financial Market Handbook	1438740271
Russia Banking & Financial Market Handbook	1433041235
Russia Banks and Financial Institutions Handbook	143874028X
Russia Banks and Financial Institutions Handbook	1433041243
Russia Beer and Non Alcoholic Beverages Producers Directory	1438740298
Russia Beer and Non Alcoholic Beverages Producers Directory	1433041251
Russia Building Materials Industry Directory	1438740301
Russia Building Materials Industry Directory	143304126X

title	ISBN
Russia Business and Investment Opportunities Yearbook	143874031X
Russia Business and Investment Opportunities Yearbook	1433041278
Russia Business and Investment Opportunities Yearbook Volume 1 Strategic Information and Opportunities	1438777728
Russia Business and Investment Opportunities Yearbook Volume 2 Leading Export-Import, Business, Investment Opportunities and Projects	1577519493
Russia Business and Investment Services Handbook	1438740328
Russia Business and Investment Services Handbook	1433041286
Russia Business Intelligence Report - Practical Information, Opportunities, Contacts	1438740336
Russia Business Intelligence Report - Practical Information, Opportunities, Contacts	1433041294
Russia Business Law Handbook - Strategic Information and Basic Laws	1438770855
Russia Business Law Handbook - Strategic Information and Basic Laws	1438740344
Russia Business Law Handbook - Strategic Information and Basic Laws	1438770855
Russia Business Law Handbook - Strategic Information and Basic Laws	1433041308
Russia Business Law Handbook Volume 2 Investment and Trade Laws Volume 2 Investment and Trade Laws	1577516958
Russia Business Survival Guide	1438740352
Russia Business Survival Guide	1433041316
Russia Charity, Religious and Non Profit organizations Directory	1438740360
Russia Charity, Religious and Non Profit organizations Directory	1433041324
Russia Clothing & Textile Industry Handbook	1438740379
Russia Clothing & Textile Industry Handbook	1433041332
Russia Coal Mining Industry Business Intelligence Report - Practical Information, Opportunities, Contacts	1438740387
Russia Coal Mining Industry Business Intelligence Report - Practical Information, Opportunities, Contacts	1433041340
Russia Coal Mining Industry Directory	1438740395
Russia Coal Mining Industry Directory	1433041359
Russia Company Laws and Regulations Handbook	1433070529
Russia Computers Video TV Electronics Producers Directory	1438740409
Russia Computers Video TV Electronics Producers Directory	1433041367
Russia Constitution and Citizenship Laws Handbook - Strategic Information and Basic Laws	1438779720
Russia Country Study Guide - Strategic Information and Developments Vol.1 History, National Identity, Politics	1433041391
Russia Country Study Guide - Strategic Information and Developments Volt 2. Economy, Industry, Regional Development	1433041375
Russia Country Study Guide - Strategic Information and Developments Volt 3. Army and National Security	1433041383
Russia Country Study Guide - Strategic Information and Developments Volume 1 Strategic Information and Developments	1438775393
Russia Country Study Guide - Strategic Information and Developments Volume 2. Economy, Industry, Regional Development	1438740417
Russia Country Study Guide - Strategic Information and Developments Volume 3. Army and National Security	1438740425
Russia Customs, Trade Regulations and Procedures Handbook	1438740433
Russia Customs, Trade Regulations and Procedures Handbook	1433041405
Russia Defense Industry Directory	1433041413
Russia Diplomatic and International Contacts Directory	1438740441
Russia Diplomatic and International Contacts Directory	1433041421
Russia Diplomatic Handbook - Strategic Information and Developments	143874045X

title	ISBN
Russia Diplomatic Handbook - Strategic Information and Developments	143304143X
Russia Ecology & Nature Protection Handbook	1438740468
Russia Ecology & Nature Protection Handbook	1433041448
Russia Ecology & Nature Protection Laws and Regulation Handbook	1433074753
Russia Economic & Development Strategy Handbook	1438740476
Russia Economic & Development Strategy Handbook	1433041456
Russia Economic, Business and Investment Statistics Yearbook	1438740484
Russia Economic, Business and Investment Statistics Yearbook	1433041464
Russia Education System and Policy Handbook	1433067730
Russia Electrical Engineering Industry Directory	1438740492
Russia Electrical Engineering Industry Directory	1433041472
Russia Electronic and Telecommunications Equipment Producers Directory	1438740506
Russia Electronic and Telecommunications Equipment Producers Directory	1433041480
Russia Energy Policy, Laws and Regulation Handbook	1433072513
Russia Energy Policy, Laws and Regulations Handbook	1438740514
Russia Energy Policy, Laws and Regulations Handbook	1433041499
Russia Energy Sector Handbook	1438740522
Russia Energy Sector Handbook	1433041502
Russia Executive Government Encyclopedic Directory	1433099756
Russia Executive Government Encyclopedic Directory	9781577515135
Russia Executive Government Encyclopedic Directory 2011 VOL 2	1438776012
Russia Executive Government Encyclopedic Directory 2011 VOL 2	1438776012
Russia Executive Government Encyclopedic Directory 2012 VOL 2	1438776039
Russia Executive Government Encyclopedic Directory VOL 1	1438740530
Russia Executive Government Encyclopedic Directory VOL 1	1433041510
Russia Executive Government Encyclopedic Directory VOL 1 2012	1438776020
Russia Executive Government Encyclopedic Directory VOL 2	073979891X
Russia Executive Government Encyclopedic Directory VOL 2 2011	1438776012
Russia Exporters and Importers Directory	1438740549
Russia Exporters and Importers Directory	1433041529
Russia Export-Import and Business Directory volt 1	1433041537
Russia Export-Import and Business Directory volt 2	1433041545
Russia Export-Import and Business Directory Volume 1	1438740557
Russia Export-Import and Business Directory Volume 2	1438740565
Russia Ferrous and Non Ferrous Metallurgy Business Intelligence Report - Practical Information, Opportunities, Contacts	1438740573
Russia Ferrous and Non Ferrous Metallurgy Business Intelligence Report - Practical Information, Opportunities, Contacts	1433041553
Russia Fishing and Fish Processing Industry	1438740581
Russia Fishing and Fish Processing Industry	1433041561
Russia Foreign Policy and Government Guide	143874059X
Russia Foreign Policy and Government Guide	143304157X
Russia Foreign Policy and National Security Yearbook Volume 1 Strategic Information and Regulations	1438745966
Russia Forestry and Timber Industry Directory	1438740603
Russia Forestry and Timber Industry Directory	1433041588
Russia Gaming Industry Investment and Business Guide - Strategic and Practical Information	1438740611
Russia Gaming Industry Investment and Business Guide - Strategic and Practical	1433041596

title	ISBN
Information	
Russia Gold Mining Industry Business Intelligence Report - Practical Information, Opportunities, Contacts	143874062X
Russia Gold Mining Industry Business Intelligence Report - Practical Information, Opportunities, Contacts	143304160X
Russia Gold Mining Industry Directory	1438740638
Russia Gold Mining Industry Directory	1433041618
Russia Government and Business Contacts Handbook	1438740646
Russia Government and Business Contacts Handbook	1433041626
Russia Government Guide: 1000+ Top Government Officials	1438738331
Russia Government Guide: 1000+ Top Government Officials	1433041634
Russia Healthcare Sector Organization, Management and Payment Systems Handbook - Strategic Information, Programs and Regulations	9781433085970
Russia Hotels Directory	143873834X
Russia Hotels Directory	1433041642
Russia Immigration Laws and Regulations Handbook - Strategic Information and Basic Laws	1438783329
Russia Industrial and Business Directory	1438738358
Russia Industrial and Business Directory	1433041650
Russia Insolvency (Bankruptcy) Laws and Regulations Handbook - Strategic Information and Basic Laws	9781433085604
Russia Intelligence & Security Activities & Operations Handbook	1438738366
Russia Intelligence & Security Activities & Operations Handbook	1433041669
Russia Internet and E-Commerce Investment and Business Guide - Strategic and Practical Information: Regulations and Opportunities	1438738374
Russia Internet and E-Commerce Investment and Business Guide - Strategic and Practical Information: Regulations and Opportunities	1433041677
Russia Investment and Business Guide - Strategic and Practical Information	1438738382
Russia Investment and Business Guide - Strategic and Practical Information	1438768575
Russia Investment and Business Guide - Strategic and Practical Information	1433041685
Russia Investment and Business Guide - Strategic and Practical Information	1438768575
Russia Investment and Business Guide Volume 2 Business, Investment Opportunities and Incentives	1577515722
Russia Investment and Trade Laws and Regulations Handbook	1433076535
Russia Justice System and National Police Handbook	1438738390
Russia Justice System and National Police Handbook	1433041693
Russia KGB Handbook: Past, Present, Future	1438738404
Russia KGB Handbook: Past, Present, Future	1433041707
Russia Labor Laws and Regulations Handbook - Strategic Information and Basic Laws	1438781520
Russia Land Ownership and Agriculture Laws Handbook	1438759835
Russia Leather Fur and Tanning Industry Directory	1438738412
Russia Leather Fur and Tanning Industry Directory	1433041723
Russia Mass Media Directory	1438738420
Russia Mass Media Directory	1433041731
Russia Medical & Pharmaceutical Industry Handbook	1438738439
Russia Medical & Pharmaceutical Industry Handbook	143304174X
Russia Metal Working Industry Directory	1438738447
Russia Metal Working Industry Directory	1433041758
Russia Metallurgy Industry Directory	1438738455
Russia Metallurgy Industry Directory	1433041766

title	ISBN
Russia Mineral & Mining Sector Investment and Business Guide - Strategic and Practical Information	1438738463
Russia Mineral & Mining Sector Investment and Business Guide - Strategic and Practical Information	1433041774
Russia Mining & Gold Mining Industry Directory	1438738471
Russia Mining & Gold Mining Industry Directory	1433041782
Russia Mining Industry Business Opportunities Handbook	143873848X
Russia Mining Industry Business Opportunities Handbook	1433041790
Russia Mining Industry Directory (Building Materials)	1438738498
Russia Mining Industry Directory (Building Materials)	1433041804
Russia Mining Laws and Regulations Handbook	1433078112
Russia National Development Strategy Handbook: Important Programs and Developments	143874076X
Russia National Security and Defense Policy Handbook	1438738501
Russia National Security and Defense Policy Handbook	1433041812
Russia Navy Handbook: History and Modern Situation	143873851X
Russia Navy Handbook: History and Modern Situation	1433041820
Russia Northern Regions Regional Investment & Business Guide	143301548X
Russia NUCLEAR INDUSTRY Business Opportunities Handbook	1438738528
Russia NUCLEAR INDUSTRY Business Opportunities Handbook	1433041839
Russia Oil & Gas Industry Business Opportunities Handbook	1438738536
Russia Oil & Gas Industry Business Opportunities Handbook	1433041847
Russia Oil & Gas Sector Business & Investment Opportunities Yearbook	1438740654
Russia Oil & Gas Sector Business & Investment Opportunities Yearbook	1433041855
Russia Oil and Gas Exploration Laws and Regulation Handbook	1433078945
Russia Oil and Gas Industry Encyclopedic Directory	1438740662
Russia Oil and Gas Industry Encyclopedic Directory	1433041863
Russia Oil and Gas Industry Producers Directory	1438740670
Russia Oil and Gas Industry Producers Directory	1433041871
Russia Oil Refining and Gas Processing Companies Handbook	1438740689
Russia Oil Refining and Gas Processing Companies Handbook	143304188X
Russia Orthodox Church Guide	1438740697
Russia Orthodox Church Guide	1433041898
Russia Parliament Encyclopedic Directory	1438740700
Russia Parliament Encyclopedic Directory	1433041901
Russia Parliament Guide	1438740719
Russia Parliament Guide	143304191X
Russia Political Atlas	1438740727
Russia Political Atlas	1433041928
Russia Political Parties Directory	1438740735
Russia Political Parties Directory	1433041936
Russia Power Industry Directory	1438740743
Russia Power Industry Directory	1433041944
Russia Precious Metals Mining Industry Business Intelligence Report - Practical Information, Opportunities, Contacts	1438740751
Russia Precious Metals Mining Industry Business Intelligence Report - Practical Information, Opportunities, Contacts	1433041952
Russia President Vladimir Putin Handbook - Foreign and Domestic Policy	1433041960
Russia President Vladimir Putin Rule: Achievements, Problems and Future Strategies	1433067749

title	ISBN
Russia Privatization Programs and Regulations Handbook	1438740778
Russia Privatization Programs and Regulations Handbook	1433041979
Russia Publishing Printing and Copying Industry Directory	1438740786
Russia Publishing Printing and Copying Industry Directory	1433041987
Russia Pulp & Paper Products Industry Directory	1438740794
Russia Pulp & Paper Products Industry Directory	1433041995
Russia Pulp and Paper Industry Directory	1438740808
Russia Pulp and Paper Industry Directory	1433042002
Russia Radio, TV and Electronic Equipment Producers Directory	1438740816
Russia Radio, TV and Electronic Equipment Producers Directory	1433042010
Russia Recent Economic and Political Developments Yearbook	1433063808
Russia Recent Economic and Political Developments Yearbook	1433063808
Russia Recent Economic and Political Developments Yearbook	1433063808
Russia Regional Economic and Business Atlas	1438740824
Russia Regional Economic and Business Atlas	1433042029
Russia Regional Economic and Business Atlas Volume 2	1577510259
Russia Regional Government Encyclopedic Directory	1438740832
Russia Regional Government Encyclopedic Directory	1433042037
Russia Regional Investment & Business Guide	1438740840
Russia Regional Investment & Business Guide	1433042045
Russia Regional Investment & Business Guide Volume 5 Siberia	1438716826
Russia Research & Development Policy Handbook	1433062801
Russia Research & Development Policy Handbook	1433062801
Russia Research & Development Policy Handbook	1433062801
Russia Research Institutions and Scientists Directory	1438740859
Russia Research Institutions and Scientists Directory	1433042053
Russia Sanitary and Bathroom Equipment Industry Directory	1438740867
Russia Sanitary and Bathroom Equipment Industry Directory	1433042061
Russia Scrap and Waste Processing Industry Directory	1438740875
Russia Scrap and Waste Processing Industry Directory	143304207X
Russia Space Agency and Programs Handbook	1438740883
Russia Space Agency and Programs Handbook	1433042088
Russia Space Programs and Exploration Handbook	1438740891
Russia Space Programs and Exploration Handbook	1433042096
Russia Special and Working Clothing Industry Directory	1438740905
Russia Special and Working Clothing Industry Directory	143304210X
Russia Starting Business (Incorporating) in Russia Guide	143304711X
Russia Starting Business (Incorporating) in....Guide	1433067757
Russia Tax Guide	1438740913
Russia Tax Guide	1433042118
Russia Taxation Laws and Regulations Handbook	143308080X
Russia Telecom & Broadcasting Equipment Producers Directory	1438740921
Russia Telecom & Broadcasting Equipment Producers Directory	1433042126
Russia Telecom Laws and Regulations Handbook	1433082381
Russia Telecommunication Industry Business Opportunities Handbook	143874093X
Russia Telecommunication Industry Business Opportunities Handbook	1433042134
Russia Telecommunication Industry Directory	1438740948
Russia Telecommunication Industry Directory	1433042142

title	ISBN
Russia Textile Industry Directory	1438740956
Russia Textile Industry Directory	1433042150
Russia Tires Rubber and Related Products Industry Directory	1438740964
Russia Tires Rubber and Related Products Industry Directory	1433042169
Russia Today Atlas: For Business and Political Decision Makers	1438740972
Russia Today Atlas: For Business and Political Decision Makers	1433042177
Russia Top Scientists and Researchers Handbook: Members of the Russian Academy of Sciences	1438740980
Russia Top Scientists and Researchers Handbook: Members of the Russian Academy of Sciences	1433042185
Russia Trade Directory: Wholesale Trading Companies	1438740999
Russia Trade Directory: Wholesale Trading Companies	1433042193
Russia Transportation Companies Directory	1438741006
Russia Transportation Companies Directory	1433042207
Russia Transportation Policy and Regulations Handbook	1433067765
Russia Universities and Colleges Directory	1438741014
Russia Universities and Colleges Directory	1433042215
Russia Vodka and Hard Liquors Industry Directory	1438741022
Russia Vodka and Hard Liquors Industry Directory	1433042223
Russia ZIP Codes Directory	1438741030
Russia ZIP Codes Directory	1433042231
Russia: Adygey Republic Regional Investment & Business Guide	1438741049
Russia: Adygey Republic Regional Investment & Business Guide	143304224X
Russia: Astrakhan Province Regional Investment & Business Guide	1438741057
Russia: Astrakhan Province Regional Investment & Business Guide	1433042258
Russia: Bashkortostan Republic Regional Investment & Business Guide	1438741065
Russia: Bashkortostan Republic Regional Investment & Business Guide	1433042266
Russia: Belgorod Province Regional Investment & Business Guide	1438741073
Russia: Belgorod Province Regional Investment & Business Guide	1433042274
Russia: Bryansk Province Regional Investment & Business Guide	1438741081
Russia: Bryansk Province Regional Investment & Business Guide	1433042282
Russia: Buryat Republic Regional Investment & Business Guide	143874109X
Russia: Buryat Republic Regional Investment & Business Guide	1433042290
Russia: Chelyabinsk Province Regional Investment & Business Guide	1438741103
Russia: Chelyabinsk Province Regional Investment & Business Guide	1433042304
Russia: Chita Province Regional Investment & Business Guide	1438741111
Russia: Chita Province Regional Investment & Business Guide	1433042312
Russia: Chuvash Republic Regional Investment & Business Guide	143874112X
Russia: Chuvash Republic Regional Investment & Business Guide	1433042320
Russia: Dagestan Republic Regional Investment & Business Guide	1438741138
Russia: Dagestan Republic Regional Investment & Business Guide	1433042339
Russia: How to Invest, Start and Run Profitable Business in Russia Guide - Practical Information, Opportunities, Contacts	9781433084379
Russia: Ingush Republic Regional Investment & Business Guide	1438741146
Russia: Ingush Republic Regional Investment & Business Guide	1433042347
Russia: Irkutsk Province Regional Investment & Business Guide	1438741154
Russia: Irkutsk Province Regional Investment & Business Guide	1433042355
Russia: Ivanovo Province Regional Investment & Business Guide	1438741162
Russia: Ivanovo Province Regional Investment & Business Guide	1433042363

title	ISBN
Russia: Karachay-Cherkess Republic Regional Investment & Business Guide	1438741170
Russia: Karachay-Cherkess Republic Regional Investment & Business Guide	1433042371
Russia: Karelian Republic Regional Investment & Business Guide	1438741189
Russia: Karelian Republic Regional Investment & Business Guide	143304238X
Russia: Kemerovo Province Regional Investment & Business Guide	1438741197
Russia: Kemerovo Province Regional Investment & Business Guide	1433042398
Russia: Khabarovsk Province Regional Investment & Business Guide	1438741200
Russia: Khabarovsk Territory Regional Investment & Business Guide	1433042401
Russia: Khakass Republic Regional Investment & Business Guide	1438741219
Russia: Khakass Republic Regional Investment & Business Guide	143304241X
Russia: Kirov Province Regional Investment & Business Guide	1438741227
Russia: Kirov Province Regional Investment & Business Guide	1433042428
Russia: Komi Republic Regional Investment & Business Guide	1438741235
Russia: Komi Republic Regional Investment & Business Guide	1433042436
Russia: Kurgan Province Regional Investment & Business Guide	1438741243
Russia: Kurgan Province Regional Investment & Business Guide	1433042444
Russia: Kursk Province Regional Investment & Business Guide	1438741251
Russia: Kursk Province Regional Investment & Business Guide	1433042452
Russia: Leningrad Province Regional Investment & Business Guide	143874126X
Russia: Leningrad Province Regional Investment & Business Guide	1433042460
Russia: Magadan Province Regional Investment & Business Guide	1438741278
Russia: Magadan Province Regional Investment & Business Guide	1433042479
Russia: Mariy El Republic Regional Investment & Business Guide	1438741286
Russia: Mariy El Republic Regional Investment & Business Guide	1433042487
Russia: Mordovian Republic Regional Investment & Business Guide	1438741294
Russia: Mordovian Republic Regional Investment & Business Guide	1433042495
Russia: Moscow City Investment & Business Guide	1438741308
Russia: Moscow City Investment & Business Guide	1433042509
Russia: Moscow Province Regional Investment & Business Guide	1438741316
Russia: Moscow Province Regional Investment & Business Guide	1433042517
Russia: Murmansk Province Regional Investment & Business Guide	1438741324
Russia: Murmansk Province Regional Investment & Business Guide	1433042525
Russia: Nizhniy Novgorod Province Regional Investment & Business Guide	1438741332
Russia: Nizhniy Novgorod Province Regional Investment & Business Guide	1433042533
Russia: North Osetian Republic Regional Investment & Business Guide	1438741340
Russia: North Osetian Republic Regional Investment & Business Guide	1433042541
Russia: Novgorod Province Regional Investment & Business Guide	1438741359
Russia: Novgorod Province Regional Investment & Business Guide	143304255X
Russia: Novosibirsk Province Regional Investment & Business Guide	1438741367
Russia: Novosibirsk Province Regional Investment & Business Guide	1433042568
Russia: Omsk Province Regional Investment & Business Guide	1438741375
Russia: Omsk Province Regional Investment & Business Guide	1433042576
Russia: Orenburg Province Regional Investment & Business Guide	1438741383
Russia: Orenburg Province Regional Investment & Business Guide	1433042584
Russia: Oryol Province Regional Investment & Business Guide	1438741391
Russia: Oryol Province Regional Investment & Business Guide	1433042592
Russia: Rostov Province Regional Investment & Business Guide	1438741405
Russia: Rostov Province Regional Investment & Business Guide	1433042606

title	ISBN
Russia: Ryazan Province Regional Investment & Business Guide	1438741413
Russia: Ryazan Province Regional Investment & Business Guide	1433042614
Russia: Sakha (Yakut) Republic Regional Investment & Business Guide	1433042622
Russia: Sakhalin Regional Investment & Business Guide	1438741421
Russia: Sakhalin Regional Investment & Business Guide	1433042630
Russia: Samara Province Regional Investment & Business Guide	143874143X
Russia: Samara Province Regional Investment & Business Guide	1433042649
Russia: Saratov Regional Investment & Business Guide	1438741448
Russia: Saratov Regional Investment & Business Guide	1433042657
Russia: Smolensk Province Regional Investment & Business Guide	1438741456
Russia: Smolensk Province Regional Investment & Business Guide	1433042665
Russia: St. Petersburg (Russia) Investment & Business Guide	1438745389
Russia: St. Petersburg Business and Investment Opportunities Yearbook	1438745397
Russia: St. Petersburg Business Law Handbook - Strategic Informtion and Basic Laws	1438745400
Russia: St. Petersburg City Business and Investment Opportunities Yearbook	1438745419
Russia: St. Petersburg City Investment & Business Guide	1438745427
Russia: St. Petersburg, Russia: A Spy" Guide"	1438745435
Russia: Stavropol Province Regional Investment & Business Guide	1438741464
Russia: Stavropol Territory Regional Investment & Business Guide	1433042673
Russia: Sverdlovsk Province Regional Investment & Business Guide	1438741472
Russia: Sverdlovsk Province Regional Investment & Business Guide	1433042681
Russia: Tambov Province Regional Investment & Business Guide	1438741480
Russia: Tambov Province Regional Investment & Business Guide	143304269X
Russia: Tatarstan Republic Regional Investment & Business Guide	1438741499
Russia: Tatarstan Republic Regional Investment & Business Guide	1433042703
Russia: Tomsk Province Regional Investment & Business Guide	1438741502
Russia: Tomsk Province Regional Investment & Business Guide	1433042711
Russia: Tula Province Regional Investment & Business Guide	1438741510
Russia: Tula Province Regional Investment & Business Guide	143304272X
Russia: Tver Province Regional Investment & Business Guide	1438741529
Russia: Tver Province Regional Investment & Business Guide	1433042738
Russia: Tyumen Province Regional Investment & Business Guide	1438741537
Russia: Tyumen Province Regional Investment & Business Guide	1433042746
Russia: Tyva Republic Regional Investment & Business Guide	1438741545
Russia: Tyva Republic Regional Investment & Business Guide	1433042754
Russia: Udmurt Republic Regional Investment & Business Guide	1438741553
Russia: Udmurt Republic Regional Investment & Business Guide	1433042762
Russia: Vladimir Province Regional Investment & Business Guide	1438741561
Russia: Vladimir Province Regional Investment & Business Guide	1433042770
Russia: Volgograd Province Regional Investment & Business Guide	143874157X
Russia: Volgograd Province Regional Investment & Business Guide	1433042789
Russia: Vologda Province Regional Investment & Business Guide	1438741588
Russia: Vologda Province Regional Investment & Business Guide	1433042797
Russia: Voronezh Province Regional Investment & Business Guide	1438741596
Russia: Voronezh Province Regional Investment & Business Guide	1433042800
Russian KGB Handbook: Past, Present, Future	143874160X
Russian KGB Handbook: Past, Present, Future	1433042819
Russian Law Firms and Legal Services Companies Directory	1438741618

title	ISBN
Russian Law Firms and Legal Services Companies Directory	1433041715
Russian Navy Handbook: History and Modern Situation	1438741626
Russian Navy Handbook: History and Modern Situation	1433042827
Russian Regional Economic and Business Atlas Volume 2 2011	9781577515142
Russian Regional Economic and Business Atlas Volume 2 2012	9781577515159
Russian Regional Investment Guide: Strategic and Practical Information (World Investment and Business Guide - Strategic and Practical Information Library)	1433000326
Russia-NATO Cooperation Handbook	1438741634
Russia-NATO Cooperation Handbook	1433042835

GLOBAL
WORLD INTERNATIONAL ORGANIZATIONS BUSINESS AND DEVELOPMENT LIBRARY

PRICE - $149.95 EACH

1. Abu Dhabi Fund for Development Handbook
2. African Development Bank Group(AfDB) Handbook
3. African Development Fund (AfDF) Handbook
4. Nigeria Trust Fund (NTF) Handbook
5. African Export-Import Bank (AFREXIMBANK) Handbook
6. Andean Community General Secretariat Handbook
7. Andean Development Corporation (CAF) Handbook
8. Arab Authority for Agricultural Investment and Development (AAAID) Handbook
9. Arab Bank for Economic Development in Africa (BADEA) Handbook
10. Arab Fund for Economic and Social Development (AFESD) Handbook
11. Arab Gulf Programme for United Nations Development Organizations (AGFUND) Handbook
12. Arab Maghreb Union (AMU) Handbook
13. Arab Monetary Fund (AMF) Handbook
14. Arab Organization for Agricultural Development (AOAD) Handbook
15. Arab Planning Institute - Kuwait Handbook
16. Arab Trade Financing Program (ATFP) Handbook
17. Asia-Pacific Economic Cooperation (APEC) Handbook
18. Asian and Pacific Coconut Community (APCC) Handbook
19. Asian Clearing Union (ACU) Handbook
20. Asian Development Bank (AsDB) Handbook
21. Association of Natural Rubber Producing Countries (ANRPC) Handbook
22. Association of South East Asian Nations (ASEAN) Handbook
23. Baltic Council of Ministers Handbook
24. Bank for International Settlements (BIS) Handbook
25. Bank of Central African States (BEAC) Handbook
26. Black Sea Trade and Development Bank (BSTDB) Handbook
27. Caribbean Centre for Monetary Studies (CCMS) Handbook
28. Caribbean Community (CARICOM) Handbook
29. Caribbean Development Bank (CDB) Handbook
30. Caribbean Regional Technical Assistance Centre (CARTAC) Handbook
31. Center for Latin American Monetary Studies (CEMLA) Handbook
32. Center for Marketing Information and Advisory Services for Fishery Products in Latin America and the Caribbean (INFOPESCA) Handbook
33. Central American Bank for Economic Integration (CABEI) Handbook
34. Central American Monetary Council (CAMC) Handbook
35. Central Bank of West African States (BCEAO) Handbook
36. Colombo Plan for Co-operative Economic and Social Development in Asia and the Pacific Handbook
37. Colombo Plan Staff College for Technician Education Handbook

38. Common Fund for Commodities Handbook
39. Common Market for Eastern and Southern Africa (COMESA) Handbook
40. Cooperation Council for the Arab States of the Gulf (GCC) Handbook
41. Council of the Baltic Sea States (CBSS) Handbook
42. Council of Europe Development Bank (CEB) Handbook
43. East African Development Bank (EADB) Handbook
44. Eastern Caribbean Central Bank (ECCB) Handbook
45. Economic Community of West African States (ECOWAS) Handbook
46. Economic Cooperation Organization (ECO) Handbook
47. European Bank for Reconstruction and Development (EBRD) Handbook
48. European Central Bank (ECB) Handbook
49. European Free Trade Association (EFTA) Handbook
50. European Investment Bank (EIB) Handbook
51. European Investment Fund (EIF) Handbook
52. European Union, The (EC) Handbook
53. Financial Fund for the Development of the River Plate Basin (FONPLATA) Handbook
54. Food and Agriculture Organization of the United Nations (FAO) Handbook
55. Fund for Co-operation, Compensation and Development (ECOWAS Fund) Handbook
56. Inter-American Development Bank (IDB) Handbook
57. Inter-American Institute for Cooperation on Agriculture (IICA) Handbook
58. Inter-Arab Investment Guarantee Corporation (IAIGC) Handbook
59. International Atomic Energy Regulations Handbook
60. International Civil Aviation Regulations Handbook
61. International Cocoa Production and Trade Regulations Handbook
62. International Coffee Production and Trade Regulations Handbook
63. International Confederation of Free Trade Unions (ICFTU) Handbook
64. International Cotton Advisory Committee (ICAC) Handbook
65. International Fund for Agricultural Development (IFAD) Handbook
66. International Grains Council Handbook
67. International Labour Organization (ILO) Handbook
68. International Lead and Zinc Study Group Handbook
69. International Monetary Fund (IMF) Handbook
70. International Olive Oil Council (IOOC) Handbook
71. International Rubber Study Group Handbook
72. International Sugar Organization (ISO) Handbook
73. International Telecommunications Union (ITU) Handbook
74. International Tropical Timber Organization (ITTO) Handbook
75. Islamic Development Bank Group (IsDB) Handbook
76. Islamic Research and Training Institute (IRTI) Handbook
77. Joint Vienna Institute (JVI) Handbook
78. Kuwait Fund for Arab Economic Development Handbook
79. Lake Chad Basin Commission (LCBC) Handbook
80. Latin American Association of Development Financing Institutions (ALIDE) Handbook
81. Latin American Economic System (SELA) Handbook
82. Latin American Energy Organization (OLADE) Handbook
83. Latin American Export Bank (BLADEX) Handbook
84. Latin American Integration Association (ALADI) Handbook
85. Latin American Reserve Fund (LARF) Handbook
86. League of Arab States Handbook
87. Mekong River Commission (MRC) Handbook
88. Nordic Development Fund (NDF) Handbook

---

89. Nordic Investment Bank (NIB) Handbook
90. OPEC Fund for International Development Handbook
91. Organisation for Economic Co-operation and Development (OECD) Handbook
92. Organisation of Eastern Caribbean States (OECS) Handbook
93. Organization of American States (OAS) Handbook
94. Organization of Arab Petroleum Exporting Countries (OAPEC) Handbook
95. Organization of the Petroleum Exporting Countries (OPEC) Handbook
96. Pacific Financial Technical Assistance Centre Handbook
97. Pacific Islands Forum Secretariat Handbook
98. Pan American Health Organization (PAHO) Handbook
99. Regional Association of Oil and Natural Gas Companies in Latin America and the Caribbean (ARPEL) Handbook
100. Regional Electrical Integration Commission (CIER) Handbook
101. Saudi Fund for Development (SFD) Handbook
102. Secretariat for Central American Economic Integration (SIECA) Handbook
103. Secretariat of the Pacific Community Handbook
104. Sectorial Commission for the Common Market of the South (MERCOSUR) - Uruguay Handbook
105. South Asian Association for Regional Cooperation (SAARC) Handbook
106. South-East Asian Central Banks (SEACEN) Research and Training Centre Handbook
107. Training Centre for Regional Integration (CEFIR) Handbook
108. United Nations African Institute for Economic Development and Planning (IDEP) Handbook
109. United Nations Conference on Trade and Development (UNCTAD) Handbook
110. United Nations Development Program (UNDP) Handbook
111. United Nations Economic and Social Commission for Asia and the Pacific (ESCAP) Handbook
112. Asian and Pacific Centre for Transfer of Technology (APCTT) Handbook
113. Regional Coordination Centre for Research and Development of Coarse Grains, Pulses, Roots and Tuber Crops in the Humid Tropics of Asia and the Pacific (ESCAP CGPRT Centre) Handbook
114. Statistical Institute for Asia and the Pacific (SIAP) Handbook
115. United Nations Economic and Social Commission for Western Asia (ESCWA) Handbook
116. United Nations Economic Commission for Africa (UNECA) Handbook
117. United Nations Economic Commission for Europe (UN/ECE) Handbook
118. United Nations Economic Commission for Latin America and the Caribbean (ECLAC) Handbook
119. United Nations Educational, Scientific and Cultural Organization (UNESCO) Handbook
120. United Nations Industrial Development Organization (UNIDO) Handbook
121. United Nations Latin American and Caribbean Institute for Economic and Social Planning (ILPES) Handbook
122. World Postal Service Handbook: Volume 1 Strategic information and basic regulations
123. West African Development Bank (BOAD) Handbook
124. West Africa Economic and Monetary Union Handbook
125. World Bank Group Handbook
126. World Food Program (WFP) Handbook
127. World Health Organization (WHO) Handbook
128. World Trade Organization (WTO) Handbook

www.ingramcontent.com/pod-product-compliance
Lightning Source LLC
LaVergne TN
LVHW080034210926
848481LV00011B/3189
* 9 7 8 1 5 7 7 5 1 9 4 9 2 *